Ponapean Reference Grammar

PALI LANGUAGE TEXTS: MICRONESIA

Social Science Research Institute
University of Hawaii

Donald M. Topping
Editor

Ponapean
Reference Grammar

KENNETH L. REHG

with the assistance of
DAMIAN G. SOHL

University of Hawaii Press
HONOLULU

The research reported herein and the publication of this book were
supported by the Government of the Trust Territory of the Pacific
Islands. Mr. Sohl's assistance was made possible through support
received from the Trust Territory Government and the Culture Learning
Institute of the East-West Center at the University of Hawai'i.

Library of Congress Cataloging-in-Publication Data

Rehg, Kenneth L   1939–
    Ponapean reference grammar.

    (PALI language texts)
    Bibliography: p.
    Includes index.
    1. Ponape language—Grammar. I. Sohl, Damian G.,
1943–   joint author. II. Title. III. Series:
Pali language texts.
PL6295.R4   499'.5   80–13276
ISBN 0–8248–0718–9

Printed by Data Reproductions Corporation

www.uhpress.hawaii.edu

Contents

Preface

My purpose in writing this book has been to provide a description of the major grammatical features of Ponapean for the reader who has had little or no training in the analysis of language. Although this work is intended primarily for native speakers of Ponapean who are bilingual in English, I hope it will also be useful to others whose interests have brought them to the study of this language.

I have endeavored throughout this volume to keep its content as clear and as simple as possible. Experience in the classroom, however, has proven that certain sections of the book are more difficult than others. Particularly challenging for some readers are those sections in which I have introduced technical terms from the field of linguistics. Generally, I have tried to minimize the usage of such terms, but where they permitted a better or more efficient explanation of the data, I have not shied away from them. I have taken care, though, to define each technical term as it is introduced and to illustrate it with numerous examples. The careful reader should thus not find unfamiliar terminology to be a serious difficulty.

The organization of this grammar is ultimately based upon the practical problem of providing a relatively nontechnical description of a language, rather than upon a particular theory of the organization of language itself. Consequently, I have drawn upon a variety of grammatical traditions in discussing this language, and I have organized the material in this grammar in essentially a cumulative way, so that understanding the material in one chapter will facilitate understanding that which follows. Chapter 1 presents some useful background information on Ponape and Ponapean. Chapter 2 examines the sound system of Ponapean. Chapter 3 explores the structure and function of words. Chapters 4 and 5 look at how words may be combined into noun phrases and verb phrases, while Chapter 6 examines how these phrases may be combined to form sentences. Chapter 7 presents a discussion of a particular speech style of Ponapean known as honorific speech. Following this chapter is an appendix that includes a summary of Ponapean spelling rules and a bibliography of selected books and articles useful in the study of Ponapean.

It is important that the reader understand that this grammar of Ponapean is by no means complete. In fact, no one has ever written a *complete* grammar of any language. Simply not enough is known about how language works to allow such a grammar. Even so, the limitations of this work cannot be overemphasized. A great deal of additional research on Ponapean remains to be done. Many aspects of this language have not yet been investigated, and, even among those dealt with in this volume, some are almost certainly misunderstood. Still, the publication of this grammar at this time is not without justification. First, the incorporation of new data in this work has made possible a number of interpretations of Ponapean grammar not previously noted by earlier students of the language. Additionally, no other work on Ponapean has been written with a Ponapean audience in mind, nor has any earlier work been easily available to the Ponapean community. Further, the introduction of bilingual education in Ponape and the emerging role of Ponapean as a medium of education necessitates a grammar such as this to serve as a springboard for the development of school grammars. Finally, the growing number of specialists in Micronesian studies insures the utility of this grammar as an aid to further research.

The pleasurable task now remains for me to acknowledge my indebtedness to the many individuals who have made this grammar of Ponapean possible. I especially wish to express my sincere appreciation to Damian Sohl, my friend and colleague, whose contributions to this work were so extensive that it could not have been written without him; to Marcelino Actouka and Ewalt Joseph, who never failed to offer their assistance and insights when the facts of Ponapean seemed hopelessly confusing; to Kim Bailey, Gideon David, Hanover Ehsa, Elaine Good, Frederick Jackson, Rodrigo Mauricio, Casiano Shoniber, Masaki Thomson, and Weldis Welley, who studied an earlier version of this grammar and suggested many improvements in its format and content; to Alan Burdick, Harold Hanlin, William McGarry, and Yasuo Yamada, who on numerous occasions brought to my attention facts about Ponapean I had not previously considered; to Sheldon Harrison, John Jensen, Kee-Dong Lee, Peter Lincoln, and Hiroshi Sugita, fellow students of Pacific languages, with whom I have had countless hours of invaluable discussion; to Paul Gallen and the staff of the Department of Education in Ponape, whose cooperation and assistance during several visits to Ponape were highly valued; to Byron Bender, George Grace, Irwin Howard, and Andrew Pawley, who contributed extensively to my understanding of language in general and Micronesian languages in particular; and finally, and especially, to Donald Topping, who carefully read through this entire text and offered many invaluable comments about its content, style, and organization. I also wish to express here my indebtedness to the authors of earlier studies of Ponapean. Their names and publications are presented in the bibliography. In addition, several have been singled out for special mention in section 1.6 of Chapter 1.

Ultimately it is impossible to name everyone who has had a part in shaping this grammar. The writings of other linguists, discussions with friends and colleagues, courses and seminars—all of these have played a role in providing me with ideas, insights, and examples, the origins of which have been lost in time. What is of value in this grammar is thus the result of the contributions of many. For the faults of this work, I alone accept full responsibility.

1 Introduction

OVERVIEW

1.1   The first chapter of this grammar provides some general background information on the context in which Ponapean is spoken. By context, I mean the physical, cultural, and historical circumstances that surround this language. Understanding the structure of any language is at one point or another so inextricably bound up with these considerations that it is impossible to ignore them. Consequently, in this chapter I have briefly taken up such questions as where Ponapean is spoken, who speaks it, what other languages it is related to, and what non-related languages have contributed to its vocabulary. Additionally, I have included a short review of some of the more important studies of Ponapean that preceded this one. Section 1.2, in which I discuss where Ponapean is spoken and who speaks it, is intended primarily for readers who are not Ponapean. The remaining sections are intended for all readers.

THE ISLAND AND THE PEOPLE

1.2   The island of Ponape, where the vast majority of Ponapean speakers reside, is located approximately half-way between Hawaii and Indonesia at 6°54′ North latitude and 158°14′ East longitude, within the geographic area known as Micronesia. Ponape and its two satellite atolls, Pakin and Ant, are also known as the Senyavin Islands. On older maps, Ponape alone is sometimes called Ascension Island.

    With a land area of approximately 129 square miles, Ponape is the largest of the islands within the group known as the Eastern Carolines. Ponape is a high island as opposed to an atoll and, like most islands in the Pacific, is of volcanic origin. No active volcanoes are now present on the island, nor apparently have there been any for a long time. The island shows evidence of considerable geological age. Its mountain tops, two of which exceed 2,500 feet, are smooth and rounded and are separated by U-shaped valleys containing numerous rivers and streams. The coastal area is flat and in most places is protected from the eroding effects of the ocean by dense mangrove swamps and a barrier reef. Occasional breaks in the reef open into well-protected harbors. Abundant rainfall, which in the interior may be as high as 400 inches per year, a tropical climate with temperatures ranging between 80 and 90 degrees, and relatively fertile soil combine to make the island one of the lushest and most beautiful in the Pacific.

During the most recent census—taken in 1973—17,259 people claimed Ponape as their usual place of residence. Perhaps less than 15,000 of these people are native Ponapeans. Also present on the island are a large number of immigrants from neighboring islands, and a comparatively small number of Americans or individuals of other nationalities, most of whom work for the government. Physically, the Ponapean inhabitants resemble Polynesians, though on the whole they are shorter in stature and more slender in build. These people primarily derive their living from subsistence agriculture, but employment with the government, commercial crops such as copra and pepper, and various private enterprises including small retail outlets, fishing, and recently tourism, provide important sources of cash. The traditional social structure of the island, and the way in which it relates to the language, is the basis for Chapter 7.

The presence of the comparatively large number of non-Ponapeans on the island is a consequence of two factors. The first is that Ponape is the site of the administrative center of one of the four states that currently comprise the Federated States of Micronesia. Many people from other islands in this state, which includes the atolls of Kapingamarangi, Nukuoro, Ngatik, Ant, Mokil, and Pingelap, have taken up residence on Ponape in order to obtain employment with the government. The second reason is that Ponape has sufficient land and resources to permit the inflow of immigrants from these atolls. Since at least the turn of the century, people from Kapingamarangi, Nukuoro, Ngatik, Pingelap, Mokil, and even from the Mortlocks in the state of Truk have moved to Ponape because of population pressures or natural disasters. Many different cultural groups thus reside on the island of Ponape and so, in fact, are there many different speech communities. Polynesian languages are spoken by the people from Kapingamarangi and Nukuoro; a related but distinct Micronesian language is spoken by the people from the Mortlocks; and varieties of speech more closely related to Ponapean are spoken by the people from Ngatik, Mokil, and Pingelap. Ponapean, however, along with English, serves as the lingua-franca for all these speech communities.

THE ORIGINS OF PONAPEAN

1.3 The origins of Ponapean, and consequently of the people who speak this language, are not known. The whole topic of how the islands of the Pacific were settled, however, has been the subject of considerable speculation. Where the original settlers came from, what prompted them to move from their homeland, and what migration patterns they followed are all questions of considerable interest, the answers to which will surely constitute an important chapter in the history of man.

The fascination that the Western world has had with these questions is in part no doubt due to the humbling realization that the peoples of this area were sailing across vast expanses of ocean at the same time Europeans clung to their shorelines. Early European voyagers were fearful that venturing out too far to sea might result in their falling off the edge of the world. The early voyagers of the Pacific, however, had no such fears. Many legends tell us that their conception of the world was quite different. They did not view the ocean as having an edge from which one might fall. Rather, they believed that sailing too far would simply result in reaching the place where the sky meets the sea. If this were to happen, then they would need only to turn around and continue their search for the land that they believed must inevitably be found.

Although the question of where the first Ponapeans came from cannot be answered at this time, this does not mean the question is unanswerable. The oral literature of Ponape which tells us how the early Ponapeans viewed the world also provides us with some interesting clues about their origins. Several stories tell of the earliest settlement of Ponape, the most widely known of which typically begins with the line: *Wahr oapwoat pwilisang sekerehn wai keilahn aio.* 'A canoe left a foreign shore long ago.'

Where this *sekerehn wai* 'foreign shore' was located is not known, but the legend tells that it was some distance from Ponape on an island called *Sapwen Eir*, which may be translated 'Southern Land'. Another legend tells that the early settlers of Ponape came from *Katau Peidak*. Since *peidak* means 'upwind', and the basic wind patterns around Ponape are from east to west, this legend suggests an eastern origin for the early Ponapeans. *Katau Peidak* is commonly thought to be the island of Kusaie. Still other legends tell of later settlements of people from the Marshall and Gilbert Islands, or from places whose identity is shrouded in mystery.

Many aspects of these legends match what modern scholars believe to be true about the settlement of Micronesia. It seems highly unlikely that any part of this area was settled by a single migration of people. No doubt there were many movements of people who, by purpose or chance, came to live on these islands. There are also reasons, that we will examine later in this section, to believe that the major migration pattern in eastern Micronesia was in fact first from the south, and then from east to west, as Ponapean legends suggest.

Contemporary scholars base their hypotheses on how the Pacific was settled on a wide variety of facts, but basic to interpreting all of these facts is the process of **comparison**. For example, by comparing the physical characteristics of people, their tools and ways of making things, their food crops, their legends, their social organizations, and their languages, one can find differences, but also a great many similarities. These similarities are of special interest because one explanation for their existence is that they have a common origin. Therefore, similarities among people living on different islands may be due to the fact that their ancestors all lived together as one people at some time in the past. Differences among these people would then be the consequence of the fact that the descendants of those ancestral people scattered to other areas and through time, which brings change, lost or replaced some features of their common heritage. The degree to which people and their cultures are similar or different can thus tell us much about the past.

Since our concern in this book is with language, and since some of the best evidence concerning the prehistory of the Pacific comes from comparing languages, we might briefly consider what can be learned from such studies. To begin, let us consider a few common words from several Micronesian languages.

Ponapean	Trukese	Kusaiean	Marshallese	Gilbertese	English
tih	*chúú*	*sri*	*di*	*ri*	'bone'
nih	*núú*	*nu*	*ni*	*nii*	'coconut'
ngih	*ngii*	*wihs*	*ñi*	*wi*	'tooth'
ngehi	*ngaang*	*nga*	*ña*	*ngai*	'I'
seng	*seng*	*tuhng*	*jañ*	*tang*	'cry'
kang	*áni*	*kang*	*kañ*	*kan*	'eat'
ihmw	*iimw*	*lohm*	*em*	*uma*	'house'
nta	*chcha*	*srah*	*da*	*rara*	'blood'
eni	*énú*	*inut*	*anij*	*ansi*	'ghost'
sahm	*saam*	*tuhma*	*jema-*	*tama*	'father'
ihn	*iin*	*ninac*	*jine-*	*tina*	'mother'

Notice that, from one language to another, many obvious similarities exist among these words. In fact, because these words are written in the standard spelling system of each of these languages (not all of which are based on the same spelling principles), hearing these words pronounced would illustrate their similarities even more vividly. So many similar words can be found among these languages that we cannot assume it is due to accident. The more likely explanation for these similarities is that all of these languages have a common ancestor. And, just as we speak of people who have a common ancestor as being related and belonging to the same family, so may we speak of languages.

Going beyond Micronesia, similarities can be found between Ponapean and many other languages. In fact, Ponapean is a member of one of the world's largest language families. The name of this language family is **Austronesian** (formerly called **Malayo-Polynesian**). It is made up of approximately 500 languages which are spoken in Micronesia, Polynesia, much of Melanesia, the Philippines, Indonesia, most of Malaysia, Madagascar, and in parts of Formosa, Vietnam, and Cambodia.

Austronesian languages are generally divided into two groups, an **Oceanic** group that includes most of the languages of Melanesia, Micronesia, and Polynesia, and a **Western** group, to which nearly all other Austronesian languages are assigned. Among the languages spoken within Micronesia, two belong to the Western group. Palauan appears to have its closest relatives in Indonesia, and Chamorro, in the Phillipines. The status of Yapese, while clearly an Austronesian language, is unclear. The remaining languages all belong to the Oceanic group, either to a

Polynesian subgroup, as in the case of Kapingamarangi and Nukuoro, or to a Micronesian subgroup.

The languages that belong to the Micronesian subgroup are Gilbertese, Marshallese, Kusaiean, the so-called Trukic and Ponapeic languages, and possibly Nauruan. Another Micronesian language, now extinct, was spoken on the island of Mapia. The Trukic languages are divided by Hiroshi Sugita into three main groups—an Eastern group which includes Lagoon Trukese, Mortlockese, Namonuito, and the varieties of speech found in the Hall Islands and in the Puluwat-Pulusuk-Pulap area; a Central group, which includes Satawalese and Saipan Carolinian; and a Western group, which includes the languages of the Ulithi-Woleai and Sonsorol/Pulo Anna/Tobi areas. Just how many languages are included within Trukic, however, is difficult to say, since within these groups it is impossible to establish meaningful language boundaries. The Ponapeic group, which consists of Ponapean, Ngatikese, Mokilese, and Pingelapese, poses a similar problem in establishing language boundaries. A more detailed discussion of the nature of this problem and of Ponapeic is the topic of section 1.4.

Information about how languages are related does, of course, provide many important clues about the history of the people who speak the languages. Findings of this nature combined with those of other fields of study, especially archeology, permit us to at least speculate about a question like where the Ponapeans came from. Such speculation is presented below. The reader is warned, though, that this discussion omits many details and by no means would be accepted by all Pacific scholars. Some of the studies listed in the bibliography, particularly those by Dyen, Grace, Howells, and Pawley, are recommended for the reader who wishes to pursue this topic in greater depth. In broad outline, then, the following events may have lead to the settlement of Ponape.

At some remote time in the past, possibly in the New Guinea/Indonesia area, a group of people lived together who spoke a language ancestral to all contemporary Austronesian languages. Linguists call this language **Proto-Austronesian**, 'proto' meaning 'the earliest form of'. Possibly as early as 4000 B.C., the people who spoke this language began to disperse to other areas in the Pacific. By approximately 3000 B.C., the ancestors of the people who speak Oceanic languages had reached at least as far as southern Melanesia, and further dispersal was taking place. Possibly by 1000 B.C., the people who spoke **Proto-Micronesian**, the ancestral language of Gilbertese, Marshallese, Kusaien, the Ponapeic and Trukic languages, and probably Nauruan, were beginning their settlement of Micronesia. Where these first Micronesians came from is unclear, but linguistic evidence indicates earlier ties with the northern New Hebrides. Their homeland was probably in the eastern part of Micronesia. An eastern homeland, which matches what Ponapean legends suggest, is based on the hypothesis that since languages change through time at approximately the same rate, earlier settlement areas should show greater linguistic diversity than later ones. If we consider Micronesia (remembering that Palauan, Yapese, and Chamorro are not Micronesian languages), then it is in the east that this diversity occurs. To the east of Ponape are such diverse languages as Kusaiean, Marshallese and Gilbertese. To the west of Ponape are the closely related Trukic languages. It is not known, however, which eastern island was settled first. Whether it was Kusaie, or whether Kusaie was settled after the Marshalls, the Gilberts, or Nauru, remains to be determined.

Obviously, many details are missing concerning the origins of the people and the language of Ponape. Even the very general sequence of events sketched above may have serious defects. But, considerable progess is being made in studying the prehistory of the Pacific. More and more pieces of the puzzle are beginning to fall into place. Work now going on at the University of Hawaii on Micronesian languages and Proto-Micronesian should prove particularly helpful.

ABOUT PONAPEIC

1.4   Throughout this book, as well as in conventional usage, the term *Ponapean* is used as the name of the indigenous language of the island of Ponape. However, there is one sense in which this usage might be too restrictive. The varieties of speech spoken on the atolls of Ngatik, Mokil, and Pingelap, respectively called **Ngatikese**, **Mokilese**, and **Pingelapese**, are similar enough to Ponapean that they, too, perhaps should be identified as being Ponapean. Therefore, it is possible that these three varieties of speech should be considered *dialects* of Ponapean.

Whether Ngatikese, Mokilese, and Pingelapese are *in fact* dialects of Ponapean depends, of course, on how one defines the term "dialect" and the related term "language." Standard definitions of these terms rely on the criterion of **mutual intelligibility**. Mutual intelligibility simply refers to whether or not people can understand each other. If two people speak differently, but can still understand each other, then we may say that they each speak a different *dialect* of the same language. If two people speak in very different ways, and they cannot understand each other, then we can say that they each speak a different *language*.

Unfortunately, the nature of language is such that the criterion of mutual intelligibility does not always work very well. If we take as an example the kind of interaction that might take place between a Ponapean and a Mokilese, then the defects of this criterion become apparent. A Ponapean who knows no Mokilese, trying to talk to a Mokilese who knows no Ponapean, will be able to understand some parts of the other's message, but there will be a great deal that he does not understand. In this case, do we want to say that Ponapean and Mokilese are different dialects or different languages?

The answer to that question is not at all obvious. Although various solutions have been offered, none are entirely satisfactory. For our purposes, let it suffice to recognize that within Ponape State there are a group of closely related varieties of speech that may collectively be labeled **Ponapeic**, a term already employed in the preceding section. Ponapeic therefore includes Ponapean, Ngatikese, Mokilese, and Pingelapese, four varieties of speech which are all mutually intelligible to varying degrees.

Unfortunately, not very much is known about Ngatikese grammar. Based on a limited amount of data, however, it seems safe to say that Ngatikese is more similar to Ponapean than either Pingelapese or Mokilese. Two of its unique features are well known to Ponapeans. One is that Ngatikese men, when speaking to each other, may employ an alternate speech style that they consider to be a pidgin English. In this style, a very large number of English words are employed. The existence of this pidgin is attributed to a tragic event in Ngatikese history when in 1837 the crew of the British cutter *Lambton* invaded the island, slaughtered the male population, and removed the surviving women and children to Ponape. Many of the Ngatikese women were subsequently taken as concubines by the ship's crew. Another characteristic of Ngatikese is that in place of the *r* sound found elsewhere in Ponapeic, it employs a sound technically described as a **voiceless velar fricative**. This is a sound made by raising the back of the tongue so close to the back of the roof of the mouth that air passing through the resulting narrow opening makes a hissing or friction-like noise. Apart from these two striking dissimilarities, Ngatikese appears to be otherwise very much like Ponapean.

A great deal more is known about Mokilese and Pingelapese. A grammar of Mokilese by Sheldon Harrison and Salich Albert is now available, and a grammar of Pingelapese by Elaine Good and Weldis Welley is currently in preparation. What is clear about these two varieties of speech is that they are more similar to each other than either is to Ponapean, though of the two, Pingelapese is closer to Ponapean. One way to verify this claim is by comparing the vocabulary of all three of these speech communities. For this purpose, linguists commonly use a standard list of 100 or 200 words that they would expect to find in any language. This list includes such common words as 'father', 'mother', 'sun', 'person', 'bird', and so on. Based on the 100 word list, the percentages of words that are shared among Ponapean, Pingelapese, and Mokilese are as follows.

1. Ponapean shares 73% with Mokilese.
2. Ponapean shares 79% with Pingelapese.
3. Pingelapese shares 83% with Mokilese.

There seem to be, however, a number of reasons to believe that Pingelapese and Mokilese are even more similar to each other and distinct from Ponapean than these percentages suggest. Four of these reasons will be considered here.

One way in which both Mokilese and Pingelapese differ from Ponapean is that where Ponapean has a *t* sound (the kind of sound called a *voiceless retroflexed affricate*, discussed in section 2.5.3), Mokilese and Pingelapese have an *s* sound. This is illustrated in the following examples.

Ponapean	Mokilese	Pingelapese	English
teh	*soa*	*se*	'leaf'
tahmw	*soamw*	*samw*	'forehead'
tamwe	*samwe*	*samwe*	'lick'
tipw	*sipw*	*sipw*	'broken'
tihti	*sihsi*	*sihsi*	'thin'
katik	*kasik*	*kasik*	'sour'
uht	*wus*	*wis*	'banana'
rot	*ros*	*ros*	'dark'

A second point of comparison involves a sound rule that occurs in Ponapean, but not in Mokilese or Pingelapese. This rule, called the **Monosyllabic Noun Vowel Lengthening Rule**, is discussed in detail in section 4.2.1. In effect, this rule predicts that all single syllable nouns will have a long vowel. The following examples, where *h* indicates the long vowel in Ponapean, illustrate that this rule does not operate in Pingelapese and Mokilese.

Ponapean	Mokilese	Pingelapese	English
pihk	*pik*	*pik*	'sand'
wahr	*war*	*war*	'canoe'
lih	*li*	*li*	'woman'
ahl	*al*	*al*	'road'
dohl	*dol*	*dol*	'mountain'
loahng	*loang*	*loang*	'fly'
ahd	*ad*	*ad*	'name'
ahu	*au*	*au*	'mouth'
dahl	*dal*	*dal*	'cup'

A third way in which both Mokilese and Pingelapese differ from Ponapean is illustrated by the following examples, where some common nouns are given as they occur with the third person singular possessive suffix meaning 'his', 'her', or 'its'. In these examples, this suffix is translated 'his' or 'its', as appropriate.

Ponapean	Mokilese	Pingelapese	English
kili	*kilin*	*kilin*	'his skin'
kode	*kodin*	*kodin*	'its horn'
kiki	*kikin*	*kikin*	'his fingernail'
edi	*adin*	*adin*	'his gall bladder'
kapehde	*kapehdin*	*kapehdin*	'his belly'

Notice that whereas the suffixed forms of these nouns all end with a vowel in Ponapean, the Mokilese and Pingelapese forms all end in the consonant *n*. There are also many Mokilese and Pingelapese nouns that, like Ponapean, end with a vowel when combined with this suffix, but there are no cases in Ponapean of final *n* ever occurring in forms like these. Details about possessive pronouns in Ponapean are presented in section 4.8.

Finally, we might consider a phenomenon that has been discussed by Sheldon Harrison in a paper called "Reduplication in Micronesian Languages." Probably all Micronesian languages employ for one grammatical purpose or another a process called **reduplication** that involves repeating all or part of a word. Harrison noted that Mokilese also employs **triplication**, in which a word or part of a word is repeated twice. Pingelapese, we may note, also employs triplication, but Ponapean does not. The various forms that a verb might have in these three varieties of speech, then, are illustrated in the examples below. The English translations, however, are only approximations of the real meanings of reduplication and triplication. The function of reduplication in Ponapean is further discussed in section 3.3.4. For further details about Mokilese, the reader is referred to the works by Harrison listed in the bibliography.

Ponapean	Mokilese	Pingelapese	English
pei	*pei*	*pei*	'float'
peipei	*peipei*	*peipei*	'floating'
	peipeipei	*peipeipei*	'still floating'
pa	*pa*	*pa*	'weave'
pahpa	*pahpa*	*pahpa*	'weaving'
	pahpahpa	*pahpahpa*	'still weaving'
kang	*kang*	*kang*	'eat'
kangkang	*kahkang*	*kahkang*	'eating'
	kangkangkang	*kahkahkang*	'still eating'
koul	*koaul*	*koaul*	'sing'
kokoul	*koahkoaul*	*koaukoaul*	'singing'
	koahkoahkoaul	*koaukoaukoaul*	'still singing'
meir	*moair*	*meir*	'sleep'
memeir	*moahmoair*	*meimeir*	'sleeping'
	moahmoahmoair	*meimeimeir*	'still sleeping'

The preceding discussion of ways in which Ponapean differs from Mokilese and Pingelapese suggests the possibility that these latter two varieties of speech might be dialects of each other which together constitute a language distinct from Ponapean. As we previously observed, however, it will be necessary to improve upon our definitions of 'language' and 'dialect' before such a claim has much validity. In subsequent parts of this book, we will thus restrict our concern with the notion of 'dialect' to the more subtle variations in speech that occur within Ponapean itself.

While on the whole the language of Ponape is fairly uniform—every Ponapean can easily understand every other Ponapean—there are some readily discernible differences between the speech of the people of the northern and southern parts of the island. Ponapean is thus generally described as having two major dialects. The **southern dialect**, or as it is more commonly known, the **Kiti dialect**, is spoken primarily in the municipality of that name. The **northern** or **main dialect** is spoken on the rest of the island. The basic differences between these two dialects are examined in section 2.6.7. Another phenomenon of Ponapean that might be thought of in terms of dialect variation are the socially determined or honorific patterns of speech that are developed in Ponapean to an extent unparalleled in the rest of Micronesia. Honorific speech is the exclusive topic of Chapter 7.

FOREIGN INFLUENCES

1.5   One fact about Ponapean that is obvious after even a brief study of the language is that it contains a considerable number of words borrowed from other languages. Linguistic borrowing of this nature, however, is by no means unusual. Probably every language has at some time or another in its history borrowed vocabulary from other speech communities. Borrowing is one of the consequences of languages coming in contact with each other. It is one of the ways in which a language keeps pace with the changes that take place in a society as a result of foreign influences.

In comparatively recent times, the contacts that have most influenced the vocabulary of Ponapean are those that have taken place with speakers of non-Austronesian languages. These contacts began only about one hundred and fifty years ago. Ponape was known to the rest of the world previous to that time—the first confirmed sighting of the island was in 1595 by the Spaniard Pedro Fernandez de Quiros—but it wasn't until 1828 that a Western voyager described the island in any detail. This description was provided by the Russian Captain Frédéric Lutké of the ship *Senyavin,* who named Ponape along with Ant and Pakin the Senyavin Islands. Lutké and his crew did not actually put ashore, but it is approximately from this period that whalers, traders, and beachcombers began to visit the island. Another date of significance in this early period of foreign contact is 1852. This is the year that the American Congregationalist missionaries arrived in Ponape. In 1885, the Spanish began to exercise their political power in the Eastern Carolines, and for the first time Ponape came under the rule of a non-Pacific nation. This period, which lasted until 1899, was marked by considerable friction and open warfare. The Ponapeans also openly resisted the Germans, whose rule began in 1899 and continued until the end of World War I. In 1918, the Japanese began their rule with the goal of making Micronesia a part of the Japanese empire. These plans were shattered by World War II, and in 1945 the political control of Micronesia passed to the hands of the Americans. Under an agreement with the United Nations, still in effect, the United States now administers this area.

It is small wonder then that Ponapean vocabulary evidences considerable borrowing, for with each of these new foreign contacts came new ideas, new trade goods, and new ways of doing things. Some of these importations were adopted by the Ponapeans. Some were forced upon them. But they all had an impact on the language. To talk about new things required that old words be used in new ways, that new words be invented, or that words be borrowed. To some extent, Ponapean employed all three of these strategies. For example, the old word *nting* 'to tattoo' also came to mean 'to write', and the phrase *weren nansapw*, literally 'canoe-of on-land', was coined to mean 'automobile'. But perhaps most often words were simply borrowed. In this process of borrowing, however, words did not always end up with the same pronunciation or meaning they had in the source language. In becoming part of the Ponapean language, these words were filtered through the Ponapean sound system, and meanings were assigned to them in terms of how they were understood by the Ponapeans. The kinds of words that were borrowed, along with their sources, are examined below. Standard spellings are employed and English translations are given for both the Ponapean borrowing and its source word in order to illustrate instances of meaning differences.

From Spanish came a relatively small number of words. Most of these were terms related to Catholicism, which was introduced to Ponape in 1886. Some examples follow.

Ponapean	English	Spanish	English
esdasion	'station of the cross'	*estacion*	'station'
kana	'to win'	*ganar*	'to win'
kandehla	'candle'	*candela*	'candle'
koronihda	'cornet, trumpet'	*corneta*	'cornet'
mahdire	'head nun'	*madre*	'mother, head nun'
medahlia	'religious medal'	*medalla*	'medal'
mihsa	'mass'	*misa*	'mass'
misiohn	'Catholic mission	*mision*	'mission'
pahdire	'priest'	*padre*	'father, priest'
pangk	'bench'	*banco*	'bench'
pehrdi	'to lose'	*perder*	'to lose'
pringihnas	'eggplant'	*berenjena*	'eggplant'
pwurkadorio	'purgatory'	*purgatorio*	'purgatory'
rosario	'rosary'	*rosario*	'rosary'
sokolahde	'chocolate'	*chocolate*	'chocolate'

The influence of the German language was minimal. Among the very few German borrowings found in Ponapean are the following.

Ponapean	English	German	English
diraht	'barbed wire'	*Draht*	'wire'
Dois	'German'	*Deutsch*	'German'
kumi	'rubber, plastic'	*Gummi*	'rubber'
mahlen	'to paint or draw'	*malen*	'to paint'
pilat	'record'	*Platte*	'record'
sunname	'surname'	*Zuname*	'surname'
sirangk	'food cabinet'	*Schrank*	'locker, cupboard'

Next to English, the language that contributed the largest number of words to Ponapean is Japanese. The *Ponapean-English Dictionary* by Rehg and Sohl contains approximately four hundred Japanese borrowings. Following are some examples that were prepared with the assistance of Hiroshi Sugita. The spelling system employed is that adopted by *Kenkyusha's New Japanese-English Dictionary,* except that long vowels are written doubled.

Ponapean	English	Japanese	English
aikiu	'to ration'	*haikyuu*	'to ration'
ami	'screen'	*ami*	'net, grill'
apwraiasi	'variety of palm'	*aburayashi*	'variety of palm'
daidowa	'war, dispute'	*Daitooa*	'Great East Asia'
dakadopi	'high jump'	*takatobi*	'high jump'
dana	'shelf'	*tana*	'shelf'
dengki	'electricity, flashlight'	*denki*	'electricity, flashlight'
iakiu	'baseball'	*yakyu*	'baseball'
impiokai	'agricultural fair'	*hinpyookai*	'agricultural fair'
kadorsingko	'mosquito coil'	*katorisenkoo*	'mosquito coil'
kairu	'toad, frog'	*kaeru*	'toad, frog'
kama	'sickle'	*kama*	sickle'
kisingai	'crazy, mad'	*kichigai*	'crazy, mad'
kiuhri	'cucumber'	*kyuuri*	'cucumber'
mai	'skillful'	*umai*	'skillful'
masinoki	'ironwood tree'	*matsu no ki*	'pine tree'
nappa	'chinese cabbage'	*nappa*	'green vegetable'
nengi	'green onion'	*negi*	'green onion'
ohdai	'bandage, gauze'	*hootai*	'bandage'
pakudang	'bomb, shell'	*bakudan*	'bomb'
sarmada	'underwear'	*sarumata*	'boxer shorts'
sasimi	'raw fish'	*sashimi*	'raw fish'
sidohsa	'automobile'	*jidoosha*	'automobile'
skohso	'airport'	*hikoojoo*	'airport'
sohri	'zories, thongs'	*zoori*	'zories, thongs'
suhmwong	'to order'	*chuumon*	'to order'
undohkai	'athletic meet'	*undookai*	'athletic meet'
waku	'embroidery hoop'	*waku*	'frame'

In some cases, words borrowed into Ponapean from Japanese had been earlier borrowed by the Japanese from English. Examples are:

Ponapean	English	Japanese	English
ampaia	'umpire'	*anpaiyaa*	'umpire'
angkasi	'handkerchief'	*hankachi*	'handkerchief'
diromkang	'oil drum'	*doramukan*	'oil drum' (from 'drum' + 'can')

kiarameru	'caramel'	*kyarameru*	'caramel'
masuku	'mask'	*masuku*	'mask'
odopai	'motorcycle, scooter'	*ootabai*	'motorcycle' (from 'auto' + 'bicycle')
pihru	'beer'	*biiru*	'beer'
pwohsdo	'post office'	*posuto*	'mail box' (from 'post')
rerei	'relay race'	*rirei*	'relay race'

The language from which Ponapean has borrowed the largest number of words is English. More than five hundred words from this source are currently included in the *Ponapean-English Dictionary*. The considerable impact that English has had on Ponapean vocabulary is primarily due to the fact that English is the language with which Ponapean has longest been in contact. During the early contact period, from approximately 1828 to 1885, Ponapeans had considerable interaction with English-speaking whalers, traders, and missionaries. The second contact period, which dates from 1945 to the present, has been one of American rule and the widespread usage of English as a second language. Borrowings took place during both of these periods, and in most cases, though not all, it is possible to determine from which period a particular borrowing dates. For example, the following words were quite likely borrowed during the first contact period.

Ponapean	English
ainpwoat	'cooking pot' (from 'iron pot')
amper	'umbrella'
dampwulo	'hold of a ship' (from 'down below')
dihn	'large can' (from 'tin')
kedilahs	'sword' (from 'cutlass')
Koht	'God'
mandolihn	'mandolin'
mete	'metal, nail, badge' (from 'metal')
misin	'mission' (particularly a Protestant mission)
nihkerehs	'cigar' (from 'Negrohead tobacco')
paipel	'Bible'
pwuhk	'book'
singiles	'T-shirt' (from 'singlet')
sukuhl	'school'
tipaker	'tobacco'
tupweiklas	'telescope, binoculars' (from 'spyglass')

The following words were borrowed during the second contact period.

Ponapean	English
daia	'tire'
daip	'to type'
daksi	'taxi'
dihsel	'diesel'
kahsilihn	'gasoline'
luhpes	'louver'
ohtehl	'hotel'
padiri	'battery'
pimpong	'pingpong'
proadkahs	'broadcast station'
redio	'radio'
skuhder	'motor scooter'
spahk	'spark plug' (from 'spark')
was	'wristwatch' (from 'watch')

Many more examples, of course, could be added. The influence of English on Ponapean is increasing, and younger speakers in particular are introducing additional borrowings at a rapid rate.

EARLIER STUDIES OF PONAPEAN GRAMMAR

1.6   Until the recent endorsement of bilingual education for Micronesia, the language policies of the nations that have ruled Ponape could all be characterized as representing, at least in practice, one form or another of linguistic imperialism. Ponapeans were expected to learn and to be educated in the language of their rulers, while at best Ponapean was the object of benign neglect. As a consequence, the existing literature on or in Ponapean is not very extensive. However, with each period of foreign contact, some outsiders came who did learn Ponapean, and there were a few who shared what they learned with others in the form of word lists, dictionaries, and grammatical studies of the language. A complete list of this literature is included in the bibliography.

Among those individuals who wrote on Ponapean grammar, there are four who deserve special mention, either because of the historical importance of their work or because of the contribution their studies made to the development of this grammar. Although all of these writers published at least several articles on Ponapean, only the most comprehensive of their works are singled out in the following brief discussions.

The first study of Ponapean grammar was written by the Rev. Luther H. Gulick, a member of the original party of missionaries who went to Ponape in 1852. Entitled "Notes on the Grammar of the Ponape Dialect," this work was first distributed in a limited edition in Honolulu in 1858. In 1880, it was published in the *American Oriental Society Journal* as part of an article entitled "A Vocabulary of the Ponape Dialect, Ponape-English and English-Ponape: With a Grammatical Sketch." Gulick's grammatical comments are devoted almost entirely to a discussion of the role of the various parts of speech in Ponapean. Although his study is quite brief, and he fails to note or misunderstands some of the more obvious features of the language, on the whole his comments are quite insightful.

A grammar of considerably more sophistication was published in 1906 by the German physician, Max Girschner. Entitled "Grammatik der Ponapesprache," this work, like Gulick's, is primarily devoted to a discussion of the role of the various parts of speech in Ponapean. But these discussions are supported with numerous examples, and a great deal more attention is paid to how words are organized to form phrases and sentences. Additionally, Girschner recognized the scope of what in this grammar is called 'Ponapeic', as well as the major dialect differences that exist on the island of Ponape itself. Although his discussion of the sound system of Ponapean is of lesser quality, the grammar is basically well done. An English translation of this work is in preparation by Syl Tulley, former Director of Public Works in Ponape.

The first scholar trained in linguistics to conduct a study of Ponapean grammar was Paul L. Garvin. Garvin was a participant in the Coordinated Investigation of Micronesian Anthropology project which was carried out at the end of World War II. His first work, entitled a *Linguistic Study of Ponapean,* presented a detailed account of the sound system, the word structure, and the syntax of this language, and also included a number of Ponapean texts along with English translations. Later, this study was expanded into a longer monograph called *A Definitional Grammar of Ponapean.* Garvin's first grammar, along with those portions of the second we have seen, have been invaluable in the preparation of this work. Unfortunately, only excerpts of

Garvin's important studies of Ponapean have been published.

Another scholar who has made important contributions to the study of Ponapean grammar is John L. Fischer. Fischer's first study, presented as his doctoral dissertation at Harvard University in 1954, was entitled "Language and Folklore in Truk and Ponape. A Study in Cultural Integration." The purpose of this work was to compare the extent to which the cultural patterns of Truk and Ponape are reflected in the patterns of their languages and folktales. In this study, Fischer presents an excellent overview of the major structural features of Ponapean, and the inclusion of the Trukese data makes this work particularly useful to linguists interested in comparative Micronesian studies. Fischer remains an active investigator of Ponapean language and culture.

Hopefully it can be said of this present grammar that it offers some new insights into Ponapean not previously included in these earlier studies. If this is true, however, it is only because this work was built on the important contributions of its predecessors.

2   The Sound System of Ponapean

2.1   This chapter presents some fundamental observations about the sound system of Ponapean. If you have never before studied a modern grammar, the amount of discussion devoted to this subject may be unanticipated. Generally, when we bother to think or talk about language, our concern is with the meaning of a word or a special way of saying something. The sounds of language, particularly those of our own language, we usually take more or less for granted. As the following pages will attempt to illustrate, however, the production of speech sounds involves some rather complex processes. Further, in Ponapean, as in every language, there are rules that govern how these sounds interact to form an essential system of the language. If we are to understand Ponapean grammar, it is important that we understand Ponapean sounds.

THE RELATIONSHIP BETWEEN SPEECH AND WRITING

2.2   As we approach this study of Ponapean speech sounds, there are several important points about the relationship between speech and writing that we must keep in mind. The first of these is that language is primarily **oral**. Literate speakers of a language sometimes think of the written language as being primary, but it is not. Every known language exists, or has existed, as a spoken language. The vast majority of these languages, however, either have never been written or have only recently been written. Language, then, clearly does not depend upon writing for its existence.

      Second, even the best writing system is imperfect as a representation of the spoken language. English provides many examples of the arbitrary nature of spelling. The letters *gh* variously represent the *f* sound in a word like 'tou*gh*', the *g* sound in a word like '*gh*ost', the *p* sound in a word like 'hiccou*gh*', and no sound at all in a word like 'thou*gh*'. In this respect, Ponapean is less confusing than English, but even in Ponapean a single letter may represent more than one sound. The letter *i*, for example, sometimes stands for a vowel sound, as in the word *sis* 'to shiver', and sometimes for a *y* sound, as in the word *pei* 'to float'. Also, as English *gh* illustrates, two or more symbols are sometimes combined in spelling to stand for one sound. In Ponapean, this is also true. The single consonant sound at the beginning of a word like *ngehi* 'I' is spelled with the two letters *ng*, and the single vowel sound in a word like *doar* 'sicker' is spelled with the two letters *oa*.

Third, no conventional writing system ever attempts to mirror all the sounds of a language. Many features of intonation, for example, are not reflected in writing and, as we shall see in this chapter, minor variations in sounds that speakers are not aware of, but nevertheless produce, are also disregarded. The goal of a standard writing system, wherein all speakers of a language write their language the same way, also means that some individual and dialectal differences in pronunciation must be ignored. In the standard writing system recommended by the Ponapean Orthography Committee (see the Appendix), spellings are basically designed to reflect the pronunciation patterns characteristic of speakers of the northern dialect area. But this does not mean that the speech of that area is superior, nor does it mean that other speakers should try to change their pronunciation to match the way words are spelled. Rather, this is just one more illustration of the ultimately arbitrary nature of spelling.

As these three points illustrate, when we study language through the means of writing, as we will in this book, it will be important not to confuse the spoken language with the way it is written. To avoid possible confusion, it will sometimes be necessary to supplement the normal writing system of Ponapean with special symbols that permit a more accurate representation of the sounds of the spoken language. These symbols will be used only when necessary, however, and they will be explained as they are introduced.

THE HUMAN SPEECH MECHANISM

2.3   Obviously not all sounds that human beings can make are used in speech. No language, for example, exploys whistling, coughing, or hand clapping as its primary medium of communication. Instead, the sounds of language are of a very special kind. They are the sounds that are made by the **human speech mechanism**, a term that refers to the various organs of the body that are used in the production of speech. To understand the sounds of Ponapean, then, it will be useful to understand this mechanism and the processes it employs.

There are four basic processes involved in the production of speech sounds. These are the **airstream process**, the **voicing process**, the **oral-nasal process**, and the **articulatory process**. Reference to the following diagram will be useful in understanding these processes and the discussion of the sounds of Ponapean that follows.

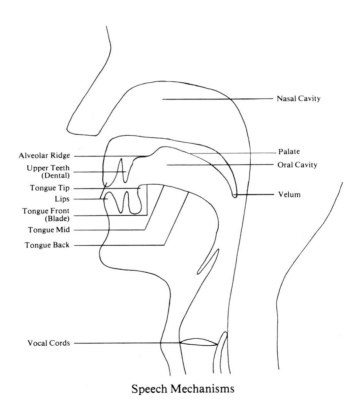

Speech Mechanisms

Figure 1

The **airstream process** involves the action of the lungs. As we exhale or breathe out, our lungs contract and a stream of air is forced out of our bodies. This airstream is essential to the production of most speech sounds. By interrupting it or redirecting it through the action of the following three processes, it is possible to produce a very wide variety of sounds.

The **voicing process** involves the action of the **vocal cords**. The vocal cords are basically two short bands of flesh that stretch from the front to the rear of the **larynx** or, as it is more commonly called, the Adam's apple. As the airstream produced by the lungs leaves the body, it passes between these two vocal cords. Because these cords are moveable, they may be held partially closed, as they are for **voiced sounds**, or they may be held apart, as they are for **voiceless sounds**. To discover for yourself the difference between these two kinds of sounds, place your fingertips against your larynx and say the vowel sound *a*. You should be able to feel some vibration. This vibration is the result of air passing between the closely held together vocal cords. This vibration produces the sound that you hear. The vowel *a* is thus a voiced sound. Now, if you again place your fingertips in this position and say a prolonged *s,* you will feel no vibration and hear no voice; *s* is thus a voiceless sound. The distinction between voiced and voiceless sounds will be important to us as we further study the sound system of Ponapean.

The **oral-nasal process** simply refers to whether the air stream from the lungs exits the body through the mouth (the **oral cavity**) or the nose (the **nasal cavity**). The direction of the airstream is controlled by the **velum**, or **soft palate**, which is the soft back part of the roof of the mouth. The velum is moveable and may be lowered to allow air to exit through the nasal passage, or it may be raised to close off this passage so that the airstream exits through the mouth. Sounds made by shutting off the oral cavity at some point and directing the airstream out through the nose are called **nasal sounds**. Examples are *m, n,* and *ng*. If while saying these sounds you pinch your nose shut, you will notice that the sound is stopped. Sounds made by directing the airstream out through the mouth are called **oral sounds**. Examples are *a, s,* and *l*. Pinching your nose shut while making these sounds does not interfere with their production.

The **articulatory process** refers to the action of the tongue and the lips during the production of speech sounds. The stream of air coming from the lungs may be interrupted in a variety of ways by the tongue and lips to produce different positions and manners of articulation. The term **position of articulation** refers to *where* in the mouth a sound is made. The term **manner of articulation** refers to *how* a sound is made. A simple example will illustrate these two terms. To make the Ponapean sound *d*, the tip of the tongue is placed against the back of the upper teeth. The position of articulation of the sound *d* is thus described as **tipdental, tip** indicating that the tip of the tongue is used, **dental** indicating that the tongue is placed against the upper teeth. Now, if you say a Ponapean *n*, you will discover that the position of articulation is the same, but the manner of articulation is different. *d* is a stop sound. In making a *d* sound, the airstream coming from the lungs is completely stopped, so that it temporarily exits neither from the mouth nor the nose. *n*, on the other hand, is a **nasal** sound. In making an *n* sound, the air is stopped in the mouth at the same position as it is for *d*, but the velum is lowered and air is allowed to escape out through the nose. There are, of course, many different possible positions and manners of articulation in addition to these we have just discussed. Those which are significant to Ponapean will be examined later in this chapter.

In summary, then, there are four basic processes involved in the production of speech sounds. The airstream process initiates the stream of air in which the sounds are made. The voicing process determines whether the sound is voiced or voiceless. The oral-nasal process directs the airstream out either through the mouth or nose, and the articulatory process determines the position and manner of articulation of a sound. Certainly, there is much more that could be said about any one of these processes, but for our purposes, the preceding discussion is adequate to provide a basis for understanding the material that follows.

THE PHONEME

2.4   The human speech mechanism, by employing the four processes previously described, is capable of producing a wide variety of sounds. Yet, speakers of a language use only a relatively small number of these possible sounds in a distinctive way. Hawaiian, for example, uses only thirteen distinctive sounds, which is one of the smallest number of such sounds in any language. The upper limit of the number of distinctive sounds in any one language is probably less than one hundred. Also interesting is the fact that

Stops

2.5.1   A **stop** involves a manner of articulation in which the outward flow of air from the lungs is completely stopped or blocked, so that it exits neither through the mouth nor the nose until a following sound or the end of the word is reached. In Ponapean there are four stops—*p, pw, d,* and *k*—all of which are voiceless and unaspirated. That is, they are produced with the vocal cords apart and without the puff of air that is characteristic of English stops in some positions.

Bilabial Stop *p*

The consonant represented by the letter *p* is called a **bilabial stop** because the outward flow of air is stopped by the two (bi-) lips (labial). The bilabial stop *p* occurs in words like these.

pihl	'water'	*lapake*	'flood'
per	'cautious'	*ngahp*	'fathom'
ape	'et cetera'	*kehp*	'yam'

Velarized Bilabial Stop *pw*

Previously it was noted that sometimes two letters are used in Ponapean to represent a single sound. The consonant represented by the letters *pw* is one such case. *pw* is a **velarized bilabial stop**. Like *p, pw* is made by stopping the flow of air from the lungs with the two lips. But *pw,* unlike *p,* is also **velarized**. Therefore, while making this sound, the back of the tongue is raised close to the back part of the roof of the mouth, called the velum. In addition, the lips are slightly rounded and protruded. *pw* occurs at the beginning and in the middle of words like these.

pwal	'to be slit'	*lapwa*	'to open, as a bag'
pwihn	'group'	*apwal*	'difficult'
pwand	'late'	*tapwur*	'to roll'

pw also occurs at the end of words, but in this position, except in very careful speech, *pw* is made without the lip rounding that occurs when *pw* is at the beginning or in the middle of words. The raising of the back of the tongue, however, still takes place. *pw* occurs at the end of words like these.

| *rihpw* | 'fungus' | *kamadipw* | 'feast' |
| *pwupw* | 'to fall' | *sahpw* | 'land' |

We may thus say that the phoneme *pw* has an unrounded velarized allophone at the end of words, and a rounded velarized allophone in all other positions.

To illustrate that *p* and *pw* are different phonemes, and thus capable of producing a difference in meaning, the following pairs of words are presented.

pai	'fortune'
pwai	'oyster'
apin	'to beat'
apwin	'to wash one's face'
kap	'bundle'
kapw	'new'

Dental Stop *d*

Like *p* and *pw*, *d* is a stop, because it is produced by completely stopping the outward air flow. *d* differs from *p* and *pw*, though, in that this stoppage takes place in the dental area rather than at the lips. The sound *d*, as we previously noted in section 2.3, is thus made by placing the tip of the tongue against the back of the upper teeth so that no air can escape. *d* occurs in words like these.

did	'to build a wall'	*kidi*	'dog'
deke	'island'	*pwoud*	'spouse'
idek	'to ask'	*kid*	'thousand'

We might note at this point that *d*, and indeed all dental sounds, are not always necessarily produced at precisely a dental position of articulation. Particularly when followed by vowels which are made in the back of the mouth, the position of articulation of dental sounds may be just a bit further back in the mouth, slightly behind where the upper teeth enter the gums. To a very minor degree, the positions of all consonants produced with the tongue are influenced by neighboring vowels, but about this we will say no more. What is of considerably more importance in Ponapean is the reverse situation, the influence neighboring consonants have on the position of vowels. We will discuss this in section 2.6.6.

Velar Stop *k*

> The stop sound represented by the letter *k* is made by placing the back of the tongue firmly against the velum so that the outward air flow is completely blocked. *k* occurs in words like these.

kang	'to eat'	*sakau*	'kava'
ke	'you'	*uhk*	'net'
lakapw	'tomorrow'	*limak*	'to bail'

Released Stops

> One further generalization may be made about the stop sounds of Ponapean. At the end of words, in careful speech, all stops in Ponapean are **released**. This means that the organs of speech involved in the production of the stop sound move from a position of articulation to a position of rest in such a manner that the air stopped up in the mouth exits with a very slight hissing noise. Released stops may be heard at the end of words like the following when they are carefully pronounced.

lahp	'guy, gal'
likedepw	'freshwater shrimp'
ohd	'species of taro'
mihk	'to suck'

> Except at the end of words in careful speech, stops are otherwise **non-released**. This means that the organs of speech involved in the production of the stop sound move apart without any resulting hissing noise.

THE FRICATIVE *s*

2.5.2   The term **fricative** describes a manner of articulation in which the airstream exiting from the lungs is obstructed enough to produce a friction-like noise. There is only one fricative sound in Ponapean. It is the sound represented by the letter *s*. In making this sound, the **blade** of the tongue (the part just behind the tip) is placed close to, but not firmly against, the **alveolar ridge**. The alveolar ridge is the bony protrusion in the front part of the roof of the mouth. As air is forced out between the tongue and this

ridge, a friction-like noise, which is the consonant *s*, results. *s* is a
voiceless sound that occurs in words like the following.

seri	'child'	*kese*	'to throw'
suk	'to pound'	*aramas*	'person'
isuh	'seven'	*os*	'to sprout'

s in Ponapean also undergoes varying degrees of **palatalization**.
This means that while *s* is being made, the middle of the tongue is
raised toward the roof of the mouth. The result is that *s* usually
sounds as if it were somewhere between English *s* (as in sip) and
sh (as in ship). The degree to which *s* is palatalized, however,
varies somewhat from speaker to speaker.

THE AFFRICATE *t*

2.5.3   An **affricate** is a combination of a stop and a fricative. There is
only one affricate in Ponapean. It is represented by the letter *t*. *t* is
made by slightly **retroflexing** or curling the tip of the tongue back
so that it touches just behind the alveolar ridge. At the same time,
the sides of the tongue are raised so that they touch against the
inner gumline of the upper teeth. As this sound is produced, the
air is first completely stopped and then, because the tongue is
moved slightly away from where it contacts the roof of the
mouth, the air escapes with the friction-like noise characteristic of
a fricative. *t* is also voiceless. It may thus be described as a
voiceless retroflexed affricate. *t* occurs in words like these.

taht	'floor'	*litok*	'hen'
tou	'contribution'	*saut*	'filthy'
ketia	'boat pole'	*maht*	'pimple'

It should be noted that for some speakers, the fricative part of the
pronunciation of *t* is very slight, so that *t* sounds more like a stop.
Like the patalization of *s*, though, this variation in pronunciation
does not seem to be restricted to a particular dialect or a
particular position in a word.

In some earlier Ponapean spelling systems, no distinction
was made between the sound now represented by the letter *d* and
the sound represented by *t*. These two sounds, though, are
separate phonemes, as illustrated by the following pairs of words.

tipw	'to be broken'
dipw	'clan'
tihti	'skinny'
dihdi	'breast'
met	'here'
med	'full'

Since it makes a difference in meaning whether we say *d* or *t*, it is useful to indicate this difference in the alphabet.

NASALS

2.5.4   There are four nasal consonants in Ponapean—*m*, *mw*, *n*, and *ng*. **Nasal**, remember, is a manner of articulation in which the outward flow of air from the lungs is directed through the nose. All nasals in Ponapean are voiced.

Bilabial Nasal *m*

The bilabial nasal *m* is made simply by holding the lips closed and allowing the air to escape through the nose. Like *p*, *m* is called bilabial because the two lips are used to make the closure. Examples of *m* are:

meir	'to sleep'	*kemeik*	'parrot fish'
mihk	'to suck'	*dahm*	'outrigger'
lemei	'cruel'	*nim*	'to drink'

Velarized Bilabial Nasal *mw*

The single consonant represented by the two letters *mw* is called a **velarized bilabial nasal**. Like *pw*, *mw* is produced with simultaneous lip closure, raising of the back of the tongue towards the velum, and some rounding and protrusion of the lips. *mw* occurs at the beginning and in the middle of words like these:

mwadong	'to play'	*tamwe*	'to lick'
mwenge	'to eat'	*amwise*	'mosquito'

Also like *pw*, *mw* has an unrounded velarized allophone at the end of words. We may thus make the generalization that both velarized consonants (*pw* and *mw*) have unrounded velarized allophones in this position. *mw* occurs word-finally in these examples.

uhmw	'stone oven'	*likamw*	'to lie'
keimw	'corner'	*tihmw*	'nose'

The following pairs of words illustrate that *m* and *mw* are separate phonemes.

mahs	'face'
mwahs	'worm'
kamam	'to enjoy kava'
kamwamw	'to exhaust'
kom	'to pull in a net'
komw	'you'

Dental Nasal *n*

n is a **dental nasal**. It is produced by placing the tip of the tongue against the back of the upper teeth and allowing the air to escape through the nose. Examples of *n* are:

nih	'coconut palm'	*onop*	'to prepare'
nohn	'too'	*lingan*	'beautiful'
eni	'ghost'	*lopwon*	'ball of something'

Before *s*, *n* is also palatalized. Therefore, it is pronounced with the additional raising of the middle of the tongue toward the center of the roof of the mouth. Examples of *n* before *s* are:

nsen	'will'	*sansal*	'clear'
ansou	'time'	*kens*	'yaws'

The reason for this palatalization is that since *s* is normally palatalized to some degree, *n* before *s* copies some of the articulatory properties of the following sound and it too becomes palatalized to the same extent that *s* is. This phenomenon of one sound becoming more like a neighboring one is a very common process in language. Linguists call it **assimilation**.

Another example of assimilation in Ponapean involves the position of articulation of *n* when it precedes *t*. *t* is a retroflexed sound. It is pronounced with the tongue tip curled back slightly and touching just behind the alveolar ridge. When *n* precedes *t*, as it does in the following examples, it too is pronounced in this retroflexed position.

nta	'blood'	*sent*	'cent'
pahnta	'variety of taro'	*kent*	'urine'

Thus, we may say that the phoneme *n* has three allophones, a palatalized one before *s*, a retroflexed one before *t*, and a plain tip dental one in all other positions.

Velar Nasal *ng*

The sound represented by the two letters *ng* is made by placing the back of the tongue against the velum, and allowing air to exit through the nose. Examples of *ng* are:

ngihl	'voice'	*kehngid*	'mango'
ngalis	'to bite'	*sohng*	'to measure'
lingan	'beautiful'	*lahng*	'sky'

LIQUIDS

2.5.5   **Liquid** is a term sometimes used to describe various kinds of *l* and *r* sounds. These two kinds of sounds are alike in that they are both oral sounds that involve partial closure in the mouth. Ponapean *l* and *r* are discussed in more detail below.

Dental *l*

The consonant *l* is made by placing the tip of the tongue against the back of the upper teeth with the blade of the tongue also touching against the alveolar ridge. The sides of the tongue, however, are lowered so that air may escape out over them. *l* is voiced and is also slightly palatalized. This consonant occurs in words like these.

laid	'to fish'	*malek*	'chicken'
litok	'hen'	*pal*	'to hack'
sali	'meat course'	*pihl*	'water'

Alveolar *r*

> The consonant *r* is an alveolar sound because it is made by placing the tip of the tongue against the alveolar ridge. In Ponapean, the *r* sound is **trilled**. This trilling is achieved by holding the tongue tip against the ridge with just the right tension so that the airstream exiting the mouth sets the tip into rapid vibration. *r,* as we have already discussed in section 2.4, has two allophones, a voiceless one at the end of words, and a voiced one elsewhere. Following are some words containing *r*.

rahr	'finger coral'	*sara*	'a species of fish'
ruk	'to hide'	*pihr*	'to fly'
lirop	'mat'	*pasur*	'to hammer'

CONSONANT CHART

2.5.6   We have now discussed how all of the twelve consonants of Ponapean are produced. For the purpose of easy reference, this information is concisely summarized in Chart 2. Notice that positions of articulation are listed horizontally across the top, while information about voicing and manners of articulation are listed vertically along the left side.

Chart 2. Ponapean Consonants

Manner of Articulation		Position of Articulation				
		Bila-bial	Dental	Alveo-lar	Retro-flex	Velar
VOICE-LESS	Stops plain	p	d			k
	velarized	pw				
	Fricative			s		
	Affricate				t	
VOICED	Nasals plain	m	n			ng
	velarized	mw				
	Liquids		l	r		

Our discussion of the consonants of Ponapean is nearly concluded; however, before we turn our attention to vowels, there is one additional property of consonants we need to look at. It is that they sometimes occur doubled.

DOUBLED CONSONANTS

2.5.7 We have observed that consonants in Ponapean may be either voiced or voiceless. As Chart 2 illustrates, there are six voiceless consonants (*p, pw, d, k, s, t*) and six voiced consonants (*m, mw, n, ng, l, r*). This distinction between voiced and voiceless consonants is useful in understanding a number of important facts about the Ponapean sound system, one of which is the occurrence of doubled consonants.

The term **doubled consonant** is used to describe two identical consonants that occur next to each other. Whether consonants are single or doubled can make a difference in meaning in Ponapean, as this example illustrates.

Single *mw*	*kamwus*	'to jerk up'
Doubled *mw*	*kammwus*	'to cause to vomit'

(Note that in Ponapean orthography doubled *mw* *(mwmw)* is written *mmw*.)

The sequence *mmw* differs from *mw* in that it is held about twice as long as the single consonant. The distinction between voiced and voiceless consonants now becomes important to us because we may make the generalization that all voiced consonants in Ponapean occur doubled. Voiceless consonants on the other hand, except under special conditions, never occur doubled.

Examples of doubled voiced consonants in the middle of words are:

m	*kommoal*	'to rest'
	kemmad	'to change into dry clothing'
mw	*lammwin*	'majestic'
	rommwidi	'to calm down'
n	*kosonned*	'rule'
	urenna	'lobster'
ng	*ngongngong*	'to be barking'

l	*arewalla*	'to return to the wild, of animals'
	lallal	'to speak incessantly'
r	*rarrar*	'to be making a static-like noise'
	rerrer	'to be trembling'

At least two of these voiced consonants also occur doubled at the ends of words in Ponapean. These are *l* and *mw,* as illustrated by the following examples.

l	*mall*	'clearing, in the forest'
	mwell	'species of shellfish'
	kull	'roach'
mw	*lemmw*	'afraid of ghosts'
	rommw	'calm'

Final doubled consonants in Ponapean, however, are somewhat uncommon.

Also uncommon are doubled consonants at the beginning of words. Only *m*, *mw*, and *ng* are found doubled in this position, and examples are rare.

m	*mmed*	'full'
mw	*mmwus*	'to vomit'
ng	*ngnget*	'to pant'

In standard Ponapean orthography, these doubled consonants are not usually written, and, in fact, probably most speakers of Ponapean do not pronounce these consonants doubled when they are at the beginning of a word. But, if we put the prefix *ka-* meaning 'to cause' before these words, the doubled consonants may be more easily heard, as illustrated below.

kammed	'to cause to be full'
kammwus	'to cause to vomit'
kangnget	'to cause to pant'

All voiced consonants thus occur doubled in the middle of words, and some voiced consonants also occur doubled at the beginning and at the end of words. Voiceless consonants though, as we have noted, do not occur doubled except under special conditions. We might examine now what these special conditions are.

One is that voiceless consonants may occur doubled in words that have been borrowed into Ponapean from other languages. Examples are:

pp	*nappa*	'Chinese cabbage'	from Japanese '*nappa*'
ss	*kiassi*	'catcher'	from English 'catcher' via Japanese '*kyatchi*'
kk	*kakko*	'putting on airs'	from Japanese 'kakkoo'

Another is that voiceless consonants sometimes occur doubled in exclamations. Two examples are:

ss	*esse*	'an exclamation of pain'
kk	*akka*	'an exclamation of surprise'

Finally, the voiceless consonants *d*, *t*, and *s* may occur doubled when a word ending in one of these consonants is followed by a suffix that begins with the same consonant. Examples are:

weid	'to walk'	*weiddi*	'to walk downwards'
saut	'filthy'	*sautte*	'just filthy'
lus	'to jump'	*lussang*	'to jump from'

Under conditions described in section 3.5, however, a vowel may occur between these doubled consonants, as in the following examples.

weididi	'to walk downwards'
sautete	'just filthy'
lusisang	'to jump from'

Except in the three circumstances named above, voiceless consonants never occur doubled. In section 2.9.5, we will examine why this is so.

THE VOWELS OF PONAPEAN

2.6.   The speech sounds represented by the letters, *a, e, i, o, oa,* and *u* are called **vowels**. Vowels are distinguished from consonants principally by the fact that they are sounds which allow a relatively free outward flow of air from the lungs. Consonants, on the other hand, are characterized by an obstruction of this air flow. About Ponapean vowels specifically, two further generalizations may be made. First, all Ponapean vowels are oral; they are produced with the velum raised to shut off the nasal passage. Secondly, all Ponapean vowels are voiced; they are produced with vibrating vocal cords. Other distinguishing features of vowels are determined by the shape of the oral cavity. This is accomplished by changing the position of the tongue, the lips, and the jaw. We shall examine these features in more detail later.

It is important first to point out that, in two respects, vowels are more difficult to discuss than consonants. First, there is some dialect variation in the vowel system of Ponapean. To alleviate possible confusion here, we will begin by examining the vowels of the northern dialect which, as we have noted, serves as the standard for Ponapean spelling. Then, in section 2.6.7, we will discuss the Kiti dialect and other subdialectal variations in vowels. A second problem is that it will be necessary in our discussion of Ponapean vowels to introduce some special symbols. This is because we shall want to talk about sound distinctions that are not represented in the spelling system. With these two points in mind, then, we may begin our discussion of the vowels of the northern dialect.

VOWEL CHART

2.6.1   The vowels of the northern dialect are illustrated in the following chart along with their approximate English equivalents. Standard alphabetic symbols are used except for the two vowels within parallel diagonal lines, /e/ and /ɛ/. Both of these are written *e* in the Ponapean spelling system.

Ponapean Vowel	As in the Ponapean Word	Approximate English Equivalent
a	*a*mwer	p*o*t
/e/	*e*sil	b*ai*t
/ɛ/	d*e*	b*e*t
i	n*i*	b*ea*t
o	r*o*ng	b*oa*t
oa	r*oa*ng	b*ou*ght
u	*u*d*u*k	b*oo*t

The positions of articulation of Ponapean vowels are summarized in Chart 3.

Chart 3.

Tongue Height	Tongue Advancement		
	Front	Central	Back
High	i		u
Mid	/e/		o
Lower-Mid	/ɛ/		oa
Low		a	

Since our discussion of vowels will be organized according to Chart 3, it is appropriate that we first say a few words about the terms it employs.

Notice that along the left side of this chart four levels of **tongue height** are indicated. Tongue height, as is implicit in the term, refers to the height of the tongue in the mouth. To get an idea of the extremes involved here, first say the high vowel *i* (as in the word *lihli*) and then the low vowel *a* (as in the word *pah*) and watch what happens to your jaw. Notice that during the pronunciation of *i* the mouth is nearly closed and the tongue is high in the mouth. When you say *a,* however, the jaw is lowered in order to get the tongue into a low position. The pronunciation of the high vowel *u* (as in the word *suhr*) followed by *a* similarly shows this difference in tongue height.

Differences in tongue height are not sufficient, however, to distinguish all Ponapean vowels from one another. If you look at the chart, you will notice that we also describe vowels according to **tongue advancement**. Tongue advancement simply refers to whether the tongue is in the front, central, or back portion of the mouth. A vowel like *i*, for example, is produced with the tongue advanced towards the front of the mouth. A vowel like *u* is produced with the tongue retracted towards the back of the mouth. If you say *i*, then *u*, and repeat these vowels in succession, *i-u, i-u*, etc., you may be able to feel your tongue changing position from the front of the mouth for *i* to the back of the mouth for *u.*

Using these terms, we will now examine in more detail the vowels presented in Chart 3. However, in the following discussion we will refer only to the basic position of articulation of these vowels and postpone our examination of vowel allophones until section 2.6.6. This is because it is possible to summarize the major vowel allophones in a few simple generalizations.

FRONT VOWELS

2.6.2   There are three **front vowels** in the northern dialect of Ponapean. These are *i*, /e/, and /ɛ/.

The High Vowel *i*

The high vowel *i* is pronounced with the tongue high and front in the mouth. Examples of *i* are:

id	'to make a fire'	*esil*	'three'
ilok	'wave'	*ni*	'at'
pil	'also'	*eni*	'ghost'

The Mid Vowel /e/ and the Lower-Mid Vowel /ɛ/

Two contrasting vowels of the northern dialect of Ponapean are represented by the single letter *e* in conventional Ponapean spelling. To distinguish between these two vowel sounds we will use the symbols /e/ and /ɛ/, enclosing these symbols or words which contain them between parallel diagonal lines (/ /) to remind you that we are talking about sound differences that the Ponapean spelling system ignores. Examples of words in which these two vowel sounds contrast are:

/pel/	'to steer'
/pɛl/	'to be in a taboo relationship'
/ser/	'hey you all'
/sɛr/	'to run aground'
/lel/	'to be wounded'
/lɛl/	'to reach or arrive at'
/les/	'to receive one's comeuppance'
/lɛs/	'to split a coconut'

The vowel /e/ differs from /ɛ/ mainly in that it is pronounced a bit higher in the mouth. /e/ is a mid vowel; it is pronounced with the tongue at a height approximately mid-way between a high and a low vowel. /ɛ/ is a lower-mid vowel; it is pronounced with the tongue a bit lower in the mouth than for /e/, but not so low as for a low vowel like *a*.

In addition to occurring in the middle of words, as the preceding examples illustrate, the vowel /e/ is also found at the beginning of words.

| /ekis/ | 'a little' | /ei/ | 'yes' |

The vowel /e/ does not occur at the end of words however. In fact, it is the only phoneme in Ponapean that does not occur in all positions within a word. All other phonemes occur at the beginning, in the middle, and at the end of words, but /e/ occurs only initially and medially.

/ɛ/, then, occurs not only medially as the previous examples illustrate, but also initially and finally. Examples are:

| /ɛni/ | 'ghost' | /dɛ/ | 'or' |
| /ɛdɛ/ | 'to sharpen' | /kɛ/ | 'you' |

In the Kiti dialect of Ponapean, as we shall discuss further in section **2**.6.7, /e/ and /ɛ/ do not contrast. Even within the northern dialect, there is some reason to believe that the contrast between /e/ and /ɛ/ is predictable (see Rehg, 1973), but the arguments for this are still tentative. For our purposes, we will recognize the existence of /e/ and /ɛ/ as contrasting vowels. You should be aware, though, that because of the dialect variations within these vowels, and because of their possible ultimate predictability, it is a strength rather than a weakness of the Ponapean orthography that it represents both these vowels with the single letter *e*.

BACK VOWELS

2.6.3   There are three **back vowels** in Ponapean. These are *u*, *o*, and *oa*. A unique characteristic of back vowels is that they are all rounded. That is, they are produced with some rounding and protrusion of the lips. Other distinguishing features of back vowels are presented below.

The High Vowel *u*

Like *i*, *u* is a high vowel; but, whereas *i* is produced in the front of the mouth, *u* is made with the tongue retracted and raised towards the velum. *u* is thus called a **high back vowel**. It occurs in words such as:

uduk	'flesh'	*mwut*	'pulverized'
urak	'to lap up'	*duhdu*	'bathe'
pwupw	'to fall'	*usu*	'star'

The Mid Vowel *o*

The vowel *o*, like /e/, is a **mid vowel**. It is made with the tongue at a mid height in the back part of the mouth. Examples of *o* are:

omw	'your, singular'	*rong*	'to hear'
onop	'to prepare'	*mehwo*	'voracious'
mwopw	'out of breath'	*uwako*	'to gag'

The Lower-Mid Vowel *oa*

In Ponapean spelling, the two letters *oa* are used to represent the lower-mid back vowel which occurs in words like these.

oale	'to wave'	*roang*	'burned'
oarong	'a species of fish'	*doakoa*	'to spear'
pwoalos	'bundle'	*pwukoa*	'responsibility'

This vowel is made with the tongue retracted towards the back of the mouth and held lower than it is for *o*, but not so low as it is for *a*. The two letters *oa* are thus combined to represent this single sound.

THE CENTRAL VOWEL *a*

2.6.4   The only **central vowel** in Ponapean is *a*. It is also the only **low vowel**. In producing *a*, the tongue is held in the central part of the mouth, and the jaw is dropped a bit in order to get the tongue into a low position. (It should be pointed out that *a* in Ponapean is not quite as low as *a* in English.) Examples are:

arep	'spear'	*tang*	'to run'
apwin	'to wash one's face'	*sawa*	'taro species'
pwar	'to appear,	*nta*	'blood'

LONG VOWELS

2.6.5 All vowels in Ponapean may occur **long** as well as **short**. This difference in vowel length is phonemic; it signals a difference in meaning. For the Ponapean spelling system, the German convention of writing *h* after a vowel to indicate length was adopted. Examples of short vs. long vowels are presented below. The vowel being contrasted for length is listed to the left and Ponapean examples are presented as they are conventionally spelled to the right.

i	*id*	'to make a fire'	*ihd*	'a species of plant'
/e/	*pei*	'to fight'	*pehi*	'altar'
/ɛ/	*ne*	'to be distributed'	*neh*	'its leg'
a	*pa*	'to weave'	*pah*	'under'
oa	*soan*	'aligned'	*soahn*	'wounded'
o	*dol*	'to mix'	*dohl*	'mountain'
u	*pwung*	'correct'	*pwuhng*	'rights'

It should be noted that long vowels might also be interpreted as a sequence of two identical vowels, or as double vowels. Thus, we might make the generalization that vowels as well as voiced consonants may occur doubled.

VOWEL ALLOPHONES

2.6.6 To account for the major allophones of the vowel phonemes we have thus far discussed, only a few simple generalizations are required. Before we may make these generalizations, though, it will be necessary to return to our discussion of consonants.

One way to classify consonants is according to their position of articulation, whether they are bilabial, dental, alveolar, etc. For the purpose of discussing vowel allophones, we may simplify this classification somewhat and merely talk about **front** and **back consonants**. These are listed below.

	Front	Back
	p	pw
	m	mw
	d	t
	l	r
	n	ng
	s	—
	—	k

Notice that all of the consonants labeled *front* involve articulation in the front of the mouth. Either they are produced at or in front of a dental position of articulation, or they involve palatalization. All of the consonants labeled *back* involve articulation in the back of the mouth. They are produced at or behind an alveolar position of articulation, or they involve velarization.

Using this front/back distinction in consonants, we may now make these statements about vowel allophones.

1. The short front vowels *i*, /e/, and /ɛ/ are backed to a central position in the environment of back consonants.

2. The short back vowels *u, o,* and *oa* are fronted to a central position in the environment of front consonants.

3. The short central vowel *a* is fronted to a front position in the environment of front consonants.

More generally, we may observe that the degree of tongue advancement of vowels is influenced by neighboring consonants. Examples where vowels are in "pure" environments, that is where the neighboring consonants are either both front or both back, are best to initially illustrate this. Such examples are provided below following a restatement of the point they exemplify.

1. The short front vowels *i*, /e/, and /ɛ/ are backed to a central position in the environment of back consonants.

Front Vowels	Between Front C's		Between Back C's	
i	pil	'also'	t*i*pw	'to be broken'
/e/	/lel/	'to be wounded'	/ngng*e*t/	'to pant'
/ɛ/	/m*ɛ*m/	'sweet'	/t*ɛ*ng/	'tight'

The italicized vowels in the above examples are the ones pro-

nounced in a central position. Thus, a vowel like /ɛ/ is pronounced as a front vowel between front consonants (phonetically
[ɛ], as in the English word 'b*e*t'), but as a central vowel between
back consonants (phonetically [ə], as in the English word 'b*u*t').

2.   The short back vowels *u, o,* and *oa* are fronted to a
central position in the environment of front consonants.

Back Vowels	Between Front C's		Between Back C's	
u	l*u*l	'to flame'	pwupw	'to be dropped'
o	p*o*s	'to explode'	ngong	'to bark'
oa	l*o*al	'deep'	roang	'burned'

As in the previous examples, the italicized vowels are the central
ones. Thus, a vowel like *u* is pronounced as a back vowel between
back consonants (phonetically [u]), but as a central vowel between front consonants (phonetically [ʉ]).

3.   The short central vowel *a* is fronted to a front position in
the environment of front consonants.

Central Vowel	Between Front C's		Between Back C's	
a	p*a*p	'to swim'	kak	'to be able'

Thus, the vowel *a* is pronounced as a central vowel between back
consonants (phonetically [ɐ], approximately as the vowel in the
English word 'top'), but as a front vowel between front consonants (phonetically [æ], as in the English word 'cap').

These examples illustrate short vowels in pure environments.
When short vowels occur in mixed environments, that is between
a front consonant and a back consonant or a back consonant and
a front consonant, the quality of the vowel is influenced by both
consonants, generally with the following consonant dominating.
An example is the word /mɛk/ 'dented'. In this word, the vowel /ɛ/
is preceded by a front consonant and followed by a back
consonant. In response to these consonants, the vowel begins in a
front position, but because of the following back consonant, the
vowel glides to a central position.

The previous statements concerning vowel allophones deal
with short vowels. Long vowels, however, are not noticeably
affected by adjacent consonants. If you listen carefully, you might
notice some slight effect of adjacent consonants on long vowels,
either at the very beginning or end of their articulation, but

basically the primary front, central, or back quality of these vowels, regardless of surrounding consonants, is preserved.

Before we conclude this discussion of vowel allophones, there are two additional points that should be noted. One is that glides (sounds like /y/ and /w/) also influence the pronunciation of vowels. We will examine this in section **2.7.4**. The second concerns the existence of a further justification for setting up a front and back series of consonants in Ponapean. Note in Chart 4 that except for *s* and *k,* front and back consonants are listed in pairs. The importance of this is that front and back consonants that are members of the same pair are almost never found within the same morpheme. (See section **3.2.1** for a definition of morpheme.) Thus, while words like *dod* and *tot* are permissible words in Ponapean, words like *dot* and *tod* are not, since *d* and *t* are members of the same pair, *d* being the front consonant of the pair and *t* the back consonant.

DIALECT VARIATION IN VOWELS

2.6.7   Thus far in our discussion of Ponapean, we have made reference to two major dialects, which we have called the northern dialect and the Kiti dialect. The consonant system of these dialects, we have noted, is the same. It is on the basis of differences in their vowel systems that we distinguish between these two dialects.

One important way in which the Kiti dialect differs from the northern dialect is that in the Kiti dialect the vowels /e/ and /ɛ/ do not contrast. Notice these pairs of words in the two dialects.

Northern Dialect	Kiti Dialect	English gloss
/pel/	/pɛl/	'to steer'
/pɛl/	/poal/	'to be in a taboo relationship'
/ser/	/sɛr/	'hey you all'
/sɛr/	/sɛr/	'to run aground'
/lel/	/lɛl/	'to be wounded'
/lɛl/	/lɛl/	'to reach or arrive at'
/les/	/lɛs/	'to receive one's comeuppance'
/lɛs/	/lɛs/	'to split a coconut'

In the Kiti dialect it is impossible to find a pair of words where the difference between the vowels /e/ and /ɛ/ results in a difference in meaning.

As the previous examples illustrate, some words which contain /ɛ/ in the northern dialect are pronounced with *oa* in the Kiti dialect. Further examples are:

Northern Dialect	Kiti Dialect	English Gloss
/dɛng/	*doang*	'taut'
/tɛp/	*toap*	'start'
/rɛirɛi/	*roairoai*	'long'
/kɛhp/	*koahp*	'yam'
/mwɛngɛ/	*mwoangoa*	'eat'
/wɛrɛk/	*woaroak*	'spouse'
/kɛhs/	*koahs*	'hook'
/mwɛkid/	*mwoakid*	'move'
/pwɛrisɛk/	*pwoarisoak*	'industrious'
/mwɛnginingin/	*mwoanginingin*	'whisper'

It is this characteristic distribution of vowels, and the lack of contrast between /e/ and /ɛ/, which most speakers of Ponapean recognize as being the distinguishing features of the Kiti dialect. In other respects, the Kiti vowel system is like the northern one. It has contrastive vowel length, and consonants affect vowel qualitites.

There are, of course, many sub-dialects within each of these two major dialect areas. Within the northern dialect, for example, there are noticeable differences between the speech of someone from the Kolonia area and someone from Awak. Within the Kiti dialect, there are also differences, for example, between the speech of someone from Wene and someone from Pehleng. These differences, though, are probably due to vowel distribution, intonation, and word choice, rather than to the actual number of contrasting vowels.

There is much more that might be said about Ponapean dialects and sub-dialects. But, unfortunately, not very much is really known about this subject. Hopefully, future investigators will add to this area of our knowledge of Ponapean.

THE GLIDES OF PONAPEAN

2.7   Thus far we have discussed the consonants and the vowels of

Ponapean. There still remain two sounds that occur in all dialects of Ponapean that we have not yet examined. These are the glides /w/ and /y/.

Glides are sounds that have properties of both consonants and vowels. Indeed, some linguists call glides semi-consonants; others call them semi-vowels. For the purposes of our discussion we will use the term glide, thus emphasizing that sounds of this type involve a moving or gliding, rather than a stationary, manner of articulation.

THE GLIDE /w/

2.7.1   Since the glide /w/ is sometimes written in Ponapean as *w* and sometimes as *u,* we will employ the usual convention of writing /w/ between diagonal lines to remind you that we are talking about the sound and not the letter.

To produce the glide /w/, as in the following words, the tongue starts from a position high and back in the mouth, as for the vowel *u,* and then glides to the position of the following vowel. Like *u,* /w/ also involves some rounding and protrusion of the lips. Examples of words containing /w/ follow.

wini	'medicine'	*weng*	'to squeeze'
wadek	'to read'	*wahr*	'canoe'

Notice that in these words, where /w/ occurs at the beginning of a word, it is spelled *w.*

When /w/ occurs in the middle of words between vowels, essentially two gliding movements are involved. The first is from the position of the preceding vowel towards the high, back part of the mouth (towards *u*); the second is from this position towards the position of the following vowel. This happens, of course, very rapidly. Examples of words in which /w/ occurs between vowels follow.

awi	'to wait'	*lawad*	'to untie'
sawa	'taro'	*ewe*	'its mouth'

Here, also, /w/ is spelled *w.*

When /w/ occurs after vowels, either at the end of a word, or before a consonant or glide, it is produced by gliding the tongue from the position of the preceding vowel towards the position of the vowel *u*. In this case, /w/ is written in standard Ponapean spelling as *u*. Notice these examples which are spelled with /w/ in the first column, and then conventionally with *u* in the second.

Spelled with /w/	Conventionally Spelled	English Gloss
/pwudaw/	*pwudau*	'sweat'
/inow/	*inou*	'promise'
/riaw/	*riau*	'two'
/pwowd/	*pwoud*	'spouse'
/mawdɛl/	*maudel*	'to yawn'
/lawd/	*laud*	'big, old'

We may summarize our observations about the spelling of this glide as follows. /w/ is written as *w* when it occurs before vowels; elsewhere, at the end of words and before consonants, it is written as *u*.

THE GLIDE /y/

2.7.2   The glide which we shall examine in this section is written in all positions in Ponapean spelling as *i*. The letter *i* thus represents both a vowel sound and a glide sound. As an example of these two uses of the letter *i*, compare the initial sounds of words like *ilok* 'wave' and *iahd* 'when'. The first word begins with a vowel, while the second begins with a glide. These two sounds, while similar, are different enough that if you substitute one for the other, the result will be unacceptable. In order to avoid confusion between the two sounds represented by the letter *i*, we will write the glide as /y/.

/y/ is a high front glide. When it occurs before vowels, the tongue starts from a position high and front in the mouth, as for the vowel *i*, and then glides to the position of the following vowel. After vowels, the process is reversed. The tongue glides from the position of the preceding vowel to the high front position. Between vowels, both the glide away from the preceding vowel and the glide towards the following vowel are heard. /y/, then, is produced much like /w/, except that /y/ is a high front glide and is unrounded while /w/ is a high back glide and is rounded. /y/ occurs in words like these:

Spelled with /y/	Conventionally Spelled	English Gloss
/yahk/	*iahk*	'crazy'

/yohla/	*iohla*	'to miscarry'
/ayo/	*aio*	'yesterday'
/lokaya/	*lokaia*	'talk'
/koayt/	*koait*	'crowded'
/ayp/	*aip*	'drum'
/loy/	*loi*	'to collide'
/mwuroy/	*mwuroi*	'pigeon'

THE SPELLING OF GLIDES

2.7.3   In the preceding sections, two rules were given about how glides are to be written. These rules, established by the Ponapean Orthography Committee, may be summarized as follows. (1) The glide /w/ is to be written *w* when it occurs before vowels; elsewhere it is to be written *u*. (2) The glide /y/ is always to be written *i*. Going from the spoken to the written language, these rules work well. Going from the written language to the spoken language, however, a problem emerges.

The nature of the problem is essentially this. When does written *u* represent /u/ and when does it represent /w/, and similarly, when does written *i* represent /i/ and when does it represent /y/? At the beginning and in the middle of words, the answer to this question is easy. The letter *u* always represents /u/ at the beginning of words; in the middle of words it represents /w/ *only* when it is preceded by a vowel (as in *laud*). The letter *i* represents /y/ *only* when it is at the beginning of a word and is followed by a vowel (as in *iahd*) or when it is in the middle of a word and is preceded by a vowel (as in *aio, aip,* or *iouiou*). At the ends of words, however, whether the letters *i* and *u* represent glides or vowels is ambiguous. This ambiguity is illustrated by the following pairs of words.

Conventionally Spelled	Phonemically Spelled	English
pei	/pey/	'float'
pei	/pei/	'fight'
leu	/lew/	'cooked'
lou	/lou/	'cooled'

Notice in the conventional spelling that final *i* represents both /y/ and /i/ and final *u* both /w/ and /u/. Proof of this is that these final sounds are pronounced differently (though this may be difficult to detect). Also, as we shall see in section **3**.3.4, pairs of words like these behave differently when they reduplicate. The Ponapean spelling system thus fails to distinguish between final glides and high vowels.

THE INFLUENCE OF GLIDES ON ADJACENT VOWELS

2.7.4   In section **2**.6.6 we noted that on the basis of a distinction between front and back consonants, it was possible to predict the major vowel allophones of Ponapean. At this point, we may extend our generalizations about the influence of front and back consonants on vowels to include glides. The observation we may make is that the glide /y/, which is a high, front glide, behaves like a front consonant; therefore, it has a fronting effect on vowels. The glide /w/, which is a high, back glide behaves like a back consonant; it has a backing effect on vowels.

THE SYLLABLE IN PONAPEAN

2.8   Our procedure thus far has been to look at the individual sounds of Ponapean. We have examined one by one the consonants, vowels, and glides of the language. Now we wish to turn to the **syllable**. Because it is easier to illustrate what a syllable is than to define it, let us begin this discussion by looking at some Ponapean words divided into syllables. A period is used in the following examples to mark syllable division.

1 Syllable	*wih*	'fat'
2 Syllables	*n.ta*	'blood'
3 Syllables	*ka.ma.dipw*	'feast'
4 Syllables	*wa.di.li.kih*	'to memorize'
5 Syllables	*pe.ri.pe.ri.ki*	'to be afraid of'

These words illustrate Ponapean words of up to five syllables in length. Some Ponapean words consist of even more than five syllables. One example is *pwu.du.pwu.dau.ke.re.ker* 'sweating', which consists of seven syllables.

Now let us attempt a definition of a syllable. Basically a syllable is a unit of speech production. It is the smallest sequence of phonemes normally uttered in slowed down speech.

If you examine the preceding examples of syllables, you will notice that one of the characteristics of a syllable is that it contains one and only one peak sound. Usually this is in the form of a vowel, but under special circumstances we will discuss below, it may also be a nasal consonant. Employing this observation, it is possible to establish three rules which will correctly mark syllable division in Ponapean. First, though, a word of caution; these rules apply to sounds and not letters. You must keep this in mind if the rules are to work.

1.   Except at the end of a word, place a syllable boundary between two adjacent consonants, between two adjacent glides, or between an adjacent consonant and a glide. Examples are:

Between Consonants

men.seng	'morning'	*mwohn.di*	'to sit down'
kam.mwus	'to make vomit'	*toan.toal*	'black'

Between Glides

wei.wei	'loincloth'	*iou.iou*	'a species of plant'
dou.iak	'type of spear-fishing'	*sei.wei*	'to paddle towards you'

Between a Glide and a Consonant

kai.kai	'chin'	*ou.dek*	'punishment'
pei.ned	'to curse'	*au.de*	'to fill'

Notice that this rule does not put a syllable boundary between final consonants or a final glide and consonant. These words, therefore, are only one syllable long.

meir	'to sleep'	*mand*	'tame'
paip	'boulder'	*kens*	'yaws'
laud	'old, big'	*emp*	'coconut crab'

This rule does correctly place a syllable boundary between an initial nasal and a following consonant.

m.pei	'bouyant'	*n.ting*	'to write'
n.sen	'will'	*ng.ked*	'to roof'

The initial vowels that are sometimes heard before words like these (for example, *mpei* is sometimes pronounced /impei/) will be discussed in section **2**.9.2.

2. Place a syllable boundary before consonants or glides which occur between vowels.

Before a Consonant

li.kan	'spider'	*i.ding*	'to grate'
deh.de	'clear'	*pa.dil*	'to paddle'

Before a Glide

da.wih	'to inspect'	*mah.win*	'war'
ma.iai	'unlucky'	*pe.iek*	'to be slid'

Because glides sound doubled between vowels in Ponapean, it is more difficult in these examples to be sure where to mark syllable division. The glide seems to belong to both syllables. For our purposes, however, we will mark syllable division before the glide.

3. Place a syllable boundary between two vowels.

wi.a	'to do'	*la.o*	'dear'
ki.epw	'species of lily'	*pa.ehl*	'four strings'

When the two words in the first column are pronounced, there is usually a glide inserted between the vowels. *Wia* for example, except in careful speech, is pronounced /wiya/. The insertion of /y/ here is predictable as a natural transition from /i/ to the following vowel. This phenomenon will be examined in further detail in section 2.9.1.

OTHER SOUND RULES

2.9 The sound rules we have examined thus far are those that describe allophones of phonemes or predict syllable structure. There are, however, still other sound rules we have not yet considered. Rules that add phonemes or delete phonemes, rules that change one phoneme to another, and rules for stress and intonation patterns are also important in describing Ponapean. Not all of these rules can be described here however. In order to understand how some sound rules work, a more sophisticated knowledge of the structure of words and phrases is necessary. Consequently, the rules presented in the following sections are limited to those for which a sufficient background has already been established. In sections **2**.9.1 and **2**.9.2 we will examine two rules which add phonemes. In

sections **2**.9.3, **2**.9.4, and **2**.9.5 we will examine five rules which
change one phoneme to another. Finally, in section **2**.9.6, references will be provided for the location of those sound rules that
are examined in subsequent chapters.

GLIDE INSERTION

2.9.1   In spoken Ponapean, a glide insertion rule is required to account
for the presence of the glide that occurs between a high vowel and
any adjacent non-high vowel. Examples involving the high vowel
/i/ follow.

Spelled	Pronounced	English
diar	/diyar/	'to find'
tie	/tiyɛ/	'to hang from the ear'
mie	/miyɛ/	'to exist'
wai	/wayi/	'to sneak'
mai	/mayi/	'skillful'
toai	/toayi/	'to have a runny nose'

The glide /y/ that is inserted in these examples is part of the
natural transition that occurs between the pronunciation of /i/
and an adjacent non-high vowel. The Ponapean Orthography
Committee's recommendation is that this glide should not be
written.
        When /u/, a high back vowel, is adjacent to a non-high
vowel, the glide /w/ is inserted. When /u/ precedes the non-high
vowel, this glide is written, as in these examples.

Spelled	Pronounced	English
suwed	/suwɛd/	'bad'
luwak	/luwak/	'jealous'
duwe	/duwɛ/	'condition'

These words could be spelled *sued*, *luak*, or *due* (as they indeed are
by many Ponapeans), but the recommendation of the orthography committee is that these inserted glides be written. If /u/
follows a non-high vowel, however, the inserted glide is not to be
written, as in these examples.

lou	/lowu/	'cooled'
sou	/sowu/	'to change residence'

pou	/powu/	'cold'

We may summarize our observations about glide insertion in the following rule.

- In speech, when a high vowel is adjacent to a non-high vowel, insert between these vowels a glide that agrees in tongue advancement with the high vowel.

If the inserted glide is /y/, it is not written. If it is /w/, it is written after *u*, but not before *u*.

PROTHETIC VOWELS

2.9.2   Consider words in Ponapean like these.

Spelled	Pronounced			English
mpe	/mpɛ/	or	/impɛ/	'beside it'
nda	/nda/	or	/inda/	'to say'
nsen	/nsɛn/	or	/insɛn/	'will'
nta	/nta/	or	/inta/	'blood'
ngkapwan	/ngkapwan/	or	/ingkapwan/	'a while ago'
mpwer	/mwpwɛr/	or	/umwpwɛr/	'twin'
ngkoal	/ngkoal/	or	/ungkoal/	'to make sennit'
ngkopw	/ngkopw/	or	/ungkopw/	'species of crab'

Notice that words like these, which begin with a nasal consonant followed by another consonant, may be pronounced in two ways. Either they may begin with the nasal consonant, or they may have a vowel before them.

A number of important observations may be made about these additional initial vowels. First, their presence is optional; they do not change the meaning of the word. Second, only one of two vowels may be added—either /i/, as in the first group of words, or /u/, as in the second group. Third, whether /i/ or /u/ will occur before a particular word is fully predictable. /u/, which is pronounced with rounded lips, occurs only before words beginning with rounded consonants (/mw/) or before words in which the first vowel is round (/oa/, /o/, or /u/). /i/ occurs elsewhere.

Predictable initial vowels like these are called **prothetic vowels** (vowels which are added to the front of words). The prothetic vowel rule may be stated as follows.

- When a word begins with a nasal consonant followed by another consonant, a prothetic vowel may optionally occur. This vowel will be /u/ before words beginning with rounded consonants or words in which the first vowel is round; elsewhere, it will be /i/.

The recommendation of the Ponapean Orthography Committee is that these prothetic vowels not be written.

NASAL ASSIMILATION

2.9.3   The two rules we will examine in this section may both be characterized as **nasal assimilation rules**. They both specify the conditions under which a nasal consonant assimilates, either partially or completely, to a following consonant. These rules are also similar in other ways. Both affect the nasal consonant *n* and both apply within a word or, in rapid speech, to adjacent consonants of different words. The second of these rules, in fact, might be viewed as a subpart of the first.

Partial Assimilation

The first of these nasal assimilation rules may be stated as follows.

- When *n* and a following consonant come together in speech, *n* may become a nasal that agrees in position of articulation with the following consonant.

This rule involves **partial assimilation**. Therefore, while *n* may assimilate to the *position* of articulation of a following consonant, it does not assimilate to the *manner;* only nasal consonants result from the application of this rule.

This rule predicts that *n* will remain *n* before dental, alveolar, or retroflex consonants (with the positional variants described in section **2.5.4**), but will become *m* before plain bilabial consonants, *mw* before velarized bilabial consonants, and *ng* before velar consonants. The words below in which the preposition *nan* 'in' is bound to a following noun illustrate this rule.

Spelled	Rapidly Pronounced	English
nanpar	/nampar/	'trade wind season'
nanpwungara	/namwpwungara/	'between them'

nanmadau	/nammadaw/	'ocean, beyond the reef'
nanmwoalehdi	/namwmwoalɛhdi/	'to rest'
nansed	/nansɛd/	'ocean'
nankep	/nangkɛp/	'inlet'

Examples involving two words are:

kisin pakas	/kisimpakas/	'small species of fish'
kilin pwihk	/kilimwpwihk/	'skin of a pig'
kilin malek	/kilimmalek/	'skin of a chicken'
tihn kidi	/tihngkidi/	'bone of a dog'
pahn ngetengete	/pahngngɛtɛngɛtɛ/	'roof of the mouth'

Complete Assimilation

The second nasal assimilation rule involves the **complete assimilation** of *n* to a following consonant. This rule specifies the conditions under which *n* will copy *both* the position and the manner of articulation of a following consonant. This rule is:

• When *n* and a following liquid consonant come together in speech, *n* may completely assimilate to that liquid.

More simply, this rule changes *nl* to *ll* and *nr* to *rr*, as illustrated by the following words.

Spelled	Rapidly Pronounced	English
nanleng	/nallɛng/	'heaven'
Kepinle	/kɛpillɛ/	'a place name'
nanrek	/narrɛk/	'season of plenty'
nanras	/narras/	'ground level of a feasthouse'

Examples with two words are:

pahn lingan	/pahllingan/	'will be beautiful'
pahn rong	/pahrrong/	'will listen'

LIQUID ASSIMILATION

2.9.4   Liquid consonants (*l* and *r*) are subject to complete assimilation under the conditions expressed in the following rule.

• When a liquid and a following coronal consonant come together as a consequence of reduplication, the liquid will completely assimilate to the following consonant.

The term **coronal consonant** is used to describe those consonants produced at dental, alveolar, or retroflex positions of articulation. The term *reduplication* was introduced in the previous chapter and is more fully discussed in section **3**.3.4.

Only two examples of this rule will be cited here. Further discussion of this rule is provided in the following section. The examples are:

Word	English	Reduplicated	From
nur	'contract'	*nunnur*	'nur + nur
lirohro	'protective'	*lillirohro*	lir + lirohro

NASAL SUBSTITUTION

2.9.5   Two similar rules exist in Ponapean that we will call **nasal substitution** rules. These rules change oral consonants to nasal ones.

Nasal Substitution in Reduplication

The first nasal substitution rule we will examine may be stated as follows.

• When two identical voiceless consonants come together as a consequence of reduplication, the first will become a nasal that agrees in position of articulation with the second.

Except when two bilabial, two velar, or two coronal consonants are involved, consonant clusters do not arise in reduplication. Instead, a vowel intervenes (discussed in section **3**.5). What happens where clusters are permitted, as well as the role nasal substitution plays in modifying these clusters, is illustrated by the chart that follows.

The consonants listed down the left side of this chart represent the first consonant of the cluster. Those listed across the top represent the second. A *V* is used to indicate that the cluster must be separated by a vowel and a dash is employed if no example exists. Otherwise, the resulting cluster is listed. (In accord with Ponapean spelling conventions, the clusters /mwpw/ and /mwmw/ are written *mpw* and *mmw* respectively.)

	Bilabials					Velars		
	p	pw	m	mw		k	ng	
p	mp	—	—	—		k	ngk	—
pw	—	mpw	—	mmw		ng	ngk	ngng
m	—	—	mm	—				
mw	—	—	—	—				

Coronals						
	s	d	t	n	l	r
s	ns	—	—	—	V	V
d	V	nd	—	V	V	—
t	V	—	nt	V	V	V
n	ns	nd	nt	nn	ll	—
l	ns	nd	nt	—	ll	—
r	ns	nd	nt	nn	ll	rr

The nasal substitution rule previously cited accounts for the fact that the clusters *pp*, *pwpw*, *kk*, *ss*, *dd*, and *tt* respectively become *mp*, *mpw* (/mwpw/), *ngk*, *ns*, *nd*, and *nt*. Examples follow.

Word	English	Reduplicated	From
pap	'swim'	*pampap*	pap + pap
pwupw	'fall'	*pwumpwupw*	pwupw + pwupw
kak	'able'	*kangkak*	kak + kak
sas	'stagger'	*sansas*	sas + sas
did	'build a wall'	*dindid*	did + did
tat	'writhe'	*tantat*	tat + tat

This rule, however, also plays a role in accounting for the observation that the clusters *ls*, *ld*, *lt*, *rs*, *rd*, and *rt* respectively become *ns*, *nd*, *nt*, *ns*, *nd*, and *nt*, as illustrated by the following examples.

Word	English	Reduplicated	From
sel	'tied'	*sensel*	sel + sel
dil	'penetrate'	*dindil*	dil + dil
tal	'click, tsk'	*tantal*	tal + tal
sar	'fade'	*sansar*	sar + sar

| *dar* | 'strike, of a fish' | *dandar* | dar + dar |
| *tir* | 'narrowing' | *tintir* | tir + tir |

Note that if we permit the liquid assimilation rule presented in section **2**.9.4 to apply *before* nasal substitution in these examples, then we can correctly account for the sound changes involved. Thus, these rules need to be ordered as follows.

Word:	*sel*	*dil*	*tal*	*sar*	*dar*	*tir*
Reduplicated:	*selsel*	*dildil*	*taltal*	*sarsar*	*dardar*	*tirtir*
Liquid Assimilation:	*sessel*	*diddil*	*tattal*	*sassar*	*daddar*	*tittir*
Nasal Substitution:	*sensel*	*dindil*	*tantal*	*sansar*	*dandar*	*tintir*

Liquid assimilation also applies to change the clusters *rn* to *nn* and *rl* to *ll*, as in these examples.

Word	English	Reduplicated	From
nur	'contract'	*nunnur*	nur + nur
lirohro	'protective'	*lillirohro*	lir + lirohro

And complete nasal assimilation accounts for the change of *nl* to *ll*, as in this example.

| linenek | 'oversexed' | lillinenek | lin + linenek |

Examples of clusters that undergo no modification are the following.

Word	English	Reduplicated
mem	'sweet'	*memmem*
nenek	'commit adultery'	*nennenek*
lal	'make a sound'	*lallal*
rer	'tremble'	*rerrer*
ngong	'bark'	*ngongngong*
sinom	'sink in'	*sinsinom*
dune	'tie together'	*dundune*
tenek	'hung up'	*tentenek*
kang	'eat'	*kangkang*

Examples of potential clusters where a vowel intervenes (at least in careful speech) are:

lus	'jump'	*lusulus*
rese	'saw'	*resirese*
set	'artificially ripen breadfruit'	*seteset*
net	'smell'	*netenet*
liduwih	'serve as female servant'	*lidiliduwih*
setik	'quick in performing action'	*setisetik*
net	'sell'	*netinet*
let	'flick'	*letelet*
rot	'dark'	*rotorot*

Except in one case, all the clusters listed in the preceding chart have been accounted for. The single exception is *mmw* from *pwmw*, illustrated by the following example.

Word	English	Reduplicated	From
mwopw	'out of breath'	*mwommwopw*	mwopw + mwopw

A second nasal substitution rule, one affecting only bilabial and velar consonants, is required to account for this example.

Nasal Substitution Affecting Bilabial and Velar Consonants

A second nasal substitution rule that affects only bilabial consonants (*p*, *pw*, *m*, and *mw*) and velar consonants (*k* and *ng*) may be stated as follows.

• When two bilabial or two velar consonants come together in the flow of speech, the first consonant will become a nasal that agrees in position of articulation and velarization with the second.

The effect of this rule is summarized in the following chart, where the consonants listed down the left side represent the first of two consonants in a cluster and those listed across the top represent the second. As in the preceding chart, the clusters /mwpw/ and /mwmw/ will be written *mpw* and *mmw* respectively.

	Bilabials				Velars		
	p	pw	m	mw		k	ng
p	mp	mpw	mm	mmw	k	ngk	ngng
pw	mp	mpw	mm	mmw	ng	ngk	ngng
m	mp	mpw	mm	mmw			
mw	mp	mpw	mm	mmw			

Note that this rule applies whenever two bilabial or two velar consonants *come together in the flow of speech.* Therefore, unlike the previous nasal substitution rule we examined, this rule is not constrained in its application to reduplicated forms. Examples of its application in a variety of word types are provided below. The clusters that result from this rule are italicized in the first column. In the second column, the parts these words are made up of are listed, and in the third column an English translation is provided.

Word	Consisting Of	English
pa*mp*ap	pap + pap	'swimming'
sa*mp*ah	sapw + pah	'world, earth'
e*mpw*oatol	ep + pwoatol	'a game'
pwu*mpw*upw	pwupw + pwupw	'falling'
li*mpw*oat	lim + pwoat	'five (oblong things)'
keh*mmw*ot	kehp + mwot	'variety of yam'
keh*mm*eirkelik	kehp + meir + kelik	'variety of yam'
mwo*mmw*op	mwopw + mwopw	'out of breath'
li*mmw*ut	lim + mwut	'five (piles)'
ki*ngk*ik	kik + kik	'kicking'

At normal conversation speed, this rule applies to final and initial consonants of separate words as well, as illustrated by the following examples. (These sound changes, however, are not conventionally written when separate words are involved.)

Sentence:	*E kalap pahn soupisek.*
Pronounced:	/e kalam pahn soupisek/
English:	'He will always be busy.'

Sentence:	*E kalap men meir.*
Pronounced:	/e kalam men meir/
English:	'He is always sleepy.'

Sentence:	*E saik kengwini.*
Pronounced:	/e saing kengwini/
English:	'He hasn't yet taken medicine.'

Sentence:	*E saik nget.*
Pronounced:	/e saing nget/
English:	'He's not yet out of breath.'

Sentence:	*Soulik kin soupisek.*
Pronounced:	/souling kin soupisek/
English:	'Soulik is (habitually) busy.'

The nasal substitution rule affecting bilabial and velar consonants thus applies whenever two bilabial or two velar consonants come together in the flow of speech. Only when a pause intervenes between the two consonants is this rule blocked.

Coronal clusters, those produced between bilabial and velar positions of articulation, do not behave in a parallel manner. Clusters of coronal consonants undergo nasal substitution in reduplicated words only. They do not undergo nasal substitution if the two consonants involved are part of separate words, as the following examples illustrate.

Sentence:	*E ekis suwed.*
Pronounced:	/e ekis suwed/
But Never:	*/e ekin suwed/
English:	'It's kind of bad.'

Sentence:	*Ke meid dangahnga!*
Pronounced:	/ke meid dangahnga/
But Never:	*/ke mein dangahnga/
English:	'Aren't you lazy!'

In words consisting of more than one part where reduplication is not involved, potential coronal clusters occur with an intervening vowel, as in the next examples.

Word	Suffixed	English
weid	*weidida*	'proceed upward'
poad	*poadedi*	'plant downward'
lus	*lusisang*	'jump from'
mwesel	*mweselisang*	'leave from'
daur	*dauridi*	'climb downward'

An exception, however, is the verb *mwohd* 'sit' when followed by the suffix -*di* 'downward.' *Mwohd*+*di* is most commonly pronounced *mwohndi*, where nasal substitution *does* apply. Quite probably, however, this is due to the fact that the verb 'to sit' so often combines with the suffix 'down' that *mwohndi* is treated as a single word. The nasal substitution that occurs in this form may then be a consequence of the fact that the nasal substitution rule that operates in reduplicated words also applied within simple words earlier in the history of the language. The exceptional nature of the form *mwohndi* is further supported by the observation that when *mwohd* is followed by other suffixes beginning with *d*, nasal substitution does not occur. Thus, *mwohd* plus *-da* 'upward' is pronounced *mwohdada* and *mwohd* plus *-do* 'toward the speaker' is pronounced *mwohdodo*.

It may finally be noted that the two nasal substitution rules examined in this section help explain why, except under the conditions described in section **2**.5.7, voiceless consonants do not occur doubled in Ponapean. The effect of these two rules is precisely to eliminate such sequences.

SOUND RULES IN SUBSEQUENT CHAPTERS

2.9.6   In this chapter we have made a number of basic observations about the sound system of Ponapean. We have discussed how sounds are made, what the distinctive sounds of Ponapean are, and how sounds form larger units called syllables. Additionally, we have examined how one sound may be changed to another and how sounds may be added to words.

Understanding this chapter will be useful to you in the materials to come, for although our attention from now on will primarily be focused on words, phrases, and sentences, we will still have frequent occasion to talk about the sound system of Ponapean. In subsequent chapters, five sections occur which are devoted specifically to the discussion of sound rules. These are: section 3.5 on *Base Vowels and Insert Vowels,* section **4**.2.1 on the *Monosyllabic Noun Vowel Lengthening Rule*, section **5**.4.6 on *Alternations in Vowel Length in the Verb Paradigm*, section **6**.3.5 on *Basic Sentence Intonation*, and section 7.5.1 on *Sound System Correlates* in honorific speech. Other observations relevant to a complete discussion of the Ponapean sound system are presented less formally as part of the general discussion of other topics, such as *Reduplication* in section **3**.3.4, *Numerals* in section **4**.4, *Possessive Constructions* in section **4**.8, *Intransitive and Transitive Verbs Sharing Common Roots* in section **5**.2.3, *Combining Forms of Verbs* in section **5**.2.4, and *Verbal Suffixes* in section **5**.4. Thus, while many rules of the Ponapean sound system are presented explicitly in this grammar, others occur only implicitly. The reason for this is that a complete, formal discussion of the sound rules of Ponapean is well beyond the scope of this work. A more thorough discussion of this topic, however, is currently in preparation by the author.

Before we proceed, it should once more be brought to your attention that a special appendix has been included at the end of this volume which sets forth Ponapean spelling conventions. Throughout this chapter and in chapters to come, various references are made to spelling rules. To facilitate your understanding of these rules, and for the purposes of easy reference, they are brought together in that appendix.

3 Words:
Their Structure And Function

3.1   Thus far in our study of Ponapean, we have focused our attention primarily upon explaining how the sound system of this language works. Our discussion of sounds, though far from complete, was probably detailed enough to permit us to record with reasonable accuracy any utterance that might occur in the language. Still, we are far short of having adequately described Ponapean. This is because every language has other kinds of important units larger than sounds. In this chapter we want to examine one of these units—the one called the word.

That it is necessary in a description of a language to talk about more than just its sound system should be obvious, particularly when you stop to think that we have still said almost nothing about meaning. And, of course, meaning is vital to language. In fact, one way to describe the task of a grammar is to say that it should explain how meaning is related to sound.

One of the ways in which meaning is conveyed is through words. However, just as we tend to take the sounds of our language for granted, so do we accept its words. Unless words happen to be unusual or unknown to us, we do not normally bother to think about them. But, as will be explored in this chapter, understanding what a word is, how words are formed, and how words pattern in a language are complex tasks to which we shall have to devote a considerable amount of attention.

Our task in the following pages, then, will be to set forth some of the major facts about the structure and function of words. We will discuss the building blocks of words called morphemes, see how morphemes combine to form various kinds of words, examine how words similar in function may be classed together into various parts of speech, and briefly note how words combine in larger grammatical units called phrases and sentences. As in the previous chapter, it will be necessary to introduce some special terminology. All new terms will be explained as they are presented, and only those terms which will contribute to our understanding of Ponapean will be employed.

MORPHEMES

3.2   Just as the phoneme is the basic unit of the sound system, the **morpheme** is the basic unit of word structure. The concept of a morpheme is very useful in describing languages.

DEFINITION OF A MORPHEME

3.2.1   One linguist, Charles Hockett, defines a morpheme as being "the smallest individually meaningful elements in the utterances of a language." To expand upon this definition, let us set up the following three criteria (suggested by Norman Stageberg in *An Introductory English Grammar*, 1966) for determining whether or not a particular element in a language is a morpheme.

1.   A morpheme is a word or a part of a word that has meaning.

2.   A morpheme cannot be divided into smaller parts without altering or destroying its meaning.

3.   A morpheme can occur in a variety of environments with essentially the same meaning.

Considering these three criteria in terms of some Ponapean words ('word' is used here in its familiar sense) should help further clarify what is meant by 'morpheme'.

Criterion one states that a morpheme may be a word. An example is *pwung* which is a word, and by all three criteria above, is also a morpheme. In accordance with criterion one, it has a meaning. It may be translated into English as 'correct'. As the second criterion requires, it cannot be divided into smaller parts without altering or destroying its meaning. If we consider just *pwu* or *ung*, for example, these units no longer mean 'correct'. And, in agreement with criterion three, *pwung* still retains the meaning of 'correct' in other environments, such as *pwungsang* 'more correct' and *uhdahn pwung* 'truly correct'. Thus, the word *pwung* meets all three criteria as a morpheme. For this reason we say *pwung* is a word consisting of a single morpheme. All words consist of at least one morpheme.

As the first criterion further states, however, a morpheme is not necessarily the same thing as a word. If you consider the word *sapwung* in relation to the word *pwung*, you will notice that *sa-* has been added before the word *pwung* and the meaning of this new word is 'not correct'. Since *pwung* means 'correct', it must therefore be *sa-* which carries the meaning of 'not'. *Sa-* is thus a meaningful unit and thereby meets the first criterion of a morpheme. It also meets the second criterion, since *sa-* cannot be divided into smaller parts like *s* or *a*, and still retain the meaning of 'not'. And, conforming with criterion three, we note that *sa-* can occur in a variety of environments and still mean 'not'. *Lelepek* means 'reliable' and *salelepek* means 'unreliable' or 'not reliable'. *Wehwe* means 'to understand' and *sawehwe* means 'to not understand'. We may conclude, then, that *sa-* is a morpheme and that a word like *sapwung* consists of two morphemes, one meaning 'not' and the other meaning 'correct'.

A morpheme, then, may be either a word or a part of a word. Morphemes are simply the building blocks of words. Many words are made up of only one part and therefore consist of only a single morpheme. Other words may be divided into more than one part, and thus consist of more than one morpheme. Some additional examples here may be helpful in reinforcing your understanding of this notion. The following words consist of only a single morpheme.

tang	'to run'	*ohd*	'mountain taro'
ohl	'man'	*rar*	'to peel'
pwili	'cowrie shell'	*sadak*	'tree species'
min	'neat'	*keteu*	'to rain'

These words may not be divided into smaller parts and still retain the same meaning. (Note, too, that these examples illustrate that a morpheme is not the same thing as a syllable. Many morphemes consist of two or more syllables.) The following words consist of two or more morphemes.

Word	Meaning	Consisting of the Morphemes	
kohdo	'to come here'	*koh-*	'to come or go'
		-do	'towards the speaker'

kaweid	'to lead'	*ka-*	'to cause'
		weid	'to proceed'
ngihlap	'molar'	*ngih*	'tooth'
		-lap	'big'
soukohp	'prophet'	*sou-*	'an expert at'
		kohp	'to prophesy'
sapeik	'disobedient'	*sa-*	'not'
		peik	'obedient'
paiki	'to consider fortunate'	*pai*	'fortunate'
		-ki	'to consider'
paikinuhk	'to consider you fortunate'	*pai*	'fortunate'
		-kin	'to consider'
		-uhk	'you'

The notion of the morpheme is very useful, since it provides us with a way to talk about parts of words.

ALLOMORPHS

3.2.2   So far we have been talking about morphemes as if all occurrences of a particular morpheme were pronounced the same way. But this is not necessarily true. In the preceding examples you may have noticed that one morpheme which was translated 'to consider' was listed in one case as *-ki*, in the example *paiki* 'to consider fortunate', and in another case as *-kin*, in the example *paikinuhk* 'to consider you fortunate'. Part of the explanation for this phenomenon involves the fact that in a manner quite parallel to the phoneme/allophone relationship, there also exists a morpheme/allomorph relationship. An **allomorph** is a variant pronunciation of a morpheme that occurs in a particular environment. The allomorph *-kin*, for example, occurs only before object pronouns like *-uhk* 'you'. (Further discussion of this morpheme is presented in section 5.4.1.)

Important here is the notion that allomorphs are determined by the *environment* in which they occur. Allomorphs should not be confused with different pronunciations that occur in different dialect areas. Allomorphs are different forms of a morpheme that are determined according to their position within the word or phrase. Some further examples will help illustrate this point.

In Ponapean there is a morpheme which may be translated into English as 'to make a demonstration of'. One pronunciation of this morpheme is *ak-* and another is *ang-*. Examples of each of these pronunciations follow.

a. **ak-**

lapalap	'high ranking'	*aklapalap*	'self-assertive'
manaman	'spiritual power'	*akmanaman*	'demonstrate spiritual power'
tikitik	'small'	*aktikitik*	'humble'

b. **ang-**

kehlail	'strong'	*angkehlail*	'demonstrate strength'
kepwehpwe	'wealthy'	*angkepwehpwe*	'demonstrate wealth'
kommwad	'brave'	*angkommwad*	'demonstrate bravery'

The two forms *ak-* and *ang-* may be explained as different pronunciations or allomorphs of the same morpheme. The environments in which these two allomorphs occur may be easily described.

> *ang-* occurs before morphemes beginning with *k*;
> *ak-* occurs elsewhere.

Since *ak-* is the more common pronunciation of this morpheme, we might wish to consider this form as the **base form**, or the form we use to name this morpheme. Starting with *ak-* as the base, we may predict the form *ang-* will occur from the application of the nasal substitution rule described in section 2.9.5 An additional point we might observe about *ak-* is that a vowel sometimes occurs between it and the following word, as in these examples.

ak*a*tantat	'to abhor'
ak*e*dei	'to engage in a throwing contest'
ak*u*pwung	'petty'

This extra vowel does not belong either to *ak-* or to the word that follows. It is a vowel that is inserted for ease of pronunciation. Inserted vowels will be examined in section 3.5.2. Further examples of the morpheme *ak-* occur in section 5.3.4.

As the examples we have thus far examined illustrate, it is usually possible to predict what allomorphs a particular morpheme will have and where they will occur. In some cases, however, why a particular allomorph occurs may not be very well understood. In the remainder of this grammar, conditioning environments for allomorphs will be explained where they may be determined. When the environment is not understood, allomorphs will simply be listed.

TYPES OF MORPHEMES

3.2.3   If we examine the morphemes presented in section **3**.2.1, there is an important observation we may make. Some morphemes, like *ngih*, *kilel*, and *ese*, may stand alone as words. Other morphemes, like *koh-*, *ka-*, and *ak-* may not. This is the basis of the distinction between free morphemes and bound morphemes.

Free Morphemes

A **free morpheme** is one which may be uttered alone with meaning. Free morphemes are always words. *Pwung* is an example of a free morpheme. Other free morphemes are:

kidi	'dog'	*loahng*	'fly'
ahk	'mangrove'	*parem*	'nipa palm'
kala	'to boast'	*suk*	'to pound'

Bound Morphemes

A **bound morpheme** is one which may not be uttered alone with meaning. Bound morphemes always occur with one or more other morphemes to form a word. The morpheme *sa-* in *sapwung* is an example of a bound morpheme. Other bound morphemes are:

Bound Morphemes	Meaning	As in the Word
ka-	'to cause'	*kamair* 'to cause to sleep'
da-	'upwards'	*lusida* 'to jump upwards'
koh-	'to come or go'	*kohla* 'to go there'
-pene	'together'	*kohpene* 'to come together'
kih-	'to give'	*kihdo* 'to give here'

AFFIXATION

3.3   As the preceding discussion has illustrated, the unit of speech that we call a word may be made up of one or more morphemes. One very important way in which morphemes may be combined to form words is through the process of **affixation**. To understand how affixation works, it will be useful to draw a distinction between **roots** and **affixes**.

ROOTS AND AFFIXES

3.3.1   A word like *tangseli* 'to run here and there' consists of two morphemes. The first morpheme *tang* carries the basic meaning of 'to run'. The second morpheme, which modifies the meaning of the first, is -*seli* meaning 'here and there'. In terms of the structure of words, each of these morphemes is of a different type. A morpheme like *tang* which carries the basic meaning in a word is called a **root**. A bound morpheme like -*seli*, which is attached to a root to modify its meaning, is called an **affix**.

While we may make the generalization that all affixes are bound morphemes, it is not true that all roots are free morphemes. Though in the previous example it is true that the root *tang* is a free morpheme—it may be uttered alone with meaning—this is not true of a root like *koh-*, as in the word *kohseli* 'to go here and there'. The morpheme *koh-* always occurs in combination with an affix. Consequently, we may say that roots may be either free or bound morphemes. Affixes, however, are always bound and are subsidiary to roots.

The combining of affixes with roots is the process called **affixation.** In Ponapean, there are three kinds of affixation, involving **prefixes**, **suffixes**, and **reduplication**. Each of these will be examined below.

PREFIXES

3.3.2   Affixes that precede roots are called **prefixes**. Some common prefixes in Ponapean are:

Prefix		Plus the Root		Yields	
sa-	'not'	*peik*	'obedient'	*sapeik*	'disobedient'
ka-	'causative'	*weid*	'to proceed'	*kaweid*	'to lead'
li-	'given to (some quality)'	*pirap*	'to steal'	*lipirap*	'thievish'
ak-	'to make a demonstration of'	*lemei*	'cruel'	*aklemei*	'tough'

Each of these prefixes is dealt with in more detail in other sections of this grammar. Checking the index will help you locate those discussions and will provide you with a list of all Ponapean prefixes.

SUFFIXES

3.3.3   Affixes that follow a root are called **suffixes**. There are considerably more suffixes in Ponapean than there are prefixes. Some common ones are:

Suffix		Plus the Root		Yields	
-pene	'together'	*wa*	'to carry'	*wapene*	'to gather'
-la	'there'	*alu*	'to walk'	*aluhla*	'to walk there'
-di	'downwards'	*pwupw*	'to fall'	*pwupwidi*	'to fall down'
-uhk	'you'	*kilang*	'to see'	*kilanguhk*	'to see you'
-ie	'superlative'	*lingan*	'pretty'	*lingahnie*	'prettiest'
-n	'of'	*ohl*	'man'	*olen*	'man of'
-sang	'from'	*tang*	'to run'	*tangasang*	'to run from'

A complete list of Ponapean suffixes is provided in the index.

REDUPLICATION

3.3.4   Another process of affixation that occurs in Ponapean is **reduplication**. Reduplication involves the total or partial repetition of a word. Its function and meaning will be examined in detail in section 5.7.3. It is perhaps enough to point out now that it is principally employed with verbs to signal on-going or durative action. Our major concern in this section is not with the meaning of reduplication, but rather with its form. Therefore, we need to consider what portion of a word is repeated in this type of affixation.

The complexities of reduplication are illustrated by the following examples.

Word	English	Reduplicated
kang	'to eat'	*kangkang*
pa	'to weave'	*pahpa*
it	'stuffed'	*itiht*
ahn	'to be accustomed to'	*aiahn*
was	'obnoxious'	*wewas*
duhp	'to bathe'	*duduhp*
alu	'to walk'	*alialu*
liahn	'outgoing'	*lihliahn*
duhpek	'starved'	*duhduhpek*
nda	'to say'	*ndinda*
rere	'to skin or peel'	*rerrere*

If you compare the forms in column one with those in column three, you will notice that there are a number of different ways in which reduplication takes place. To reduplicate a word like *kang*, for example, the entire word is repeated, resulting in *kangkang*. A word like *duhp*, on the other hand, is reduplicated by repeating only the first two segments, *d* and *u*, resulting in *duduhp*.

In the following pages, we will examine eleven patterns of reduplication. While it may be possible to combine some of these patterns, it is also possible that other patterns exist. Still, one can almost always predict which pattern of reduplication a particular word will employ. The most important consideration in making such predictions is the phonemic shape of the word; therefore, the pattern of consonants and vowels employed in the word determines the way it will be reduplicated.

Pattern I: The first pattern of reduplication that we will consider is one where the entire word is repeated. This kind of reduplication is called **total reduplication**. It applies to one syllable words of the shape CVC or CVG (where C stands for consonant, V stands for vowel, and G stands for glide). Following are examples where the root word is of the shape CVC.

Word	English	Reduplicated
lal	'to make a sound'	*lallal*
rer	'to tremble'	*rerrer*
mem	'sweet'	*memmem*
kang	'to eat'	*kangkang*

Notice that one of the effects of this pattern of reduplication is to create consonant clusters. The clusters that result in the examples above are permissible in Ponapean, as was discussed in section **2**.5.7. However, if the resulting clusters are not permissible, then one of two things will happen. Either the cluster will be changed or a vowel will intervene between the consonants. Examples where the cluster is changed are:

pap	'to swim'	*pampap*
pwupw	'to fall'	*pwumpwupw*
mwopw	'to be out of breath'	*mwommwopw*
dod	'frequent'	*dondod*
dil	'to penetrate'	*dindil*
dar	'to strike, of a fish'	*dandar*
sis	'to speak with an accent'	*sinsis*
sel	'to be tied'	*sensel*
sar	'to fade'	*sansar*
tat	'to writhe'	*tantat*
tal	'to make a click-like sound'	*tantal*
kik	'to kick'	*kingkik*

The changes that result here are, of course, a consequence of the application of the nasal substitution rules we examined in section **2**.9.5. Where these nasal substitution rules do not apply, then a vowel may intervene between the consonants, as in these examples.

pwil	'to flow'	*pwilipwil*
ped	'to be squeezed'	*pediped*
lop	'to be cut'	*lopilop*
ker	'to flow'	*kereker*
ned	'to smell'	*nedened*
par	'to cut'	*parapar*

Notice that the intervening vowel in the reduplicated forms of these words cannot be predicted from the unaffixed forms. In particular, consider the following examples.

tep	'to kick'	*tepetep*
tep	'to begin'	*tepitep*

Here, even though both root words are pronounced /tɛp/, the

vowel that intervenes is /ɛ/ in one case and /i/ in the other. To know how to reduplicate words like these, therefore, also involves knowing what vowel will intervene. Further discussion of vowels like these, called **base vowels**, is presented in section **3**.5.

Words of the shape CVG also reduplicate by this pattern, as the following examples illustrate.

dou	'to climb'	*doudou*
pwei	'hardy, of plants'	*pweipwei*
tei	'to be torn'	*teitei*
ngai	'to bay, of dogs'	*ngaingai*

Since no consonant clusters are created here, the complications of nasal substitution and intervening vowels are not encountered, but one difficulty of a different nature does arise. This difficulty is illustrated by the following pairs of words.

pei	'to float'	*peipei*
pei	'to fight'	*pepei*

Both of these roots are normally written the same way, but they reduplicate differently. An explanation for this we already considered in section **2**.7.3 is that in the word 'to float', the *i* represents the glide /y/, while in the word 'to fight' the *i* represents the vowel /i/. Thus, these two words may be represented as /pɛy/ 'to float' and /pɛi/ 'to fight'. This explains why /pɛy/ reduplicates by this pattern (which applies to words of the shape CVG), but /pɛi/ does not. Additionally, it offers evidence that /i/ and /y/ are separate phonemes in Ponapean. Similarly, we may note that /u/ and /w/ differ in final position, though in this position they are both spelled *u*, as in these examples.

leu	'to be cooked'	*leuleu*
lou	'cooled'	*lolou*

Here we assume that the first word, to which reduplication Pattern I applies, is /lew/ while the second, which reduplicates differently, is /lou/. The pattern of reduplication applicable to the vowel final words /pɛi/ and /and /lou/ is Pattern VI, which will be examined later.

Pattern II: Words of the shape CV reduplicate according to the pattern CV → CVhCV.

pa	'to weave'	*pahpa*
mi	'to exist'	*mihmi*
pu	'bent, crooked'	*puhpu*
lo	'to be caught'	*lohlo*
du	'to dive'	*duhdu*

Pattern III: Words of the shape VC reduplicate according to the pattern VC →VCVhC.

el	'to rub or massage'	*elehl*
it	'stuffed'	*itiht*
uk	'fast'	*ukuhk*
us	'to pull out'	*usuhs*
up	'to shield from the weather'	*upuhp*

Notice that the effects of Patterns II and III are essentially the same. Reduplication creates a two syllable word, one vowel of which is long, while the other is short.

Pattern IV: One syllable words beginning with a long vowel reduplicate according to the pattern VhC→ViVhC, where *i* represents the glide /y/.

ahn	'to be accustomed to'	*aiahn*
ehd	'to strip off'	*eiehd*
oaht	'to order'	*oaioaht*
ohn	'hungover'	*oiohn*

When words of this shape contain a high vowel, then both this pattern and VhC → VCVhC are commonly employed. Examples follow.

Word	English	Reduplicated	Spelled
ihk	'to inhale'	/iyihk/	*iihk*
		or /ikihk/	*ikihk*
ihr	'to string'	/iyihr/	*iihr*
		or /irihr/	*irihr*
uhk	'to lead'	/uyuhk/	*uiuhk*
		or /uwuhk/	*uwuhk*
		or /ukuhk/	*ukuhk*

Notice in the last example that the glide /y/ alternates with the glide /w/. The pattern VhC → VCVhC is apparently formed analogous to Pattern III.

Pattern V: One syllable words beginning with a glide followed by a short vowel and an optional consonant reduplicate by the pattern GV(C) → GeGV(C), where *e* is a mid vowel. Examples are:

wa	'to carry'	*wewa*
was	'obnoxious'	*wewas*
iang	'to accompany'	*ieiang*
wal	'able to be thrown far, of a stick'	*wewal*

Words of this shape also occur with other patterns of re-duplication. Perhaps because words of this phonological shape are rare, this pattern is being lost from the language. These alternate patterns are examined at the end of this section.

Pattern VI: Words of the following shapes reduplicate by repeating the first two segments.

(a)	*duhp*	'to dive'	*duduhp*
	mihk	'to suck'	*mimihk*
	mwahu	'good'	*mwamwahu*
	iahk	'insane'	*iaiahk*
	wehk	'to confess'	*wewehk*
	wihn	'to win'	*wiwihn*
(b)	*laud*	'big, old'	*lalaud*
	reid	'to stain'	*rereid*
	pain	'to incite'	*papain*
	weid	'to walk'	*weweid*
(c)	*pou*	'cold'	*popou*
	pei	'to fight'	*pepei*
	wai	'to sneak'	*wawai*
	lou	'cooled'	*lolou*
(d)	*mand*	'tame'	*mamand*
	pwand	'late'	*pwapwand*
	lengk	'acrophobic'	*lelengk*
	kens	'to ulcerate'	*kekens*

Under (c) are listed those forms to which reference was previously made in the discussion of Pattern I.

Pattern VII: Polysyllabic words (words of more than one syllable) that begin with a vowel are reduplicated by repeating the first two segments and inserting the vowel *i*. Examples follow:

alu	'to walk'	*alialu*
arekarek	'gritty'	*ariarekarek*
uhtohr	'independent'	*uhiuhtohr*
inen	'straight'	*inihnen*
urak	'to wade'	*uruhrak*

Notice in the second last example that *inihnen* results from *in + i + inen*. In the last example, the sequence *iu* becomes *uh*; therefore, *ur + i + urak* becomes *uruhrak*.

Pattern VIII: Words of more than one syllable which begin with a consonant followed by *i* or *uw* plus another vowel reduplicate by repeating the first consonant and lengthening the first vowel, as these examples illustrate.

liahn	'outgoing'	*lihliahn*
riahla	'to be cursed'	*rihriahla*
luwak	'jealous'	*luhluwak*
luwet	'weak'	*luhluwet*

Pattern IX: Under this pattern we will consider two types of reduplication, both of which affect polysyllabic words that begin with a consonant or glide followed by a long vowel. Which type of reduplication is employed depends upon the nature of the second syllable. If the second syllable contains a long vowel, then only the initial CV is repeated.

luhmwuhmw	'to be sick'	*luluhmwuhmw*
mahsahs	'cleared, of vegetation'	*mamahsahs*
tohrohr	'to be independent'	*totohrohr*
wahntuhke	'to calculate'	*wawahntuhke*

Conversely, if the second syllable contains a short vowel, then the initial CVh is repeated.

duhpek	'starved'	*duhduhpek*
mehlel	'true'	*mehmehlel*

| *noahrok* | 'greedy' | *noahnoahrok* |
| *pehse* | 'to be acquainted' | *pehpehse* |

Pattern X: Words that begin with doubled consonants or with a nasal consonant followed by an oral consonant produced in the same position (and are thus considered polysyllabic—see section **2**.8) reduplicate by repeating the first two consonants and inserting either *i* or *u*. As with prothetic vowels, *u* is employed before *mmw* or *mpw* or when the first vowel of the word is round; otherwise *i* occurs.

(a)	*mmed*	'full'	*mmimmed*
	ngnget	'to pant'	*ngngingnget*
	ngngar	'to see'	*ngngingngar*
	mmwus	'to vomit'	*mmwummwus*

As we noted in section **2**.5.7, doubled consonants at the beginning of words are difficult to hear and are often not written. In the middle of words, though, as in the reduplicated forms above, they are easily recognized.

Following are examples of words beginning with a nasal consonant followed by an oral consonant produced in the same position.

(b)	*mpek*	'to look for lice'	*mpimpek*
	nda	'to say'	*ndinda*
	nsehn	'to snare'	*nsinsehn*
	nting	'to write'	*ntinting*
	ngkoal	'to make sennit'	*ngkungkoal*
	mpwul	'to flame'	*mpwumpwul*

Pattern XI: Other polysyllabic words reduplicate by repeating the first three segments. Examples are:

rere	'to skin or peel'	*rerrere*
dune	'to attach in a sequence'	*dundune*
deied	'to eat breakfast'	*deideied*

This pattern, like the first pattern of reduplication we examined, may have the effect of creating consonant clusters. If the cluster that results is an impermissible one, then it will be modified, either to make it acceptable or to break it up. These words, for example, undergo nasal substitution when they are reduplicated.

dilip	'to mend thatch'	*dindilip*
sile	'to guard'	*sinsile*
sarek	'to uproot'	*sansarek*
pepe	'to swim to'	*pempepe*

In the following words, the consonant cluster is broken up by an **insert vowel**.

siped	'to shake out'	*sipisiped*
taman	'to remember'	*tamataman*
tepek	'to kick'	*tepetepek*
wasas	'to stagger'	*wasawasas*

The preceding examples illustrate the use of the type of insert vowels called **copy vowels**. The following examples illustrate a second type, called **excrescent vowels**. The parentheses signify that their presence is optional.

loange	'to pass across'	*loang(i)loange*
katohre	'to subtract'	*kat(i)katohre*

These two types of insert vowels are examined in section 3.5.

Possibly there are still other productive ways of reduplicating words in Ponapean that have been overlooked in the preceding discussion, but certainly most forms may be accounted for by one of the preceding eleven patterns. There are, though, a number of words that seem to be exceptions to these patterns. These may be accounted for in one of the following three ways.

For some words, there are alternate patterns of reduplication. For example, *was* 'obnoxious' is normally reduplicated according to Pattern V to produce *wewas*; however, a competing pattern of reduplication, Pattern I, is also employed by some speakers to produce *wasawas*. A few other words exhibiting alternate patterns of reduplication follow. In each case, the expected pattern is listed first. The alternate pattern follows.

amas	'raw'	Pattern VII	*amiamas*
		Pattern XI	*amahmas*

ewetik	'abstemious'	Pattern VII	*ewiewetik*
		Pattern XI	*ewehwetik*
iahk	'mentally disturbed'	Pattern VI	*iaiahk*
		Pattern V	*ieiahk*
wahsek	'to enlarge an opening'	Pattern IX	*wahwahsek*
		Pattern V	*wewahsek*

Some speakers, perhaps, will consider certain of these alternants as incorrect. Nevertheless, they do occur, particularly with words that begin with vowels or glides.

A second reason why a word might not reduplicate as predicted by one of the preceding patterns is that the word may be made up of more than one morpheme. For some words containing more than one morpheme, only the first morpheme is considered in determining which pattern of reduplication is to apply. Consider, for example, a word like *adsuwed* 'to have a bad reputation'. Since the reduplicated form of *arekarek* is *ariarekarek* by Pattern VII, one might expect the reduplicated form of *adsuwed* to be *adiadsuwed*, but this reduplicated form is incorrect. Instead, the correct form is *adahdsuwed*. The word *adsuwed* consists of two morphemes, *ad* 'name' and *suwed* 'bad'. For this word, only the morpheme *ad* is considered for the purpose of reduplication, and it reduplicates according to Pattern III to produce *adahd*. Two other examples, where the internal structure of the word is important in determining the correct pattern of reduplication, follow.

Word	Consisting of:	English	Reduplicates
soupisek	*sou + pisek*	'busy'	*sosoupisek*
meirkelik	*meir + kelik*	'deep in sleep'	*memeirkelik*

For words like these, reduplication may be difficult to predict. Notice in these cases, however, that if only the first morpheme is considered, reduplication is regular.

A third reason why some words appear to be irregularly reduplicated is that they are **inherently reduplicated**. Therefore, they do not occur unreduplicated as a free form, at least with the same meaning or as the same part of speech. In many cases, these words exhibit patterns of reduplication that are no longer productive in Ponapean. These non-productive patterns of reduplication are examined in the next section.

FOSSILIZED AFFIXES

3.3.5   There are a number of affixes in Ponapean which in the past were
used productively in the process of word formation, but today are
no longer employed. Affixes of this type are called **fossilized
affixes**. Because fossilized affixes are generally preserved in only a
relatively small number of words, and because native speakers of
the language usually do not recognize these affixes as being
separate morphemes, it is sometimes difficult to recognize these
fossilized forms. In this section, we will examine fossilized patterns of reduplication and provide cross-references to subsequent
discussions of other fossilized affixes.

Fossilized Patterns of Reduplication

Among the easiest of the fossilized affixes to recognize are
fossilized patterns of reduplication. These are essentially of two
types, which are described below.

Type I

makiaki	'to sob'	*lohpwelipwel*	'to make a good catch'
dikeriker	'healthy looking, of plants'	*malekelek*	'fish species'
lahpweseisei	'waterspout'	*peiruhru*	'clay'
dangahnga	'lazy'	*pwidikidik*	'tiny'
liapiap	'snare noose'	*sinopwunopw*	'fat, healthy'

These words illustrate a fossilized pattern of reduplication in
which the last rather than the first part of the word is reduplicated. Reduplication in these words does not signal durative
aspect, as it did for the words examined in the preceding section.
Rather, these words are inherently reduplicated; they have no
corresponding unreduplicated forms that have the same grammatical function or meaning. Also inherently reduplicated and
exhibiting non-productive patterns of reduplication are words
like the following.

Type II

dikadik	'one's image'	*tipwatipw*	'brittle'
edied	'cloudy'	*emiemw*	'to wash one's hands'

lepalep	'to doze'	*idaid*	'to be under pressure'
eliel	'to rub'	*iroir*	'to look in the distance'
kisakis	'gift'	*ekiek*	'to be hidden'

These words appear to have undergone a process of total reduplication.

Durative aspect is indicated with words of these two types by different methods. For words of Type I, which reduplicate finally, one of the patterns that we described in the preceding section will apply. Therefore, *makiaki* 'to sob' is reduplicated by Pattern XI to produce *mak(i)makiaki* 'to be sobbing'. Words of Type II, however, may not be further reduplicated. Instead the verb *wie* 'to do' is employed. *Lepalep* means 'to doze'; *wie lepalep* means 'to be dozing'. The reduplicated form of *lepalep*, **lepelepalep*, is not possible.

It is probable that both types of words exhibit the same fossilized pattern of final reduplication, which involves repetition of the last two syllables of a word. To illustrate what may have happened to forms like these, let us consider a word of Type I like *dikeriker* 'healthy, of plants' and a word of Type II, like *eliel* 'to massage'. Evidence exists that at some earlier point in time these words were pronounced *dikeri* and *eli*. Further, it is a well-established fact that, at some time in the past, final vowels were lost in Ponapean. (See Rehg, 1973.) If we reduplicate the last two syllables of these words and delete the final vowels, we may correctly derive the forms of these words as they occur today.

	dikeri	*eli*
	dikeri	*eli*
Final Reduplication	*dikerikeri*	*elieli*
Loss of Final Vowel	*dikeriker*	*eliel*

To summarize, let us consider a verb like *el* 'to massage' that illustrates both productive and unproductive patterns of reduplication, as well as the use of *wie*. *El* is a transitive verb. Its intransitive form, historically derived by final reduplication, is *eliel*. Durative aspect is indicated for *el* by the use of reduplication Pattern III to produce *elehl* 'to be massaging someone'. For *eliel*, *wie* is used to produce *wie eliel* 'to be massaging'. The following diagram summarizes these observations.

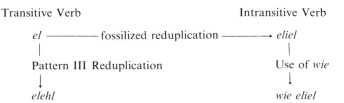

The use of reduplication to derive intransitive verbs, apparently no longer a productive device, is examined further in sections **3**.7.4 and **5**.2.3.

Other Fossilized Affixes

In addition to fossilized patterns of reduplication, there are also other fossilized affixes in Ponapean. An effective discussion of these other affixes, however, depends on the reader's understanding of concepts not yet introduced. Consequently, these affixes will be examined in subsequent sections of this grammar. In particular, the fossilized prefix *sou-* will be examined in section **3**.7.4. The fossilized prefix *pV-* and the fossilized suffix *-ek* will be examined in section **5**.2.3.

ENCLITICS

3.4   Similar to affixes, particularly suffixes, are a set of forms we will label **enclitics**. In Ponapean, all enclitics belong to one of three word classes. These are:

1. *Demonstrative Modifiers*: Examples are *-et* 'this', *-en* 'that, by you', and *-o* 'that, away from you and me'. (Section **4**.5.1)

2. *Numeral Classifiers*: Examples are *-men* 'animate object', *-pwoat* 'long object', and *-kis* 'bit'. (Section **4**.4.4)

3. *Sentence Adverbs*: The single enclitic in this word class is *-te* 'just' or 'still'. (Section **6**.3.3)

Detailed discussions of these enclitics are presented in the sections for which references have been provided above. What is of particular interest here is why it is necessary to distinguish enclitics from suffixes.

Like suffixes, enclitics always occur bound to a preceding root, but enclitics and suffixes are unlike each other in two respects. One way in which they differ is illustrated by the following examples, where the enclitic *-et* 'this' is employed in the (a) set of examples while the suffix *-t* 'our' is used in the (b) set.

a) *wahret*   'this canoe'
    wahr kalaimwunet   'this large canoe'
    wahr kalaimwun me pwoaret   'this large canoe
                                      that is cracked'

b) *warat wahr*   'our canoe'
    warat wahr kalaimwun   'our large canoe'
    warat wahr kalaimwun me pwoar 'our large canoe
                                      that is cracked'

Note that the positions of the enclitic *-et* and the suffix *-t* in these examples are different. Whereas *-t* always follows the first word in the sentence, *-et* always occurs at the end of the phrase. One basic difference between suffixes and enclitics in Ponapean, then, is that suffixes follow particular morphemes, while enclitics follow entire phrases.

A second way in which enclitics differ from suffixes is illustrated by the next set of examples, where the enclitic *-et* and the suffix *-niki* are employed.

a) *wahr*   'canoe'
    wahret   'this canoe'

b) *wahr*   'canoe'
    waraniki   'to possess (of canoes or, more
                   generally, vehicles)'

The free form of the morpheme meaning 'canoe' is *wahr*. Note in the examples after (a) that this is also the form that occurs in combination with the enclitic *-et*. The suffix *-niki*, however, is found with a different form of this morpheme, *wara-*. Enclitics and suffixes thus also differ in terms of which allomorph of a particular morpheme they may occur with.

The evidence presented here points to the necessity of distinguishing enclitics from suffixes. Further comments about enclitics are presented in the next section, as well as in those sections on the particular classes of enclitics for which references have already been provided.

BASE VOWELS AND INSERT VOWELS

3.5   In several preceding sections of this grammar it was noted that when two morphemes are combined, a vowel may occur between the two morphemes that does not obviously seem to be a part of either. We encountered such cases, for example, in discussions of two patterns of reduplication. Therefore:

Pattern I—Total Reduplication

Root	English	Reduplication
tep	'to kick'	tep*i*tep
tep	'to begin'	tep*e*tep

Pattern XI—Reduplication of the Initial Three Segments

| taman | 'to remember' | tam*a*taman |
| katohre | 'to subtract' | kat(*i*) katohre |

The italicized vowels in the reduplicated words listed under Pattern I we previously labeled **base vowels**, while those occurring in the reduplicated words under Pattern XI we called **insert vowels**. The purpose of the following discussions is to set forth some preliminary observations on the conditions under which base vowels and insert vowels occur. The word *preliminary* must be given special emphasis, however, since these conditions are not at all well understood.

Base Vowels

3.5.1   Two conditions under which base vowels may occur are:

1) when a root is totally reduplicated by Pattern I.
2) when a root is followed by a suffix.

Consider, for example, the following pair of words which were cited in the introduction to this section.

Root	English	Reduplicated
tep	'to begin'	tep*i*tep
tep	'to kick'	tep*e*tep

The base vowels in these examples are the italicized vowels that occur in the reduplicated forms. Clearly, it is not possible to predict the quality of these base vowels simply by examining the roots as they occur in column one. Both of these roots, we previously noted, are pronounced alike. However, a clue to the explanation of these vowels was already presented in section 3.3.5, where we noted that, historically, final vowels were lost in Ponapean. If we assume that the roots of these words are in fact *tepi* and *tepe*, we reduplicate them and then drop the final vowel, the reduplicated forms that occur above result. Thus:

Root	*tepi*	*tepe*
Reduplicated	*tepitepi*	*tepetepe*
Loss of Final Vowel	*tepitep*	*tepetep*

Further evidence that these vowels should be considered to belong to the roots of these words is provided by related words. Both of the words above are intransitive verbs. The transitive forms of these verbs are *tapi* 'to begin' and *tepek* 'to kick'. (Intransitive and transitive verbs are discussed in section 5.2.) These transitive forms contain the same final vowels that were set forth above as belonging to the roots of the intransitive forms.

Vowels like these that must be considered part of a morpheme are called **base vowels**; they are vowels that are present in the most basic form of the morpheme. Base vowels that occur at the end of a morpheme, therefore, may be absent in the free form of the morpheme, but present when the morpheme is completely reduplicated and where the absence of the vowel would lead to an impermissible consonant cluster. Final base vowels may also surface when a morpheme is followed by a suffix.

Certain nouns in Ponapean may be changed to verbs through the use of a suffix -*niki*, which means 'to possess' the kind of thing characterized by the noun. This suffix is examined in more detail in section 3.7.4. Here it is necessary only to consider what happens when this suffix is attached to a noun, as illustrated by the following examples.

Noun	English	Suffixed by -*niki*
kihl	'skin'	kil*i*niki
ngihl	'voice'	ngil*e*niki
dihp	'sin'	dip*a*niki

There is no way that the vowels that occur immediately before the suffix -*niki* can be predicted either by considering the free forms of these nouns or the suffix. Again, the explanation is that these vowels are *base vowels*. The base vowels present in the suffixed forms of these nouns are not present in the free forms, due to the operation of the rule which deletes final vowels. Therefore:

Root	*kili*	*ngile*	*dipa*
Loss of Final Vowel	*kil*	*ngil*	*dip*

In the case of these nouns, one additional rule applies that results in the long vowel that appears in the free forms of these nouns— *kihl*, *ngihl*, and *dihp*. This rule, called the **monosyllabic noun vowel lengthening rule**, is further discussed in sections 3.7.3 and 4.2.1.

At this point we may note a seeming dilemma that arises if we accept a rule that deletes final vowels. The problem is, how are the many Ponapean words that end in vowels to be accounted for? For example, why have the final vowels of words like *nta* 'blood' and *kehke* 'stem of a fruit' not been dropped? The answer is that they have. Consider these two words as they occur alone and suffixed by *-niki*.

Free Form	Suffixed by *-niki*
nta	*ntahniki*
kehke	*kehkehniki*

We may assume that the roots of these two nouns are *ntah* and *kehkeh*. As we have previously noted, long vowels may be thought of as a sequence of two vowels. Therefore, *ah* might also be represented as *aa*. If we restrict final vowel loss to the deletion of only one short vowel, then we may relate these roots to the free forms as follows.

Root	*ntaa*	*keekee*
Loss of Final Vowel	*nta*	*keeke*

These forms thus do not constitute exceptions to the loss of final vowels.

There are two additional observations about base vowels that may be made. The first is that not all vowels may occur as final base vowels. Thus far, only the vowels /i/, /ɛ/, and /a/ have been found. The second is that not all morphemes have final base vowels. Before any definitive statement may be made about which morphemes have these final base vowels, a great deal more

research will need to be done. However, a few tentative generalizations may be made at this point.

1. Only native Ponapean morphemes have final base
    vowels in their root forms that are not present in their
    free forms.

    Final base vowels have their origins in older pro-
    nunciations of words. Borrowed words do not share this
    history. Therefore, we may assume that the root of a
    borrowed word like *peht* 'bed' is the same as its free form,
    since no final vowel occurs with this word in the source
    language. Further discussion of such borrowed words is
    presented in section **4**.9.

2. Only morphemes that may combine with suffixes or that
    reduplicate by Pattern I have final base vowels in their
    root forms that are not present in their free forms.

    Note that the only way final base vowels are preserved is
    when they are followed by other phonemes in the same
    word. Being no longer in final position, they are thus
    prevented from undergoing the final vowel deletion rule.

The two classes of words that commonly occur with suffixes
or that reduplicate are nouns and verbs. For each of these classes
of words, the more specific constraints governing the preservation
of final vowels are:

1. Nouns have final base vowels in their root forms not
    present in their free forms if:

    (a) they may combine with possessive suffixes.

    (b) they may combine with the adjective forming suffix
         -n (discussed in section 3.7.4).

    (c) they undergo the monosyllabic noun vowel length-
         ening rule.

Except for (b) above, further discussion of these base vowels is
presented in chapter 4, *Nouns and Noun Phrases*.

2. Verbs have final base vowels in their root forms not
    present in their free forms if:

(a) they undergo Pattern I reduplication of the type previously described.

(b) they have a corresponding transitive form which preserves the final base vowel.

Further discussion of final base vowels in verb roots occurs in chapter 5, *Verbs and Verb Phrases.*

INSERT VOWELS

3.5.2 Whereas base vowels are part of a particular morpheme, insert vowels are not. **Insert vowels** are vowels that are inserted into a word for the purpose of making its pronunciation easier.

Ponapean is a language in which the preferred sequence of sounds is basically one in which every consonant or glide is followed by a vowel. As we noted in chapter 2, however, certain sequences of consonants are possible. Excluding borrowed words and exclamations, two consonants may appear in sequence when:

(1) both consonants are voiced and have the same position of articulation.

(2) the first consonant is nasal and the following consonant is produced at the same position of articulation.

Except in these cases, other clusters of consonants are subject to being broken up by an insert vowel.

The typical instance in which consonant clusters arise is when a morpheme ending in a consonant is combined with one beginning with a consonant. Examples of the creation of such clusters have already been presented in section 3.3.4 in the discussion of reduplication Pattern XI, which involves the reduplication of the first three segments of a word. Examples are:

Root	Meaning	Reduplicated
taman	'to remember'	tam*a*taman
katohre	'to subtract'	kat(*i*)katohre

The italicized vowels in these examples are insert vowels. In the first example, the insert vowel is a copy of the vowel that follows. This type of insert vowel is called a **copy vowel.** It must occur in this form. In the second example, the insert vowel is *i.* It is not a copy vowel, and its use is optional; hence, it is included in parentheses. This type of insert vowel is called an **epenthetic vowel.** The rules that govern whether a copy vowel or an epenthetic vowel will be used to break up a consonant cluster are by no means well understood. However, some basic observations about each of these kinds of insert vowels are possible.

Copy Vowels

Three considerations are involved in determining whether a copy vowel will be employed. These are:

(1)   the nature of the cluster.
(2)   the types of morphemes involved.
(3)   the sounds before and after the cluster.

The only permissible clusters, we will assume, are those previously described. However, this may be an oversimplification. Other kinds of clusters might be permissible based on principles not currently understood. Further, there seems to be considerable variation among different speakers as to what kinds of consonant clusters will be tolerated. In the speech of speakers of Ponapean who are also fluent in English, one will hear clusters of consonants that would never occur in the speech of monolingual speakers of the language. As to the kinds of morphemes involved, the fundamental distinction appears to be between those clusters that arise through the process of affixation as opposed to the clusters created by the use of enclitics. The importance of the sounds before and after clusters that arise in these two instances appears to be somewhat different.

When an impermissible consonant cluster is created through the process of affixation (prefixation or reduplication—suffixation involves base vowels), a copy vowel will be inserted to break up the cluster when:

(1) the next syllable is closed; that is, when it ends with a consonant or a glide. For example:

ak + dei   *akedei*
ak + pwung   *akupwung*
ak + tantat   *akatantat*

Note that a copy vowel is *not* inserted in these next forms.

ak + lapalap	*aklapalap*
ak + manaman	*akmanaman*
ak + tikitik	*aktikitik*
ak + papah	*akpapah*

(2) before CVCVC #, where # represents the end of the word and where neither V is high. For example:

tam + taman	*tamataman*
tep + tepek	*tepetepek*
pad + padahk	*padapadahk*
kad + kadall	*kadakadall*

But note:

ngal + ngalis	*ngal(i)ngalis*
pir + pirap	*pir(i)pirap*
kil + kiles	*kil(i)kiles*
sop + sopuk	*sop(u)sopuk*

Only an excrescent vowel appears in these forms.

The conditions under which copy vowels are inserted before *enclitics* may be tentatively characterized as follows.

Insert a copy vowel after a word ending in a consonant preceded by a non-high vowel and before an enclitic of the shape CV(C).

Therefore, if we consider an enclitic like *men* meaning 'a (of animate beings)', we find that it is sometimes preceded by a copy vowel. This copy vowel is conventionally written together with the following enclitic and separate from the preceding word, as in these examples.

Word	English	Word + Clitic *men*
kaht	'cat'	*kaht emen*
pwehk	'bat'	*pwehk emen*
malek	'chicken'	*malek emen*
litok	'hen'	*litok emen*
aramas	'person'	*aramas emen*
elimoang	'mangrove crab'	*elimoang emen*

A copy vowel does not occur before the enclitic *men* in the following examples.

kihr	'fish species'	*kihr men*

pwihk	'pig'	*pwihk men*
mwuhn	'squirrelfish'	*mwuhn men*
kitik	'rat'	*kitik men*
mahulik	'variety of parrotfish'	*mahulik men*
parakus	'fish species'	*parakus men*

A copy vowel is not employed in these examples, since the vowel preceding the cluster is a high vowel. A copy vowel also does not occur before an enclitic like *pali* 'a (section)', since it is not of the shape CV(C). Therefore:

| *pelienmwomw* | 'school of fish' | *pelienmwomw pali* |

Further information about how enclitics interact with preceding words and how they are conventionally written is presented in sections **4.4.4**, **4.5.1**. and **6.3.3**.

Epenthetic Vowels

Probably all impermissible consonant clusters not subject to the insertion of a copy vowel may be broken up by the insertion of an **epenthetic vowel**. Epenthetic vowels are only of two qualities— either *i* or *u*. The vowel *u* is employed before round consonants, or before a consonant followed by a round vowel. The vowel *i* is employed elsewhere. (Note that this is the same rule that governed the selection of prothetic vowels.) Epenthetic vowels are never stressed and they are often reduced to the point that identifying their quality becomes extremely difficult. They are also optional, their optionality depending at least in part on the rate of speech. Therefore, in slow, careful speech they are less likely to be employed than in rapid, less careful speech. Examples of the insertion of epenthetic vowels follow.

ak + suwei	ak(*u*)suwei
loang + loange	loang(*i*)loange
pwihk + men	pwihk(*i*)men
kitik + men	kitik(*i*)men

Epenthetic vowels are also used to break up clusters of consonants that occur in words which are borrowed into Ponapean. The following words borrowed from English illustrate this phenomenon.

English Word	Pronounced in Ponapean
school	s(u)kuhl
screw	s(u)k(u)ru
stamp	s(i)damp
silk	sil(i)k

Many younger speakers of Ponapean who have studied English do not insert the epenthetic vowels in these borrowed words.

WORDS

3.6   Thus far we have been using the word 'word' in its familiar sense, without having formally defined it. That there is such a unit in language, however, can scarcely be questioned. Teachers make up lists of words, lexicographers write dictionaries consisting mainly of words, and, as we read, we recognize words by the white spaces between them. Still, deciding what a word is can be a troublesome task. In written Ponapean, for example, there is a great deal of inconsistency in the way different writers divide up units of speech into words. As an example, let us consider a sentence which in English might be translated as 'I have gone with them to Kolonia many times.' The authors have observed both of the following spellings for this sentence.

(a)   *I iangiraillahr Kolonia pak tohto.*
(b)   *I iang iraillahr Kolonia pak tohto.*

Notice in sentence (a) that *iangiraillahr* 'to have gone with them' is written as one word, while in sentence (b) it is written as two, *iang iraillahr*. The correct spelling, according to the recommendations of the Ponapean Orthography Committee, is the one that occurs in sentence (a), where *iangiraillahr* is written as a single word. The basis for selecting this spelling lies in how a word is to be defined.

DEFINITION OF A WORD

3.6.1   We have already defined a free morpheme as being a morpheme that can be uttered alone with a complete meaning. From this definition we might go on to define a word as being a free form that can be uttered alone with complete meaning and that cannot be divided wholly into smaller free forms without a change in meaning. By this definition, with reference to our previous examples, we may conclude that *iraillahr* is not a word, since uttered alone it does not have a complete meaning; *iangiraillahr*, on the other hand, is a word, since it does have a complete meaning and it cannot be divided wholly into other free forms. Therefore, while *iang* and *irail* may stand alone as free forms, the remaining part of this word *-lahr* may not. This way of defining a word will normally help us in determining what a word is when we are writing. There are, though, in Ponapean spelling, a few exceptions to this generalization. These are noted in the Appendix.

TYPES OF WORDS

3.6.2   There are three types of words in Ponapean. These we will call **simple words**, **complex words**, and **compound words**.

A **simple word** is one that consists of only a single root. Another way to define a simple word is to say that it is a single free morpheme. All of the following words are simple words.

kidi	'dog'	*seri*	'child'
keteu	'rain'	*moahd*	'echo'
ahl	'road'	*pwek*	'to lift'
pwihl	'gum'	*us*	'to pull out'
tuhke	'tree'	*dairuk*	'to bow'

A **complex word** is one which consists of a single free or bound root plus one or more affixes. Examples where the root is a free morpheme follow. The root is italicized in the second column.

Complex Word	Consisting of	English
tangseli	*tang* + seli	'to run here and there'
lipirap	li + *pirap*	'thief'
sapwung	sa + *pwung*	'incorrect'
kamwahuih	ka + *mwahu* + ih	'to improve'

In these next examples, the root is a bound morpheme.

kihdo	*kih-* + do	'to give here'
kohsang	*koh-* + sang	'to come from'
keidi	*kei-* + di	'to move downwards'

Since a single root may sometimes combine with up to four, five, or more affixes, complex words in Ponapean may be quite long.

A **compound word** is one which consists of two or more roots, with or without affixes. A distinguishing feature of a compound word is that its meaning is usually somewhat different from what one would expect if the meaning of each of its roots were considered individually. For example, the two roots *sohp* 'ship' and *pihr* 'to fly' combine to form the compound word *sompihr*. But, the meaning of this word is not literally 'flying ship'; rather, it is 'airplane'. The meaning of a compound word is thus generally somewhat different from the sum of its parts. Other examples of compound words follow.

	Compound Word	English		From	
(a)	*Pohnpei*	'Ponape'		*pohn*	'on top of'
				pehi	'altar'
	ngensuwed	'devil'		*ngehn*	'spirit'
				suwed	'bad'
	daldod	'to drink kava out of turn, one cup after another'		*dahl*	'coconut cup'
				dod	'frequent'
	kisiniei	'fire'		*kisin*	'bit of'
				ahi	'fire'
	ahdomour	'of a stream, rising and fast flowing'		*ahd*	'current'
				mour	'alive'
(b)	*kote kehp*	'first feast of the yam season'		*kote*	'to cut'
				kehp	'yam'
	rahn mwahu	'to greet, greeting'		*rahn*	'day'
				mwahu	'good'
	wahn sahpw	'agricultural products'		*wahn*	'fruit of'
				sahpw	'land'
	lepin lokaia	'word'		*lepin*	'piece of'
				lokaia	'talk'
	kisin likou	'letter'		*kisin*	'bit of'
				likou	'cloth'

Notice that the first five words, those listed under (a), are written together; the second five, those listed under (b), are not. This is because the words listed under (a) involve sound changes when the parts of which they are composed come together. The words listed under (b) do not. The Ponapean Orthography Committee has recommended that only those compound words that involve sound change should be written together. Of course, it is sometimes difficult to decide if two or more words form a compound word, but the native speaker of Ponapean can generally rely on his intuition here.

DIVIDING WORDS INTO CLASSES

3.6.3   In addition to being able to sort words into types according to their composition, it is also possible to group words into classes based on their meaning and how they are used in sentences. A classification scheme of this type is common in any grammar and is usually considered under a label such as "parts of speech." The consideration here, then, is how do we class words into groups like nouns, verbs, pronouns, prepositions, and so forth? In Ponapean, as in most languages, this is a somewhat troublesome task, but we may simplify this undertaking from the outset by dividing words into three basic classes—**major word classes, minor word classes**, and **interjections**.

The words that we shall consider under **major word classes** are those that are traditionally labeled as nouns and verbs. One distinguishing feature of major word classes is that they form *open sets*. That is, the number of words belonging to a major word class is very large, and new words may readily be added or lost. The vast majority of words that have been borrowed into Ponapean belong to one of these two major word classes.

Minor word classes include words that are traditionally labeled pronouns, numerals, prepositions, and so on. These classes are called minor, not because they are unimportant—in fact it is impossible to speak a language without the words of these classes—but because they form *closed sets*. In Ponapean, no words from other languages have been borrowed into these classes, and the total number of words contained in these classes is relatively small. In this grammar, we will attempt to list all minor words. The listing of all major words, however, will not be attempted, since this would involve creating a dictionary, and that is quite a separate task.

Interjections are words or expressions that are distinguished from other word classes by the fact that they never occur as part of larger grammatical units. Two major types of interjections are those which are used to convey emotions or express greetings. Words of this class form an *open set*. New interjections are freely borrowed into Ponapean from other languages.

With these basic divisions among types of word classes in mind, we may now begin to examine the individual word classes of Ponapean. Our intention here will not be to study each of these classes in depth. Rather, the purpose of the following sections is to set forth the names of the word classes, along with some of their major characteristics. Usually further discussions of each of these classes occur elsewhere in the grammar. References to these discussions will be included where appropriate.

MAJOR WORD CLASSES

3.7   Only two major word classes are recognized in Ponapean. These are **nouns** and **verbs**.

NOUNS

3.7.1   For the purposes of the present discussion, we will simply describe **nouns** as being words that (1) may occupy a position in the sentence that can be labeled 'subject' or 'object' and (2) generally correspond to nouns in other languages, where they name or designate a person, place, or thing. There are a very large number of words in Ponapean that we may consider nouns. Examples follow.

Ewalt	'a personal name'	*ihmw*	'house'
Nahlaimw	'a title'	*karangahp*	'tuna'
Wene	'a place name'	*sakau*	'kava'
ahlek	'species of reed'	*limpwel*	'species of crab'
karer	'citrus'	*madep*	'species of sea cucumber'
lukouk	'small hand net'	*mwahs*	'worm'
padil	'paddle'	*nahna*	'mountain'
saip	'sardine'	*ahd*	'current'
Uh	'a place name'	*pwoahr*	'hole, cave'
Dauk	'a title'	*wahr*	'canoe'

We could easily add many more words to this list. There are thousands of nouns in Ponapean, and more—like *sompihr* 'airplane', *spahk* 'spark plug', and *dihsel* 'diesel'—are being invented or borrowed all the time. In the next chapter of this book we will examine nouns in more detail.

VERBS

3.7.2　　　**Verbs** can be described as words which designate an action, event, state, condition, or quality. Following are some examples of verbs.

ede	'to sharpen'	*kapahtou*	'sad'
ale	'to take or get'	*likih*	'to trust'
iang	'to accompany'	*mworourou*	'fat, stout'
ingirek	'smelly'	*pain*	'to incite'
kading	'to tickle'	*saloh*	'nervous'
ned	'to smell'	*seng*	'to cry'
pahng	'to enumerate'	*war*	'worthy'
rese	'to saw'	*doaloa*	'to mix'
urahki	'to pull'	*inen*	'straight'
kapat	'to add'	*woakih*	'to whip'

Notice that the list of examples of verbs above includes a number of words that might more conventionally be labeled adjectives. These are words like *ingirek* 'smelly', *kapahtou* 'sad, and *mworourou* 'fat, stout'. These words are indeed adjectives, but they are included here since in this grammar adjectives will be dealt with as a subclass of verbs, rather than as a separate word class. The arguments supporting this position are included in the more detailed discussion of verbs that occurs in section **5**.2.

WORDS WHICH FUNCTION BOTH AS NOUNS AND VERBS

3.7.3　　　A considerable number of words in Ponapean function both as nouns and verbs. *Rasaras*, for example, means both 'a saw' and 'to saw', as the following sentences illustrate.

> *Rasaraso keng.*
> 'That saw is sharp.'

> *Ihs me pahn rasaras?*
> 'Who is going to saw?'

Of course, this is similarly true of the word 'saw' in English as well as of a great many other English words, particularly those which are only one syllable long. 'Hit', 'throw', 'kiss', 'knock', 'punch', 'walk', 'hammer', 'file', 'vomit', 'jump', 'slap' and 'cut' are just a few examples of English words that function both as nouns and verbs. Among the many Ponapean words that have this dual function are the following.

	Word	As a Noun	As a Verb
(a)	*wini*	'medicine'	'to take medicine'
	mwaramwar	'garland'	'to wear a garland'
	suht	'shoes'	'to wear shoes'
	aip	'drum'	'to play a drum'
(b)	*kapwat*	'decoration'	'to decorate'
	didmwerek	'phosphorescence'	'phosphorescent'
	enihep	'mildew'	'mildewed'
	sakau	'kava'	'to be intoxicated'
	peinakapw	'young female'	'young, of females'

In these examples, notice that when the word in question is used as a noun, it refers to a physical object or being. When used as a verb, it either refers to an activity usually associated with the object, as in the (a) examples, or it describes a quality or condition associated with the object, as in the (b) examples. Now consider these words.

(c)	*akamai*	'argument'	'to argue'
	asi	'sneeze'	'to sneeze'
	doadoahk	'work'	'to work'
	esingek	'breath'	'to breathe'
	kahlek	'dance'	'to dance'
	kapakap	'prayer'	'to pray'
	lokaia	'speech'	'to speak'
	pilipil	'selection'	'to select'
	sawas	'help'	'to help'

A great many words that may function as both nouns and verbs behave like the above. As verbs, these words describe an activity, condition, or state. As nouns, they simply name the activity, condition, or state. There are many words like this in Ponapean. In fact, most of the kinds of verbs that we will discuss as intransitive verbs in section 5.2.1 may be used as both nouns and verbs.

Since so many words in Ponapean may function either as nouns or verbs, one might be tempted to simply eliminate this distinction in favor of a broader label like **universal** or **major word** to indicate all those words that may function either as nouns or verbs. There are, however, a number of unsatisfactory consequences of this position.

One is that to discard the distinction between nouns and verbs is to ignore the intuition of the native speaker, who in many cases feels there is a difference between when a word *is* a noun, and when it is being *used* as a noun, or when a word *is* a verb, and when it is being *used* as a verb. For example, probably all of the words in examples (a) and (b) are thought of primarily as nouns, while those listed under (c) might be more commonly thought of as verbs. No doubt this correlates with the fact that (a) and (b) words as nouns are concrete, while (c) words are not. Still, the distinction between nouns and verbs seems valid.

Another reason that we want to maintain nouns and verbs as separate word classes is that, except through the processes of derivation we will discuss in section 3.7.4, there are some nouns that may not be used as verbs, and similarly, there are some verbs that may not be used as nouns. A few examples of nouns that may not be used as verbs follow.

adohl	'a variety of coconut palm'
kailok	'hatred'
kalahp	'Pacific green back turtle'
elimoang	'mangrove crab'
lohs	'mat'

Among the verbs which may not be used as nouns are:

lang	'to be hung up'
karasapene	'to compare'
adih	'to take by force'
ainpene	'to be handcuffed'
likahde	'to caress'

We also need to maintain the distinction between nouns and verbs because without it we are unable to capture an important generalization about Ponapean. In Ponapean, there are a number of morphemes that have two allomorphs—one where the first vowel is long when the morpheme stands alone, and one where this same vowel is short when certain affixes are attached. But not all morphemes show this alternation. Here are some examples, where the first set of morphemes shows the alternation, and the second set does not.

	Unaffixed	English	Affixed	English
(1)	*ohl*	'man'	*olen*	'man of'
	pihk	'sand'	*piken*	'sand of'
	pwehl	'earth'	*pwelin*	'earth of'
(2)	*tang*	'run'	*tangen*	'running of'
	dik	'skip'	*diken*	'skipping of'
	dil	'penetrate'	*dilin*	'penetrating of'

Notice that the first three forms, precisely those that we would wish to call nouns, show the alternation, while the second three, those that we want to call verbs, do not. What is demonstrated here is the monosyllabic noun vowel lengthening rule to which we already made reference in section 3.5.1. This rule applies only to nouns. We will examine this rule in more detail in section 4.2.1.

The distinction that we have drawn between nouns and verbs, while not without its difficulties, is a useful one that we will refer to throughout this grammar. Both nouns and verbs are examined in much greater detail in the following two chapters.

CHANGING MAJOR WORD CLASSES

3.7.4   In the preceding discussion, we considered some of the problems involved in determining to which class, noun or verb, a particular major word belongs. The difficulty we encountered was due to the fact that there are many nouns that may be used as verbs, and similarly there are many verbs that may be used as nouns. In the examples we looked at thus far, this changing of a word from one class to another required no additional morphemes. Therefore, a word like *kamadipw* may be both a noun 'a feast' and a verb 'to feast' without further affixation. To describe this kind of changing of word classes, the term **conversion** is sometimes employed. That is, some major morphemes may be converted to another word class simply by using them as that part of speech.

Currently, we do not know very much about what major words may undergo conversion, except to say that there clearly seems to be some correlation between the meaning of a word and its ability to function as both a noun and a verb. For example, probably all words designating titles or ranks may be used as nouns to name the title or rank, or as verbs meaning to hold that title or rank. Similarly, words designating feasts may be used as nouns to name the feast, or as verbs meaning to prepare the feast. Words designating articles of clothing may be used as nouns to name the article of clothing, or as verbs meaning to wear the clothing, and words designating kinds of magic may be used as nouns to name the kind of magic, or as verbs meaning to employ the magic. Other classes of words that work both as nouns and verbs are those designating tools, dances, games, meals, types of fishing, and diseases. Further study of what major words may undergo conversion would be an interesting and worthwhile task, but it is one that is beyond the scope of this grammar.

What we do wish to consider here is the process of changing word classes called **derivation.** Derivation, unlike conversion, involves the use of affixation. Of the seven kinds of derivation we will examine here, six involve the use of suffixes, while only one involves the use of a prefix.

Our discussion of derivation will be divided into two parts—the changing of nouns to verbs, and conversely, the changing of verbs to nouns. Before we begin this discussion, however, it should be noted that in some instances grammatical terms which have not yet been defined are employed. References to where these terms are explained are provided, though in most cases lack of familiarity with them should not seriously interfere with your understanding.

Nouns to Verbs

There are at least five productive derivational ways of changing nouns to verbs in Ponapean, all of which involve suffixation. Each of these is considered below.

Noun + *n*: Many, but not all, nouns in Ponapean may be suffixed by -*n* to produce the particular subclass of verbs that we will label adjectives. The general meaning of this suffix is 'having the thing or quality named by the noun in abundance'. The English suffix -*y* may often be employed in translating these forms, as some of the following examples illustrate.

Noun	Noun + *n*	As in the Sentence
ahng	*angin*	*E pahn angin lakapw.*
'wind'	'windy'	'It will be windy tomorrow.'
ilok	*ilokin*	*E nohn ilokin rahnwet.*
'wave'	'wavy'	'It's too wavy today.'
pihl	*pilen*	*Wasaht me pilen.*
'water'	'watery'	'This place is watery.'
dihp	*dipan*	*Kitail koaros me dipan.*
'sin'	'sinful'	'We are all sinful.'
mwahs	*mwasan*	*Met me mwasan.*
'worm'	'wormy'	'This one is wormy.'

The vowel that occurs before the sufix -*n* is a base vowel. The alternation of vowel length, as in the forms *dihp* and *dipan*, is due to the monosyllabic noun vowel lengthening rule.

Some adjectives in Ponapean have also been derived from nouns by the process of reduplication. Reduplication for this purpose, though, is probably no longer in use; therefore, adjectives like these illustrate a fossilized way of deriving adjectives. The productive way is the one described above. Usually, where an adjective derived by this fossilized use of reduplication survives in the language, it is preferred over the form derived by the use of -*n*. Following are some examples.

Noun	Preferred	Also Possible
pihk	*pikapik*	*piken*
'sand'	'sandy'	'sandy'
dihpw	*dipwidipw*	*dipwen*
'grass'	'grassy'	'grassy'
loahng	*loangoaloang*	*loangen*
'fly'	'full of flies'	'full of flies'

In some instances, the adjective derived by reduplication has shifted in meaning so that both the reduplicated and -*n* forms may occur, but with different meanings.

Noun	Reduplicated	Suffixed by -*n*
ahl	*alahl*	*alan*
'road, path'	'striped'	'full of roads or paths'

mwahs	*mwasamwas*	*mwasan*
'worm'	'rotten'	'full of worms'

It thus seems safe to say that the suffixing of *-n* to nouns is a productive process of deriving adjectives in Ponapean and has replaced reduplication which once served this purpose.

Noun + *niki*: Any noun which may take possessive suffixes (see section **4**.8) may be suffixed by *-niki* to function as a transitive verb meaning 'to have or to own' the kind of thing characterized by the noun. Examples follow.

Noun	Noun + *niki*	As in the Sentence
wahr	*waraniki*	*I waraniki sidohsa silipwoat.*
'canoe or vehicle'	'to own (of vehicles)'	'I own three automobiles.'
ihmw	*imwaniki*	*Lahpo imwaniki ihmw riau.*
'house or building'	'to own (of buildings)'	'That guy owns two houses.'
sahpw	*sapweniki*	*Ohlo sapweniki wasaht.*
'land'	'to own (of land)'	'That man owns this place.'
ulung	*ulunganiki*	*Liho ulunganiki uluhl siluh.*
'pillow (archaic)'	'to own (of pillows)'	'That woman owns three pillows.'
moange	*moangeniki*	*I men moangeniki moangeho.*
'head (his her, or its)'	'to own (of heads)'	'I want to possess his head.'

The vowels that occur before *-niki* are, as noted in section **3**.5.1, base vowels. Notice that in these examples, as in the ones in the preceding discussion, the long vowel in monosyllabic nouns shortens when followed by *-niki*. It may be possible that the suffix *-niki* should be thought of as a combination of the derivational suffix *-n* plus the suffix *-ki*, examined next, but this remains unclear.

Noun + *ki*: Some nouns may be suffixed by *-ki* to form transitive verbs. In this case, the suffix might be translated as 'with' or more idiomatically, depending on the verb, 'to use as' or 'to consider as'. Following are some examples.

Noun	Noun + *ki*
uhr	*Soulik pahn uriki ahk.*
'pole'	'Soulik will use mangrove for posts.'
pahpa	*E pahpahki ohlo.*
'father'	'He considers that man as a father.'
dahm	*I pahn damiki tuhkeht.*
'outrigger'	'I will use this log as an outrigger.'
dahl	*I daliki tehnmeiet.*
'plate'	'I used this breadfruit leaf as a plate.'

The suffix -*ki*, a highly productive verbal suffix, is examined in further detail in section 5.4.1. In the examples above, the nouns employed are ones which, except by derivation, never function as verbs. Of course, most nouns which may function as verbs as a result of conversion also take this suffix. This is similarly true of the next two derivational suffixes we will examine.

Noun + *ih*: The suffix -*ih* may be added to some nouns to form transitive verbs. Examples are:

Noun	Noun + *ih*	As in the Sentence
aditik	*aditikih*	*I aditikih serio.*
'nickname'	'to nickname'	'I nicknamed that child.'
ain	*ainih*	*Soulik ainih lahpo.*
'handcuffs'	'to handcuff'	'Soulik handcuffed that guy.'

This suffix is further examined in section 5.2.3.

Noun + *la*: Some nouns combine with the suffix -*la* to form verbs like the following.

Noun	Noun + *la*	As in the Sentence
ais	*aisla*	*Pihlo pahn aisla.*
'ice'	'to become ice'	'That water will become ice.'
lohpwu	*lohpwuala*	*Sises lohpwuala.*
'cross'	'to be crucified'	'Jesus was crucified.'
ohl	*ohlla*	*Ehu rahn, pwutako pahn ohlla.*
'man'	'to become a man'	'Someday, that boy will become a man.'

The general meaning of -*la* in these examples is 'to become'. This suffix also has other meanings and usages which are discussed in section 5.4.3.

Verbs to Nouns

Two patterns of affixation are employed in Ponapean to derive nouns from verbs. One of these involves the use of two kinds of suffixes in combination, while the other involves the use of a prefix. Each of these types of derivation is considered below.

Verb + *pa* + Possessive Pronoun Suffix: Some verbs combine with the suffix -*pa* plus a possessive pronoun suffix (see section 4.7.4) to form nouns. For example, the verb *akamai* means 'to argue'. When suffixed by -*pa* plus the possessive pronoun suffix -*mwa* 'you, two', the result is the noun *akamaipamwa* which means 'an argument concerning you two'. Other possessive pronoun suffixes, of course, might also be employed. Therefore, the verb *akamai* might have all the following derived noun forms.

Verb + *pa* + Poss. Pronoun	Meaning 'an argument concerning . . . '
akamaipei	'me'
akamaipemw	'you'
akamaipe	'him, her, or it'
akamaipat	'us, but not you'
akamaipata	'us, two'
akamaipatail	'us, three or more'
akamaipamwa	'you, two'
akamaipamwail	'you, three or more'
akamaipara	'them, two'
akamaiparail	'them, three or more'

Notice that the suffix -*pa* occurs as -*pe* in the singular forms above. Further information about this kind of vowel alternation is presented in section 4.7.4.

Other examples of nouns similarly derived from verbs follow. Only the form with -*pe*, 'him, her, or it' is listed. The remaining forms parallel those above.

Verb	Verb + *pa* + Possessive Pronoun
sawas	*sawasepe*
'to help'	'care of him, her, or it'

kosou	*kosoupe*
'to predict'	'prediction about him, her, or it'
koasoai	*koasoaiepe*
'to talk'	'story about him, her, or it'
kasuwed	*kasuwedpe*
'to ruin'	'bad effect of him, her, or it'
kasarawi	*kasarawipe*
'to sanctify'	'sanctification of him, her, or it'
kalingana	*kalinganepe*
'to beautify'	'beauty of him, her, or it'

Notice in some instances there is a shift in meaning between the verb and its derived noun.

sou + Verb: The prefix *sou-* meaning 'an expert at' occurs in combination with a few verbs in Ponapean to produce derived nouns like the following.

Verb	*sou* + Verb
kohp	*soukohp*
'to prophesy'	'a prophet'
	(an expert at prophesy)
mwet	*soumwet*
'to clear land'	'a farmer'
	(an expert at clearing land)
pal	*soupal*
'to carve or hack'	'a canoe builder'
	(an expert at carving—sometimes used
	to refer to any kind of expert)

In some instances, this prefix also occurs with nouns, as in *soused* 'an expert fisherman' (from *sehd* 'sea'). In the case of *souse* 'an expert carpenter', the meaning of the morpheme to which *sou-* is attached (*se*) is not known. The use of *sou-* is not very productive and appears to be limited largely to describing expertise in traditional Ponapean skills. Probably it is safe to say that the use of *sou* to derive nouns from verbs is fossilized.

   Much more productive is the use of this prefix in combination with the construct suffix *-n* 'of'. (See section **4.9** for further discussion of this suffix.) This combination results in *soun*, the meaning of which, rather than being 'an expert at', is perhaps closer to 'a practitioner of'. In standard Ponapean spelling, *soun* is written attached to the root it precedes. Thus, *soun* plus *pei* 'to fight' is written *sounpei* 'soldier'. It is incorrect to think of *soun* as a prefix, however, since the construction of *sounpei* is analogous, for example, to *olen pei*, literally 'man-of-fight' or more idiomatically 'fighting man'. *Olen pei*, though, is always written as two words. The writing of *soun* with the root that follows is simply the consequence of an orthographic rule. This rule may be justified, however, because in many cases *soun* plus a verb results in a noun which has a somewhat unpredictable meaning. Thus, a *sounpei* is not just a 'practitioner of fighting', but is more specifically a 'soldier'. Other examples follow.

Verb	*soun* + Verb
kapakap	*sounkapakap*
'to pray'	'a prayer leader'
mwadong	*sounmwadong*
'to play'	'an athlete'
sawas	*sounsawas*
'to help'	'an attorney or defender'
padahk	*sounpadahk*
'to preach'	'a teacher'
lokaia	*sounlokaia*
'to talk'	'a spokesman'

Some speakers of Ponapean pronounce *soun* as *sohn*, but the former pronunciation is more common.

One additional related point here is the fact that *tohn*, which means a 'participant, member, or inhabitant of', is treated analogous to *soun*. Therefore, it is written attached to the word it precedes. It is commonly found in combination with both nouns and verbs, as in these examples.

Word	*tohn* + Word
sukuhl	*tohnsukuhl*
'school'	'student'
sarawi	*tohnsarawi*
'holy'	'church member'

lahng	*tohnleng*
'heaven, sky'	'angel'
ihmw	*tohnihmw*
'house'	'resident of a house'

Sometimes *toun* is heard as an alternant of *tohn*.

MINOR WORD CLASSES

3.8 Minor word classes, as we noted in section **3**.6.3, include the kinds of words that are traditionally labeled pronouns, demonstratives, prepositions, and so on. For Ponapean, we will recognize nine minor word classes. It should again be emphasized here that the purpose of this section is not to provide detailed information about these classes. Rather, its purpose is largely one of providing their names in one place. The more detailed discussions of minor words, for which references are provided below, occur in other sections of this grammar. This kind of organization is employed because it is easier to understand the meaning and function of minor words in terms of their relationship to major words and larger grammatical units such as the phrase and the sentence. Following are the names, along with brief definitions and examples, of the nine minor word classes.

PRONOUNS

3.8.1 **Pronouns** are words that are used as replacements or substitutes for nouns or noun phrases. Words such a *i* 'I', *ke* 'you, *e* 'he, she, or it', and *me* 'one' are pronouns. A full discussion of pronouns is presented in sections **4**.6 and **4**.7.

NUMERALS

3.8.2 **Numerals** are words or combinations of words that are used to express numbers. Examples are *ehu* 'one', *limau* 'five', and *eisek* 'ten'. Numerals are examined in more detail in section **4**.4.

DEMONSTRATIVES

3.8.3 **Demonstratives** are words that point to the location or identity of a person, thing, happening, etc. by indicating its distance, either physical or psychological, from the speaker or hearer or both. Words like *met* 'here', *men* 'there by you', and *mwo* 'there, away from both of us' are demonstratives. Demonstratives are examined in section **4**.5.

ASPECT MARKERS

3.8.4   **Aspect markers** are words used with verbs to mark the time contour of an event. There are two aspect markers in Ponapean. These are *pahn*, which signals unrealized aspect, and *kin*, which signals habitual aspect. These aspect markers are examined along with affixes which may be used to indicate aspect in section **5**.7.

PREPOSITIONS

3.8.5   **Prepositions** are words used to form phrases that typically express temporal or spatial relationships. The words that we will call prepositions are *ni* 'to or at' and *nan* 'in or on'. Discussions of these prepositions occur in sections **6**.3.1. and **6**.3.2.

CONJUNCTIONS

3.8.6   **Conjunctions** are words that link phrases and sentences. These are of two types, coordinators and subordinators. **Coordinators** are words like *oh* 'and' and *de* 'or'. **Subordinators** are words like *ma* 'if' and *pwe* 'because'. Conjunctions are examined in section **6**.5.1.

INTERROGATIVES

3.8.7   **Interrogatives** are words that are used to ask questions. Words like *ia* 'where or what', *dah* 'what', *iahd* 'when', and *depe* 'how many' are interrogatives. These words are discussed in section **6**.4.3.

NEGATORS

3.8.8   **Negators** are used in negative sentences. Some of the negators are *kaidehn* 'not', *sohte* 'not', *saikinte* 'not yet', and *sohla* 'no longer'. Negators are discussed in section **6**.4.4.

ADVERBS

3.8.9   Words which occur as part of larger grammatical units like phrases or sentences, but do not belong to one of the preceding word clases, we will call **adverbs**. Adverbs are of three basic types. These are **preverbal adverbs** like *inenen* 'very' and *nohn* 'too', **sentence adverbs** like *dene* 'it is said that' and *mwein* 'perhaps', and **conjunctive adverbs** like *lao* 'until' and *apw* 'and then'. Preverbal adverbs are discussed in section **5.6**, sentence adverbs in section **6.3.3**, and conjunctive adverbs in section **6.5.1**.

INTERJECTIONS

3.9   **Interjections** are words or expressions that are distinguished from other word classes by the fact that they never occur as part of larger grammatical units. Two major types of interjections are those that express emotions and greetings. Because of the grammatical isolation of interjections, they are not discussed elsewhere in this grammar. Consequently, the list of examples included here will be somewhat more lengthy than in preceding sections.

Examples of interjections which are used to express or convey emotions follow.

Ahk!	'an expression of disgust'
Ahka!	'Of course!', 'Indeed!'
Akka!	'an exclamation of surprise'
Ehk!	'an expression of pain'
Ekei!	'an exclamation conveying wonder or surprise'
Esse!	'an expression of much pain'
Iddai!	'Ouch!' (from Japanese)
Kampare!	'Do your best!' (from Japanese)
Kasaroh!	'Too bad!', 'You lose!'
Keti!	'Wow!'
Luhl!	'an expression used to drive away sharks'
Oh!	'Oh!'
Okei!	'O.K.!' (from English)
Pakadanah!	'Alas, you are a fool!' (from Japanese)
Pakehro!	'You fool!' (from Japanese)
Pwakel!	'What a knockout!'
Set!	'Shit!' (from English, a mild expletive in Ponapean)
Sokko!	'That's admirable!' (from Japanese)

| *Oh tier!* | 'Oh dear!' (from English, used by both male and female speakers in Ponapean) |
| *Wei!* | 'an exclamation of surprise' |

As these examples suggest, many interjections have been borrowed into Ponapean from both Japanese and English.

Also included in the class of interjections are greetings or conversation initiating expressions, a few of which follow.

Kaselel!	'Hi!' or 'Bye!'
Kaselehlie!	'Hello!' or 'Goodbye!'
Iau?	'What's up?'

WORDS IN COMBINATION

3.10   Our principal concerns thus far in this grammar have been with sounds and words. We have examined the kinds of sounds that occur in Ponapean, and we have seen how sounds by themselves or in combination with other sounds form morphemes, and how morphemes by themselves or in combination with other morphemes form words. In the next three chapters of this grammar, we will turn our attention to how words by themselves or in combination with other words form phrases, how phrases in combination form sentences, and how sentences combine with each other to form larger sentences.

Just as there are rules about how sounds and morphemes may be combined, so are there rules about permissible combinations of words. These rules may not be obvious to the speaker of a language, but that such rules exist may easily be demonstrated. Consider, for example, a simple Ponapean sentence like the following.

> *Ohl riemeno kin kalapw seiloak.*
> 'Those two men frequently travel.'

If there were no rules about how the words in this sentence were to be combined, then a sentence like the following would be just as good as the one above.

> **Kalapw kin riemeno seiloak ohl.*
> 'frequently habitually two-those travel man'

No speaker of Ponapean, however, would ever consider this sentence to be acceptable. It is not a sentence. It is merely a string of words. To combine these words into an acceptable sentence, several rules must be observed. The first is that the words that specify what is being talked about must precede the words that comment on the subject. What is being talked about are 'those two men'; the comment about these two men is that they 'frequently travel'. Still, this rule is not enough. Considering only this rule, an unacceptable sentence like the following is still possible.

*Riemeno ohl seiloak kin kalapw.
'two-those man travel habitually frequently'

Additional rules are necessary which specify that in the first phrase, the noun *ohl* must precede the numeral *riemen* and the enclitic demonstrative *-o* must be at the end of the phrase. In the second phrase, the aspect marker *kin* must precede the adverb *kalapw*, and both of these words must precede the verb *seiloak*.

Thus we see that there are rules governing how words may be combined to form both phrases and sentences. If for the sentence we have been discussing we label the first phrase which contains a noun, a **noun phrase**, and the second phrase which contains a verb, a **verb phrase**, then we may characterize the correct structure of this sentence with the following diagram.

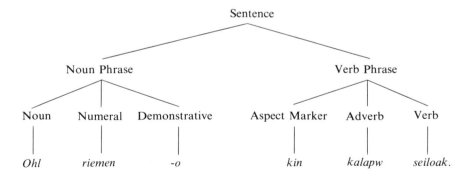

The task of the next three chapters of this grammar will be to examine in more detail first noun phrases, then verb phrases, and subsequently sentences.

4 Nouns and Noun Phrases

OVERVIEW

4.1   A **noun phrase** consists of a noun and, depending upon the type of noun and the nature of the utterance, other modifiers which may serve to clarify the meaning or identity of the noun. Since it is nouns that are at the heart of noun phrases, we will begin our discussion in this chapter by examining words which belong to this part of speech. We will then move on to see how nouns may be modified by affixes or by words which belong to other parts of speech. This discussion will lead us into an examination of numerals and demonstratives. Pronouns will subsequently also be considered, since they may replace nouns or noun phrases. Finally, we will examine the role possessive and construct constructions play in noun phrases.

NOUNS

4.2   As noted in chapter 3, nouns are words that (1) may occupy a position in the sentence that can be labeled 'subject' or 'object' and (2) generally correspond to nouns in other languages, where they name or designate a person, place, or thing. A few examples of the kinds of words that are called nouns follow.

aramas	'person'	*lih*	'woman'
Dauk	'a title'	*Limwei*	'a name'
deke	'island'	*lioal*	'lightning, electricity'
dihpw	'grass'	*loahng*	'fly'
ehd	'bag'	*mahr*	'preserved breadfruit'
ihmw	'house'	*nahn*	'pus'
kaikai	'chin'	*pahs*	'nest'

kalahp	'green back turtle'	*rahn*	'day'
kasap	'frigate bird'	*sahl*	'rope'
lapwed	'salt water eel'	*sewi*	'conch shell'

MONOSYLLABIC NOUN VOWEL LENGTHENING RULE

4.2.1   There is one sound rule in Ponapean which applies uniquely to nouns. In chapter 3 we identified this rule as the **monosyllabic noun vowel lengthening rule**. The effect of this rule is to lengthen vowels in certain monosyllabic (single syllable) nouns. The application of this rule is illustrated by the following examples, where a number of nouns are listed in both their free forms and followed by the construct suffix *-n* 'of'. The vowels that occur before *-n* are base vowels.

pwihl	'gum'	*pwilin*	'gum of'
ngehn	'spirit'	*ngenin*	'spirit of'
sahpw	'land'	*sapwen*	'land of'
loahng	'fly'	*loangen*	'fly of'
pwohng	'night'	*pwongen*	'night of'
uhs	'net float'	*usen*	'float of'

Notice that in the unaffixed forms of these nouns, the vowels are long. Because these forms are monosyllabic, the monosyllabic noun vowel lengthening rule has applied. The corresponding vowels in the suffixed forms of these nouns, however, are short. These nouns are bisyllabic (containing two syllables); therefore, the lengthening rule does not apply.

While it is convenient to talk about this rule affecting monosyllabic nouns, evidence from other Micronesian languages suggests a different explanation. Apparently, this rule is older than the rule that deletes final vowels (discussed in sections 3.3.5 and 3.5.1). Therefore, it is believed that, originally, lengthening applied to the first vowel of two syllable nouns. More specifically, it lengthened the first vowel of nouns of the shape (C) VCV, (C) VGV, (G) VCV, or (G) VGV. Later, final vowels were lost. If we assume that at some time in the past the word *pwihl* was pronounced **pwili* and the word *ngehn* was pronounced **ngeni*, we may derive the current pronunciation of these words by the application of these rules.

Older Free Form	**pwili*	**ngeni*
Vowel Lengthening	*pwihli*	*ngehni*
Vowel Deletion	*pwihl*	*ngehn*

The older form of the construct suffix was *-ni*. The current suffixed forms of these nouns may thus be derived as follows.

Older Form	*pwili+ni*	*ngeni+ni*
Vowel Lengthening	—	—
Vowel Deletion	*pwilin*	*ngenin*

In these suffixed forms, the final vowels (the base vowels) of the noun roots are retained, since they are not in final position. The final vowel of *-ni* is deleted. The vowel lengthening rule does not apply to these forms since, in combination with the suffix, they are not of one of the shapes described above.

In contemporary Ponapean, almost every noun that has a free form of the shape (C)VC, (C)VG, (G)VC, or (G)VG has a long vowel in that form. Nouns like the following, however, that are monosyllabic do not contain a long vowel, since they are not of one of these shapes.

emp	'coconut crab'	*kent*	'urine'
kengk	'coconut, containing no nut'	*mall*	'grassy area'

There are a few nouns in Ponapean which seem to be exceptions to the lengthening rule. Four examples follow.

pil	'bill'	*wil*	'will (the document)'
pis	'pitch, tar'	*dipw*	'clan'

Most exceptional nouns of this nature are ones which have been borrowed from English. True Ponapean examples are rare.

There are also some nouns which have long vowels in both their free forms and their suffixed forms. Examples are:

ihpw	'spear handle'	*ihpwin*	'spear handle of'
kehp	'yam'	*kehpin*	'yam of'
rahn	'day'	*rahnin*	'day of'
moahd	'echo'	*moahdin*	'echo of'
pwohr	'carton'	*pwohrin*	'carton of'
uhp	'plant species'	*uhpin*	'plant species of'

Nouns like these have *inherently* long vowels. The vowel that occurs before *-n* in these forms is probably not a base vowel. We will discuss nouns like these further in section **4**.9.

4.2.2   Another fact about nouns that we need to consider is that they may be divided into different classes. These classes may be determined by either of two basic criteria. One is meaning and the other is function. Using the criterion of meaning, we might, for example, consider all nouns naming living things to belong to one class, all nouns naming oblong things to belong to another class, all nouns naming food to belong to still another class, and so on. With the criterion of function, we might class nouns according to their ability to combine with a certain affix or to appear in a certain kind of grammatical construction.

Both of these criteria for grouping nouns into different classes will be useful to us in various parts of this grammar. When we discuss numerals and possession, for example, we will find it helpful to divide nouns up into classes according to their meanings. Functional classes will be useful, for example, in our discussion of temporal and locative phrases in chapter 6.

The grouping of nouns into classes is something that we will do as our need for understanding these classes arises. Consequently, our discussion of noun classes here is by no means intended to be exhaustive. Rather, the purpose of this brief section is to establish that we may divide nouns into various classes and that talking about these classes is sometimes useful to us in describing Ponapean grammar. For our immediate purposes, we need only consider the distinction between the two classes of nouns which we will label proper nouns and common nouns.

Proper Nouns

The words listed below are all **proper nouns**.

Wene	'name of a community'
Marce	'name of a person'
Spam	'name of a product'
Kolonia	'name of a town'
Kirismas	'name of a holiday (Christmas)'
Sapahn	'name of a country (Japan)'

Notice that all of these nouns we have called proper nouns are names. Each designates a single, individual entity. A noun like *Wene* is the name of a single place, *Marce* is the name of an individual person, and *Spam* is the name of a specific product.

Common Nouns

These nouns are all **common nouns**.

ohl	'man'
ihmw	'house'
limwakatantar	'millipede'
resires	'shoal'
tih	'bone'
kemisik	'fresh water eel'

These nouns, rather than being names of individual entities, refer to classes of things. The noun *ohl* is not the name of a particular man. It may be used to refer to any man. Similarly, a noun like *ihmw* refers to the whole class of objects we call houses. Nouns that refer to classes of things, therefore, are called common nouns.

The distinction that we have made here between proper and common nouns is a useful one. It will be especially helpful in understanding noun phrases, the subject to be considered next.

NOUN PHRASES

4.3   As a first step towards understanding what a noun phrase is, let us consider the subjects of the following sentences, all of which are noun phrases.

(a) *Soulik*
    'Soulik

(b) *Pwutako*
    'That boy

(c) *Pwutak silimeno*
    'Those three boys

(d) *Pwutak reirei silimeno*
    'Those three tall boys

(e) *Pwutak silimen me lalaido*
    'Those three boys who are fishing

(f) *Nei pwutak silimeno*
    'My three sons there

kohdo aio.
came yesterday.'

Notice in these examples that the noun phrase in sentence (a) consists of only a single noun, while those in sentences (b) through (f) consist of the noun *pwutak* 'boy' plus other modifying elements. Based on these examples, let us define a noun phrase as follows. A **noun phrase** consists of a noun plus any other words or word groups that belong with the noun and in some way modify its meaning. The noun being referred to is called the **head** of the noun phrase; the other words or morphemes present help the speaker specify or make reference to the identity or meaning of the head noun.

If the identity of whatever is referred to in the noun phrase is understood by the listener(s), then either a single noun or an entire noun phrase may be replaced by a pronoun. Pronouns will be examined later in this chapter. First, we will consider noun phrases consisting of a single noun, and then those containing modifiers.

NOUN PHRASES CONSISTING OF A SINGLE NOUN

4.3.1   As we saw in sentence (a) in the preceding section, a noun phrase may consist of only a single noun. For example, in each of the following sentences the first word is a noun phrase.

Soulik pwurodo.
'Soulik returned.'

Spam sohte iou.
'Spam isn't delicious.'

Pohnpei inenen lingan.
'Ponape is very beautiful.'

Hawaii pil lingan.
'Hawaii is also beautiful.'

Damian pahn ese.
'Damian will know.'

Limwei pwupwidi.
'Limwei fell down.'

Ewalt kohla laid.
'Ewalt went fishing.'

In all these sentences, the noun that occurs alone is a proper noun. With proper nouns, modifiers to establish the identity of the thing in question are not necessary. This is because a proper noun, as we earlier observed, refers to a single unique entity. It is possible, though, for proper nouns to be used with modifiers, as in *Johnet; kaidehn John kau.* 'This John, not those Johns'. But, here it is a group of individuals named 'John' that is involved, and the word 'John' is no longer really functioning as a proper noun. Under these circumstances, it is better considered a common noun. Such a usage of proper nouns, however, is somewhat rare. Normally, proper nouns stand alone as noun phrases.

Common nouns, on the other hand, normally occur in noun phrases with other modifying words or morphemes, since by themselves they refer to a whole class of objects. Only when one wishes to refer to the whole class of things named by the noun, or when the identity of a particular member of the class is unimportant, may common nouns stand alone in noun phrases. Some examples of where this might be the case follow.

When common nouns are used **generically** to refer to the entire class of objects being named, they stand alone. Examples are:

Menpihr kak pihr.
'Birds can fly.'

Aramas kin mehla.
'People die.'

Pwihk kin ngopwongopw.
'Pigs grunt.'

Seri kin sengiseng.
'Children cry.'

Mwahmw kin dahr.
'Fish school during spawning season.'

Kamadipw me kasoupisek.
'Feasts cause one to be busy.'

Emp me iou.
'Coconut crabs are delicious.'

Seir me pwohmwahu.
'Seir (a tree species) smells good.'

In all these sentences, what is being talked about is not a particular object or being, but the entire class of things named by the noun.

Common nouns are also used alone in contrastive sentences, where what is being emphasized is not the identity of a particular item, but the fact that the object in question belongs to one class as opposed to another. The following sentences illustrate this usage.

Wahr me i anahne, kaidehn *sidohsa.*
'It's a *canoe* that I need, not a *car.*'

Sompihr me kohdo, kaidehn *sohpw.*
'An *airplane* came, not a *ship.*'

Mwahmw iousang *kou.*
'*Fish* is more delicious than *beef.*'

E wahdo *uhp*, kaidehn *uhpw.*
'He brought *fish poison*, not a *drinking coconut.*'

Similarly, when one's concern is with establishing the existence of something, common nouns by themselves function as noun phrases, as in these sentences.

Mie *kahs*?
'Is there gas?'

Sohte *mwenge.*
'There is no food.'

Mie nei *pwihk.*
'I have a pig.'

In summary, proper nouns normally occur alone as noun phrases. Common nouns, too, may occur alone, but only when they are being used in one of the ways illustrated above.

NOUN PHRASES CONTAINING MODIFIERS

4.3.2   In sentences (b) through (f) of section 4.3, noun phrases consisting of a head noun plus other modifiers were presented. For convenience, those noun phrases are repeated here.

(b) *pwutako*
     'that boy'

(c) *pwutak silimeno*
     'those three boys'

(d) *pwutak reirei silimeno*
     'those three tall boys'

(e) *pwutak silimen me lalaido*
     'those three boys who are fishing'

(f) *nei pwutak silimeno*
     'my three sons there'

Noun phrases (b) through (f) are alike in having the same noun
pwutak 'boy' as their head. They differ in the kinds of modifiers
they employ. In sentence (b), the head noun is modified by the
demonstrative *-o* 'that, away from you and me' and in sentence
(c) it is additionally modified by the numeral *silimen* 'three'. In
(d), the adjective *reirei* 'tall' is added, while in (e) the relative
clause *me lalaid* 'who are fishing' is employed. In (f), a possessive
construction is employed.

Since noun phrases of the types illustrated in (d) and (e)
include elements dealt with later in this book (adjectives and
relative clauses are examined in section 6.5.2), we will postpone
discussion of these. The other kinds of elements illustrated in
these noun phrases are examined in the remainder of this chapter.
Numerals are our next topic.

NUMERALS

4.4   A **numeral** is a word or a combination of words used to express a
           number. In a phrase like *takai riau* 'two stones', the word *riau* is a
           numeral that expresses the number '2'. Similarly, in a phrase like
           takai eisek riau, the words *eisek riau* express the number '12',
           eisek meaning '10' and *riau* meaning '2'.
               In Ponapean, as in most Micronesian languages, there are a
           number of elaborations in the use of numerals that do not occur
           in a language like English. To illustrate this, let us begin by
           considering the following Ponapean numerals, the meanings of
           which are represented by the numbers in the left column.

	I	II	III
1	ehu	emen	oumw
2	riau	riemen	rioumw
3	siluh	silimen	siluhmw
4	pahieu	pahmen	pahumw
5	limau	limmen	limoumw
6	weneu	wenemen	wenoumw
7	isuh	isimen	isuhmw
8	waluh	welimen	weluhmw
9	duwau	duwemen	duwoumw
10	eisek	ehk	ngoul

The first and most obvious observation we might make from an examination of these numerals is that there is more than just a single way to count in Ponapean. In fact, there are at least thirty ways. This multiplicity of counting systems is due to the existence of **numeral classifiers**. Every concrete noun in Ponapean belongs to one or more classes. When we use a numeral with a noun, an appropriate numeral classifier must be employed. More simply stated, the choice of the numeral system one uses is dependent upon what one is counting. For example, the first counting system above, the one beginning with *ehu*, is a general counting system, often used to count things which have the property of being round. The second counting system, beginning with *emen*, is used to count animate things. The third system, beginning with *oumw*, is used to count certain foods which are baked. As we shall see, with some exceptions, the choice of which counting system is to be used with a particular noun is based upon meaning considerations like these.

To better understand what numeral classifiers are, let us examine the words for the numbers one through nine in the preceding three counting systems. In each of these systems, these numerals consist of two morphemes. This is illustrated below, where the division between morphemes is shown by the use of a plus sign. (In some cases, what is normally written *uh* in Ponapean is treated here as a sequence of the two vowels $u + u$.)

	I	II	III
1	eh + u	e + men	o + umw
2	ria + u	rie + men	rio + umw
3	silu + u	sili + men	silu + umw

4	pahie + u	pah + men	pah + umw
5	lima + u	lim + men	limo + umw
6	wene + u	wene + men	weno + umw
7	isu + u	isi + men	isu + umw
8	walu + u	weli + men	welu + umw
9	duwa + u	duwe + men	duwo + umw

Notice that the first set of numerals ends with -u, the second set with -men, and the third set with -umw. These final morphemes, -u, -men and -umw, are the numeral classifiers. These classifiers are suffixes which are attached to the numeral stems representing the numbers one through nine. Therefore, the numeral stems are, in the first system for example, *eh-*, *ria-*, *silu-*, etc. These numeral stems vary in pronunciation depending upon which classifier follows. In a more complete grammar of Ponapean we would wish to explore the rules which cause the variations in pronunciation, but for our purposes here we will simply note that these variations exist. The more important point is that the numerals one through nine in each case consist of a numeral stem plus a numeral classifier.

In all there are at least twenty-nine numeral classifiers in Ponapean. (As we will see later, there is one counting system that does not employ classifiers, thus accounting for thirty counting systems.) Through the use of these classifiers, there are at least twenty-nine ways of saying one, twenty-nine ways of saying two, etc. With these systems, however, there are only three ways of saying ten. These three words for ten, given in the first set of counting systems we examined, are *eisek*, *ehk*, and *ngoul*.

One way to organize further discussion of these counting systems is to group them together according to which word they employ for ten. This system of organization will be employed in the following sections. Therefore, we will discuss first those counting systems which take *eisek* as the numeral for ten, then those that take *ehk*, and finally those that take *ngoul*. You should be cautioned, though, that there is considerable disagreement among native speakers about which of these words for ten is correct for some of these systems. The choices made here represent what some older speakers believe to be correct; where variation commonly exists, it is pointed out.

Eisek CLASSIFIERS

4.4.1   There are at least thirteen counting systems that take *eisek* as their word for ten. Some speakers, particularly younger ones, use *ehk* with all of these systems except the first one that we will discuss, the one employing the classifier *-u*. *Ngoul* is an alternant for the systems employing the classifiers *-pak* and *-sou*. All thirteen systems are listed below, the more common ones being presented first. Each system is named according to the classifier employed.

-u Numerals

If asked to count from one to ten, most native speakers of Ponapean would respond with the following numerals plus *eisek*.

1	*ehu*	4	*pahieu*	7	*isuh*
2	*riau*	5	*limau*	8	*waluh*
3	*siluh*	6	*weneu*	9	*duwau*

This is probably the most common counting system in Ponapean. Although some native speakers attribute the characteristic of roundness to things counted with the *-u* classifier, in actuality it is used with inanimate nouns of many types. Some examples are *uhpw riau* 'two drinking coconuts', *pwuhk siluh* 'three books', *wihk weneu* 'six weeks', and *pwopwoud limau* 'five married couples'. Even some animate nouns, which are usually counted with the *-men* numerals discussed in section **4.4.2**, are counted with these numerals. Examples are *wehi riau* 'two turtles', *karangahp duwau* 'nine tuna', *merer siluh* 'three parrot fish' and *kemeik isuh* 'seven *kemeik* (a species of fish)'. Other nouns like this are *kihs* 'octopus' and *liht* 'jellyfish'. It should be pointed out, however, that some speakers of Ponapean feel sea creatures like these would be counted with *-u* only when they are part of a catch. When free in the ocean, they may be counted with *-men*. In any case, *-u* numerals are used with more than just nouns which have the semantic characteristic of roundness.

-pak Numerals

1	*apak*	4	*pahpak*	7	*isipak*
2	*riapak*	5	*limpak*	8	*welipak*
3	*silipak*	6	*wenepak*	9	*duwapak*

These numerals occur with *pahn* 'times' as in these examples: *pahn riapak* 'two times', *pahn silipak* 'three times'. Some speakers prefer the constructions *pahn pak riapak* or *pahn pak silipak*.

-mwut Numerals

1	*emwut*	4	*pahmwut*	7	*isimwut*
2	*riemwut*	5	*limmwut*	8	*walimwut*
3	*silimwut*	6	*wenemwut*	9	*duwamwut*

These numerals are used with *mwutin* 'heap or pile of' plus a following noun, as in *mwutin dihpw pahmwut* 'four heaps of grass'. As we shall see, this kind of construction, where the classifier plus the construct suffix *-n* 'of' precedes the noun being counted, is quite common.

-lep Numerals

1	*elep*	4	*pahlep*	7	*isilep*
2	*rielep*	5	*limelep*	8	*wellep*
3	*sillep*	6	*wenlep*	9	*duwelep*

This system occurs with expressions employing *lepin* 'oblong piece of' as in *lepin tuhke sillep* 'three oblong pieces of wood' or *lepin sika rielep* 'two cigarette butts'. This classifier is also used interchangeably with *-sop*, discussed later.

-pit Numerals

1	*epit*	4	*pahpit*	7	*isipit*
2	*riepit*	5	*limpit*	8	*walipit*
3	*silipit*	6	*wenepit*	9	*duwapit*

These numerals are restricted to expressions involving *piten* 'strip or strand of' as in *piten peilirop riepit* 'two strips of pandanus for weaving mats' or *pitenwel isipit* 'seven strands of hair'.

-el Numerals

1	*ehl*	4	*pahiel*	7	*isiel*
2	*riehl*	5	*limiel*	8	*weliel*
3	*siliel*	6	*weniel*	9	*duwehl*

This counting system seems to be restricted to phrases involving the noun *ehl* 'garland', as in *elin seir riehl* 'two garlands of *seir* (a type of fragrant flowering tree)' or *elin kapwat pahiel* 'four garlands or leis'.

-*sop* Numerals

1	*osop*	4	*pahsop*	7	*isisop*
2	*riasop*	5	*limisop*	8	*welisop*
3	*silisop*	6	*wensop*	9	*duwasop*

These numerals are used to count 'stalks' as in *sehu silisop* 'three stalks of sugarcane'. They also occur in constructions involving *sopin* as in *sopin tuhke pahsop* 'four pieces of wood'. The classifier -*sop*, as we have noted, is used interchangeably with - *lep*.

-*sou* Numerals

1	*esou*	4	*pahsou*	7	*isisou*
2	*riesou*	5	*limisou*	8	*welisou*
3	*silisou*	6	*wensou*	9	*duwesou*

This system is used only with the noun *pwise* 'feces' and is used to count 'heaps' or 'piles'. It is used in phrases like *pwise riesou* 'two piles of feces' or *pwise pahsou* 'four piles of feces'.

-*mwodol* Numerals

1	*emwodol*	4	*pahmwodol*	7	*isimwodol*
2	*riemwodol*	5	*limwomwodol*	8	*welimwodol*
3	*silimwodol*	6	*wenemwodol*	9	*duwemwodol*

These numerals are used to count small, round objects. Examples are *kisin kehp reimwodol* 'two small round yams' and *mwodolen pilawa pahmwodol* 'four small round loaves of bread'.

-*tumw* Numerals

1	*otumw*	4	*pahtumw*	7	*isitumw*
2	*riotumw*	5	*limatumw*	8	*welitumw*
3	*silitumw*	6	*wenetumw*	9	*duwetumw*

These numerals are used only to count 'gusts of wind' as in the expression *tumwenieng riotumw* 'two gusts of wind'.

-dip Numerals

1	*edip*	4	*pahdip*	7	*isidip*
2	*riadip*	5	*limadip*	8	*welidip*
3	*silidip*	6	*wenedip*	9	*duwadip*

These numerals are used for counting slices, chips, or shavings of something, as in the phrases *dipen mei riadip* 'two slices of breadfruit' or *dipen pilein pahdip* 'four shavings from a plane'.

-dun Numerals

1	*odun*	4	*pahdun*	7	*isidun*
2	*riadun*	5	*limadun*	8	*welidun*
3	*silidun*	6	*wendun*	9	*duwadun*

These numerals occur only in noun expressions employing *dunen* 'bundle of (food, tied together with a string)' as in *dunen mei riadun* 'two bundles of breadfruit'.

-i Numerals

Only two forms have been recorded for this counting system—*ih* 'one' and *riai* 'two'. Apparently these numerals are used only with the noun *ih* 'bunch' as in *ihn uht ih* 'one bunch of bananas'. This classifier system is rare. Most younger speakers of Ponapean use the *-u* system to count 'bunches'; therefore, *ihn uht ehu* is also possible.

Ehk CLASSIFIERS

4.4.2   There are at least twelve counting systems that take *ehk* as their numeral for ten. Four of these systems, those employing the classifiers *-par*, *-ka*, *-pwuloi*, and *-sel*, also occur with *eisek*. The system employing the classifier *-pa* sometimes occurs with *ngoul*.

-men Numerals

1	*emen*	4	*pahmen*	7	*isimen*
2	*riemen*	5	*limmen*	8	*welimen*
3	*silimen*	6	*wenemen*	9	*duwemen*

These numerals are used exclusively to count animate beings. Examples are *pwihk riemen* 'two pigs', *ohl limmen* 'five men', *seri pahmen* 'four children' and *kidi isimen* 'seven dogs'. Some nouns, though, like *wehi* 'turtle', although they designate animate beings, are counted with the *-u* system (as noted in section **4.4.1**).

-pwoat Numerals

1	*oapwoat*	4	*pahpwoat*	7	*isipwoat*
2	*rioapwoat*	5	*limpwoat*	8	*welipwoat*
3	*silipwoat*	6	*wenepwoat*	9	*duwoapwoat*

These numerals are used to count objects having the common characteristic of 'longness'. Some examples are *tuhke rioapwoat* 'two trees', *dinapw limpwoat* 'five boards', *sika silipwoat* 'three cigarettes'. Vehicles are also counted with this system; thus, *wahr welipwoat* 'eight canoes', *sidohsa limpwoat* 'five automobiles', and *sompihr pahpwoat* 'four airplanes'. This counting system is also used with nouns such as *koul* 'song', as in *koul rioapwoat* 'two songs', *mehlel* 'truth' as in *mehlel oapwoat* 'a truth', or *koasoai* 'speech or story' as in *koasoai silipwoat* 'three stories'.

-pali Numerals

1	*apali*	4	*pahpali*	7	*isipali*
2	*riapali*	5	*limpali*	8	*welipali*
3	*silipali*	6	*wenepali*	9	*duwepali*

This system is used to count body extremities, as in *peh riapali* 'two hands'. It also occurs with the noun *pali* itself which has the general meaning 'part, division, or side' as in *pelien mete limpali* 'five sheets of tin roofing' or *pelien mwomw pahpali* 'four schools of fish'. When the noun *pali* is used to mean 'side' however, as the 'side of something', the *-u* system is employed; therefore, *pali siluh* 'three sides'.

-poar Numerals

1	*oapoar*	4	*pahpoar*	7	*isipoar*
2	*rioapoar*	5	*limpoar*	8	*welipoar*
3	*silipoar*	6	*wenepoar*	9	*duwoapoar*

These numerals are restricted to expressions employing *poaren* 'long, thin piece or strip of'. Examples are *poaren dinapw rioapoar* 'two pieces of board' and *poaren karangahp silipoar* 'three strips of tuna'.

-*te* Numerals

1	*ete*	4	*pahte*	7	*isite*
2	*riete*	5	*limete*	8	*welite*
3	*silite*	6	*wente*	9	*duwete*

This system occurs only with the noun *teh* 'leaf or sheet'. Examples are *tehn tuhke riete* 'two leaves' or *tehn doaropwe isite* 'seven sheets of paper'.

-*par* Numerals

1	*apar*	4	*pahpar*	7	*isipar*
2	*riapar*	5	*limpar*	8	*welipar*
3	*silipar*	6	*wenepar*	9	*duwapar*

These numerals are used to count flat things, as in *pelien mete silipar* 'three sheets of tin roofing'.

-*kap* Numerals

1	*akap*	4	*pahkap*	7	*isikap*
2	*riakap*	5	*limakap*	8	*welikap*
3	*silikap*	6	*wenakap*	9	*duwakap*

These numerals occur only with expressions involving *kap* 'sheaf or bundle'. Some examples are *kepen sehu welikap* 'seven sheaves of sugar cane' and *kepen tuwi riakap* 'two sheaves of firewood'.

-*ka* Numerals

1	*aka*	4	*pahka*	7	*isika*
2	*riaka*	5	*limaka*	8	*welika*
3	*silika*	6	*weneka*	9	*duwaka*

These numerals are used with the noun *kahng* 'row or line' or with phrases containing the bound stem *kah-* meaning 'a row or group of kava stones in a feasthouse'. Examples are *kahngen nih weneka* 'six rows of coconut trees', *kahngen aramas riaka* 'two lines of people', and *kahn takai aka* 'one group of kava stones'.

-pa Numerals

1	*apa*	4	*pahpa*	7	*isipa*
2	*riapa*	5	*limpa*	8	*welipa*
3	*silipa*	6	*wenepa*	9	*duwapa*

This system is used to count 'fronds' as in the phrase *pahn nih riapa* 'two coconut fronds'.

-ra Numerals

1	*ara*	4	*pahra*	7	*isira*
2	*riara*	5	*limara*	8	*welira*
3	*silira*	6	*wenera*	9	*duwara*

These numerals occur only with the noun *rah* 'branch' in phrases like *rahn tuhke limara* 'five tree branches'.

-pwuloi Numerals

1	*opwuloi*	4	*pahpwuloi*	7	*isipwuloi*
2	*riopwuloi*	5	*limpwuloi*	8	*welipwuloi*
3	*silipwuloi*	6	*wenpwuloi*	9	*duwopwuloi*

These numerals are used to count sections from joint to joint of cane-like plants, as in *sehu limpwuloi* 'five sections of sugar cane' or stanzas of a song, as in *pwuloin koul riopwuloi* 'two stanzas'.

-sel Numerals

1	*esel*	4	*pahsel*	7	*isisel*
2	*riesel*	5	*limesel*	8	*welisel*
3	*silisel*	6	*wenesel*	9	*duwesel*

These numerals are used for counting sennit, as in *kisin pwehl pahsel* 'four balls of sennit'.

NGOUL CLASSIFIERS

4.4.3   Four counting systems have been recorded that commonly take *ngoul* as their word for 'ten'. Except with the system that employs the classifier *-umw*, other words for 'ten' are possible. These are noted in the discussions below.

-umw Numerals

1	*oumw*	4	*pahumw*	7	*isuhmw*
2	*rioumw*	5	*limoumw*	8	*weluhmw*
3	*siluhmw*	6	*wenoumw*	9	*duwoumw*

These numerals are used to count yams and bananas, foods that are traditionally prepared in an *uhmw* 'stone oven'. The classifier *-umw* no doubt derives from *uhmw*. Examples of the use of this counting system are *kehp isuhmw* 'seven yams' and *uht siluhmw* 'three bunches of bananas'.

-pwong Numerals

1	*opwong*	4	*pahpwong*	7	*isipwong*
2	*rioapwong*	5	*limpwong*	8	*welipwong*
3	*silipwong*	6	*wenepwong*	9	*duwoapwong*

These numerals occur only with the noun *pwohng* 'night'. Therefore *pwohng silipwong* means 'three nights'; *pwohng limpwong* means 'five nights'. Many speakers feel that *koadoangoul*, used with the *ehd* counting system discussed in section **4.4.5**, is the correct word for ten for these numerals.

-wel Numerals

1	*ewel*	4	*pahwel*	7	*isiwel*
2	*riewel*	5	*limewel*	8	*welewel*
3	*siliwel*	6	*wenewel*	9	*duwewel*

These numerals are used in counting plants like hibiscus, bamboo, or sugarcane that have a single root, but several stalks. Examples are *welin keleu riewel* 'two hibiscus bushes', *welin sehu siliwel* 'three sugar cane plants' or *welin pehri limewel* 'five bamboo plants'. Some speakers of Ponapean also use *ehk* or *eisek* with this counting system rather than *ngoul*.

-kis Numerals

1	*ekis*	4	*pahkis*	7	*isikis*
2	*riakis*	5	*limakis*	8	*welikis*
3	*silikis*	6	*wenekis*	9	*duwakis*

This counting system is used to count small pieces or fragments of things, as in *kisin kehp riakis* 'two small pieces of yam' or *kisin tuhke pahkis* 'four small pieces of wood'. It is also used to count *dinak*, which is a section of a thatch roof measuring one armspan in width and from the eave to peak in length. A building which is described as being *pahkis*, therefore, would be approximately twenty-four feet long. In this latter usage, most native speakers agree that the number for ten is *ngoul*. In the first usage that we presented, both *eisek* and *ehk* are used.

THE USE OF NUMERAL CLASSIFIERS

4.4.4   In the preceding pages we listed a total of twenty-nine different counting systems, each of which was named according to the classifier it employs. These systems were divided into three sets according to the numeral for ten with which they usually occur. For purposes of reference, these sets are summarized below.

eisek	*ehk*	*ngoul*
-u	-men	-umw
-pak	-pwoat	-pwong
-mwut	-pali	-wel
-lep	-poar	-kis
-pit	-te	
-el	-par	
-sop	-kap	
-sou	-ka	
-mwodol	-pa	
-tumw	-ra	
-dip	-pwuloi	
-dun	-sel	
-i		

In most instances, the choice of which of these counting systems to use is determined by the meaning of the noun being counted. There are, however, many nouns which occur with more than just a single counting system. Consider for example the noun *mahi* 'breadfruit'. *Mahi* is used with -*u* numerals, as in *mahi riau* 'two breadfruit', when counting the fruit of the tree. When counting trees rather than fruit, -*pwoat* numerals are used, as in *mahi rioapwoat* 'two breadfruit trees'. The meaning of the noun *mahi* is thus modified according to which classifier is employed. A few additional examples of nouns that occur with more than one counting system follow.

sika	*sika limau*
'cigarette'	'five packs of cigarettes'
	sika limpwoat
	'five cigarettes'
uht	*uht riau*
'banana'	'two bananas'
	uht rioapwoat
	'two banana trees'
	uht rioumw
	'two bunches of bananas'
karangahp	*karangahp riau*
'tuna'	'two tuna (part of a catch)'
	karangahp riemen
	'two tuna (in the sea)'

In these examples, the selection of the classifier depends upon which aspect of the noun a speaker wishes to emphasize.

Another important point concerning the use of numeral classifiers is that they may be used without numeral prefixes with a meaning analogous to the English indefinite article 'a'. In Ponapean spelling, classifiers used for this purpose are written as separate words, but in fact they are enclitics (discussed in section 3.4). Further information concerning the spelling practices associated with these enclitic classifiers follows. Consider first these examples.

Written	Pronounced	English
seri men	/serihmen/	'a child'
tuhke pwoat	/tuhkehpwoat/	'a tree'
kairu men	/kairuhmen/	'a toad'

Here, where the word preceding the classifier ends in a vowel, that vowel lengthens before the enclitic. This lengthening is not represented in the spelling. In the next examples, the classifier follows a word ending either in a glide or a consonant.

	Written	Pronounced	English
(a)	*mahu men*	/mahumen/	'a parrot fish'

(b)	*pwihk men*	/pwihkmen/	'a pig'
(c)	*naip pwoat*	/naimpwoat/	'a knife'
(d)	*malek emen*	/malekemen/	'a chicken'

In examples (a) and (b), no sound change occurs. In (c), a nasal substitution rule applies, but notice that the resulting sound change is not written. In (d), the copy vowel insertion rule applies. This vowel *is* written. Notice that the copy vowel plus the classifier results in a form identical to that of the numeral stem for 'one' plus the classifier—*emen*. These forms are not always identical however. To say 'a small party', one would say /kisin tehpelikis/. Here the copy vowel is *i*, resulting in *ikis*, while the numeral for 'one' in this system is *ekis*. One final point is that the general classifier -*u* without a numeral prefix occurs as *ieu*, as in *pwuhk ieu* 'a book.'

Many of the classifiers previously examined are rarely employed. The considerable confusion that exists concerning what the correct word for 'ten' is with some counting systems is a result of this fact. Many speakers of Ponapean have consequently expressed concern that the rich system of numeral classifiers is in a state of decay and that many counting systems are in danger of being lost from the language. This danger may be real, but it is probably overestimated. It seems quite likely that many numeral classifiers have *never* been commonly employed. At the present time, some classifiers are so restricted in their usage that they may be employed with only a few nouns, while others are generally found only in formal speech or in poetic language. This situation may always have been true. The ability to accurately employ some of the rarer classifiers is now, and may always have been, the mark of an individual who has a better than average command of his language. Thus, the concern that the elaborate numeral classifier system of Ponapean is being reduced to a few common classifiers may not be well founded.

THE *ehd* COUNTING SYSTEM

4.4.5   The counting systems we have examined thus far have all involved the use of a numeral stem plus a classifier. Therefore a numeral like *silipwoat* consists of the numeral stem *sili-* 'three' plus the classifier -*pwoat*. There is one counting system, however, called here the *ehd* system after its word for 'one', which does not employ classifiers. Instead, the numeral stems occur after an initial vowel to produce the following forms. Alternate forms are included in parentheses.

1	*ehd*	4	*epeng*	7	*eis*
2	*ari (are)*	5	*alim (alem)*	8	*ewel*
3	*esil*	6	*oun (aun)*	9	*adu (edu)*

The numeral for 'ten' in this system is *koadoangoul*, also pronounced *kedingoul*.

These numerals function as a general counting system; therefore, since no numeral classifiers are involved, they may be used to enumerate objects of any sort, in the sense of counting them off—one, two three, four, five, etc. These numerals are not used in phrases after a noun. Therefore, *kidi ari is not correct. Also, they do not occur with higher numerals.

The first five of these numerals combine with the preposition *ni* 'at or in' to name five days of the week; thus, *Niehd* 'Monday', *Niari* 'Tuesday', *Niesil* 'Wednesday', *Niepeng* 'Thursday', and *Nialim* 'Friday'.

HIGHER NUMERALS

4.4.6   Thus far in our discussion of Ponapean numerals we have focused our attention on the numbers 'one' through 'nine', making reference to the number 'ten' only for the purpose of organizing our discussion of these lower numerals. Let us now turn our attention to numerals higher than nine.

There are three sets of numerals representing ten and multiples of ten to ninety. For counting systems employing *eisek* these are:

10	*eisek*	40	*pahisek*	70	*isihsek*
20	*rieisek*	50	*limeisek*	80	*welihsek*
30	*silihsek*	60	*weneisek*	90	*duweisek*

The morpheme representing 'ten' here is *-isek* which combines with the lower numeral stems *e-*, *rie-*, *sili-*, *pah-*, *lime-*, *wene-*, *isi-*, *weli-*, and *duwe-*, representing the numerals one through nine. Thus, a numeral like 'twenty' is formed of *rie + isek*, literally 'two + ten'.

For counting systems employing *ehk*, these higher numerals are somewhat irregular, as the following forms illustrate.

10	*ehk*	40	*pehk*	70	*isiakan*
20	*riehk*	50	*limehk*	80	*weliakan*
30	*siliakan*	60	*wenehk*	90	*duwehk*

Here, the morpheme *-akan* is used after the numeral stems for 'three' *sili-*, 'seven' *isi-*, and 'eight' *weli-*, all of which end in the vowel *i*. The other numeral stems, all of which end in some vowel other than *i*, combine with *-ek* to produce the remaining forms.

For counting systems employing *ngoul*, the numerals representing multiples of ten are as follows:

10	*ngoul*	40	*pahngoul*	70	*isingoul*
20	*riengoul*	50	*limengoul*	80	*welingoul*
30	*silingoul*	60	*wenengoul*	90	*duwengoul*

A special use of these numerals is to count coconuts by multiples of one hundred. Therefore, when counting coconuts, *ngoul* means not 'ten', but 'one hundred', *riengoul* means 'two hundred', etc. All higher numerals are also then increased by multiples of 'ten' so that 'one hundred' means 'one thousand' and so on.

Except in this special counting system, the morpheme representing 'hundred' is *-pwiki*. It combines with lower numeral stems to produce these forms:

100	*epwiki*	400	*pahpwiki*	700	*isipwiki*
200	*riepwiki*	500	*limepwiki*	800	*welipwiki*
300	*silipwiki*	600	*wenepwiki*	900	*duwepwiki*

All counting systems employ these numerals. This is similarly true of the following numerals representing numbers higher than 'hundred'.

1,000	*kid*
10,000	*nen*
100,000	*lopw*
1,000,000	*rar*
10,000,000	*dep*
100,000,000	*sapw*
1,000,000,000	*lik*

These numerals may stand for 'one' of this number (therefore *kid* may mean 'one thousand'), or they may combine with the lower numeral stems for two through nine to produce multiples of these numbers. With the numerals *kid, nen, lopw, dep* and *lik* the forms of these lower numeral stems are *rie-, sili-, pah-, lime-, wene-, isi-, weli-*, and *duwe-*. With *rar* and *sapw*, the forms of these stems are *ria-, sili-, pah-, lima-, wene-, isi-, weli-*, and *duwa-*. Thus, 'two thousand' would be *riekid*; 'two-hundred million' would be *riasapw*. Obviously these higher numerals, particularly those higher than 'thousand', are not commonly used, and indeed it is an intriguing question as to what their origin might be. Girschner, in his *Grammatik der Ponapesprache*, suggests they were introduced by missionaries.

One important final observation we may make about higher numerals is that they do not combine with numeral classifiers. Therefore *riepwiki*, meaning 'two-hundred', may be used to mean two-hundred of anything. Numeral classifiers occur only in lower numerals. Therefore, 'two-hundred men' is *ohl riepwiki*. 'Two-hundred and seven men' is *ohl riepwiki isimen*. Further examples follow.

wahr riehk silipwoat	'twenty-three canoes'
pwuhk eisek limau	'fifteen books'
seri kid pahpwiki wenemen	'one thousand, four hundred and six children'
aramas rienen limpwiki	'twenty thousand, five hundred people'
kid duwepwiki isihsek limau	'1975'

FRACTIONS

4.4.7   Fractions, like two-thirds or three-fourths, are composed of two parts, a numerator and a denominator. In a fraction like two-thirds (2/3) two is the numerator and three is the denominator. To form fractions in Ponapean, the denominator is expressed by employing a numeral plus the classifier *-kis*. The numerator, which follows the denominator, uses a numeral plus the general classifier *-u*. Thus to express two-thirds, one would say *silikis riau*. Other examples are:

1/4	*pahkis ehu*
2/5	*limakis riau*
3/4	*pahkis siluh*
7/8	*welikis isuh*

One exception to this formulation of fractions is 1/2. Here, either the word *apali* or *elep* is employed. *Apali* is used with objects divided vertically or by their length, and *elep* is used with objects divided horizontally or by their width. Thus, the following two sentences are possible.

> *Wahdo mahs apalihn tuhkeho.*
> 'Please bring half (split from top to bottom) of that log.'

> *Wahdo mahs elepen tuhkeho.*
> 'Please bring me half (cut crosswise) of that log.'

As these sentences illustrate, fractions combine with the construct suffix *-n* 'of' and precede nouns. Some additional examples are:

> *pahkis ehuwen orenso*
> 'one-fourth of that orange'

> *pahkis siluhwen mahio*
> 'three-fourths of that breadfruit'

> *pahkis siluhwen mahi kau*
> 'three-fourths of those breadfruit'

ORDINAL NUMERALS

4.4.8   **Ordinal numerals** are used to express order or sequence. Examples of ordinal numerals in English are 'first', 'second', 'third', 'fourth', etc. In Ponapean, ordinal numerals are formed with the prefix *ka-*. With the general counting system employing the *-u* classifier, the following forms result.

keieu	'first'	*keweneu*	'sixth'
kariau	'second'	*keisuh*	'seventh'
kesiluh	'third'	*kawaluh*	'eighth'
kapahieu	'fourth'	*keduwau*	'ninth'
kelimau	'fifth'	*keisek*	'tenth'

(Notice that *ka-* is also pronouced *ke-* in some forms.) This prefix may also be used with other counting systems, but 'first' in all cases is *keieu*. Examples with *-men* and *-pwoat* follow.

keieu	*keieu*	'first'
keriemen	*kerioapwoat*	'second'
kesilimen	*kesilipwoat*	'third'

With less common counting systems, however, it is not clear whether or not ordinal numerals are possible. Typically, the general counting system forms are used.

We will also include here among ordinals the bound morpheme *tei-* 'other' which always occurs in combination with demonstrative modifiers. Like ordinal numerals, it expresses order. Compare these examples:

ohl keriemeno	'that second man'
ohl teio	'that other man'
naip kerioapwoatet	'this second knife'
naip teiet	'this other knife'

PREPOSED NUMERALS

4.4.9   Except for fractions, the normal position of numerals is following the head noun of a noun phrase. Numerals, though, may also be **preposed** (placed before the head noun) as these examples illustrate.

Following Numeral	Preposed Numeral
seri men	*emen seri kau*
'a child'	'one of those children'
tuhke rioapwoato	*rioapwoat tuhke kau*
'those two logs'	'two of those logs'
elin seir riehlo	*riehl elin seir kau*
'those two garlands of *seir*'	'two of those garlands of *seir*'
ohl keriemeno	*keriemenen ohlo*
'that second man'	'the second man from that man'

In the last example, which employs an ordinal numeral, the construct suffix is used when the numeral is preposed. In all of these examples, the preposing of the numeral indicates that one is talking about a certain number of some larger group.

QUANTIFIERS

4.4.10   Two additional words that we will consider here in our discussion of numerals are the words *ekei* 'some' and *koaros* 'all'. These two words, which express an indefinite quantity, we will call **quantifiers**. Like numerals, these words may occur after nouns in phrases like these.

aramas koaros	'all the people'
aramas ekei	'some people'

These words may also modify an entire noun phrase, as in these examples.

ekei aramas ehket
'some of these ten people'

koaros aramas ehket
'all of these ten people'
aramas ehket koaros
'all of these ten people'

Notice in these phrases that *ekei* precedes the noun phrase while *koaros* may either precede or follow it.

Other words which express an indefinite quantity, like *tohto* 'many' and *kidalap* 'a great many' do not modify noun phrases and are probably better treated as adjectives in Ponapean.

DEMONSTRATIVES

4.5   **Demonstratives** may be broadly defined as morphemes or words whose function is to help limit the range of what is being talked about by establishing its location relative to the speaker and the listener. In this section we will examine the various kinds of demonstratives that occur in or replace noun phrases in Ponapean. They are of three basic types which we will call **demonstrative modifiers, pointing demonstratives**, and **demonstrative pronouns**. Examples of each of these three types of demonstratives are presented in the following sentences.

Sentence	Type of Demonstrative
Wahr kalaimwun*et* pwoar. '*This* large canoe cracked.'	demonstrative modifier
Iet noumw pinselen. '*Here* is your pencil.'	pointing demonstrative
Met pahn mengila. '*This* will wither.'	demonstrative pronoun

Further information about these three types of demonstratives is presented in the following sections.

4.5.1   **Demonstrative modifiers** are used to modify nouns. Demonstrative modifiers always occur as the last element in a noun
phrase, where they function as enclitics. There are two basic sets
of demonstratives of this type: non-emphatic forms and emphatic
forms.

Non-Emphatic Forms

          Non-emphatic forms of demonstrative modifiers are listed in the
          chart below.

Singular		Plural	
-e(t)	'this, by me'	*-ka(t)*	'these, by me'
-en	'that, by you'	*-kan*	'those, by you'
-o	'that, away from you and me'	*-kau, -koa,* or *-ko*	'those, away from you and me'

          Notice that there is a three-way distinction of location in these
          forms. The location specified may be either physical or
          psychological. Thus, the first form indicates either a physical
          location near the speaker or something in the mind of the
          speaker. The second form indicates a physical location near the
          listener(s) or something in the mind of the listener(s). The third
          form indicates a physical location away from both the speaker
          and the listener(s), or something in the minds of both the speaker
          and the listener(s). This three-way distinction parallels the distinc-
          tions of person in pronouns (*i* 'I', *ke* 'you' and *e* 'he, she, or it')
          and the distinctions of direction in verbal suffixes (*-do* 'toward
          me', *-wei* 'toward you' and *-la* 'away from you and me').
          All of the demonstrative modifiers listed above have alter-
          nate pronunciations. Some of these are indicated in the preced-
          ing chart. Therefore, *-e(t)* and *-ka(t)* are listed with the final
          consonant *t* in parentheses because *t* occurs optionally; in casual
          speech it is normally not pronounced. Also notice that three
          forms, *-kau, -koa* and *-ko*, are listed for the plural demonstrative
          indicating 'those, away from you and me.' There seems to be
          some evidence that the form *-ko* was once employed to indicate
          a location remote from the speaker and hearer. It is still used by
          nearly all speakers in the greeting *Kaselehlie maing ko*! 'Hello
          gentlemen (or ladies)!', and in expressions like *Ohl oko*! which

may be used to politely attract the attention of two or more men. Except in these fixed expressions, many speakers use *-kau* and *-ko* interchangeably. The form *-koa* is commonly heard in the municipality of Uh and may be used elsewhere.

All singular demonstrative modifiers are written attached to the word they follow. Each of these modifiers has two allomorphs, conditioned by the nature of the last segment of the preceding root. The forms that were listed in the chart occur after words ending in consonants, glides (written *i* and *u* in final position)*,* or high vowels. Examples follow.

After Words Ending in Consonants

pwihk	'pig'	*pwihke(t)*	'this pig'
		pwihken	'that pig by you'
		pwihko	'that pig away from you and me'
ihmw	'house'	*ihmwe(t)*	'this house'
		ihmwen	'that house by you'
		ihmwo	'that house away from you and me'

After Words Ending in High Vowels

kidi	'dog'	*kidie(t)*	'this dog'
		kidien	'that dog by you'
		kidio	'that dog away from you and me'
kulu	'plover'	*kuluwe(t)*	'this plover'
		kuluwen	'that plover by you'
		kuluwo	'that plover away from you and me'

The use of *w* in the *u* final forms here and below is consistent with the spelling conventions described in the Appendix.

After Words Ending in Glides

tehi	'sheet'	*tehie(t)*	'this sheet'
		tehien	'that sheet by you'
		tehio	'that sheet away from you and me'
likou	'cloth'	*likowe(t)*	'this cloth'
		likowen	'that cloth by you'

| *likowo* | 'that cloth away from you and me' |

When singular demonstrative modifiers follow words ending in non-high vowels (*e, a, oa,* and *o*), then (1) the final non-high vowel is lengthened, and (2) the following allomorphs of the singular demonstrative modifiers are employed.

-(t)	'this, by me'
-n	'that, by you'
/-w/	'that, away from you and me'

The Ponapean Orthography Committee did not set forth a recommendation concerning how the allomorph /-w/ should be orthographically represented, except that after the plural morpheme *ka* it is to be spelled -*u*; thus *kau*. In other environments, this allomorph is conventionally written as both -*u* and -*o*; -*u* is most commonly written after words ending in the vowel *o* (presumably to avoid *oho* sequences), while -*o* is typically written elsewhere. These same conventions will be employed in this grammar, as illustrated by the following examples.

After Words Ending in Non-High Vowels

mete	'nail'	*meteh(t)*	'this nail'
		metehn	'that nail by you'
		meteho	'that nail away from you and me'
wasa	'place'	*wasah(t)*	'this place'
		wasahn	'that place by you'
		wasaho	'that place away from you and me'
pwukoa	'duty'	*pwukoah(t)*	'this duty'
		pwukoahn	'that duty you know of'
		pwukoaho	'that duty we know of'
pako	'shark'	*pakoh(t)*	'this shark'
		pakohn	'that shark by you'
		pakohu	'that shark away from you and me'

Plural demonstrative modifiers are also enclitics. However, in standard Ponapean spelling these forms are written as separate words according to the principles illustrated by the following examples.

	Noun	Pronounced	But Written
(a)	*dihng* 'ti plant'	/dihngka(t)/ 'these ti plants' /dihngkan/ 'those ti plants by you' /dihngkau/ 'those ti plants away from you and me'	*dihng ka(t)* *dihng kan* *dihng kau*

No sound changes are involved in the forms above, but in the ones below, the copy vowel insertion rule applies.

(b)	*ohl* 'man'	/ohlaka(t)/ 'these men' /ohlakan/ 'those men by you' /ohlakau/ 'those men away from you and me'	*ohl aka(t)* *ohl akan* *ohl akau*

By spelling convention, the copy vowel is written attached to the demonstrative. (Note that this spelling rule is the same as that established for copy vowels before enclitic numeral classifiers.) The choice of the consonant initial demonstrative, as in (a), or the vowel initial form, as in (b), should present no problem for the native speaker of Ponapean. He need only write the form he says. This is somewhat analogous to the situation in English where two forms 'a' and 'an' are used for the indefinite article.

Changes in pronunciation that occur in the root when plural demonstrative modifiers follow are not to be written, as the following examples illustrate.

pwihk 'pig'	/pwihngka(t)/ 'these pigs' /pwihngkan/ 'those pigs by you' /pwihngkau/ 'those pigs away from you and me'	*pwihk kat* *pwihk kan* *pwihk kau*

Though in the spoken language *kk* becomes *ngk* by a nasal substitution rule, this change is not written. Similarly with vowel final words, where the final vowel is lengthened before these enclitics, vowel lengthening is not written. This spelling convention is illustrated using the demonstrative *-ka(t)*.

kidi	/kidihka(t)/	*kidi ka(t)*
'dog'	'these dogs'	
deke	/dekehka(t)/	*deke ka(t)*
'island'	'these islands'	
wasa	/wasahka(t)/	*wasa ka(t)*
'place'	'these places'	
pwukoa	/pwukoahka(t)/	*pwukoa ka(t)*
'responsibility'	'these responsibilities'	
pako	/pakohka(t)/	*pako ka(t)*
'shark'	'these sharks'	
kulu	/kuluhka(t)/	*kulu ka(t)*
'plover'	'these plovers'	

Notice that all vowels lengthen before plural demonstratives, whereas with the singular forms only the non-high vowels do.

The plural demonstrative modifiers listed above consist of two morphemes, with *-ka* marking an indefinite plural number and the suffixes *-(t)*, *-n*, and /*-w*/ representing location. Thus *-ka(t)* is from *-ka+(t)*, *-kan* is from *-ka+n*, and *-kau* is from /*-ka+w*/. This analysis is justified in part by the fact that *-ka* may occur without locational suffixes in time phrases like *ni menseng ka*, as in the sentence *Ni menseng ka, i kin pirida kuloak isuh.* 'In the morning (meaning every morning), I get up at seven o'clock.'

After definite numerals like *riemen* 'two animate things', singular demonstrative modifiers are employed, as illustrated in these examples.

pwihk riemenet	'these two pigs'
seri riemenen	'those two children by you'
ohl riemeno	'those two men, away from you and me'

These singular demonstrative forms also combine with numeral classifiers as we shall examine next.

Emphatic Forms

Emphatic demonstrative modifiers are formed by combining non-emphatic singular forms with numeral classifiers and non-emphatic plural forms with the morpheme *pwu-*. Using the animate classifier *-men* for the purposes of illustration, the following set of emphatic demonstrative modifiers result.

Singular		Plural	
mene(t)	'this here, by me'	*pwuka(t)*	'these here, by me'
menen	'that there, by you'	*pwukan*	'those there, by you'
meno	'that there, away from you and me'	*pwukau*	'those there, away from you and me'

With the classifier *-pwoat*, used for counting long, thin things, the following forms result, with meanings parallel to those above.

pwoate(t)	*pwuka(t)*
pwoaten	*pwukan*
pwoato	*pwukau*

With the general classifier *-u*, only the singular form *wet* is common. (The forms preceded by question marks are questionably acceptable.)

we (t)	*pwuka* (t)
(?) wen	*pwukan*
(?) wo	*pwukau*

Regardless of which classifier is chosen, the plural forms all combine with *pwu-* which, apart from signaling emphasis, has no obvious meaning.

The emphatic nature of these forms, while difficult to capture in translation, is revealed by a comparison of the following phrases.

Non-Emphatic		Emphatic	
ohlet	'this man'	*ohl menet*	'this man here'
ohl akat	'these men'	*ohl pwukat*	'these men here'

POINTING DEMONSTRATIVES

4.5.2   In addition to demonstrative modifiers, there is a set of demonstratives in Ponapean that we will call **pointing demonstratives**. Pointing demonstratives also have both non-
emphatic and emphatic forms.

Non-Emphatic Forms

	Singular		Plural	
ie(t)	'here, by me'	*ietakan/iehkan*	'here, by me'
ien	'there, by you'	*ienakan*	'there, by you'
io	'there, away from you and me'	*iohkan*	'there, away from you and me'

Unlike demonstrative modifiers, which occur as a modifying
element in a noun phrase, pointing demonstratives stand alone in
noun phrases. In essence, they are demonstrative nouns. They are
used in sentences of the type that we will call equational (section
6.2.1), as these examples illustrate.

Iet noumw naipen.	*Ietakan noumw naip akan.*
'Here is your knife.'	'Here are your knives.'
Ien noumw pinselen.	*Ienakan noumw pinsel kan.*
'There is your pencil.'	'There are your pencils.'
Io sounpadahko.	*Iohkan sounpadahk kau.*
'There is that teacher.'	'There are those teachers.'

These forms also commonly occur as one word sentences, with
the following meanings.

Iet!	'Here it is!'
Ietakan!	'Here they are!'
Ien!	'There it is! (by you)'
Ienakan!	'There they are! (by you)'
Io!	'There it is! (away from you and me)'
Iohkan!	'There they are! (away from you and me)'

Emphatic Forms

Emphatic pointing demonstratives are formed with the morpheme *-kenen*. Examples follow.

Singular		Plural	
ietkenen or *iehkenen*	'here, by me'	*ietkenenkan* or *iehkenenkan*	here, by me'
ienkenen	'there, by you'	*ienkenenkan*	'there, by you'
iohkenen	'there, away from you and me'	*iohkenenkan*	'there, away from you and me'

The morpheme *-kenen* also occurs in a shortened form as *-ken*, resulting in the following forms, the meanings of which parallel those above.

Singular	Plural
ieteken/iehken	*ietekenakan/iehkenakan*
ieneken	*ienekenakan*
iohken	*iohkenakan*

In the plural forms, some speakers reverse the order of the morphemes *-ken* and *-kan*, to produce the following emphatic demonstratives.

Plural
ietakaneken/iehkaneken
ienakaneken
iohkaneken

The additional vowels that occur in all of these emphatic forms are copy vowels. Therefore, *iet + ken* is pronounced *ieteken*, *iet + ken + kan* is pronounced *ietekenakan*, etc.

The morpheme *-kenen* is also alternately shortened to *-nen* in these forms.

Singular	Plural
iehnen	*iehnenkan*
iohnen	*iohnenkan*

Notice that the shortened form *-nen* only occurs with vowel final demonstrative roots; therefore, it combines with *ieh-* and *ioh-*, but not with *iet* and *ien*.

Some speakers also pronounce *-kenen* and its shortened forms *-ken* and *-nen* as *-kinin*, *-kin*, and *-nin*.

4.5.3   The demonstratives we will examine here are those that we will
call **demonstrative pronouns**. Their function is to replace noun
phrases. As with the other demonstratives we have examined,
both non-e mphatic and emphatic forms of these demonstratives
occur.

Non-Emphatic Forms

Singular		Plural	
me(t)	'this, by me'	*metakan*	'these, by me'
		or *mehkan*	
men	'that, by you'	*menakan*	'those, by you'
mwo	'that, away from you and me'	*mwohkan*	'those, away from you and me'

An uncommon alternant of *me(t)* is *meteht*. However, *mehkan*,
which is listed as an alternate form of *metakan*, is frequently used.
Sentences illustrating the usage of these pronouns follow.

Met ohla.	*Metakan ohla.*
'This is broken.'	'These are broken.'
Men ohla.	*Menakan ohla.*
'That is broken.'	'Those are broken.'
Mwo ohla.	*Mwohkan ohla.*
'That is broken.'	'Those are broken.'

The singular forms of these pronouns also occur in locative
phrases (discussed in section **6**.3.1) with the following meanings.

Pronoun	As in the Sentence
met	*E wahdo met.*
'here'	'He brought it here.'
men	*E wahwei men.*
'there, by you'	'He took it there by you.'
mwo	*E wahla mwo.*
'there, away from you and me'	'He took it there away from you and me.'

The first form listed above is also used in temporal phrases (discussed in section **6**.3.2).

me(t)   *E pampap met.*
'now'   'He is swimming now.'

In sentences containing both locative and temporal phrases, *met* may be used to represent one or the other of the phrases, but not both. Therefore, these sentences are acceptable.

E wie doadoahk wasaht met.
'He is working here now.'

E wie doadoahk met ansowet.
'He is working here now.'

The following sentence, though, is not acceptable.

*E wie doadoahk met met.

Emphatic Forms

Like pointing demonstratives, demonstrative pronouns combine with the morpheme *-kenen* to form emphatic demonstratives. These are listed below.

Singular		Plural	
metkenen or *mehkenen*	'this one here, by me'	*metkenenkan* or *mehkenenkan*	'these here by me'
menkenen	'that one there, by you'	*menkenenkan*	'those there, by you'
mwohkenen	'that one there, away from you and me'	*mwohkenenkan*	'those there, away from you and me'

The alternate forms of *-kenen* (*-ken, -nen, -kinin, -kin,* and *-nin*) also occur with these forms in a manner parallel to that described for pointing demonstratives.

A CHART OF PONAPEAN DEMONSTRATIVES

4.5.4   We may now summarize our discussion of demonstratives in the following chart. For the purpose of easy presentation, alternate pronunciations of these forms are ignored. Only full forms are given. Also, English translations are not provided, since the meanings of these forms have already been presented. *Cl* is used to stand for a numeral classifier. The (a) forms are non-emphatic. The (b) forms are emphatic.

Demonstrative Modifiers

	Singular	Plural
(a)	*-et*	*-kat*
	-en	*-kan*
	-o	*-kau*
(b)	*Cl+et*	*pwukat*
	Cl+en	*pwukan*
	Cl+o	*pwukau*

Pointing Demonstratives

	Singular	Plural
(a)	*iet*	*ietakan*
	ien	*ienakan*
	io	*iohkan*
(b)	*ietkenen*	*ietkenenkan*
	ienkenen	*ienkenenkan*
	iohkenen	*iohkenenkan*

Demonstrative Pronouns

	Singular	Plural
(a)	*met*	*metakan*
	men	*menakan*
	mwo	*mwohkan*
(b)	*metkenen*	*metkenenkan*
	menkenen	*menkenenkan*
	mwohkenen	*mwohkenenkan*

THE REPLACIVE PRONOUN *ME*

4.6   The demonstrative pronouns we previously examined and the personal pronouns we will examine in the next section all have a similar function; they replace noun phrases. There is one pronoun in Ponapean, however, that only replaces nouns. This is the **replacive pronoun** *me*, which is sometimes translated as 'one'. Its usage is illustrated in the following noun phrases, where in the phrases in the left-hand column a noun is used, and in the right-hand column the pronoun *me* replaces that noun.

pwutak reireio	*me reireio*
'that tall boy'	'that tall one'
pwutak silimen	*me silimen*
'three boys'	'three (animate ones)'
pwutak reirei silimeno	*me reirei silimeno*
'those three tall boys'	'those three tall ones'

Like nouns, *me* may be followed by a classifier without a numeral prefix in indefinite noun phrases. In this case, since classifiers used alone are bound to the preceding word, the vowel in *me* becomes long. This long vowel, however, according to the convention established in section **4.4.4**, is not written and the classifier is written as a separate word. Examples follow.

Pronounced	But Written
/mehmen/	*me men*
/mehpwoat/	*me pwoat*
/mehkis/	*me kis*
/mehpak/	*me pak*

Me also combines with the morphemes *-kot* and *-kei* to produce these forms.

mehkot	*mehkei*
'something, anything'	'some (things)'

The morphemes *-kot* and *-kei* are also used with the question word *dah* 'what'. Question words are examined in section **6.4.3**.

It seems likely that the demonstrative pronouns examined in section **4.5.3** were historically formed by combining the replacive pronoun *me* with the *-t, -n,* and /*-w*/ set of allomorphs of the singular demonstrative modifiers. However, if this is true, it is not an explanation that can be used to describe the current forms of the demonstrative pronouns. Consider, for example, the following sentence, where the demonstrative pronoun *met* is employed in sentence (a) and the replacive pronoun *me* plus the demonstrative modifier *-t* is used in sentence (b).

a)   *Met ohla.*
       'This is broken.'

b)   *Meht ohla.*
       'This one is broken.'

Notice that the vowel of the replacive pronoun *me* lengthens in combination with the enclitic *-t*. The form that results is different from *met*. Also note that the replacive pronoun *me* in combination with /-w/ results in *meho*, whereas the correponding demonstrative pronoun is *mwo*.

Words pronounced *me* occur in four other contexts in Ponapean.

1.   There is a stative marker *me* that is used with adjectives.

     E me kehlail!
     'He is strong!'

This stative marker is discussed in section **5**.2.1.

2.   *Me* is used in sentences with focused noun phrases.

     Ih me kehlail.
     'He is the one who is strong.'

Focusing is examined in section **6**.4.2.

3.   *Me* is used in relative clauses.

     Mwahmw me e wahdo aioh mat.
     'The fish that he brought yesterday is spoiled.'

Relative clauses are discussed in section **6**.5.2.

4.   *Me* is used before finite clauses.

     Soulik rong me serepeino sohte mwahukinuhk.
     'Soulik heard that girl doesn't like you.'

Finite clauses are examined in section **6**.5.3.

It is clear that the stative marker *me* is distinct from the replacive pronoun *me*. They are different morphemes. Whether the other words *me* used in the sentences above are related to or distinct from the pronoun *me* is less clear.

PERSONAL PRONOUNS

4.7   **Personal pronouns** are so named because, unlike other pronouns that have thus far been examined, they show distinctions of person. Three distinctions are made:

> 1st person—the speaker
> 2nd person—the person(s) spoken to
> 3rd person—the person(s) spoken about

These pronouns also exhibit three distinctions in number:

> Singular —one person
> Dual—two persons
> Plural—three or more persons

Two other important characteristics of Ponapean personal pronouns are:

1. No distinctions of gender are made. Therefore, while in a language like English it is necessary to choose between the forms 'he', 'she', or 'it', depending upon who or what is being talked about, such distinctions are irrelevant to Ponapean.

2. Except for the third person singular forms of the personal pronouns, these pronouns are normally employed only when making reference to human beings or to domestic animals.

There are four sets of personal pronouns in Ponapean. These are the **independent pronouns**, the **subject pronouns**, the **object pronouns**, and the **possessive pronouns**. We will begin our study of these pronouns by first examining the independent set.

<small>INDEPENDENT PRONOUNS</small>

4.7.1   The **independent pronouns** are listed in the chart below.

	1st	*ngehi*	'I'
Singular	2nd	*kowe/koh*	'you'
	3rd	*ih*	'he, she, it'
Dual/Plural	1st excl.	*kiht*	'we, exclusive'
	1st incl.	*kita*	'we two, inclusive'
Dual	2nd	*kumwa*	'you two'
	3rd	*ira*	'they two'
	1st incl.	*kitail*	'we three or more, inclusive'
Plural	2nd	*kumwail*	'you three or more'
	3rd	*irail/ihr*	'they three or more'

Notice that the second person singular pronoun *kowe* has an alternate form *koh*. *Ihr* is listed as an alternate form of *irail*, but most speakers additionally use *ihr* as an alternant of *ira*. Thus, with this form, the dual/plural distinction in number is seldom (if ever) maintained. A dual/plural distinction is clearly never made with the pronoun *kiht*. *Kiht* is simply a non-singular form that may be used with two or more people.

All other non-singular pronouns maintain the dual/plural distinction. Further, they all consist of more than one morpheme. If you examine these pronouns, you will observe that all the dual forms end in *-a*, while all the plural forms end in *-ail*. We may deduce that the roots for both the dual and plural forms of these pronouns are *kit-* for 1st person, *kumw-* for 2nd person, and *ir-* for 3rd person, to which the dual number marker *-a* may be added to give the dual forms, and the plural number marker *-ail* may be added to give the plural forms.

Another distinction that has been made in the chart above is between **inclusive** and **exclusive** forms of pronouns. Thus, the pronouns *kiht, kita,* and *kitail* all translate into English as 'we'; *kiht* is labeled as *exclusive*, while *kita* and *kitail* are called *inclusive*. The term exclusive simply means that the speaker is excluding the person or persons he is speaking to; *kiht* means 'we, but not you.' How many people are included in the 'we', whether two or more, is not important. *Kita* and *kitail*, on the other hand, are inclusive; therefore, they include the person or persons being spoken to. Thus *kita*, which is a dual pronoun, means 'we' in the sense of 'you and I.' *Kitail* means 'we three or more', including the person or persons being spoken to.

SUBJECT PRONOUNS

4.7.2   The **subject pronouns** are listed in the following chart.

Singular	1st	*i*	'I'
	2nd	*ke*	'you'
	3rd	*e*	'he, she, it'
Dual/Plural	1st excl.	*se*	'we, exclusive'
Dual	1st incl.	*kita*	'we two, inclusive'
	2nd	*kumwa*	'you two'
	3rd	*ira*	'they two'
Plural	1st incl.	*kitail*	'we three or more, inclusive'
	2nd	*kumwail*	'you three or more'
	3rd	*irail/re*	'they three or more'

Notice that the last six of these pronouns are identical to the independent set, except that in the subject set the alternant of *irail* is *re*, not *ihr*. *Re*, in a manner parallel to *ihr*, is additionally used as an alternant of *ira* by most speakers.

Like independent pronouns, subject pronouns replace noun phrases. These pronouns differ in function from the independent set, however, in two important ways.

First, whereas independent pronouns may stand alone as one word sentences, subject pronouns may not. Therefore, in response to a question like *Ihs me pahn wahdo rais?* 'Who will bring rice?', one could respond with the independent pronoun *ngehi* (literally 'I'), but not with the corresponding subject pronoun *i*. Similarly, *kowe* could be used, but not *ke*, nor for that matter *koh*, the shortened form of *kowe*. (*Ihr*, the shortened form of *irail*, would also not be possible here.) Thus, independent pronouns may be used independently, without other elements of the sentence being present. It is from this distinctive usage that independent pronouns derive their name.

Second, subject pronouns always occur in sentences that

contain verbs. Independent pronouns occur in the kinds of sentences called **equational** (discussed in section **6**.2.1). Example equational sentences follow.

> *Ngehi mehn Pohnpei.*
> 'I am a Ponapean.'
>
> *Ih sounpadahk men.*
> 'He is a teacher.'
>
> *Kowe ohl loalekeng.*
> 'You are an intelligent man.'

Subject pronouns occur in **verbal** sentences like the following.

> *I tangala ni oaroahro.*
> 'I ran to the shore.'
>
> *Ke pahn nohn soupisek.*
> 'You will be too busy.'
>
> *E wahdo kilelo.*
> 'He brought that picture.'

Independent pronouns occur in sentences which contain verbs, but only when the subject of the sentence is **focused**. Focused sentences, as we will note in section **6**.4.2, are in fact special kinds of equational sentences. The subject of the last sentence in the preceding examples may be focused as follows.

> *Ih me wahdo kilelo.*
> 'He is the one who brought that picture.'

Therefore, although both subject and independent pronouns may replace subject noun phrases, they occur in different sentence types. As we shall discuss in the next chapter, subject pronouns in fact function as part of the verb phrase. Object pronouns, which are examined next, also occur as part of the verb phrase.

OBJECT PRONOUNS

4.7.3   The third set of pronouns, the **object pronouns**, occur as suffixes to verbs. A detailed discussion of the function and alternate forms of these pronouns is presented in section **5**.4.2. Here, our primary concern will be with the basic forms of these pronouns. These are listed below.

	1st	*-ie*	'me'
Singular	2nd	*-uhk*	'you'
	3rd	*-∅*	'him, her, it'
Dual/Plural	1st excl.	*-kit*	'us, exclusive'
	1st incl.	*-kita*	'us two, inclusive'
Dual	2nd	*-kumwa*	'you two'
	3rd	*-ira*	'them two'
	1st incl.	*-kitail*	'us three or more, inclusive'
Plural	2nd	*-kumwail*	'you three or more'
	3rd	*-irail*	'them three or more'

The 3rd person singular form is listed in this chart as ∅, meaning that when one wants to indicate a 3rd person object (him, her, or it), no suffix is used.

POSSESSIVE PRONOUNS

4.7.4   One way in which possession is indicated in Ponapean is by the use of **possessive pronouns**. Like object pronouns, possessive pronouns are suffixes. But, determining the forms of these pronouns is somewhat troublesome. The basic problem may be illustrated by a consideration of the following paradigms that first list the unpossessed form of a noun and then all its possessive forms.

		ihn 'mother'	*kihl* 'skin'	
	1st	*inei*	*kili*	'my___'
Singular	2nd	*inemw*	*kilimw*	'your___'
	3rd	*ine*	*kili*	'his, her, its___'

Dual/Plural	1st excl.	*inat*	*kilit*	'our___' but not yours'
	1st incl.	*inata*	*kilita*	'our___'
Dual	2nd	*inamwa*	*kilimwa*	'your___'
	3rd	*inara*	*kilira*	'their___'
	1st incl.	*inatail*	*kilitail*	'our___'
Plural	2nd	*inamwail*	*kilimwail*	'your___'
	3rd	*inarail*	*kilirail*	'their___'

The question here is what part of a possessed form represents the root, and what part the suffix? There are a number of possible solutions that we could employ, two of which are considered below.

The first solution would be to consider the noun roots of the preceding examples to be *in-* 'mother' and *kil-* 'skin.' The possessive suffixes that occur with *in-* are therefore *-ei, -omw, -e, -at, -ata,* etc. With *kil-,* they are *-i, -imw, -i, -it, -ita,* and so on. Many native speakers believe this solution to be the correct one, and thus it merits consideration. The trouble with this solution, however, is that it requires setting up for these two nouns two different sets of possessive suffixes. And, when we consider other nouns, still other sets of possessive pronouns will be required. This solution thus leads to numerous sets of possessive suffixes and accordingly is somewhat inefficient.

An alternate solution, and one that seems historically correct, is to consider the noun roots to be *ina-* and *kili-,* where the final vowels of these roots are base vowels. If we take this approach, the effect is to reduce the variety of possessive suffixes. This is illustrated below, where a plus sign (+) is placed between the noun roots and the possessive suffix. (Note that the final vowel of *ina-* is pronounced *e* before singular possessive suffixes. Further information about this change in vowel quality is presented in section **4.8.2.**)

		ihn 'mother'	*kihl* 'skin'
	1st	ine + i	kili + $\emptyset$
Singular	2nd	ine + mw	kili + mw
	3rd	ine + $\emptyset$	kili + $\emptyset$

Dual/Plural	1st excl.	ina + t	kili + t
	1st incl.	ina + ta	kili + ta
Dual	2nd	ina + mwa	kili + mwa
	3rd	ina + ra	kili + ra
	1st incl.	ina + tail	kili + tail
Plural	2nd	ina + mwail	kili + mwail
	3rd	ina + rail	kili + rail

We will adopt this second solution because it simplifies our analysis of the possessive suffixes in a justifiable way. Still, it is necessary to recognize two first person singular suffixes. If you examine the two paradigms previously presented, you will note that for the noun *ihn* 'mother' there is a difference between the first person singular form *inei* 'my mother' and the third person singular form *ine* 'his, her, or its mother'. This is not true of a noun like *kihl* 'skin', however. For this noun, both the first and third person singular forms are the same—*kili*. If still other nouns are examined, a generalization can be made that all nouns which do not distinguish between 1st and 3rd person singular forms have roots with -*i* as the final base vowel. Noun roots that end in the base vowels *e* or *a* do distinguish between these forms. To predict how noun roots interact with possessive suffixes, it will be useful to divide nouns into three classes, according to their final base vowel. These classes are discussed in section **4**.8.2. Here, let us only summarize the forms of the possessive pronoun suffixes that we have established. These are listed in the following chart.

	1st	-*i*, -∅	'my'
Singular	2nd	-*mw*	'your'
	3rd	-∅	'his, her, or its'
Dual/Plural	1st excl.	-*t*	'our, but not yours'
	1st incl.	-*ta*	'our, mine and yours'
Dual	2nd	-*mwa*	'your, two'
	3rd	-*ra*	'their, two'
	1st incl.	-*tail*	'our, three or more'
Plural	2nd	-*mwail*	'your, three or more'
	3rd	-*rail*	'their, three or more'

For the 1st person singular form, two suffixes are listed for the reasons noted above; *-∅* is to be used only with noun roots ending in *i*; *-i* is used with roots ending in other vowels.

It should also be pointed out that both the dual and plural possessive pronouns are themselves composed of two morphemes. Remember that in section **4**.7.1 we established that the dual morpheme was *-a* and that the plural morpheme was *-ail*. If these morphemes are separated from the dual and plural possessive suffixes, then what remains is *-t-*, which marks 1st person non-singular, *-mw-*, which marks 2nd person non-singular, and *-r-*, which marks 3rd person non-singular. A word like *kilimwail* 'your skin, three or more' may thus be divided into three morphemes; *kili-* is the noun root 'skin', *-mw-* marks 2nd person non-singular, and *-ail* marks plurality.

Although our concern with possessive pronouns thus far has been primarily focused on their forms, there is much more to be said about these pronouns. One thing we will need to examine is how these suffixes modify the nouns to which they are attached. This issue, along with the other very important matter of how these forms function in Ponapean, will be considered in the following section which deals more generally with all types of possession.

POSSESSIVE CONSTRUCTIONS

4.8   To begin our discussion of possessive constructions, let us consider the following phrase:

> *nimei uhpw*
> 'my drinking coconut'

This phrase represents a possessive construction. A **possessive construction** is one which consists of two or more morphemes or words, at least one of which represents the possessor (in the above example, *nimei* 'my'), while another represents the thing possessed (*uhpw* 'drinking coconut'). A possessive construction may stand alone as a noun phrase when it is being used indefinitely, as in a sentence like *Mie nimei uhpw*. 'I have a drinking cocout.' Otherwise, it must occur with a demonstrative modifier to form a noun phrase, as in the sentence, *Nimei uhpwo pwupwsang pohn tehpelo*. 'My drinking coconut (there) fell from that table.' In this section, our purpose will be to examine the kinds of possessive constructions that occur in Ponapean. To start, it will be useful to distinguish between two basic patterns which we will call *direct* and *indirect* possession.

DIRECT AND INDIRECT POSSESSION

4.8.1   Possession in Ponapean is indicated in one of two basic ways. Either the part of the possessive construction representing the possessor precedes the noun representing the thing possessed, or it follows it. To illustrate, let us consider the two nouns *moahng* 'head' and *uhpw* 'drinking coconut'. To indicate possession with these nouns, different patterns of possession must be employed. If a possessive pronoun is used, *-i* 'my' for example, the following constructions result.

> *moangei*   *nimei uhpw*
> 'my head'   'my drinking coconut'

In the first example, the pronoun *-i* is suffixed directly to the noun root *moange-*. In the second example, however, *-i* is suffixed not to the noun *uhpw*, but rather to the root *nime-* which precedes *uhpw*. Roots like *nime-* we will call **possessive classifiers**. There are a number of these in Ponapean which we shall examine in section **4.8.3**.

If a noun or noun phrase is used to represent the possessor instead of a pronoun, again two patterns of possession occur. In the following examples, the phrase *ohlo* 'that man' represents the possessor.

> *moangen ohlo*   *nimen ohlo uhpw*
> 'that man's head'   'that man's drinking coconut'

In the first example, *ohlo* follows the noun root *moange-* which is suffixed by the construct suffix *-n*. In the second example, *ohlo* precedes the noun *uhpw* and in turn is preceded by the possessive classifier *nime-* plus the construct suffix *-n*.

Thus, whether the possessor is represented by a pronoun or a noun, two patterns of possession occur. One places the possessor *after* the thing possessed. This type of possession we will call **direct possession**. The other places the possessor *before* the thing possessed. This kind of possession we will call **indirect possession**. Each of these types of possession are investigated in more detail below. We begin with direct possession.

4.8.2   **Direct possession** in Ponapean is characteristically employed where the relationship between the possessor and the thing possessed is viewed as permanent and indestructible. It is difficult, if not impossible, to formulate a rule that will predict which nouns will be directly possessed, but some generalizations may be made.

Nouns employed to express part-whole relationships are usually directly possessed. Included here are body parts, both of people and animals, as well as parts of plants and things. Some examples follow, where possession is illustrated either with the pronoun 'my' or 'its'.

Body Parts

moangei	'my head'
kili	'my skin'
pahi	'my arm'
mesei	'my face'
kiki	'my nail'
pwusei	'my navel'
dengei	'my thigh'
mwasahlei	'my intestines'
ntahi	'my blood'
iki	'its tail'
kopwenadi	'its breast, of a chicken'
ede	'its gill'
wine	'its feather'

Parts of Plants and Things

pwili	'its gum or sap'
ili	'its sucker, as of a banana tree'
paki	'its replantable part'
owe	'its sprout, of a yam'
kesenge	'its fork, of a tree'
inoande	'its main tuber, of a yam'
kapi	'its bottom'
keile	'its edge'
imwi	'its top'
koadoki	'its peak'
deme	'its outrigger, of a canoe'

Nouns denoting personal attributes are also directly possessed.

Personal Attributes

edei	'my name'
mwarei	'my title'
irei	'my state of health'
dipei	'my sin'
ngorei	'my dialect'
mouri	'my life'
paiei	'my luck'

Also some nouns designating kinship relations are directly possessed.

Kinship

semei	'my father'
inei	'my mother'

As noted, though, these generalizations about meaning are not sufficient to predict without exception which nouns will be directly possessed. For example, listed above is a directly possessed form of the word *sahm* 'father'. Another more common word for 'father', however, is *pahpa*, which is *indirectly* possessed. Thus, to say 'my father' one may say either *semei* or *ahi pahpa*. In this example, two words with the same meaning enter into different patterns of possession.

Let us now examine in further detail how direct possession is accomplished, first with pronouns and then with nouns.

Direct Possession with Pronouns

In section **4.7.4**, we examined the possessive pronoun suffixes of Ponapean. The forms established were as follows.

Singular	1st	*-i, -∅*	'my'
	2nd	*-mw*	'your'
	3rd	*-∅*	'his, her, its'
Dual/Plural	1st excl.	*-t*	'our'
Dual	1st incl.	*-ta*	'our'
	2nd	*-mwa*	'your'
	3rd	*-ra*	'their'

	1st incl.	*-tail*	'our'
Plural	2nd	*-mwail*	'your'
	3rd	*-rail*	'their'

In order to predict how these possessive suffixes will interact with noun roots, it is useful to divide nouns into different classes, these classes being determined by the final base vowel of the root. Almost all nouns that may take possessive suffixes belong to one of the following three classes.

(1) *i* roots, where the final base vowel is *i*
(2) *e* roots, where the final base vowel is *e* (/ɛ/)
(3) *a* roots, where the final base vowel is *a*

To determine to which root class a particular noun belongs, the easiest test is to suffix *-niki* to the noun. The form of the noun that appears before the suffix is the root.

Noun	Suffixed by *-niki*	Root	Class
kihl	*kiliniki*	*kili-*	*i* root
ngihl	*ngileniki*	*ngile-*	*e* root
dihp	*dipaniki*	*dipa-*	*a* root

Each of these classes of nouns is examined in further detail in the sections that follow.

Class I—i Root Nouns

Nouns which have *i* as the final base vowel in their roots, we have already noted, are distinguished by the fact that they have identical first and third person singular forms. Examples are:

kili   'my skin'
kili   'his, her, or its skin'

To determine other possessed forms of this noun, one need only suffix those pronouns previously listed to the root *kili-*. To illustrate, the entire possessive paradigm for *kihl* is listed below.

Possessive Pronouns	Suffixed to *kili-*	English
-∅	*kili*	'my skin'
-mw	*kilimw*	'your skin'

-∅	*kili*	'his, her, or its skin'
-*t*	*kilit*	'our skin (excl.)'
-*ta*	*kilita*	'our skin (dual)'
-*mwa*	*kilimwa*	'your skin (dual)'
-*ra*	*kilira*	'their skin (dual)'
-*tail*	*kilitail*	'our skin (plural)'
-*mwail*	*kilimwail*	'your skin (plural)'
-*rail*	*kilirail*	'their skin (plural)'

Relatively few nouns belong to this class. Additional examples are provided below, where the free forms of these nouns are given in the first column, the third person singular forms in the second column, and translations of the free forms in the third column.

Free Form	3rd Person Sing.	English
kihk	*kiki*	'nail'
kumwut	*kumwuti*	'fist'
mohngiong	*mohngiongi*	'heart'
mour	*mouri*	'life'
ngehn	*ngeni*	'soul, spirit, shadow'
wahl	*wali*	'head'
pwihl	*pwili*	'gum, of a tree'
sikihr	*sikihri*	'tail bone'
ngih	*ngih*	'tooth'

For these nouns, the third person singular form of the noun is identical to the root of the noun. Therefore, one can determine all other possessed forms of these nouns by adding the possessive suffixes to these third person singular forms.

Class II—e Root Nouns

Examples of nouns belonging to Class II—nouns which have *e* (/ɛ/) as their final base vowel—are presented in the paradigms below. For the sake of brevity, translations of the suffixed forms are not given, since they parallel those previously described.

ngihl	*nsen*	*sahpw*
'voice'	'feelings'	'land'
ngilei	*nsenei*	*sapwei*
ngilemw	*nsenemw*	*sapwomw*

ngile	*nsene*	*sapwe*
ngilet	*nsenet*	*sapwet*
ngilata	*nsenata*	*sapwata*
ngilamwa	*nsenamwa*	*sapwamwa*
ngilara	*nsenara*	*sapwara*
ngilatail	*nsenatail*	*sapwatail*
ngilamwail	*nsenamwail*	*sapwamwail*
ngilarail	*nsenarail*	*sapwarail*
moahng	*ngohr*	*pwuhs*
'head'	'dialect'	'navel'
moangei	*ngorei*	*pwusei*
moangemw	*ngoremw*	*pwusemw*
moange	*ngore*	*pwuse*
moanget	*ngoret*	*pwuset*
moangata	*ngorata*	*pwusata*
moangamwa	*ngoramwa*	*pwusamwa*
moangara	*ngorara*	*pwusara*
moangatail	*ngoratail*	*pwusatail*
moangamwail	*ngoramwail*	*pwusamwail*
moangarail	*ngorarail*	*pwusarail*

The roots of these nouns are also identical to the third person singular forms. Note, however, that before possessive suffixes containing the vowel *a*, the final base vowel of the root also becomes *a*. Compare, for example, the third person singular and the third person dual forms of these nouns.

Nouns	3rd Person Singular	3rd Person Dual
ngihl	*ngile*	*ngilara*
sahpw	*sapwe*	*sapwara*
pwuhs	*pwuse*	*pwusara*

All of the non-singular possessive suffixes except the first person exclusive form (-*t*) contain the vowel *a*. Therefore, the final base vowel *e* changes to *a* before all these suffixes. However, some speakers even change *e* to *a* before -*t*. Thus, alternants like the following exist for the exclusive forms of all Class II nouns.

ngilet	*nsenet*	*sapwet*	*moanget*	*ngoret*	*pwuset*
or	or	or	or	or	or
ngilat	*nsenat*	*sapwat*	*moangat*	*ngorat*	*pwusat*

Further discussion of these alternate forms is presented in the section on Class III nouns.

The base vowel *e* before the second person singular suffix *-mw* is sometimes written *o* in non-standard spelling. Therefore, *ngilemw* is sometimes also written *ngilomw*. The basis of the confusion about how these forms are to be spelled lies in the fact that when *e* is followed by the back rounded consonant *mw*, it is pronounced farther back in the mouth and is somewhat rounded sounding nearly like, but not identical to, *o*. Between two back rounded consonants, however, *e* does become *o*, as in *sapwomw*.

Additional examples of nouns of this class follow. Only the free form of the noun is translated. The third person singular form means 'his, her, or its____'.

Free Form	3rd Person Singular Form	English
kapehd	*kapehde*	'belly'
kehke	*kehkeh*	'stem of a fruit'
lahk	*lake*	'penis'
mangil	*mangile*	'handle'
moahl	*moale*	'fleeting appearance'
mwahr	*mware*	'title'
mwasahl	*mwasahle*	'intestine'
mwohmw	*mwomwe*	'appearance'
pwise	*pwiseh*	'feces'
uduk	*uduke*	'flesh'

Class III—a Root Nouns

Perhaps most nouns that may take possessive suffixes belong to Class III. These nouns have *a* as their final base vowel. Four example paradigms of nouns belonging to this class are presented below.

dihp	*ihn*	*ihmw*	*lihpw*
'sin'	'mother'	'house'	'trace or track'
dipei	*inei*	*imwei*	*lipwei*
dipemw	*inemw*	*imwomw*	*lipwomw*
dipe	*ine*	*imwe*	*lipwe*
dipat	*inat*	*imwat*	*lipwat*
dipata	*inata*	*imwata*	*lipwata*
dipamwa	*inamwa*	*imwamwa*	*lipwamwa*

dipara	*inara*	*imwara*	*lipwara*
dipatail	*inatail*	*imwatail*	*lipwatail*
dipamwail	*inamwail*	*imwamwail*	*lipwamwail*
diparail	*inarail*	*imwarail*	*lipwarail*

The roots of these nouns are *dipa-* (*dipaniki*), *ina-* (*inaniki*), *imwa-* (*imwaniki*), and *lipwa-* (*lipwaniki*). Note, however, that the final base vowel *a* is pronounced *e* (/ɛ/) before all singular possessive suffixes. The result is that Class II and Class III paradigms are almost identical, as illustrated in these examples.

Class II	Class III
ngihl	*dihp*
'voice'	'sin'
ngilei	*dipei*
ngilemw	*dipemw*
ngile	*dipe*
ngilet	*dipat*
ngilata	*dipata*
ngilamwa	*dipamwa*
ngilara	*dipara*
ngilatail	*dipatail*
ngilamwail	*dipamwail*
ngilarail	*diparail*

These paradigms differ only in the base vowel that occurs before *-t*; therefore:

ngilet	*dipat*

Thus, the rule affecting Class II nouns which changes the final base vowel *e* to *a* before suffixes containing *a*, and the rule affecting Class III nouns, which changes the final base vowel *a* to *e* before singular possessive suffixes, interact to make the resulting paradigms identical except in the first person exclusive forms. And even these forms are identical for some speakers. As we noted, *ngilat* is an acceptable alternative to *ngilet* for many speakers. By changing this single form, the final base vowels in Class II paradigms parallel those of Class III. No doubt the alternants that exist for Class II nouns result from the similarities between these two paradigms.

Class III nouns, however, also differ from Class II nouns in one additional way. Consider the following Class III paradigms.

dahng	*irap*	*mahs*	*sahm*	*ahd*
'thigh'	'anything sat upon'	'face'	'father'	'name'
dengei	*irepei*	*mesei*	*semei*	*edei*
dengemw	*irepemw*	*mesemw*	*sememw*	*edemw*
denge	*irepe*	*mese*	*seme*	*ede*
dangat	*irapat*	*masat*	*samat*	*adat*
dangata	*irapata*	*masata*	*samata*	*adata*
dangamwa	*irapamwa*	*masamwa*	*samamwa*	*adamwa*
dangara	*irapara*	*masara*	*samara*	*adara*
dangatail	*irapatail*	*masatail*	*samatail*	*adatail*
dangamwail	*irapamwail*	*masamwail*	*samamwail*	*adamwail*
dangarail	*iraparail*	*masarail*	*samarail*	*adarail*

The roots of these nouns are *danga-* (*danganiki*), *irapa-* (*irapaniki*), *masa-*(*masaniki*), *sama-* (*samaniki*), and *ada-* (*adaniki*). Note in the paradigms for these nouns that not only the *final a* of the root changes to *e*, but that *all a*'s do. This provides another basis for drawing a distinction between Class II and Class III nouns. Compare the following singular forms of the nouns below.

	Class II	Class III
Free Form	*mwahr*	*sahm*
English	'title'	'father'
Root	*mware-*	*sama-*
1st Person Sing.	*mwarei*	*semei*
2nd Person Sing.	*mwaremw*	*sememw*
3rd Person Sing.	*mware*	*seme*

The vowel *a* is never changed to *e* in Class II nouns. For Class III nouns, we may make the generalization that all *short a*'s change to *e* before singular possessive suffixes.

The word *short* is included in the preceding generalization, because *long* vowels are not similarly affected. The following partial paradigms for two Class III nouns—*kahu* 'buttocks' and *nta* 'blood'—illustrate the difference between short and long *a*'s.

Free Form	*kahu*	*nta*
Root	*kahwa-*	*ntah-*
1st Person Sing.	*kahwei*	*ntahi*
2nd Person Sing.	*kahwomw*	*ntahmw*
3rd Person Sing.	*kahwe*	*ntah*

The final short vowel of the root *kahwa-* changes to *e* (or *o*) in the forms above, but the long vowel *ah* does not. Similarly, the long vowel of the root *ntah-* is unaffected by following suffixes.

Additional examples of nouns that belong to Class III follow.

Free Form	3rd Person Singular Form	English
keisar	*keisere*	'pancreas'
likarak	*likereke*	'louse'
pahs	*pese*	'nest'
pwais	*pweise*	'responsibility'
pwuri	*pwurie*	'core'
tahmw	*temwe*	'forehead'
wakar	*wekere*	'pubic hair'

Irregular Paradigms

Most nouns in Ponapean which may be directly possessed fit into one of the three classes described above. There are, however, some paradigms which seem irregular, for which no obvious generalizations may be made. One of these is the paradigm for *adi* 'bile, of the liver' which follows.

edi	*edimwa*
edimw	*edira*
adi	*editail*
adit	*edimwail*
edita	*edirail*

The possessed forms of the noun *dehu* 'rank, area' seem particularly confusing to most speakers of Ponapean, and at least these four different paradigms occur.

dewi	*doai*	*dowei*	*doahi*
dewumw	*domw*	*dowomw*	*dohmw*
dewe	*dowe*	*dowe*	*dowe*
dewat	*doht*	*dowet*	*dowat ~ dowt*
dewta	*dota*	*doweta*	*dowta*
dewmwa	*domwa*	*dowimwa*	*dowamwa ~ dohmwa*
dewra	*dora*	*dowera*	*dowra*
dewtail	*dowatail*	*dowetail*	*dowtail*
dewmwail	*domwail*	*dowimwail*	*dowamwail ~ dohmwail*
dewrail	*dorail*	*dowerail*	*dowrail*

These are just two irregular paradigms. Others will be examined in section **4.8.3**, and there are possibly still others that we are not yet aware of.

Direct Possession with Nouns

All of the instances of direct possession we have thus far examined involved the use of possessive pronouns. It is also possible to represent the possessor with a noun, as in the following examples.

Unpossessed	English	Possessed	English
kihl	'skin'	*kilin serio*	'that child's skin'
mour	'life'	*mourin aramaso*	'that person's life'
mahs	'face'	*mesen ohlo*	'that man's face'
dahng	'thigh'	*dengen pwutako*	'that boy's thigh'
dahm	'outrigger'	*demen wahro*	'that canoe's outrigger'
ahd	'name'	*eden lahpo*	'that guy's name'
sahm	'father'	*semen ohlo*	'that man's father'
tihmw	'nose'	*timwen serio*	'that child's nose'
moahng	'head'	*moangen liho*	'that woman's head'
mwahliel	'brain'	*mwahlielen pwihko*	'that pig's brain'
mwahr	'title'	*mwaren ohlo*	'that man's title'
nta	'blood'	*ntahn maleko*	'that chicken's blood'

Notice that in possessive constructions like these, the construct suffix is employed with the head noun representing the thing possessed, while the noun representing the possessor follows. All the phrases in the third column above, therefore, consist of a noun suffixed by the construct suffix followed by a noun phrase.

The **construct form** of these nouns involves adding -*n* to a form of the noun identical to the third person singular possessed form. This is illustrated below, using the nouns from the preceding examples.

Unpossessed	3rd Person Singular Form	Construct Form
kihl	*kili*	*kilin*
mour	*mouri*	*mourin*
mahs	*mese*	*mesen*
dahng	*denge*	*dengen*
dahm	*deme*	*demen*
ahd	*ede*	*eden*
sahm	*seme*	*semen*
tihmw	*timwe*	*timwen*
moahng	*moange*	*moangen*
mwahliel	*mwahliele*	*mwahlielen*
mwahr	*mware*	*mwaren*
nta	*ntah*	*ntahn*

Nouns Which Always Occur Possessed

There are many nouns in Ponapean which have no free forms. These nouns always occur either with a possessive pronoun suffix or in a construct form, in one of the possessive constructions previously described. These nouns, which always occur possessed, belong to all three root classes. Examples from each class follow.

3rd Person Singular	Meaning 'his, her, or its. . . . .'
Class I	
imwi	'top'
menipinipi	'sideburn'
padi	'eyebrow'
paki	'replantable part (of a plant)'
pahnadi	'chest'
kapi	'bottom'
adi	'vapor'
edi	'core (as of a boil)'

Class II

pwopwe	'shoulder'
sike	'fin (of a fish)'
teke	'thorn'
uhre	'muscle (of a clam)'
apere	'shoulder (honorific)'
dipere	'flake, chip'
duwe	'nature, manner'
takain were	'Adam's apple'
kode	'horn'
enge	'claw (as of a crab)'

Class III

ienge	'companion'
ire	'condition'
isepe	'fee'
keile	'edge'
kidipe	'cover'
koadoke	'peak'
lime	'hand (honorific)'
neme	'taste'
pelie	'peer'
pwere	'lower abdomen'
uhsepe	'continuation'

There is no sure way to predict which nouns will have no free forms. Since all classes are included in nouns of this type, we cannot tell from the way they are pronounced if they will behave this way, and even in terms of meaning we can make no accurate generalizations. While it is true that most nouns that always occur possessed are ones expressing part-whole relationships, including many body parts, there are other nouns expressing these relationships which do have free forms. Examples are *moahng* 'head' and *tihmw* 'nose'.

Nouns With Partial Possessive Paradigms

A number of nouns normally only occur with the third person singular possessive suffix or the construct suffix. Therefore, a noun like *keimw* can occur in these forms:

keimwi	'its corner'
keimwin koakono	'the corner of that box'

For reasons of meaning, first and second person suffixes are not normally employed with *keimw*. Also, because third person dual and plural suffixes are employed only with reference to human beings or some domestic animals, these suffixed forms also do not occur. Some other nouns that have only partial paradigms are:

	Free Form	English	3rd Person Singular Form
Class I			
	pwihl	'gum, of a tree'	*pwili*
	seuseu	'small tuber of a yam'	*seusewi*
Class II			
	kehke	'stem, of a fruit'	*kehkeh*
	mangil	'handle, of a tool'	*mangile*
Class III			
	pahs	'nest'	*pese*
	kasang	'fork of a tree'	*kesenge*

Also, as one might expect, some nouns with partial paradigms always occur possessed. Some examples are listed below in their third person singular forms.

Class I		
	kapi	'bottom'
	paki	'replantable part (of a plant)'
Class II		
	kode	'horn'
	inoande	'main tuber of a yam'
Class III		
	keile	'edge'
	koadoke	'peak'

INDIRECT POSSESSION

4.8.3   While some nouns in Ponapean may be directly possessed, the majority occur in indirect patterns of possession. Indirect possession is employed with nouns representing things other than those which label parts of a whole, body parts, and kinship relations. Nouns like these involve a less immediate kind of possessor relationship.

The key fact about indirect possession is that it requires the use of possessive classifiers, as these examples illustrate.

nei	*seri*	'my child'
kenei	*mwenge*	'my food'
nimei	*saida*	'my soda'
werei	*pwoht*	'my boat'

Here, the nouns *seri*, *mwenge*, *saida*, and *pwoht* represent the thing possessed. The possessor, represented by the possessive pronoun -*i* 'my' does not suffix directly to these nouns, however, as in direct possession. Rather, it suffixes to *ne-*, *kene-*, *nime-*, and *were-*, all of which are possessive classifiers. Since classifiers play such an important role in possession of this type, it is appropriate that we first familiarize ourselves with the various possessive classifiers that occur in Ponapean.

Possessive Classifiers

The use of classifiers in Ponapean should already be familiar to you. In section **4**. 4, in our discussion of numerals, we noted that there were at least twenty-nine different numeral classifiers, the use of which was determined in part by the meaning of the noun being counted, and in part by a decision on the part of the speaker as to what aspect of the noun being counted he wished to emphasize. The use of possesssive classifiers is similarly determined.

Before we go on, it might be useful to list some of the possessive classifiers that occur in Ponapean. For purposes of illustration, twenty-one are given here. In fact, how many there are in Ponapean is difficult to determine, for reasons we will discuss later. In the following list, in the first column, each classifier is given as it occurs with the 3rd person singular possessive pronoun, indicating 'his, her, or its'. In the second column, an example of its use is presented. In the third column, a generalization, if possible, is made about what other kinds of nouns one might expect the classifier to occur with. For the sake of convenience, all possessors will simply be translated 'his', except where 'her' is more appropriate.

Classifier	Example	Generally Used With
ah	*ah pwoud* 'his spouse'	(see below)
nah	*nah seri* 'his child'	(see below)
kene	*kene uht* 'his banana'	edible things
nime	*nime uhpw* 'his drinking coconut'	drinkable things
sapwe	*sapwe deke* 'his island'	land
imwe	*imwe nahs* 'his feasthouse'	buildings
were	*were sidohsa* 'his car'	vehicles
kie	*kie lohs* 'his mat'	things to sleep on
ipe	*ipe tehi* 'his sheet'	things to cover with
ulunge	*ulunge uluhl* 'his pillow'	pillows
rie	*rie pwutak* 'his brother'	siblings
kiseh	*kiseh ohl* 'his male relative'	relatives
ullepe	*ullepe ohl* 'his maternal uncle'	maternal uncles
wahwah	*wahwah serepein* 'his niece'	nephews, nieces
sawi	*sawi pwutak* 'his boy clansmember'	clan members
pelie	*pelie ohl* 'his male peer'	peers, counterparts, opponents

seike	*seike ah* 'his catch of mullet'	catch, sea or land
pwekidah	*pwekidah pwihk* 'his share of pig'	share of food at a feast
mware	*mware mwaramwar* 'his garland'	garlands, names, titles
ede	*ede aditik* 'his nickname'	names
tie	*tie kisin kohl* 'her gold earring'	earrings

The generalizations made in the third column about what other kinds of nouns one might expect these classifiers to be used with vary somewhat in their accuracy. In the case of the first classifier listed above, *ah*, no attempt at a generalization was made. This classifier is best characterized as a 'general classifier' because it is impossible to accurately associate this classifier with a particular group of nouns, all of which share some common area of meaning. Some examples of nouns that occur with this classifier are listed below.

pwoud	'spouse'	*ketia*	'boat pole'
pahpa	'father'	*tuhke*	'tree'
nohno	'mother'	*rausis*	'trousers'
tehpel	'table'	*palangk*	'porch'
sirangk	'cabinet'	*sehr*	'chair'
sohri	'zorie'	*lisoarop*	'hat'
seht	'shirt'	*sarmahda*	'underwear'

While it is generally true that items such as clothing or large personal possessions occur with this classifier, probably the best way to describe the use of *ah* is to say that is is employed with nouns which do not fall into one of the other classes.

The use of the *nah* classifier is also difficult to characterize, though it might be called a 'dominant' classifier. This is because *nah* is generally used with people or things over which the possessor has a dominant relationship. It is also used with small items and things considered to be precious to the possessor. Some examples of nouns that occur with the *nah* classifier follow.

seri	'child'	*pinsel*	'pencil'
kaht	'cat'	*dengki*	'flashlight'
kidi	'dog'	*masis*	'match'
dahl	'dish'	*pwihk*	'pig'

With the remaining classifiers, it is easier to make accurate predictions about what kinds of nouns they will be used with. With the classifier *kene*, which is normally used with edible things (as *kene mahi*, 'his breadfruit' or *kene uht*, 'his banana'), there are two unexpected inclusions. These are *sakau* 'kava' and *sika* 'cigarette'. Therefore, both of these nouns are treated as edibles in terms of possession.

Another important point about possessive classifiers is that, as with numeral classifiers, a single noun may occur with more than one classifier with changes in meaning. Thus one may say *kene mahi*, meaning 'his breadfruit (to eat)'; however, *ah mahi* is also possible, meaning 'his breadfruit tree'. It is for this reason that we remarked earlier that the classifier employed may indicate what aspect of the noun the speaker wishes to emphasize. Other examples of a single noun occurring with more than one classifier are given below.

pwihk	'pig'	*nah pwihk*	'his pig, alive'
		ah pwihk	'his pig, butchered'
		kene pwihk	'his pig, to eat'
kehp	'yam'	*nah kehp*	'his yam, unharvested'
		ah kehp	'his yam, harvested'
		kene kehp	'his yam, to eat'
uht	'banana'	*nah uht*	'his banana, the tree'
		ah uht	'his banana, harvested'
		kene uht	'his banana, to eat'

Here, notice that the classifier *nah* is used with these nouns when they are in their natural state; *ah* is used after they have been butchered or harvested; and, when they are to be eaten, *kene* is used. With some nouns, however, this distinction does not hold, as illustrated by the following example.

mahi	'breadfruit'	*ah mahi*	'his breadfruit, the tree'
		ah mahi	'his breadfruit, harvested'

| *kene mahi* | 'his breadfruit, to eat' |

Another important instance where the choice of a classifier may affect the meaning of a possessed noun is with kinship terms, as in these examples.

pwutak 'boy'	*nah pwutak*	'his son'
	rie pwutak	'his brother'
	kiseh pwutak	'his boy relative'
	wahwah pwutak	'his nephew'
	sawi pwutak	'his boy clansmember'

The noun *pwutak* might also occur with other classifiers, as:

| *pelie pwutak* | 'his boy peer' |
| *ah pwutak* | 'his boy friend' |

When the relationship between the possessor and the thing possessed is viewed as being of a temporary nature, the general classifier *ah* may be employed, as in these examples.

nah moahl	'his kava pounding stone that he owns'
ah moahl	'his kava pounding stone that he is working with'
were sidohsa	'his automobile that he owns'
ah sidohsa	'his automobile that he is working on'

One additional point about possessive classifiers is that since they may be suffixed by possessive pronouns—and this we shall examine in more detail in the next section—they are probably best considered to be a special class of noun roots which may be directly possessed. Indeed, it is difficult, if not impossible, to set up precise criteria that will tell us whether a particular root is to be considered a possessive classifier or simply a directly possessed noun. Still, these classifiers are treated as a unique class in this grammar for the following reasons.

First, possessive classifiers suffixed by possessive pronouns may appear before any of a number of nouns with which that possessive classifier may be appropriately employed. Thus, we have seen that the third person singular form of the possessive

classifiers *ah*, *nah*, and *kene* may occur with a variety of nouns.
This is also true of the other possessive classifiers.

Classifier	Used with Nouns Like:	
nime	*pihl*	'water'
	uhpw	'drinking coconut'
	pihru	'beer'
sapwe	*sahpw*	'land'
	deke	'island'
	eiker	'acre'
imwe	*ihmw*	'house'
	nahs	'feasthouse'
	sidohwa	'store'
were	*wahr*	'canoe'
	pwoht	'boat'
	odopai	'motorcycle'
kie	*lohs*	'mat'
	madires	'mattress'
ipe	*tehi*	'sheet'
	pilangkes	'blanket'

These examples illustrate just a few of the possessive classifiers
previously listed, along with just a few of the nouns with which
they may occur. What is important here is the ability of possessive
classifiers to occur with more than just a single following noun.
This is one of the characteristics of classifiers not shared by other
nouns which may be directly possessed. Directly possessed nouns,
however, may occur in similar structures as illustrated below,
where a free form of a noun follows its possessed form.

moange moahng	'his head'
kili kihl	'his skin'
ewe ahu	'his mouth'
timwe tihmw	'his nose'

Although these phrases are grammatically acceptable, they normally do not occur since they are redundant. And they are
redundant precisely because only one noun may normally follow.
With possessive classifiers, as we have seen, this is not true.

Apparently, though, any noun which may take possessive suffixes may come to function as a possessive classifier, given the proper context. For example, the noun *mahs* 'face' is used as a classifier by some speakers when talking about masks, as in *mese masuku* 'his catcher's mask' or 'his welding mask'. Similarly, the noun *ahu* 'mouth' may be used as a possessive classifier, as in the phrase *ewe aupwal* 'his hairlip'.

Another reason why we want to recognize a certain group of roots as possessive classifiers is that whereas all directly possessed nouns have nouns as their roots, this is apparently not true of possessive classifiers. The classifier *nime* for drinkable things, for example, clearly comes from the verb *nim* 'to drink'. In the case of some other classifiers such as *ah*, *nah*, and *kie*, the root morpheme appears to have no function except as a classifier.

The problem of precisely defining possessive classifiers is difficult, but this is a problem not only in Ponapean, but in many Oceanic languages. Let us now turn our attention to the various forms that these classifiers may take when they are suffixed by possessive pronouns.

Indirect Possession with Pronouns

As we have already noted, in patterns of indirect possession the possessive pronouns are suffixed to possessive classifiers. For each possessive classifier, therefore, there is a paradigm parallel to one of those we previously established for nouns which may be directly possessed. Except for the two classifiers *ah* and *nah*, which have irregular paradigms, all of the classifiers listed in the preceding section belong to one of the three root classes established for nouns which may be directly possessed. The root classes these classifiers belong to are specified as follows.

Class I—i Roots: The only classifier which belongs to this class is the one for 'clan membership', which has as its third person singular form *sawi*, meaning 'his or her clan'. The entire paradigm of this classifier is presented below.

sawi	'my clan'
sawimw or *soumw*	'your clan'
sawi	'his or her clan'
sawit	'our clan (exclusive)'
sawita or *souta*	'our clan (dual)'

sawimwa or *soumwa*	'your clan (dual)'
sawira or *soura*	'their clan (dual)'
sawitail or *soutail*	'our clan (plural)'
sawimwail or *soumwail*	'your clan (plural)'
sawirail or *sourail*	'their clan (plural)'

Note that a number of the above forms have alternate pronunciations, where *-awi-* (as in *sawimw*) is also pronounced *-ou-* (as in *soumw*).

Class II—e Roots: Three classifiers belong to Class II. Both the roots and the third person singular form of these classifiers follow.

Root	3rd Person Singular	Used With
sapwe-	*sapwe*	land
mware-	*mware*	titles
kiseh-	*kiseh*	relatives

The full paradigms for these classifiers parallel the paradigms given for Class II nouns in section **4**.8.2

Class III—a Roots: Fifteen classifiers belong to Class III. The roots as well as the third person singular forms of these classifiers follow.

Root	3rd Person Singular	Used With
kana-	*kene*	edible things
nima-	*nime*	drinkable things
imwa-	*imwe*	buildings
wara-	*were*	vehicles
kia-	*kie*	things to sleep on
ipa-	*ipe*	things to cover with
ulunga-	*ulunge*	pillows
ria-	*rie*	siblings
ullapa-	*ullepe*	maternal uncles
wahwah-	*wahwah*	nephews, nieces
pelia-	*pelie*	peers, counterparts, opponents
seika-	*seike*	catch, sea or land
pwekidah-	*pwekidah*	share of food at a feast
ada-	*ede*	names
tia-	*tie*	earrings

The full paradigms for these classifiers parallel the paradigms given for Class III nouns in section **4**.8.2.

The paradigms of two classifiers—*ah* the general classifier and *nah* the dominant classifier—are somewhat irregular and do not fit into any of the three preceding classes. These paradigms are listed below with common alternate pronunciations where they occur.

ahi or *ei*	*nei*
ahmw or *omw*	*noumw*
ah or *e*	*nah*
aht or *at*	*nait*
ata	*neita*
amwa	*noumwa*
ara	*neira*
atail	*neitail*
amwail	*noumwail*
arail	*neirail* or *nair*

The alternate forms in the first paradigm, *ei*, *omw*, and *e* (some speakers prefer *eh*), occur in casual speech only when a noun or noun phrase follows, as in these examples.

Careful Speech		Casual Speech		English
ahi	*seht*	*ei*	*seht*	'my shirt'
ahmw	*seht*	*omw*	*seht*	'your shirt'
ah	*seht*	*e*	*seht*	'his shirt'

The casual speech forms may not occur when the following noun or noun phrase is deleted. Therefore, one might say *Ahiet laudsang ahmwen* 'Mine is bigger than yours', or simply *Ahi* 'Mine' in response to a question like *En ihs met?* 'Whose is this?'. But, the use of *ei* in either of these sentences is ungrammatical.

Indirect Possession with Nouns

As with direct possession, the possessor in indirect patterns of possession may also be represented by a noun or a noun phrase. Some examples follow.

kenen ohlo mahi	'that man's breadfruit'
nimen ohlo pihl	'that man's water'

imwen ohlo nahs	'that man's feasthouse'
weren ohlo wahr	'that man's canoe'
wahwahn ohlo pwutak	'that man's nephew'
seiken ohlo ah	'that man's catch of mullet'

Notice in these constructions that the possessive classifier is followed by the construct suffix *-n*. Then comes the noun phrase representing the possessor, followed by the noun representing the thing possessed.

With the two most common classifiers *ah* and *nah*, an additional optional element may occur in this construction, as illustrated by these examples.

en ohlo (ah) seht	'that man's shirt'
nein ohlo (nah) rasaras	'that man's saw'

Notice that between the noun phrase representing the possessor and the noun representing the thing possessed, a third person form of the possessive classifier may occur. In the above examples, the third person singular form is listed, but the dual and plural forms may also be employed, as in these examples.

en ohl akau (ara) seht	'those men's shirts (dual)'
en ohl akau (arail) seht	'those men's shirts (plural)'
nein ohl akau (neira) rasaras	'those men's saws (dual)'
nein ohl akau (neirail) rasaras	'those men's saws (plural)'

With other possessive classifiers, constructions like these are also grammatically possible, but rarely occur. With *ah* and *nah*, though, constructions using a third person form of the classifier as above are quite common.

NOUNS POSSESSED BOTH DIRECTLY AND INDIRECTLY

4.8.4   Although the majority of nouns in Ponapean are restricted in the way they may be possessed to either direct or indirect patterns of possession, there are some nouns with which both patterns of possession may be employed. Some examples follow, where the possessor is represented by the first person singular pronoun 'my'.

Noun	Possessed Directly	Possessed Indirectly
kilel	*kilelei*	*nei kilel*
'picture'	'picture of me'	'my picture'
rohng	*rongei*	*ahi rohng*
'news'	'news of me'	'my news'
pwuhk	*pwukei*	*nei pwuhk*
'book'	'book about me'	'my book'
kihl	*kili*	*nei kihl*
'skin'	'my skin'	'my skin (as an animal skin)'

These examples once more illustrate the basic meaning distinctions between these two patterns of possession. In the direct patterns listed above, the possession that is referred to is one that is essentially permanent, over which the possessor has no control. Therefore, when a noun like *kilel* 'picture' enters into a direct pattern of possession, the result is *kilelei*, meaning 'my picture' in the sense of 'a picture of me'. Here the relationship between the possessor and the thing possessed is one over which the possessor has no obvious control. With an indirect pattern of possession, like *nei kilel* 'my picture' in the sense of 'the picture that I own', one can see that the relationship between the possessor and the thing possessed is quite different. Here the possessor does have control over the possession. The ownership here is one that may be easily transferred to another possessor.

MULTIPLE POSSESSIVE CONSTRUCTIONS

4.8.5   The noun phrase representing the possessor in a possessive construction may itself be a possessive construction. This is illustrated by the following two phrases where the noun phrase *ohlo* 'that man' in the first phrase is replaced by the possessive noun phrase *semen ohlo* 'that man's father' in the second.

> *nein ohlo nah pelik*   'that man's coconut grater'
> *nein semen ohlo nah pelik*   'that man's father's coconut grater'

Constructions like the second one above which contain more than one possessive construction we will call **multiple possessive constructions**.

In multiple possessive constructions both indirect and direct patterns of possession may occur. For example, in an indirect construction like *nein ohlo nah pwuhk* 'that man's book', the noun phrase *ohlo* 'that man' which represents the possessor may be replaced by either an indirect or a direct possessive construction. Therefore, the indirect construction *en ohlo ah pwoud* 'that man's wife' or *ei pwoudo* 'my wife' might replace *ohlo*, as in these examples.

>*nein en ohlo ah pwoud nah pwuhk*
>'that man's wife's book'
>
>*nein ei pwoudo nah pwuhk*
>'my wife's book'

Or, direct constructions like *semen ohlo* 'that man's father' or *semeio* 'my father' might replace *ohlo*, as in these examples.

>*nein semen ohlo nah pwuhk*
>'that man's father's book'
>
>*nein semeio nah pwuhk*
>'my father's book'

Within a direct possessive construction like *kilin ohlo* 'that man's skin' the same substitutions are possible, as in these examples.

>*kilin en ohlo ah pwoud*
>'that man's wife's skin'
>
>*kilin ei pwoudo*
>'my wife's skin'
>
>*kilin semen ohlo*
>'that man's father's skin'
>
>*kilin semeio*
>'my father's skin'

All of the examples of multiple possessive constructions we have examined thus far have involved the insertion of a single possessive construction within another. Still even more complex constructions are possible. Therefore, starting with the possessive construction *nein ohlo nah pwuhk* 'that man's book', we may substitute for *ohlo* 'that man' the possessive construction *rien ohlo pwutak* 'that man's brother'. This results in the following phrase.

> *nein rien ohlo pwutak nah pwuhk*
> 'that man's brother's book'

And, we may again substitute a possessive phrase for *ohlo*, for example *en ohlo ah kompani* 'that man's friend' to produce the following phrase.

> *nein rien en ohlo ah kompani pwutak nah pwuhk*
> 'that man's friend's brother's book'

It should be noted, however, that while multiple possessive constructions involving a single substitution of a possessive construction for a noun phrase are common in conversation, those involving two or more substitutions, while grammatical, are rarely used. They are difficult, even for a native speaker, to understand.

THE USE OF THE CONSTRUCT SUFFIX IN REFERENTIAL NOUN PHRASES

4.9   In our preceding discussion of possession in Ponapean, we examined the use of the construct suffix *-n* in both direct and indirect constructions. We noted that if a noun rather than a pronoun is used to represent the possessor, then constructions like the following result.

> *kilin ohlo*   'that man's skin'
> *en ohlo ah pwoud*   'that man's wife'

In the first phrase, a direct construction, the construct suffix is attached to the noun naming the thing possessed. In the second phrase, an indirect construction, the construct suffix is attached to the possessive classifier.

Still another use of the construct suffix is in **referential noun phrases**, where the noun or phrase following the noun to which the construct suffix is attached indicates the origin, source, location, content, or purpose of the thing being talked about. Examples follow:

olen Pohnpei	'Ponapean man'
dengki en Sapahn	'Japanese flashlight'
nahsen Wene	'Wene feasthouse'
pwohren sika	'cigarette carton'
misihn en deidei	'sewing machine'

(The treatment of the construct suffix here, being either attached to the preceding word or written separately, is consistent with the orthography conventions described in the Appendix.) The usage of the construct suffix in these examples differs from its use in direct or indirect constructions. Whereas in possessive constructions the noun phrase introduced by the construct suffix may be replaced by a pronoun, in referential constructions it may not. Therefore, the noun phrase *ohlo* 'that man' in a possessive construction like *kilin ohlo* 'that man's skin' may be replaced by a pronoun. The result is *kili* 'his skin.' In a referential construction, like *nahsen Wene* 'the feast house of Wene', the noun phrase *Wene* may not be similarly replaced.

All nouns may occur in referential noun phrases. Apparently, except for nouns which may be directly possessed or which undergo the monosyllabic noun vowel lengthening rule, the vowel that occurs before the construct suffix *-n* is an insert vowel. This insert vowel may be either *i* or *e* ($/\varepsilon/$), as illustrated by the following construct forms of monosyllabic nouns which have inherently long vowels.

Free Form	English	Construct Form
ihpw	'spear handle'	*ihpwin* or *ihpwen*
peht	'bed'	*pehtin* or *pehten*
pweht	'lime'	*pwehtin* or *pwehten*
kahp	'curve'	*kahpin* or *kahpen*
moahd	'echo'	*moahdin* or *moahden*
pwohr	'carton'	*pwohrin* or *pwohren*
uhp	'plant species'	*uhpin* or *uhpen*

It may be that the vowel *i* is chosen when *-n* is treated as a suffix, and *e* when it is treated as an enclitic. However, at this point this explantation is only speculative.

5   Verbs and Verb Phrases

OVERVIEW

5.1   In the preceding chapter we examined one of the major kinds of phrases which occurs in Ponapean sentences—the noun phrase. In this chapter we will turn our attention to what we noted in section 3.10 to be a second major phrase type—the **verb phrase**.

Just as every noun phrase must contain a noun (or a word substituting for a noun), so must every verb phrase contain a verb. Consequently, we will begin our study of the verb phrase by examining verbs, considering first what a verb is, what classes of verbs there are, and what affixes may combine with verbs. We will then examine what a verb phrase is and consider in detail two additional classes of words that may occur with verbs in a verb phrase—**adverbs** and **aspect markers**.

The material in this chapter in combination with the content of the preceding chapter will provide the foundation for the study of sentences—the subject of chapter 6.

VERBS

5.2   Verbs, as we previously noted in section 3.7.2, are words whose characteristic function is one of predication. That is, they name actions, events, states, conditions, or qualities. Words like the following are verbs.

dou	'to climb'	*daper*	'to catch'
leke	'to slash'	*lawalo*	'to be wild'
perek	'to unroll'	*pang*	'to be crooked'
duhp	'to bathe'	*lisoi*	'to nod'
reirei	'to be long'	*noahrok*	'to be greedy'

tang	'to run'	*rese*	'to saw'
alu	'to walk'	*oh*	'to start'
laid	'to fish'	*ihkose*	'to pleat'
edied	'to be cloudy'	*sarek*	'to dodge'

Like nouns, verbs may be divided into different classes according to similarities in function or meaning. At this point, it will be convenient to introduce a classification of verbs that depends upon how many noun phrases they may occur with. According to this classification, we will divide verbs into two types. Verbs like *duhdu* 'to bathe', *tang* 'to run', and *noahrok* 'to be greedy' which occur with only a preceding noun phrase, as in the sentences below, we will call **intransitive verbs**.

(a) *Lahpo duhdu.*
    'That guy bathed.'

(b) *Pwutako tang.*
    'That boy ran.'

(c) *Ohlo noahrok.*
    'That man is greedy.'

Verbs like *kang* 'to eat', *daper* 'to catch', and *rese* 'to saw' which may occur with a following noun phrase, as in the next sentences, we will call **transitive verbs**.

(d) *Lahpo kang raiso.*
    'That guy ate that rice.'

(e) *Pwutako daper mpweio.*
    'That boy caught that ball.'

(f) *E rese tuhke rioapwoato.*
    'He sawed those two logs.'

This distinction between intransitive and transitive verbs allows us to correctly predict that a sentence like the following is ungrammatical.

*Liho duhdu serio.
woman-that bathe child-that.

Because *duhdu* is an intransitive verb, it may not be followed by a noun phrase like *serio*. To make this sentence grammatical, the transitive verb *duhp* must be employed, as follows.

> *Liho duhp serio.*
> woman-that bathe child-that
> 'That woman bathed that child.'

Intransitive and transitive verbs are examined in detail in the sections that follow.

INTRANSITIVE VERBS

5.2.1   Intransitive verbs are of two basic types: **general intransitive verbs** and **adjectives**. Examples of verbs of these two types follow.

General Intransitives		Adjectives	
mwenge	'to eat'	*kehlail*	'to be strong'
iohla	'to miscarry'	*sapan*	'to be generous'
alu	'to walk'	*lelepek*	'to be reliable'
lidip	'to trap'	*katik*	'to be bitter'
marer	'to hiccough'	*dir*	'to be overcrowded'
men	'to wink'	*kaparapar*	'to be fertile'
ngarahk	'to laugh heartily'	*kapw*	'to be new'
tang	'to run'	*kesempwal*	'to be valuable'
seng	'to cry'	*mwotomwot*	'to be short'
sis	'to shiver'	*oaritik*	'to be detailed'
paker	'to punch'	*pweipwei*	'to be stupid'

Further details about each of these types of verbs, along with reasons why in Ponapean we want to consider adjectives as a subclass of intransitive verbs, are presented in the following discussions.

General Intransitive Verbs

Nearly all general intransitive verbs are of the type that we will call activity verbs. **Activity verbs** are verbs which express actions or events. We may divide activity verbs into three subtypes, according to whether thay are **active**, **resultative**, or **neutral**. Examples of verbs of these three subtypes are given below.

	Subtype	Verb	As in the Sentence
(a)	active	*mwenge*	*I pahn mwenge.*
		'to eat'	'I will eat.'
		laid	*I pahn laid.*
		'to fish'	'I will fish.'
(b)	resultative	*langada*	*Lampo pahn langada.*
		'to be hung up'	'That lamp will be hung up.'
		ritidi	*Wenihmwo pahn ritidi.*
		'to be closed'	'The door will be closed.'
(c)	neutral	*deidei*	*Liho pahn deidei.*
		'to sew or	'That woman will sew.'
		to be sewed'	*Sehto pahn deidei.*
			'That shirt will be sewed.'
		pirap	*Ohlo pahn pirap.*
		'to steal or	'That man will steal.'
		to be stolen'	*Pwuhket pahn pirap.*
			'This book will be stolen.'

With active verbs, the preceding noun phrase names the actor or agent that carried out the action. With resultative verbs, this noun phrase names the person or object affected by the action. With verbs which are neutral, therefore either active or resultative, the preceding noun phrase may have either of these functions.

Notice that the active/resultative distinction here is not the same as the active/passive distinction in English. Therefore, passive sentences in English like 'This book was read by John' involve transitive verbs. Resultative verbs in Ponapean, though, are intransitive. In fact, there is no active/passive voice distinction in Ponapean comparable to that in English.

With neutral verbs, there is some potential for ambiguity. In a sentence like *Sehto pahn deidei* 'That shirt will be sewed', we assume that the noun phrase *sehto* 'that shirt' represents what is being sewed, rather than what is doing the sewing. But there are some verbs where out of context we cannot know what the role of the noun phrase is. Therefore, a sentence like *Ohlo pahn kilel* may be translated either 'That man will take a photograph' or 'That man will be photographed.'

Some additional examples of verbs of each of these three subtypes are provided below.

	Active		Resultative
ding	'to drip'	*dol*	'to be severed'
dipwahk	'to eat'	*irihrla*	'to be erased'
ihk	'to inhale'	*irisek*	'to be rubbed'
ingihng	'to whisper'	*leu*	'to be cooked'
lipahrok	'to spy'	*lop*	'to be cut'
mehn	'to kiss'	*peserek*	'to be yanked'
pap	'to swim'	*sansar*	'to be sliced'
nget	'to pant'	*ep*	'to be pulled, of a rope'
pwedehk	'to buzz'	*weweti*	'to be whipped'
pwupwidi	'to fall down'	*dou*	'to be woven, of a net'

Neutral

kasawa	'to hatch'	'to be hatched'
ked	'to cut open'	'to be cut open'
les	'to split'	'to be split'
lukom	'to wrap around'	'to be wrapped around'
ngked	'to roof'	'to be roofed'
peipei	'to weave'	'to be woven'
peleng	'to dry'	'to be dried'
pwal	'to slit'	'to be slit'
serek	'to sail'	'to be sailed'
sihp	'to shave'	'to be shaved'

In addition to activity verbs like those above, there are also a number of general intransitive verbs in Ponapean that we will label **non-activity verbs**. These are verbs which name states or conditions which may exist without the involvement of an actor or agent. A few examples follow.

mi	'to exist'	*kahiep*	'to be empty-handed'
ikmwir	'to be last in a sequence'	*pat*	'to be together'

Adjectives

Adjectives in Ponapean are intrasitive verbs which typically name qualities. Following are some examples.

akuh	'boastful'	*lingeringer*	'angry'
dehde	'clear, evident'	*luwak*	'jealous'

deng	'taut'	*maledek*	'roomy'
dir	'overcrowded'	*mat*	'ripe'
it	'stuffed'	*mem*	'sweet'
kala	'boastful'	*min*	'neat, clean'
kapw	'new'	*ngelingel*	'stinking'
kehl	'very hot'	*sahliel*	'dizzy'
lemei	'cruel'	*tihti*	'skinny'
limek	'bent, smashed'	*was*	'obnoxious'

In this grammar, adjectives are treated as a subclass of intransitive verbs because adjectives have essentially the same grammatical properties as other intransitives. Their similarities are illustrated by the following pairs of sentences, where the adjective *lemei* 'cruel, belligerent, tough' is employed in the (a) sentences, while the general intransitive verb *tang* 'to run' is used in the (b) sentences.

(1)   (a)   *E pahn lemei.*
              'He will be cruel.'

       (b)   *E pahn tang.*
              'He will run.'

(2)   (a)   *E lemelemei.*
              'He is being cruel.'

       (b)   *E tangatang.*
              'He is running.'

(3)   (a)   *Lemei!*
              'Be cruel!'

       (b)   *Tang!*
              'Run!'

(4)   (a)   *E lamai pwutako.*
              'He is cruel to that boy.'

       (b)   *E tenge pwutako.*
              'He ran to that boy.'

The sentences listed after (1) illustrate that both adjectives and general intransitive verbs (hereafter abbreviated as GIV's) may occur with subject pronouns (like *e*) and with aspect markers (like *pahn*). The sentences listed after (2) show that adjectives and GIV's may both reduplicate. In (3), it is shown that in many cases both adjectives and GIV's may be used in commands, and in (4) we see that some adjectives, like some GIV's, have transitive counterparts.

Based on the examples we have examined thus far, it would seem appropriate simply to classify adjectives as non-activity general intransitive verbs. However, there are reasons why we want to consider adjectives as distinct from verbs of this type. One reason is that only those kinds of words that we call adjectives may occur with the **stative marker** *me*. Therefore, while adjectives may occur alone in a verb phrase, they may also occur with *me*, as illustrated by the following sentences.

E kehlail.	*E me kehlail!*
'He is strong.'	'He is strong!'
E mwahu.	*E me mwahu!*
'He is good.'	'He is good!'
E suwed.	*E me suwed!*
'He is bad.'	'He is bad!'

The difference in meaning between a sentence using *me* and one not using *me* is primarily one of emphasis. This difference is indicated in the translations above by the kind of punctuation employed. This emphasis, though, is not one of intensity, but rather one of factuality. Therefore, a sentence like *E me kehlail* is perhaps best translated 'He is strong, no doubt about it' as opposed to 'He is really strong.'

With general intransitive verbs, the stative marker *me* may not be used. All the sentences in the right-hand column below are ungrammatical.

E mwenge.	**E me mwenge.*
'He ate.'	
E dol.	**E me dol.*
'It was severed.'	
E mi mwo.	**E me mi mwo.*
'It exists there.'	

The stative marker *me* should not be confused with the replacive pronoun *me*. With the pronoun *me*, these sentences are possible.

Ih me kehlail.
he one strong
'He is the strong one.'

Ih me mwenge.
he one eat
'He is the one who ate.'

Ih me dol.
it one severed
'It is the one that was severed.'

These sentences, which necessarily employ independent rather than subject pronouns, are equational sentences. Sentences like these will be examined further in section **6**.4.2.

Another characteristic of adjectives that sets them apart from general intransitive verbs is that most, perhaps all, may occur with the **superlative suffix** -*ie*. Examples follow.

lingan	*lingahnie*
'beautiful'	'the most beautiful'
kadek	*kadehkie*
'kind'	'the kindest'
roson	*rosohnie*
'healthy'	'the healthiest'
sakanakan	*sakanakahnie*
'bad'	'the worst'
kaselel	*kaselehlie*
'precious'	'the most precious'

Notice that when this suffix is used, the final vowel in the adjective root lengthens. Adjectives also occur in comparative constructions with the suffix -*sang*. This usage of -*sang* is further examined in section **5**.4.4.

Still one more characteristic of adjectives that distinguishes them from other intransitive verbs is the way they behave when functioning as modifiers in noun phrases. Compare the following sentences.

(a) *Ohl mworourou silimeno kerenieng duhla.*
     man fat three-there near-to drown
     'Those three fat men nearly drowned.'

(b) *Ohl silimen (me) duhduo kerenieng duhla.*
man three (one) diving-there near-to drown
'Those three men who were diving nearly drowned.'

Notice in sentence (a) that the adjective *mworourou* 'fat' precedes the numeral *silimen* 'three', while in sentence (b) the general intransitive verb *duhdu* 'diving' (optionally preceded by *me*) follows the numeral. For adjectives, this position is optional; therefore, the following sentence where the adjective follows the numeral is also possible.

Ohl silimen (me) mworourowo kerenieng duhla.
'Those three men who are fat nearly drowned.'

For general intransitive verbs, however, the position following the numeral is obligatory. A sentence like the following is therefore ungrammatical.

*Ohl duhdu silimeno kerenieng duhla.

Further discussion of modification of this type occurs in section **6**.5.2.

Before we go on to examine transitive verbs, it might be useful to summarize the various subclasses of intransitive verbs thus far established. Such a summary is provided in the following chart.

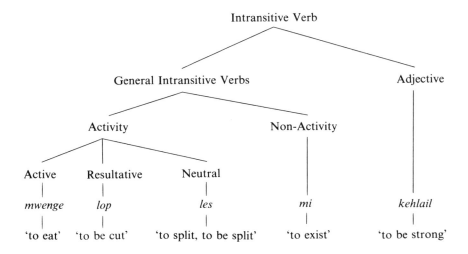

5.2.2   **Transitive verbs** are characterized by their ability to occur with
more than one noun phrase. Transitive verbs, therefore, occur in
sentences like the following.

> *Kidiet ngalis pwutako.*
> 'This dog bit that boy.'
>
> *Ohlo parok kidiet.*
> 'That man caught this dog.'
>
> *Kitail pahn kang kidiet.*
> 'We will eat this dog.'

In these sentences, in addition to the subject noun phrase, an
object noun phrase occurs which names the direct and immediate
goal or receiver of the action. Some additional examples of
transitive verbs are listed below.

amwer	'to crumple'	*mwoanok*	'to peep at'
ede	'to sharpen'	*ned*	'to smell'
eker	'to call or summon'	*padik*	'to squeeze'
ingid	'to braid'	*palang*	'to dry'
ipir	'to blow at'	*pwaik*	'to split'
kakil	'to stare at'	*rese*	'to saw'
kate	'to stone'	*siken*	'to push'
koduhpwal	'to cover up'	*dolung*	'to pick from the stalk'
limwih	'to sponge off'	*uhpe*	'to poison, as of fish'
manih	'to wink at'	*wehk*	'to confess'

INTRANSITIVE AND TRANSITIVE VERBS SHARING COMMON ROOTS

5.2.3   While many verb roots in Ponapean are used only intransitively
or only transitively, a considerable number of roots occur in verbs
of both these types. Some examples follow.

Intransitive		Transitive	
poad	'to be planted'	*poadok*	'to plant'
kehsek	'to mate'	*kehsekih*	'to mate with'
ihkos	'to pleat'	*ihkose*	'to pleat'
der	'to strike, of fish'	*dar*	'to strike, of fish'

eliel	'to massage'	*el*	'to massage'
emwirek	'to be crumpled'	*emwir*	'to crumple'
pehse	'to know each other'	*ese*	'to know'

As these examples illustrate, the intransitive and transitive forms of these verbs are not all related in the same way. In the first example, the transitive form has a final *-ok* not present in the intransitive form. In the second example, the transitive form has an additional *-ih*, and so on. Our task here will be to examine the more common of these relationships. Seven types will be described and labeled according to what seems to be their major characteristic. Where meaning apparently plays no role in understanding the relationship, only transitive verb forms will be translated.

I. *-VC* Final Transitives

	Intransitive	Transitive	English
(a)	*poad*	*poadok*	'to plant'
	kumw	*kumwur*	'to alert by pounding'
	id	*iding*	'to make fire by friction'
(b)	*pek*	*pakad*	'to defecate'
	ped	*padik*	'to squeeze'
	inou	*inaur*	'to lash with sennit'
(c)	*duhdu*	*duhp*	'to bathe'
	idaid	*idang*	'to mash'
	dapadap	*daper*	'to catch'

All of these pairs of verbs have a final *VC* (*V*owel, *C*onsonant) in the transitive form that does not occur in the intransitive form. Historically, the intransitive forms of these verbs were probably derived from the transitive form, in case (a) by deleting the final *VC*, and in case (b) by the same deletion plus a change in the quality of the vowel *a* to either *e* or *o*. In case (c), reduplication is also involved. Here we may assume that the final consonant was dropped, the form was reduplicated, and then the final vowel was deleted. This may be illustrated as follows:

Transitive Verb	*duhp*	*idang*
Delete Final C	*duh*	*ida*

Reduplicate	*duhduh*	*idaida*
Delete Final V	*duhdu*	*idaid*

In the case of *daper* to *dapadap*, the same steps are involved—
thus, *daper* → *dape* → *dapedape* → *dapedap* — but additionally,
the vowel *e* which occurs in the middle of this word was changed
to *a* to agree with the following *a*, thus producing *dapadap*.

There are many pairs of verbs in Ponapean which are of this
type, but the following type is also very common.

II. *-ih* Final Transitives

	Intransitive	Transitive	English
(a)	*deiad*	*deiadih*	'to embroider'
	kehsek	*kehsekih*	'to mate'
	mahlen	*mahlenih*	'to draw'
(b)	*sel*	*salih*	'to tie'
	dou	*dawih*	'to inspect'
	engieng	*angiangih*	'to be angry at'
(c)	*limwilimw*	*limwih*	'to sponge off'
	erier	*arih*	'to stir, to probe'

The basic difference between the intransitive and transitive verbs
here is that the transitive forms have a final *-ih* not present in the
intransitive forms. This is illustrated in the (a) examples. In the
(b) examples, there is additionally a change in the vowel *a* in the
transitive roots to *e* or *o* in the intransitive forms. In the (c)
examples, the intransitive form is reduplicated with, in some
cases, a change in vowel quality in the root. Notice that these
three subtypes parallel those we established for Type I.

The final *-ih* that occurs with the transitive forms here is a
transitive suffix. Therefore, it is added to intransitive verb roots to
form transitive verbs. This suffix seems to be used quite productively in Ponapean. It is suffixed to many borrowed intransitive verbs, as these examples illustrate.

Intransitive	Transitive	English
kuk	*kukih*	'to cook'
ain	*ainih*	'to iron'
deip	*deipih*	'to tape'

Borrowed verb roots which are used both intransitively and transitively are generally of this type (or the next) rather than Type I. One exception, however, is the verb 'to kick' which has as its intransitive form *kik* and as its transitive form *kikim*, as in the sentence *Lahpo kikim Soulik* 'That guy kicked Soulik.' This verb would seem to be of Type I, since its transitive form contains a final *-VC* not present in the intransitive form. Probably, though, the *-im* of *kikim* is from the English 'him' and speakers of Ponapean incorrectly interpreted this as the transitive ending.

III. Final Short Vowel Transitives

	Intransitive	Transitive	English
(a)	*lang*	*langa*	'to hang up'
	lek	*leke*	'to slash'
	perek	*pereki*	'to unroll'
(b)	*dok*	*doakoa*	'to spear'
	pal	*pele*	'to hack'
	likidar	*likidere*	'to scavenge'
(c)	*rasaras*	*rese*	'to saw'
	adahd	*ede*	'to sharpen'

In all of these examples, the transitive forms contain a final short vowel (either *i*, *a*, *e* (phonetically [ɛ]) or *oa*) not present in the intransitive forms. In the (b) examples, there is also a difference in the quality of one of the vowels of the verb root. In the (c) examples, reduplication as well as a change of vowel quality in the root may be involved. Verbs of this type are also very common, but it is difficult with this type to say which form of the verb is the basic one and which is derived.

One curious point here is that the final short vowel *-i* apparently occurs only after roots ending in the consonant *-k*. Additional examples follow.

peiek	*peieki*	'to slide'
dipwahk	*dipwahki*	'to eat'
elingek	*elingeki*	'to carry repeatedly'
kalehk	*kalehki*	'to fast'

Other short vowels as well as the transitive suffix *-ih* also occur after *-k* roots, though, as in these examples.

(a)	*lek*	*leke*	'to slash'
	dok	*doakoa*	'to spear'
(b)	*dik*	*dikih*	'to skip across the water'
	kehsek	*kehsekih*	'to mate'
	nenek	*nenekih*	'to commit adultery'

Why -*i* should occur only after -*k* final roots is not clear. It may be that the final *ki* of these verbs has been confused with the suffix -*ki*, discussed in section 5.4.1.

Verb roots involving a short final vowel in the transitive form not present in the intransitive form are quite common in Ponapean. Even some borrowed English roots are of this type, as the following examples illustrate.

Intransitive	Transitive	English
oaht	*oahte*	'to order'
sapwel	*sapwele*	'to shovel'

IV. Ablauted Intransitives

Intransitive	Transitive	English
epid	*apid*	'to carry on one's side'
der	*dar*	'to strike, of fish'
ngked	*ngkad*	'to roof with thatch'
lemei	*lamai*	'to be cruel'
peleng	*palang*	'to dry'
periper	*par*	'to cut'

With some verbs, the difference between the intransitive and transitive forms is signaled by a change in vowel quality, with *e* (/ɛ/) occurring in the intransitive form and *a* occurring in the transitive form. The word used to refer to changes in vowel quality like this is **ablaut**. Notice that reduplication may also be involved, as in the last example.

V. Reduplicated Intransitives

Intransitive	Transitive	English
pilipil	*pil*	'to choose'
eliel	*el*	'to massage'
popohr	*pohr*	'to slap in anger'

pipihs	*pihs*	'to urinate'
usuhs	*us*	'to pull out'

A few verbs in Ponapean involve only reduplication of the transitive root to form the intransitive. Verbs like these are uncommon.

VI. *-ek* Intransitives

Intransitive	English	Transitive	English
dilipek	'to be mended, of a thatch roof'	*dilip*	'to mend, of a thatch roof'
emwirek	'to be crumpled'	*amwir*	'to crumple'
dierek	'to be found'	*diar*	'to find'

Intransitive verbs of this type are formed by adding the suffix *-ek* to the transitive root. Where the transitive form of the verb contains the vowel *a*, the intransitive form contains a corresponding *e* ($[\varepsilon]$). This change in vowel quality is possibly a result of assimilation to the *e* in the suffix *-ek*. This suffix is probably fossilized. It does not seem to be used productively in Ponapean, nor do most speakers of Ponapean recognize it as being a separate morpheme.

The function of the *-ek* suffix was probably to form resultative intransitive verbs from transitive roots. If you examine the English gloss provided for the *-ek* intransitives above, you will notice this to be the case. Further verification of this comes from the fact that there are a number of transitive verbs in Ponapean which have two intransitive forms, one formed by *-ek* and the other by means of one of the other methods we previously discussed. Some examples are:

Transitive	*wengid*	'to wring'
Intransitive	*wengiweng*	'to wring'
Intransitive	*wengidek*	'to be twisted'
Transitive	*widinge*	'to deceive'
Intransitive	*widing*	'to deceive'
Intransitive	*widingek*	'to be deceitful'

These verbs are particularly illustrative of the function that *-ek* originally must have had.

It is not the case in contemporary Ponapean, however, that all verb roots suffixed by *-ek* are resultative. In an unpublished paper on Ponapean verbs, Robert Sarazen pointed out that there are a few verb roots suffixed by *-ek* that are active. Examples are:

Intransitive	English	Transitive	English
epwinek	'to wash one's face'	*apwin*	'to wash (one's face)'
pengidek	'to blow one's nose'	*pangid*	'to blow (one's nose)'
tuwelek	'to sway one's body'	*tuwel*	'to sway (one's body)'

Sarazen further points out that all verbs of this nature name activities done to or with the body.

VII.   *pV-* Intransitives

Intransitive	English	Transitive	English
pidilin	'to pull each other's hair'	*dilin*	'to pull hair'
pekekil	'to stare at each other'	*kakil*	'to stare at'
pehse	'to know each other'	*ese*	'to know'
pisiken	'to push each other'	*siken*	'to push'
paiahn	'to be used to each other'	*ahn*	'to be used to'

The prefix *pV-*, like the suffix *-ek*, is probably fossilized in Ponapean. Its function, though, seems to have been to form **reciprocal verbs**. Therefore, while *dilin* means 'to pull hair', *pidilin* means 'to pull each other's hair'. The action described by the intransitive verb is a reciprocal one. A sentence like *E pahn dilin liho* 'She's going to pull that woman's hair' is possible, but a sentence like *E pahn pidilin* is not. Instead, one would have to use a dual or plural subject here in order to include the idea of 'each other'; therefore, one might say *Re pahn pidilin* 'They are going to pull each other's hair'.

The shape of this prefix is described as *pV-*, where *V* represents a vowel that is a copy of the first vowel of the intransitive root. In most cases, this is the same vowel as in the transitive form—therefore *dilin, pidilin*—but in some cases, as we have noted previously, where the transitive form of the verb contains a short *a*, the intransitive might contain *e*. Thus, *kakil* 'to stare' has as its intransitive form *pekekil*.

With some verbs, the function of this prefix is less obvious. For example, the transitive verb *kadeik* 'to investigate' has an intransitive form *pakadeik*. The meaning of *pakadeik*, though, is 'to be investigated'. Thus, one may say *I pahn pakadeik*, 'I am going to be investigated'. The transitive verb *kaus* 'to exile someone' has an intransitive form *pekousla* which means 'to be exiled'. In both of these cases, however, while the reciprocal notion 'each other' is not present in the intransitive forms of these verbs, 'by another' is. It may be, then, that the function of *pV*-was not precisely to form reciprocal verbs, but was to form verbs where at least two participants were implicit.

Other Types

Most verbs which occur both intransitively and transitively are of one of the seven preceding types. There are some that are not. A few examples follow.

Intransitive	Transitive	English
koroiroi	*korehd*	'to scrape off'
repen	*rapahki*	'to find'
uhpaup	*uhpe*	'to poison fish'
wai	*waine*	'to sneak'

These verbs are irregular with respect to the types established above.

COMBINING FORMS OF VERBS

5.2.4   Many verb roots in Poapean that have transitive forms also have **combining forms** (a term first suggested by Sheldon Harrison). Combining forms of verbs combine with nouns to form two-word verbs. To illustrate, let us consider the verb 'to pleat'. This verb has a transitive form which is *ihkose* and an intransitive form which is *ihkos*. These two sentences are then possible.

(a) *I pahn ihkose likou ehu.*
     'I will pleat a dress.'

(b) *I pahn ihkos.*
     'I will pleat.'

But, a third sentence similar to sentence (a) is also possible.

(c) *I pahn ihkoslikou.*
     'I will dress-pleat.'

This sentence illustrates this verb root in a combining form; *ihkos* combines with the noun *likou* to produce the two-word verb *ihkoslikou*.

There are at least three points about a construction like *ihkoslikou* that we need to consider: the form of the verb that occurs, its relationship to the noun that it combines with, and the kind of translation that is appropriate. In order to consider each of these points in more detail, let us examine other verbs that have combining forms. Following are some examples.

Transitive	Intransitive	Combining Form	English
leke	*lek*	*lek-*	'to slash or castrate'
ngkoale	*ngkoal*	*ngkoal-*	'to make sennit'
peieki	*peiek*	*peiek-*	'to slide'
pereki	*perek*	*perek-*	'to unroll'

The combining forms of these verbs may occur with nouns to form two-word verbs, as in these examples.

Noun	English	With a Verb	English
pwihk	'pig'	*lekpwihk*	'to pig-castrate'
pwehl	'sennit'	*ngkoalpwehl*	'to sennit-make'
tuhke	'stick, log'	*peiektuhke*	'to log-slide'
lohs	'mat'	*pereklos*	'to mat-unroll'

In the case of these verbs, the combining form of the verb is identical to the form of the intransitive verb. This is not always the case, though, as these verbs illustrate.

Transitive	Intransitive	Combining Form	English
daper	*dapadap*	*dap-*	'to catch'
par	*pereper*	*per-*	'to cut'
rese	*rasaras*	*ras-*	'to saw'

Examples of the combining forms of these verbs in combination with a noun follow.

Noun	English	With a Verb	English
mpwei	'ball'	*dapmpwei*	'to ball-catch'
sumwumw	'trochus'	*persumwumw*	'to trochus-cut'
tuhke	'log, stick'	*rastuhke*	'to log-saw'

The intransitive and combining forms of these verbs differ. Whereas the intransitive form of the verb is reduplicated, the combining form is not. Verbs like these illustrate that combining forms of verbs are not the same as intransitive forms. Further proof of this is provided by the following transitive verbs.

Transitive Form	Combining Form	English
kang	*keng-*	'to eat'
mwowe	*mwoh-*	'to offer as a first fruit'

Combining forms of these verbs with following nouns are:

Noun	English	With a Verb	English
wini	'medicine'	*kengwini*	'to medicine-eat'
dipwisou	'thing'	*mwohdipwisou*	'to thing-offer'

These transitive verbs have no corresponding intransitive forms, but they do have combining forms. More often, however, combining forms are found with verb roots which have both transitive and intransitive forms.

While some combining forms of verbs are identical to intransitive forms, others, as we have seen, are not. In fact, combining forms seem to have more in common with transitive than with intransitive forms. Combining forms are found only with verbs which occur transitively, and like transitives, they may be followed by a noun. For these reasons, some linguists have called combining forms of verbs **pseudo-transitives**. This is not an inappropriate name; however, for the sake of simplicity we will continue to employ the term 'combining form' in this grammar.

Intransitive verb forms, as we have previously noted, do not occur with following nouns or noun phrases which function as objects of the verb. Combining forms and transitive forms do. There are several important differences, however, between the kinds of objects that occur with combining forms and with transitive forms. Consider these two sentences.

(a) *I pahn pereki lohso.*
     'I will unroll that mat.'

(b) *I pahn pereklos.*
     'I will mat-unroll.'

In sentence (a), which employs the transitive verb *pereki* 'to unroll', the noun *lohs* 'mat' follows in combination with the demonstrative modifier *-o*. In sentence (b), which employs the combining form of this verb, *perek-*, the same noun follows. But notice in this sentence that: (1) no demonstrative modifier is employed; (2) the word for mat is *los* with a short vowel (whereas in sentence (a) it is long); and (3) *los* is written attached to the verb.

In the case of sentence (a), the demonstrative modifier *-o* is actually optional. Thus, both of these sentences are grammatical.

I pahn pereki lohso.
'I will unroll that mat.'

I pahn pereki lohs.
'I will unroll mats.'

The second sentence, which employs the noun *lohs* in a generic sense, might be used to describe the kind of work one will do in a warehouse full of mats. With a noun following a combining form of a verb, however, the use of a demonstrative modifier is not permitted. A sentence like **I pahn perekloso* is ungrammatical. More generally, we might say that only a noun can be used with a combining form of a verb, never a noun phrase.

The difference in the length of the vowel of *lohs* in the phrases *pereki lohs* and *pereklos* is a consequence of the fact that a noun following a combining form of a verb is usually tightly bound to that verb in a manner analogous to compounding. Thus, the monosyllabic noun vowel lengthening rule that produces a form like *lohs* does not apply here, since *los* is part of the verb and is not standing alone as an independent word. This is one reason why combining forms of verbs are commonly written together with the nouns that follow them.

It is not true, however, that the lengthening of the vowels of monosyllabic nouns never takes place in constructions of this type. In forms like the following, lengthening does occur.

Noun	English	Combining Form	English
uhk	'net'	*dowuhk*	'to net-weave'
uht	'banana'	*sapuht*	'to banana-harvest'

With the construct suffix, the vowels in these nouns are short, as demonstrated below.

Noun	English	Construct Form	English
uhk	'net'	*ukin*	'net of'
uht	'banana'	*utun*	'banana of'

The fact that these vowels remain long with combining forms of verbs is somewhat unexpected. This may be due to the difference in the degree to which the native speaker thinks of these two-word verbs as single units. In some instances, of course, the length of the vowel of a monosyllabic noun in a combining form is due to the fact that the vowel is inherently long. Thus, one says *lekpwihk* 'to pig-castrate' where the vowel in the word *pwihk* is long. But the vowel in this word is always long, even in the construct form, which is *pwihken*.

The important point here is that the noun which follows a combining form of a verb is quite different in terms of its relationship with that verb than a noun or noun phrase which follows a transitive verb. Because the noun that follows a combining form of a verb has the various properties described above, it is sometimes called an **incorporated object**. That is, the noun is incorporated as part of the verb, both phonologically and in terms of meaning.

In terms of meaning, we have generally described combining forms of verbs plus their incorporated object as two-word verbs. A few more words about the translations we have given these constructions might now be appropriate. Consider two sentences like the following.

(a)   *I pahn pereki lohs.*

(b)   *I pahn pereklos.*

We previously examined these two sentences; the translations that we gave them were for sentence (a) 'I will unroll mats' and for sentence (b) 'I will mat-unroll.' The difference in meaning between these two sentences is not great, but it might be characterized in the following way. In sentence (a), the action that is being engaged in is one of unrolling. What is being unrolled are mats, as opposed to sheets, blankets, sails, etc. In sentence (b), however, the action that is being engaged in is one that is named by the speaker as mat-unrolling, where both the idea of unrolling and mats share in describing the action. The translation of these kinds of construction has generally been accomplished by placing the noun before the verb to produce verbs like 'net-weave', 'banana-harvest', and 'pig-castrate'. These verbs are very much like the English verbs 'to babysit' or 'to flycast'. However, whereas verbs like these are not very common in English, there are many such constructions in Ponapean.

One final point about combining forms of verbs is that when verbal suffixes occur with these forms, they are placed after the incorporated object, as these examples demonstrate.

(a) *I kengwiniher.*
'I have medicine-taken.'

(b) *I kengwinihla.*
'I completed my medicine-taking.'

In these sentences, the verbal suffixes -*ehr* and -*la* are placed after *kengwini*. (The meaning of these suffixes and their allomorphs will be explained in section 5.4.) When the transitive verb form *kang* is used, these suffixes must be placed immediately after the verb.

(a) *I kangehr winio.*
'I have taken that medicine.'

(b) *I kangala winio.*
'I took all of that medicine.'

These facts provide one more reason why we wish to treat combining forms of verbs plus their incorporated objects as single units in Ponapean.

VERBAL PREFIXES

5.3   There are five verbal prefixes in Ponapean: the causative prefix *ka-*, the two negative prefixes *sa-* and *sou-*, and two other meaning modifying prefixes, *ak-* and *li-*. The order of these prefixes before a verb root is summarized in the following chart.

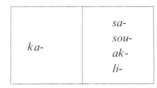

As this chart illustrates, only the prefix *ka-* may co-occur with another prefix, and, if it does, it occurs first. Therefore, while *ka-* may precede any one of the prefixes of the second position, no examples have been found of second position prefixes in combination with each other. Further information about each of these prefixes is presented in the following discussions.

THE CAUSATIVE PREFIX *ka-*

5.3.1   We previously encountered the prefix *ka-* in the discussion of numerals, where we described its function as being one of forming ordinal from cardinal numerals. Therefore, *kapahieu* 'fourth' comes from *ka-* plus *pahieu* 'four'. In combination with verbs, however, *ka-* functions as a **causative prefix**.

To understand why *ka-* is called a causative prefix, let us consider its function with a verb of the subclass we labeled adjective. An adjective like *luwak* 'jealous' may be used in a sentence like the following.

> *Liho luwak.*
> 'That woman is jealous.'

Combined with the prefix *ka-*, two other forms of this adjective are possible, as the following sentences illustrate.

(a) *Liho kaluwak.*
     'That woman was caused to be jealous.'

(b) *Liho kaluwaka lihet.*
     'That woman caused this woman to be jealous.'

The translations of the two forms *kaluwak* and *kaluwaka* are somewhat awkward in English, but the reason why *ka-* is called a causative prefix should be apparent. In sentence (a) *ka* + *luwak* results in a resultative intransitive verb which we might translate as 'to be caused to be jealous.' In sentence (b) *ka* + *luwak* plus the transitivizing element *a* results in the transitive verb *kaluwaka*, which we may translate as 'to cause another to be jealous.' With both of these verbs, the notion of causation is obvious.

Among the verbs that combine with the causative prefix, only adjectives and a few resultative intransitive verbs have both intransitive and transitive causative forms. Some examples follow, where the roots listed under (a) are adjectives, while that listed under (b) is resultative.

	Verb	English	Intransitive	Transitive
(a)	*ketiket*	'to be numb'	*kaketiket*	*kaketiketih*
	mer	'to be rusty'	*kamer*	*kamere*
	tikitik	'to be small'	*katikitik*	*katikitikih*
	lelepek	'to be reliable'	*kalelepek*	*kalelepekih*
(b)	*pang*	'to be crooked'	*kapang*	*kapanga*

Only one active intransitive verb has been found which has both an intransitive and a transitive causative form when it combines with *ka-*. This is the verb *mwenge* 'to eat' which has a transitive form *kamwenge* 'to cause another to eat' or 'to feed' and an intransitive form *kamweng* which means 'to cause to be fed'.

The majority of intransitive verbs have only a transitive causative form, as these examples illustrate.

Verb	English	Transitive
mwotomwot	'to be short'	*kamwotomwotih*
pweipwei	'to be stupid'	*kapweipwei*
ok	'to be started'	*kaoke*
peserek	'to be yanked'	*kapeserekih*
lisoi	'to nod'	*kalisoi*
weid	'to walk'	*kaweid*
dir	'to be filled'	*kadirih*
dol	'to be severed'	*kadolih*

The causative prefix *ka-* also occurs with some transitive verbs, as in these examples.

ned	'to smell'	*kanedih*
reid	'to stain'	*kareidih*

Generally, though, *ka-* is more commonly found with intransitive roots. There are some intransitives, however, with which it does not occur. Among these are:

Verb	English
asi	'to sneeze'
del	'to swarm'
kahk	'to step'
lolok	'to frown'
sikel	'to tiptoe'
tip	'to be full'
ingirek	'to be smelly'
sapan	'to be generous'

Which verbs may be prefixed by *ka-* and which may not is impossible to predict at this time. Based upon the examples cited thus far, however, we may note that *ka-* occurs with some transitive verbs and many, but not all, intransitive verbs. Among the classes of intransitive verbs established in section 5.2.1, *ka-* may be prefixed to most adjectives and some resultative verbs to form both active intransitive verbs and transitive verbs. Many active and resultative intransitive verbs only combine with *ka-* to form transitive verbs. No examples have been found of either neutral or non-activity intransitive verbs prefixed by *ka-*. It may also be noted that if a verb root combines with *ka-* to form an active intransitive verb, then it will also combine with this prefix to form a transitive verb.

All the transitive causative verbs that we have examined thus far are of three types, as summarized below:

(1) *ka_____ih*

      Example: *ketiket*   *kaketiketih*
                  'to be numb'   'to cause to be numb'

Here, the causative prefix *ka-* is used in combination with the transitivizing suffix *ih-*.

(2) *ka_____plus a vowel*

      Example: *ok*   *kaoke*
                  'to be started'   'to cause to start'

The causative prefix here combines with a final vowel, either *e* or *a*, to produce the transitive form.

(3) *ka*_____∅

      Example: *weid*   *kaweid*
                  'to walk'   'to cause to walk, to lead'

With verbs like these, only the causative prefix is employed to produce a transitive form.

In all of the examples of the causative prefix we have examined thus far, this prefix has occurred only as *ka-*. But other pronunciations of this morpheme also exist, as the following examples illustrate.

Causative Form	English	Related to the Verb	English
kerir	'secret sweetheart'	*rir*	'hidden'
kedirepw	'busy, bothersome'	*direpw*	'nosy'
koasoai	'talk, story'	*soai*	'to tell a tale'
kodoudou	'to trace one's ancestry'	*dou*	'to climb'
kopwung	'trial'	*pwung*	'right, correct'

In the words in the first column, the causative prefix is pronounced *ke-* ([kɛ-]), *koa-*, or *ko-*, depending upon the quality of the first vowel of the following verb. It is probable that in these forms the causative prefix has become fused to the verb. Most native speakers fail to immediately recognize that a causative prefix is present in these words. Note also that the meanings of these words may not easily be predicted as a combination of *ka-* 'to cause to' plus the meaning of the verb. While *rir* means 'hidden', *kerir* does not mean 'to cause to be hidden', but rather 'secret sweetheart'. To say 'to cause to be hidden' *karirala* would be employed, where *ka-* is used. Generally, one might conclude that *ka-* is employed where this prefix is used productively with a predictable causative meaning. Alternate pronunciations of this prefix occur when it has become fused to the verb root, and the entire unit is treated as a single word. Some verbs like *pwung* 'to be right or correct' occur both with *ka-*, as *kapwung* 'to correct', and with an alternate form of this prefix, as *kopwung*, which has the somewhat unpredictable meaning of 'trial'.

Still, there are some cases in which alternate pronunciations of *ka-* are used where the meanings of the resulting causative forms are largely predictable. Two such examples follow.

Verb	English	Causative Form	English
pou	'to be cold'	*kopou*	'to cause to be cold'
deng	'to be taut'	*kedeng*	'to cause to be taut'

Perhaps in cases like these the causative prefix occurs so often in combination with these verbs that the causative form is treated as a single morpheme.

THE NEGATIVE PREFIX *sa-*

5.3.2   The function of the prefix *sa-* is to negate the meaning of the verb to which it is attached. Following are some examples of the usage of this prefix.

Verb	English	With *sa-*	English
kadek	'kind'	*sakadek*	'unkind'
wehwe	'to understand'	*sawehwe*	'to not understand'
pwung	'correct'	*sapwung*	'incorrect'
lelepek	'reliable'	*salelepek*	'unreliable'
peik	'obedient'	*sapeik*	'disobedient'
ese	'to know'	*sehse*	'to not know'
ahn	'to be accustomed to'	*sahn*	'to not be accustomed to'

In the last two examples, *sa* + *ese* becomes *sehse* and *sa* + *ahn* becomes *sahn*.

Alternate pronunciations of this prefix occur in forms like the following.

kehohla	'fragile'	*sekehohla*	'not fragile'
loalekeng	'intelligent'	*soaloalekeng*	'not intelligent'
koluhla	'penitent'	*sokoluhla*	'not penitent'

As with the prefix *ka-*, these alternate pronunciations of *sa-* — *se-* ([*sɛ-*]), *soa-*, and *so-* — probably occur as a result of these forms being treated as single morphemes.

In section **5**.3, the prefix *ka-* was described as coming before *sa-* when both prefixes are used with the same verb. Only a single example of such a combination has, in fact, been found. This example is *koasoakoahiek* 'inappropriate', which is from the verb *koahiek* 'to be competent'. However, note that alternate forms of both these prefixes are involved. Whether or not these prefixes may occur together as *kasa-* is not known.

The productivity of the prefix *sa-* apparently varies somewhat from one dialect area to another. In most areas, however, it seems to occur regularly with only a relatively small number of verbs, the more normal pattern of negation being that involving a separate negative marker like *sohte*. Patterns of negation like this are examined in section **6.4.4**.

THE NEGATIVE PREFIX *sou-*

5.3.3   Like *sa-*, the prefix *sou-* negates the meaning of the verb to which it is attached. However, there seems to be a subtle distinction between the function of these two prefixes. Whereas *sa-* may be translated 'not', *sou-* seems to mean 'the opposite of'. The verb *kadek* 'kind' prefixed by *sa-*, as in *sakadek*, means 'not kind'; but, it does not mean 'cruel'. On the other hand, the prefix *sou-* attached to a verb like *pisek* 'idle' does not simply mean 'not idle', but rather the opposite of idle—'busy'. Since no examples have been found of the two prefixes *sa-* and *sou-* occurring with the same verb, it is difficult to be sure if this distinction in meaning is correct.

The prefix *sou-* is limited in its productivity and occurs with only a relatively small number of verbs. Among these are the following.

Verb	English	With *sou-*	English
nsenoh	'concerned'	*sounsenoh*	'careless'
mahk	'constrained'	*soumahk*	'bold, brazen'
mwahu	'good'	*soumwahu*	'ill'
kautih	'concerned'	*soukautih*	'indifferent'

Some speakers of Ponapean also pronounce this prefix as *soh-*. Whether this is peculiar to a particular dialect or is simply an alternate pronunciation is not know.

Some verbs that may take the prefix *sou-* also occur with *ka-* as these examples illustrate.

With *sou-*	English	With *ka-*	English
soupisek	'busy'	*kasoupisek*	'to cause to be busy'
soumwahu	'ill'	*kasoumwahu*	'to cause to be ill'
soumahk	'bold, brazen'	*kasoumahk*	'to cause to be bold, brazen'

In addition to the prefix *sou-*, there is also a word *sou* which is used in negative questions. It is examined in section **6**.4.4.

THE PREFIX *ak-*

5.3.4   The prefix *ak-* 'to make a demonstration of' was previously examined in some detail in section **3**.2.2. There we noted that *ak-* may occur as *ang-* before velar consonants (as in *angkehlail* 'to rape') or with an insert vowel between it and the following root (as in *akatantat* 'to abhor'). Some additional examples of its usage follow.

lemei	'cruel, tough'	*aklemei*	'demonstrating cruelty, doing something to embarrass another'
suwei	'boastful'	*aksuwei*	'demonstrating boastfulness'
manaman	'magical, spiritual'	*akmanaman*	'to demonstrate magical or spiritual power'
inen	'straight'	*akinen*	'to demonstrate being straight (as in throwing) or proper'
uh-	'to be loyal'	*akuh*	'demonstrating loyalty'

The prefix *ak-* normally combines with adjectives, as in the first four examples above, but it does occur with a few verbs like *uh-* (normally found as *uhki*, as in *I uhki ei pwoudo* 'I'm loyal to my wife.') The resulting forms may be adjectives, as in the first, second, and fifth examples above, or they may be active verbs, as in the third and fourth examples.

The prefix *ak-* may be preceded by the causative prefix *ka-* (resulting in *kahk-*), as in the following example.

Soulik kahklapalapiala ohlo.
'Soulik caused that man to be cocky.'

THE PREFIX *li-*

5.3.5   The prefix *li-* 'given to' may be prefixed to adjectives, active intransitive verbs, or transitive verbs. All resulting forms are adjectives. Examples are:

Verb	Verb Type	English	With *li-*	English
tikitik	adjective	'little'	*litikitik*	'given to pettiness'
pirap	active intr.	'to steal'	*lipirap*	'given to stealing'
ahn	transitive	'to be used to'	*liahn*	'outgoing'

Some verbs occur with *li-* only in their reduplicated forms, as these exampes illustrate.

pei	'to fight'	*lipepei*	'given to fighting'
kouruhr	'to laugh'	*likokouruhr*	'given to laughing'

The prefix *ka-* may appear before *li-*, as in the following sentence.

Ohlo kalipirapiala pwutako.
'That man caused that boy to become given to stealing.'

VERBAL SUFFIXES

5.4   The verbal suffixes of Ponapean are listed in the following chart. This chart illustrates that following a verb there are seven positions of suffixation as well as one position which is labeled as intermediate. Suffixes of the same position may not occur together, nor may suffixes of the intermediate position co-occur with suffixes of the third and fourth positions. A vertical dotted line between suffixes of the intermediate position and suffixes of the fifth position is employed to indicate that only some suffixes of these positions may combine. While some disagreement exists among speakers as to which combinations are permissible, most informants agree that *-pene* may combine with both *-ehng* and *-sang*, *-peseng* may combine with *-sang*, but not with *-ehng*, while *-seli* never combines with either *-ehng* or *-sang*. Potentially, a verb could simultaneously occur with as many as seven suffixes, but, in fact, verbs occurring with more than three suffixes at a time are rare.

1st	2nd	3rd	4th	5th	6th	7th
-ki	*-ie*	*-da*	*-la*	*-ehng*	*-ie*	*-ehr*
	-uhk	*-di*	*-do*	*-sang*	*-uhk*	
	-∅	*-iei*	*-wei*		*-∅*	
	-kit	*-long*			*-kit*	
	-kita				*-kita*	
	-kumwa	Intermediate			*-kumwa*	
	-ira				*-ira*	
	-kitail	*-pene*			*-kitail*	
	-kumwail	*-peseng*			*-kumwail*	
	-irail	*-seli*			*-irail*	

The basic meanings or functions of each of these suffixes follow.

1st Position:
    -ki   'instrumental suffix'

2nd and 6th Positions:
    Object Pronouns

3rd Position:
    -da   'upwards'
    -di   'downwards'
    -iei   'outwards'
    -long   'inwards'

4th Position:
    -la   'there, away from you and me'
    -do   'here, by me'
    -wei   'there, by you'

5th Position:
    -ehng   'to'
    -sang   'from'

Intermediate Position:
    -pene   'together'
    -peseng   'apart'
    -seli   'scattered'

7th Position:
    -ehr   'completive suffix'

Most of these suffixes have more than one allomorph. The procedure to be employed in the following sections will be to examine each suffix individually, along with all of its allomorphs except those involving alternations in vowel length. The latter will be dealt with in section 5.4.6.

THE SUFFIX *-ki*

5.4.1   The suffix *-ki* is highly productive in Ponapean. It has at least three functions, depending upon the type of verb to which it is suffixed.

With active intransitive and transitive verbs, *-ki* functions as an **instrumental suffix**. Therefore, verbs of these types followed by *-ki* may be used in sentences where an instrument associated with the action described by the verb is expressed. An example follows.

> *I pahn ntingki pehnet.*
> I will write-with pen-this.
> 'I will write with this pen.'

Here the active intransitive verb *nting* 'to write' is suffixed by *-ki* so that the instrument used in performing the action of writing may be stated. Other examples of *-ki* with active intransitive verbs follow.

Verb	As in the Sentence
laid	*I pahn laidiki uhket.*
'to fish'	'I will fish with this net.'
pereper	*I pahn pereperiki naipet.*
'to cut'	'I will cut with this knife.'
duhdu	*I pahn duhduhki lihmwet.*
'to bathe'	'I will bathe with this sponge.'
mahlen	*I pahn mahleniki pinselet.*
'to draw'	'I will draw with this pencil.'
inou	*I pahn inouki kisin pwehlet.*
'to lash'	'I will lash with this sennit.'
doadoahk	*I pahn doadoahngki sapwelet.*
'to work'	'I will work with (use) this shovel.'

As these examples illustrate, when *-ki* is suffixed to verbs, a number of sound changes of types we have already discussed may take place. Vowel insertion may occur, as in *laid + ki* resulting in *laidiki*; vowel lengthening may occur, as in *duhdu + ki* resulting in *duhduhki*, or nasal substitution may occur, as in *doadoahk + ki* resulting in *doadoahngki*.

With active transitive verbs, a sentence like the following is possible.

> *I pahn duhpiki seriet lihmwet.*
> I will bathe-with child-this sponge-this.
> 'I will bathe this child with this sponge.'

In the sentence above, the transitive verb *duhp* 'to bathe' is suffixed by *-ki* to permit the expression of the instrument with which the bathing is done, in this case a 'sponge'. It should be noted that in sentences like the above, the order of the noun phrases expressing the object of the verb and the instrument makes no difference. Thus, the previous sentence might also be expressed this way, with the same meaning.

> *I pahn duhpiki lihmwet seriet.*
> 'I will bathe this child with this sponge.'

Common sense or the context of the situation determines whether this sentence means 'I will bathe this child with this sponge.' or 'I will bathe this sponge with this child.' Other examples of transitive verbs with *-ki* follow.

Verb	As in the Sentence
daper	*I pahn daperiki mpweio kuropet.*
'to catch'	'I will catch that ball with this glove.'
rese	*I pahn resehki tuhkeho rasaraset.*
'to saw'	'I will saw that log with this saw.'
inaur	*I pahn inauriki wahro kisin pwehlet.*
'to lash'	'I will lash that canoe with this sennit.'
weir	*I pahn weiriki pwoahro sapwelet.*
'to dig'	'I will dig that hole with this shovel.'
leke	*I pahn lekehki sahlo naipet.*
'to slash'	'I will slash that rope with this knife.'

> *par*   *I pahn pariki tuhkeho sileht.*
> 'to cut'   'I will cut that log with this adze.'

Any active intransitive verb or transitive verb that one can imagine being used with an instrumental noun phrase may take the suffix *-ki*.

With adjectives, the function of *-ki* is somewhat different. Suffixed to *lingan* 'pretty', for example, the following sentence is possible.

> *I linganiki serepeino.*
> 'I consider that girl to be pretty.'

This usage of *-ki* is perhaps best translated as 'to consider another to have the quality of.' Therefore, *lingan + ki* is used in the preceding sentence to mean 'to consider that girl to have the quality of being pretty.' This usage of *-ki* is highly productive. Following are other examples:

Verb	As in the Sentence
dehde	*I dehdehki ahmw koasoaien.*
'clear'	'I consider your story to be clear.'
edied	*I ediediki rahnwet.*
'cloudy'	'I consider today to be cloudy.'
pai	*I paiki lahpo.*
'fortunate'	'I consider that guy to be fortunate.'
lawalo	*I lawalohki pwihko.*
'wild'	'I consider that pig to be wild.'
noahrok	*I noahrongki liho.*
'greedy'	'I consider that woman to be greedy.'
tikitik	*I tikitingki wahro.*
'small'	'I consider that canoe to be small.'
sapan	*I sapaniki Soulik.*
'generous'	'I consider Soulik to be generous.'

With some adjectives, particularly those which describe emotions, *-ki* is used to mark the person, object, or event that brought about the state or condition described by the verb. The adjective *luwak* 'to be jealous', for example, may be used with -*ki* as in the following sentence.

> *I luwangki ohlo.*
> 'I am jealous of that guy.'

In this sentence, the quality of jealously is attributed to the subject of the sentence, not the object. Other verbs that work like this are:

Verb	As in the Sentence
nsensuwed	*I nsensuwediki lahpo.*
'sad'	'I am sad about that guy.'
peren	*I pereniki ohlo.*
'happy'	'I am happy for that guy.'
mwahu	*I mwahuki pwutako.*
'good'	'I like that boy.'
loaloaid	*I loaloaidiki Pohnpei.*
'homesick'	'I am homesick for Ponape.'

The meanings attributed to the sentences listed above are normally the first ones the native speaker recognizes, though it is probably possible to interpret most of these sentences as attributing the quality described by the verb to another. Thus, *I pereniki lahpo* might conceivably also be interpreted as 'I consider that guy to be happy', but this is not the first interpretation of this sentence.

For a few verbs there are two forms with -*ki*, depending upon whether the speaker attributed the quality expressed by the verb to himself or to the object of the verb. One example is *pwang* 'tired' which may occur in these sentences.

> (a) *I pwangki ohlo.*
> 'I consider that man to be tired.'

> (b) *I pwangahki ohlo.*
> 'I am tired of that man.'

In sentence (b), notice, *pwang* + *ah* + *ki* is used to mean 'to be tired of.' The function of *ah* + *ki* here is not very well understood, but it appears to be a device for deriving special transitive forms from both intransitive and transitive verbs. Some further examples are:

Transitive Verb

iang   'to accompany'   *iangahki*   'to include'

Intransitive Active Verb

rop   'to search'   *rapahki*   'to search for'

Intransitive Resultative Verb

lang   'to be hung'   *langahki*   'to hang with'

The suffix *-ki* has still other functions in addition to those we have listed above. One of these we already examined in section **3**.7.4, where it was shown that *-ki* may be used to derive verbs from nouns. It is also used in forming 'why' questions, as we shall see in section **6**.4.3. The suffix *-ki*, then, is highly productive in Ponapean.

Two alternate pronunciations of the suffix *-ki* occur when it is followed by other verbal suffixes. These alternants are illustrated in the following sentences.

(a)   *I mwahukinuhk.*
       'I like you.'

(b)   *I laidikihla uhket.*
       'I fished there with this net.'

Here we note that *-ki* also occurs as *-kin* and *-kih*; *-kin* occurs only when an object suffix of the second position follows, while *-kih* often occurs when other verbal suffixes follow. The precise conditions which lead to the vowel lengthening here (the presence of the *h*) are quite complex. They will be examined further in section **5**.4.6.

OBJECT PRONOUN SUFFIXES

5.4.2   Object pronoun suffixes occur in the 2nd and 6th positions of the verb paradigm. We already noted the basic forms of these pronouns in sections **4**.7.3 and **5**.4, but since we wish to discuss these pronouns here in further detail, it will be convenient to list them again.

	1st	*-ie*	'me'
Singular	2nd	*-uhk*	'you'
	3rd	*-0̸*	'him, her, it'
Dual/Plural	1st excl.	*-kit*	'us, exclusive'
	1st incl.	*-kita*	'us two, inclusive'
Dual	2nd	*-kumwa*	'you two'
	3rd	*-ira*	'them two'
	1st incl.	*-kitail*	'us three or more, inclusive'
Plural	2nd	*-kumwail*	'you three or more'
	3rd	*-irail*	'them three or more'

Although the forms of the object suffixes in either the 2nd or 6th positions after a verb are identical, their functions are different. Object pronouns of the 2nd position are used to replace noun phrases that are direct objects of transitive verbs or are introduced through the use of the suffix *-ki*. Examples are:

Kidio ngalisie.
'That dog bit me.'

I perenikinuhk.
'I am happy for you.'

Object pronouns of the 6th position are used only to replace noun phrases introduced by the two suffixes of the 5th position, *-ehng* and *-sang*. Examples are:

I kihengirailehr koakono.
'I have given them that box.'

I pahn tangasanguhk.
'I will run away from you.'

The kinds of noun phrases that may be introduced by *-ehng* and *-sang* will be examined in section 5.4.4.

One point not previously noted concerning object pronoun suffixes is that, when they are directly suffixed to verb roots ending in short vowels, the glide /y/ (spelled *i*) occurs between the root and the following suffix. The occurrence of this glide is illustrated in the following examples, where the object pronoun -*kumwail* 'you, plural' is employed.

ise	'to pay tribute'	*iseikumwail*	'to pay tribute to you'
wa	'to carry'	*waikumwail*	'to carry you'
doakoa	'to spear'	*doakoaikumwail*	'to spear you'

This *i* occurs with these verbs only when object pronouns directly follow.

We may also make some additional observations about each of the singular suffixes that we listed above. The first person form, spelled -*ie* 'me', has two pronunciations. One of these is /-yɛ/ and the other is /-iyɛ/. /-yɛ/ occurs after vowels or the glide /y/; /-iyɛ/ occurs elsewhere. Examples follow.

Verb	English	Conventionally Spelled with Suffix	Pronounced
mahlenih	'to draw'	*mahlenihie*	/mahlɛnihyɛ/
doakoa	'to spear'	*doakoaie*	/doakoayyɛ/
duhp	'to bathe'	*duhpie*	/duhpiyɛ/

The second person singular object pronoun also has two pronunciations. These are /-yuk/, spelled -*iuk*, and /-uhk/, spelled -*uhk*. /-yuk/ occurs after vowels or the glide /y/; /-uhk/ occurs elsewhere. Examples are:

Verb	English	Conventionally Spelled with Suffix	Pronounced
mahlenih	'to draw'	*mahlenihiuk*	/mahlenihyuk/
doakoa	'to spear'	*doakoaiuk*	/doakoayyuk/
duhp	'to bathe'	*duhpuhk*	/duhpuhk/

Finally, note that the third person singular form is listed in the preceding chart as Ø, meaning that when one wants to indicate a third person singular object (him, her, or it), no suffix is attached to the verb. Following are examples.

I wahla mwo.
'I carried (him, her, or it) there.'

I doakoa.
'I speared (him, her, or it).'

I duhp.
'I bathed (him, her, or it).'

5.4.3   Suffixes of the third, fourth, and intermediate positions are
directional suffixes. For easy reference, these suffixes are again
listed here.

3rd		4th	
-da	'upwards'	*-la*	'there, away from you and me'
-di	'downwards'	*-do*	'here, by me'
-iei	'outwards'	*-wei*	'there, by you'
-long	'inwards'		

Intermediate

-pene	'together'
-peseng	'apart'
-seli	'scattered'

All of these suffixes indicate physical locations or directions
which are indicated by the translations supplied above. In addition to these directional usages, however, many of these suffixes
have still other functions.

To discuss the various functions of these suffixes, it will be
useful to divide Ponapean verbs into two classes, based upon their
meanings. These two classes are **motion verbs** and **non-motion
verbs**. Examples of verbs of each of these classes are listed below.

Motion Verbs		Non-Motion Verbs	
tang	'to run'	*lingeringer*	'to be angry'
lus	'to jump'	*kilang*	'to see'
alu	'to walk'	*lingan*	'to be pretty'
mwemweit	'to visit'	*sar*	'to fade'
kerep	'to crawl'	*rek*	'to be abundant'

The significance of these two classes is this: with motion verbs, directional suffixes usually combine freely and have directional meanings. With non-motion verbs, the usage of directional suffixes is much more restricted, and with these verbs these suffixes usually have meanings different from their directional ones. This distinction may be illustrated by using the first verbs listed in the two columns above.

(a) *E pahn tangada.*
     'He will run upwards.'

(b) *E pahn lingeringerada.*
     'He will get angry.'

In sentence (a), which contains a verb of motion, the suffix *-da* has its literal directional meaning 'upwards'. In sentence (b), which contains a non-motion verb, the suffix *-da* has an **inchoative** meaning, indicating the onset of a state, in this case, 'anger'.

Not all directional suffixes have meanings other than directional ones, but five do. In the following discussion we will examine each of these suffixes in some detail, considering first its directional meaning and then, where relevant, its other functions. (Many examples of the figurative usages of these suffixes are from Lee, 1973.)

The Suffix *-da*

With verbs of motion, the suffix *-da* has the directional meaning of 'up' or 'upwards'. Some examples follow.

Verb	English	Plus *-da*	English
dou	'to climb'	*douda*	'to climb upwards'
alu	'to walk'	*aluhda*	'to walk upwards'
tang	'to run'	*tangada*	'to run upwards'
lang	'to be hung'	*langada*	'to be hung up'
lus	'to jump'	*lusida*	'to jump upwards'

With non-motion verbs, *-da* has at least four general figurative meanings, each of which is examined below.

(a) With adjectives, *-da* has an inchoative meaning, expressing the onset of a state. It is perhaps best translated into English as 'to get', as in these examples.

katik	'bitter'	katikada	'to get bitter'
angin	'windy'	anginada	'to get windy'
karakar	'hot'	karakarada	'to get hot.
lokalok	'restless'	lokalokada	'to get restless'
rot	'dark'	rotada	'to get dark'

(b) Another common usage of *-da* is to indicate that an action or activity has been carried through to its logical conclusion. Which verbs may take *-da* with this meaning is largely determined by the meaning of the verb. For example, verbs whose meanings are related to cooking combine with *-da* to indicate that the process of cooking has been completed and the thing being cooked is ready to be eaten, as illustrated by the following sentences.

I kukih raiso.
'I cooked that rice.'

I kukihda raiso.
'I cooked up that rice (and it is ready to be eaten).'

Other verbs of cooking that may take *-da* are listed below.

umwun	'to bake'	ainpwoate	'to cook in an iron pot'
inim	'to cook, roast, etc.'	pwoaile	'to boil'
piraine	'to fry'	suhpwih	'to make soup of'

Verbs whose meanings involve the idea of detaching something also combine with *-da* to indicate the completion of an activity, as the following sentences show.

I lapwad sahlo.
'I untied that rope.'

I lapwadida sahlo.
'I untied that rope (and it is completely united).'

Other verbs of detaching are:

| kodom | 'to husk' | kederwina | 'to scale or pluck' |
| rere | 'to skin or peel' | tehr | 'to tear' |

dolung	'to pick'	*ke*	'to remove with the teeth, to bite'

With verbs of wearing, *-da* is employed to mean that the action of putting on an item of clothing has been carried out, as illustrated by the contrast between these two sentences.

I pahn seht.
'I will wear a shirt.'

I pahn sehtda.
'I will put on a shirt.'

Examples of other verbs that work like *seht* are listed below.

rausis	'to wear trousers'	*sekid*	'to wear a jacket'
suht	'to wear shoes'	*lisoarop*	'to wear a hat'
likou	'to wear clothing'	*sidakin*	'to wear stockings'

Another group of verbs that combines with *-da* to indicate that the action named by the verb has been carried through to its logical conclusion are those whose meanings relate to acquisition or selection. For example:

I pwain dengki pwoat.
'I bought a flashlight.'

I pwainda dengki pwoat.
'I bought a flashlight (and it is in my possession).'

Other verbs of acquisition or selection are:

pil	'to choose'	*saik*	'to catch'
pwek	'to adopt'	*ahniki*	'to possess'
ale	'to take'	*naitiki*	'to be the parent of'

(c)   A third function of *-da* is illustrated by its interaction with verbs of perception or thinking, where it signals that the thing being perceived or thought of has suddenly come into one's consciousness. This function is illustrated by the verb *taman* 'to remember' in the following pair of sentences.

I taman ohlo.
'I remembered that man.'

I tamanda ohlo.
'I suddenly remembered that man.'

Examples of other verbs that interact with *-da* like *taman* are listed below.

kilang	'to see'	*leme*	'to believe'
rong	'to hear'	*dehm*	'to feel around for'
song	'to try'	*kehn*	'to feel, to experience'
ned	'to smell'	*medewe*	'to think'

(d)   Still one other function of *-da* is its use to indicate that an action was performed accidentally. Generally, this usage of *-da* occurs with verbs which name bodily activities over which one normally has control. A verb like *kang* 'to eat' may be used for purposes of illustration.

I kang rais.
'I ate rice.'

I kangada loahngo.
'I accidentally ate that fly.'

Other verbs which combine with *-da* with an accidental meaning follow.

mwohd	'to sit'	*sok*	'to step'
nim	'to drink'	*tiak*	'to step'

Further study will perhaps reveal additional figurative usages of this suffix. The discussion here is by no means complete, nor in fact are any of the following discussions of the figurative usages of directional suffixes. The study of these usages remains a rich area for future research.

The Suffix *-di*

With verbs of motion, the suffix *-di* has the directional meaning of 'down' or 'downwards', as illustrated by these examples.

Verb	English	With *-di*	English
pwupw	'to fall'	*pwupwidi*	'to fall down'

lus	'to jump'	*lusidi*	'to jump down'
kiris	'to slip'	*kirisidi*	'to slip down'
dou	'to climb'	*doudi*	'to climb down'
kese	'to drop'	*kesehdi*	'to drop down'

With some non-motion verbs, *-di* is used like *-da* to indicate that an action has been carried through to its logical conclusion. This usage of *-di* is largely restricted to verbs whose meanings are related to confining or securing, as illustrated by the following two sentences.

E pwakih tieho.
'He chased that deer.'

E pwakihdi tieho.
'He chased down that deer.'

Other verbs of confining or securing are:

ilewe	'to secure a canoe'	*lidipih*	'to trap'
pile	'to pick with a pole'	*parok*	'to catch something animate'
doakoa	'to spear'	*salih*	'to tie'
daper	'to catch'		

The Suffix *-iei*

With verbs of motion, the suffix *-iei* means 'out' or 'outwards'. This suffix has a number of alternate pronunciations that are illustrated below.

After vowels and glides, this suffix is pronounced /-yey/, as these examples illustrate.

Verb + iei	Pronounced	Spelled	English
koh + *iei*	/kohyey/	*kohiei*	'to go out'
wah + *iei*	/wahyey/	*wahiei*	'to carry out'

After consonants, one possible pronunciation of this suffix is /-iyey/, as shown by these examples.

| *lus* + *iei* | /lusiyey/ | *lusiei* | 'to jump out' |
| *tang* + *iei* | /tangiyey/ | *tangiei* | 'to run out' |

Another pronunciation that occurs after consonants is /-ehy/, as in these examples.

lus + iei	/lusehy/	*lusehi*	'to jump out'
tang + iei	/tangehy/	*tangehi*	'to run out'

Both /-iyey/ and /-ehy/ are apparently used by most speakers of Ponapean.

Still one other pronunciation of this suffix that sometimes occurs when other suffixes follow is *-ih*. This alternant is illustrated in the following examples, where the suffix *la* 'there, away from us' is used after *-iei*.

koh + iei + la	/kohyeyla/	*kohieila*	'to go out there'
	or	or	
	/kohihla/	*kohihla*	
lus + iei + la	/lusiyeyla/	*lusieila*	'to jump out there'
	or	or	
	/lusihla/	*lusihla*	

The usage of *-ih* as an alternant of *-iei*, as these examples illustrate, is not dependent upon whether the verb stem ends in a consonant or vowel. Rather, it depends upon the presence of a following suffix. Some speakers of Ponapean, however, report that they never employ the alternate form *-ih*.

Unlike the previous two suffixes, no examples of this suffix with a figurative usage were found.

The Suffix *-long*

The suffix *-long* is used with verbs of motion to indicate the direction 'inwards' or 'into'. Examples of the use of this suffix follow.

Verb	English	Plus *-long*	English
alu	'to walk'	*aluhlong*	'to walk into'
duwal	'to squeeze through'	*duwallong*	'to squeeze through into'
ir-	'to penetrate'	*irilong*	'to penetrate into'
tang	'to run'	*tangolong*	'to run into'

Like *-iei*, *-long* has not been found to occur with figurative meanings.

The Suffix *-la*

With verbs of motion, the suffix *-la* indicates the direction 'there, away from you and me'. Examples of the use of this suffix are presented below where, for the sake of brevity, it is simply translated 'there'.

daur	'to climb'	*daurla*	'to climb there'
koh-	'to come or go'	*kohla*	'to go there'
sangk	'to commute'	*sangkila*	'to commute there'
tang	'to run'	*tangala*	'to run there'
weid	'to walk'	*weidila*	'to walk there'

With non-motion verbs, *-la* has at least three common figurative usages.

a) With adjectives, *-la* is used to indicate that a new state exists that has come about as a result of a gradual change from some previous state. This usage of *-la* is illustrated by the contrast between the following pairs of sentences.

Soulik mworourou.
'Soulik is fat.'

Soulik mworouroula.
'Soulik became fat.'

The first sentence simply describes the condition of Soulik as being 'fat'. The second sentence indicates that the state of being fat came about over a period of time, and there was some previous time when Soulik was not fat. Other adjectives that combine with *-la* in this way follow.

laud	'big or old'	*laudala*	'to become big or old'
reirei	'long or tall'	*reireila*	'to become long or tall'
tihti	'skinny'	*tihtihla*	'to become skinny'
tikitik	'small'	*tikitikala*	'to become small'
suwed	'bad'	*suwedala*	'to become bad'
luwet	'weak'	*luwetala*	'to become weak'

(b) The suffix *-la*, like both *-da* and *-di*, is used with some non-motion verbs to indicate that the action or activity named by the verb has been carried through to its logical conclusion. This usage is common with verbs whose meanings are broadly related to the loss or disappearance of something, as illustrated by the contrast between these two sentences.

E sar.
'It faded.'

E sarala.
'It completely faded.'

Examples of other verbs like *sar* are:

sehse	'to not know'	*sehsehla*	'to completely not know'
kese	'to throw'	*kesehla*	'to discard'
salong	'hard to find'	*salongala*	'to be invisible'

There are also some verbs whose meanings are not related to the loss or disappearance of something that behave with this suffix in a parallel manner. Examples are:

kang	'to eat'	*kangala*	'to completely eat'
nim	'to drink'	*nimala*	'to completely drink'
nek	'to finish'	*nekila*	'to completely finish'

c)   Still one other highly productive use of the suffix *-la* is to indicate that an action or activity is carried out without undue delay. For example, when talking about someone who was seasick, we might say *E mmwusila; eri, e solahr soumwahu.* 'He went ahead and vomited; consequently, he is no longer sick.' Notice that when *-la* is suffixed to *mmwus* 'vomit', the resulting form means 'go ahead and vomit.' This usage of *-la* is highly productive and commonly occurs in commands, as in the following examples.

mwenge	'to eat'	*Mwengehla!*	'Go ahead and eat!'
sukusuk	'to pound kava'	*Sukusukila*	'Go ahead and pound kava!'
doaloa	'to mix'	*Doaloahla!*	'Go ahead and mix it!'
lokaia	'to talk'	*Lokaiahla!*	'Go ahead and talk!'

In the beginning of this discussion of verbal affixes, we noted that suffixes of the same position may not occur together. Therefore, one can not use both -*da* 'upwards' and -*di* 'downwards' with the same verb. Such a combination would make no sense. It is possible, however, for the suffix -*la* to occur with other suffixes of the fourth position when it is employed in the sense described here of urging one to carry out an action. Therefore, commands like the following are possible.

Komw ketdohla!
'Come on and come here!'

Wahweila pwuhke mwo!
'Go ahead and take this book there!'

In these examples, the suffix -*la* follows -*do* 'here, by me' and -*wei* 'there, by you' which like -*la* are suffixes of the fourth position. This combining of fourth position suffixes occurs only when -*la* has this particular figurative function.

The derivational function of -*la* was already discussed in section 3.7.4. It is mentioned here only as a reminder that this is still one additional usage of this suffix.

The Suffix -*do*

The suffix -*do* is used with verbs of motion with the directional meaning 'here, by me'. Examples of this usage of -*do* follow.

pei	'to float'	*peido*	'to float here'
mwemweit	'to visit'	*mwemweitdo*	'to visit here'
sei	'to paddle'	*seido*	'to paddle here,
kese	'to throw'	*kesehdo*	'to throw here'
alu	'to walk'	*aluhdo*	'to walk here'

No figurative usages of -*do* have been discovered.

The Suffix -*wei*

The suffix -*wei* is used with verbs of motion to indicate the direction 'there, by you'. Examples follow.

tang	'to run'	*tangewei*	'to run there by you'
padok	'to plant'	*padokewei*	'to plant there by you'

moahl	'to pass by'	*moahlewei*	'to pass by there by you'
tapwur	'to roll'	*tapwurewei*	'to roll there by you'
kerep	'to creep'	*kerepewei*	'to creep there by you'

Like *-do*, *-wei* has not been found to occur with figurative meanings.

The Suffix *-pene*

With verbs of motion, the suffix *-pene* may be translated as 'toward one another' or 'together'. Examples are:

koh-	'to come or go'	*kohpene*	'to come toward one another'
wa	'to carry'	*wapene*	'to carry together, to gather'
kih-	'to give or take'	*kihpene*	'to take together, to gather'
alu	'to walk'	*alupene*	'to walk toward one another'
pihr	'to fly'	*pihrpene*	'to fly toward one another'

With many verbs which marginally denote motion, *-pene* has essentially this same meaning. 'Together' is usually the best translation for *-pene* with these verbs, as the next examples illustrate.

salih	'to tie'	*salihpene*	'to tie together'
pouse	'to connect'	*pousepene*	'to connect together'
ingid	'to braid'	*ingidpene*	'to braid together'
lim	'to fold'	*limpene*	'to fold together'
rukoa	'to chew'	*rukoapene*	'to chew together'

With adjectives, the suffix *-pene* has at least three distinct meanings, depending upon the meaning of the adjective involved. With those expressing qualities, *-pene* has a reciprocal meaning and might be translated as 'to or of each other'. For example:

mwahu	'good'	*mwahupene*	'good to each other'
luwak	'jealous'	*luwakpene*	'jealous of each other'
suwed	'bad'	*suwedpene*	'bad to each other'
materek	'lucky'	*materekpene*	'lucky for each other'

maiai	'unfortunate'	maiaipene	'unfortunate for each other'

With many other adjectives expressing qualities, where a reciprocal meaning would be meaningless, *-pene* is used to indicate 'totality', that all the items being described have a particular quality. This usage is illustrated by the following sentence.

Uht kau matpene.
'Those bananas are all ripe.'

Other examples of adjectives that combine with *-pene* with this meaning are:

soumwahu	'sick'	*soumwahupene*	'all sick'
lukuluk	'asthmatic'	*lukulukpene*	'all asthmatic'
mah	'old'	*mahpene*	'all old'

With adjectives expressing size, *-pene* may be employed to indicate a decrease in size, as these examples illustrate.

tihti	'skinny'	*tihtipene*	'to get skinnier'
tikitik	'small'	*tikitikpene*	'to get smaller'
menipinip	'thin'	*menipinimpene*	'to get thinner'
tehtik	'narrow'	*tehtikpene*	'to get narrower'

The Suffix *-peseng*

With motion verbs, the suffix *-peseng* has the directional meaning of 'apart', indicating that two or more things are moving away from each other. This meaning is illustrated in the following sentence, where *-peseng* is suffixed to the verb *alu* 'to walk'.

Ira alupeseng.
they walk-apart
'They walked away from each other.'

Examples of the use of *-peseng* with other verbs follow.

tang	'to run'	*tangpeseng*	'to run apart'
sei	'to paddle'	*seipeseng*	'to paddle apart'
sepe	'to cut'	*sepepeseng*	'to cut apart'

suk	'to pound'	*sukpeseng*	'to pound apart'
tehr	'to tear'	*tehrpeseng*	'to tear apart'
lapwad	'to untie'	*lapwadpeseng*	'to untie apart'

For many of these examples, the translation 'into pieces' is also appropriate. Therefore, *tehrpeseng* may be translated either 'to tear apart' or 'to tear into pieces'.

With adjectives expressing size, *-peseng* is used to indicate an increase in size, as in the next examples.

lapala	'large'	*lapalapeseng*	'to get larger'
moasul	'thick'	*moasulpeseng*	'to get thicker'
tehlap	'wide'	*tehlampeseng*	'to get wider'
laud	'big'	*laudpeseng*	'to get bigger'
reirei	'long'	*reireipeseng*	'to get longer'

Notice that the meaning of *-peseng* here is opposite that of *-pene*, which is used to indicate a decrease in size.

The Suffix *-seli*

The suffix *-seli* used in combination with verbs of motion indicates scattered, random movement, without definite direction. It may be translated into English as 'around' or 'here and there'. Examples of the use of this suffix follow.

tang	'to run'	*tangseli*	'to run around'
mwemweit	'to visit'	*mwemweitseli*	'to visit around'
alu	'to walk'	*aluseli*	'to walk around'
seisei	'to paddle'	*seiseiseli*	'to paddle around'
pekipek	'to beg'	*pekipekseli*	'to go around begging'

No figurative usages of this suffix have been found.

Summary of the Figurative Usages of Directional Suffixes

In the preceding pages, we examined ten directional suffixes. Of these, five were found to occur with figurative meanings, while five were not, as summarized below.

With Figurative Meanings	No Figurative Meanings
-da	*-iei*
-di	*-long*

-la	-do
-pene	-wei
-peseng	-seli

Since the figurative usages that we established thus far are quite numerous, and, in some instances, overlapping, the following summary of these usages is provided.

Figurative Meaning	Suffix	Verb Type
(a) to get	-da	adjectives
(b) to become	-la	adjectives
(c) to signify that an action or activity has been carried through to its logical conclusion	-da	verbs of cooking, detaching, wearing, acquiring and selecting
	-la	verbs of loss or disappearance
	-di	verbs of confining or securing
(d) to signal a thought or sense has come into one's consciousness	-da	verbs of perception or thinking
(e) accidental action	-da	verbs of bodily activities
(f) to signal an action or activity is carried out without undue delay	-la	intransitive verbs
(g) reciprocal meaning	-pene	adjectives
(h) totality	-pene	adjectives expressing qualities where a reciprocal meaning makes no sense
(i) decrease in size	-pene	adjectives of size
(j) increase in size	-peseng	adjectives of size

The distinction made between the first two of these figurative meanings, which have been translated as 'to get' and 'to become', is rather subtle and deserves further comment. Basically, both of these figurative meanings involve a change of state. However, -da indicates the onset of a new state, while *-la* is used to indicate that a new state exists that came about over a period of time. This contrast in meaning is illustrated by following sentences, where these two suffixes are employed with the adjective *lengk* 'acrophobic'.

> *Soulik lengkida eh lel nan koadoken mahio.*
> 'Soulik got acrophobic when he reached the top of the breadfruit tree.'

> *Soulik lengkila eh mahla.*
> 'Soulik became acrophobic as he grew older.'

The usage of these two suffixes to indicate a change of state is very productive. They may be combined with any adjective where the resulting meaning makes sense.

In the case of the third figurative meaning that we listed, that of signifying that an action or activity has been carried through to its logical conclusion, three suffixes are involved. These are *-da*, *-la*, and *-di*. The choice of which of these suffixes to use is largely determined by the meaning of the verb involved. Some of the meaning classes which determine this choice are listed above. Here, though, our discussion remains far from complete. Almost certainly, not all verbs that may take one of these three suffixes to indicate completed action fit into one of the classes listed above. Providing more detailed information here is one of the many tasks that remains for future investigators of Ponapean.

No doubt, with further work in this area, still other figurative usages of directional suffixes will be found. That it will be possible to make accurate generalizations about all figurative usages of directional suffixes, though, is highly unlikely. In many instances the meaning that results when a verb is combined with one of these suffixes is **idiomatic**. For example, the verb *tiak* means 'to step on'. In combination with *-di* 'downwards', however, the meaning of this verb shifts. Therefore, *tiakidi* means 'to interrupt some serious activity'. Other examples follow.

pwupw	'to fall'	*pwupwala*	'to be lost'
padok	'to plant'	*padokewei*	'to speak the truth'
awih	'to wait'	*awihedi*	'to await someone at a point approximately halfway to his/her destination'

eng	'to spend the night'	*engida*	'to have sexual intercourse'
isik	'to set fire to'	*isikala*	'to propitiate a spirit'

THE SUFFIXES -*ehng* AND -*sang*

5.4.4   The two verbal suffixes found in the fifth position of the verb paradigm are -*ehng* and -*sang*. A unique feature of these morphemes, however, is that in addition to functioning as suffixes, they may also occur as separate words. More detailed examinations of each of these suffixes follow.

The Suffix -*ehng*

Before we consider the meaning of the suffix -*ehng*, let us examine its various allomorphs. These may be described as follows.

The allomorph -*ehng* (/-ɛhng/) occurs after verb roots or preceding verbal suffixes ending in consonants. Examples with consonant final verb roots follow.

Verb	English	With -*ehng*
nehk	'to distribute'	*nehkehng*
mwadong	'to play'	*mwadongehng*
liseian	'to be pregnant'	*liseianehng*
mweid	'to allow'	*mweidehng*
lopuk	'to cut'	*lopukehng*

The next examples involve consonant final suffixes.

duhp + *irail*	'to bathe them'	*duhpirailehng*
tang + *long*	'to run into'	*tangolongehng*

After verbs or verbal suffixes ending in vowels or glides, the situation is more complex. After such verbs, this suffix is pronounced either -*ieng* (/-yɛng/) or -*weng* (/-wɛng/), -*weng* being the more common form after final -*o*, -*u*, or -*w*. Examples follow.

limwih	'to sponge'	*limwihieng*
nehne	'to distribute'	*nehnehieng*
wa	'to carry'	*wahieng*

doakoa	'to spear'	*doakoahieng*
koh-	'to come or go'	*kohweng* or *kohieng*
tu	'to meet'	*tuhweng* or *tuhieng*
mwahu	'to be good'	*mwahuweng* or *mwahuieng*

Following vowel final suffixes of the first and second positions of suffixation, these same allomorphs occur, as in these examples.

nting + *ki*	'to write + with'	*ntingkiieng*
mahlenih + *ira*	'to draw + them'	*mahlenihiraieng*

With verbal suffixes of the third or fourth positions ending in high vowels (*di* is in fact the only example) this same description of allomorphs applies. However, after verbal suffixes of these positions ending in non-high vowels or glides, still other allomorphs occur. These alternants are illustrated in the following examples.

tang + *da*	'to run + upwards'	*tangadahng*
tang + *la*	'to run + there'	*tangalahng*
tang + *do*	'to run + here'	*tangodohng*
tang + *iei*	'to run + out'	*tangieiieng*
tang + *wei*	'to run + there'	*tangewehng*

After suffixes of these positions ending in non-high vowels (*a* and *o* in these examples), the form of this suffix is not *-ieng*, as it was after verbs and suffixes of the second position ending in these vowels, but rather the forms *-dahng*, *-lahng*, and *-dohng* result. Another peculiarity is that following the suffix *-iei*, *-ieng* is employed, but after the suffix *-wei*, *-wehng* occurs, *-weiieng* not being possible.

Describing the forms of this suffix, as we have seen, is somewhat complicated. Also complex are its functions. In general, we may say that this suffix permits the expression of an additional noun phrase with any verb to which it is suffixed. With intransitive motion verbs, *-ehng* normally occurs in combination with one of the directional suffixes of the third or fourth positions to mean 'to' or 'towards', as in these sentences.

I pahn alulahng ohlo.
I will walk-there-to man-that
'I will walk to that man.'

I pahn seilahng mwahmw akau.
I will paddle-there-to fish those
'I will paddle to those fish.'

I papalahng wahro.
I swim-there-to canoe-that
'I swam to that canoe.'

Here -*ehng* is employed with a following noun phrase to express the **goal** of the motion; therefore, the motion has some purpose in relation to what is expressed in the following noun phrase. With intransitive non-motion verbs, the function of -*ehng* to express purpose is more obvious, as these sentences illustrate.

Lampo langehng wiesakau.
lamp-that hung-for do-kava
'That lamp was hung for the kava preparation.'

Naipet adahdehng doadoahk en lakapw.
knife-this sharpen-for work of tomorrow
'This knife was sharpened for tomorrow's work.'

Pwuhket wiawidahng mehn Pohnpei.
book-this do-for one-of Ponape
'This book was written for Ponapeans.'

Used with adjectives, -*ehng* may also be translated 'for' in the sense of 'in relation to', as in these examples.

Sehto laudehng lahpo.
shirt-that big-for guy-that
'That shirt is big for that guy.'

Doadoahko mwahuweng ohlo.
work-that good-for man-that
'That work is good for that man.'

E pahieng ah lisoaropo.
he suited-for his hat-that
'He is suited for that hat.' or 'He looks good in that hat.'

With transitive verbs, which require a following noun phrase representing the object of the verb, the suffix -*ehng* permits the expression of a second noun phrase which expresses the one who benefits from or is the recipient of the action expressed by the verb. Examples follow.

> *I pahn lopukehng ohlo sehu.*
> I will cut-for man-that sugarcane
> 'I will cut sugarcane for that man.'

> *I kak walahng ohlo koakono.*
> I can carry-for man-that box-that
> 'I can carry that box for that man.'

> *I en kihieng lahpo pwuhket.*
> I should give-to guy-that book-this
> 'I should give this book to that guy.'

This suffix, as we noted, may also occur as a separate word. In this case, it is pronounced /oang/, but it is usually spelled *ong*. An example follows.

> *Ong mehn wai, e pahn apwal.*
> for one-of abroad, it will difficult
> 'For foreigners, it will be difficult.'

A more common way to say this sentence, though, is as follows.

> *E pahn apwalehng mehn wai.*
> 'It will be difficult for foreigners.'

Examples where *ong* is found as a separate word are rather rare. They generally occur only when the main verb of the sentence is a common adjective like *mengei* 'easy', *apwal* 'difficult', or *sakanakan* 'bad', or as part of a phrase that might be used as an introduction to a memo or an announcement, as in *ong mehn Pohnpei koaros* 'to all Ponapeans'.

The Suffix *-sang*

The suffix *-sang*, like *-ehng*, permits the expression of an additional noun phrase with any verb to which it is suffixed. Its meanings, however, are essentially opposite those of *-ehng*.

With intransitive motion verbs, *-sang* is used to express the source of an action, and may be translated 'from' as in these examples.

I aluhlahsang ohlo.
I walk-there-from man-that
'I walked away from that man.'

I papasang wahro.
I swim-from canoe-that
'I swam away from the canoe.'

I tangasang sounpadahkᴏ.
I run-from teacher-that
'I fled from that teacher.'

With adjectives, *-sang* means 'in opposition to' and is used in **comparative** constructions. Examples follow.

Pwihke laudsang pwihko.
pig-this big-in-opposition-to pig-that
'This pig is bigger than that pig.'

Nih reireisang uht.
coconut tall-in-opposition-to banana
'Coconut trees are taller than banana trees.'

Sahpw kesempwalsang mwohni.
land important-in-opposition-to money
'Land is more important than money.'

In section 5.2.1 we noted that superlative forms may be formed by the suffix *-ie*. Another way to form the superlative is by use of the ordinal numeral *keieu* 'first'. Thus, the full range of comparative constructions in Ponapean is illustrated by the following sentences.

Pwihke laudsang pwihko.
'This pig is bigger than that pig.'

Pwihke lahudie.
'This pig is the biggest.'

Pwihke me keieu laud.
'This pig is the biggest.'

The use of this suffix with transitive verbs is largely confined to verbs whose meanings are related to 'removing', 'separating', or 'taking away', where it may be translated 'from' or 'off'. Some examples follow.

Resehsang imwin tuhkehn.
saw-off end-of board-by-you
'Saw off the end of the board.'

E sepehsang nehn pwihko.
he cut-off leg-of pig-that
'He cut off that pig's leg.'

Other transitive verbs which may combine with -*sang* with this same meaning follow.

rakih	'to claw'	*widen*	'to wash'
ripe	'to move, of lids'	*rihs*	'to break'
us	'to pull out'	*sapwad*	'to untie'
siped	'to shake out'	*tehr*	'to tear'

Like -*ehng*, the suffix -*sang* sometimes occurs as a separate word. As with -*ehng*, examples like this are found when -*sang* is suffixed to common adjectives. Thus, the following two sentences are posible, though the first is considered by some speakers to be more correct.

Sehte, I mwahukihsang sehto.
I mwahuki sehte sang sehto.
'I like this shirt better than that shirt.'

Sang also occurs as a separate word in 'from . . . to' expressions involving distance or duration, as these examples illustrate.

Ahlo sakanakan sang irepen wehin Uh kohkohla.
road-that bad from border-of state-of Uh going
'The road is bad from the Uh border on.'

Soulik sohte pahn doadoahk sang Niehd lel Niepeng.
Soulik not will work from Monday reach Thursday
'Soulik will not work from Monday until Thursday.'

Sang also functions as an independent word when it is used to denote the source or origin of things, as the following examples illustrate.

Re kin wiahda likou sang ni nih oh mahi.
they habitually make-up cloth from at coconut and breadfruit
'They make cloth from coconut and breadfruit trees.'

> *Ih ansou me re tepin wiahda sakau sang ni nih.*
> it time one they begin-to make-up intoxicating-drink from at coconut
> 'That was the time when they began to make an intoxicating drink from coconut trees.'

> *Aramas akan tepidahr wapene pwehl oh takai sang ni deke doh teikan.*
> person those begin-up-perfective bring-together earth and rock from at island distant other-plural
> 'Those people had begun to gather earth and rocks from other distant islands.'

THE PERFECTIVE SUFFIX *-ehr*

5.4.5   The suffix *-ehr* occurs in the seventh and final position of the verb paradigm. Used to indicate completed action, it is often best translated into English as 'have . . . already'. Notice the difference in meaning between the following two sentences, where this suffix used in combination with *-la* is pronounced *-lahr*.

> *I tangala Kolonia.*
> 'I ran to Kolonia.'

> *I tangalahr Kolonia.*
> 'I have already run to Kolonia.'

The suffix *-ehr* has more than one prononunication. In fact, its range of forms parallels those of *-ehng*, as summarized below.

Allomorph	Position	Example
-ehr	After consonants	*mwadongehr* 'to have already played'
-ier	After verb roots and non-directional suffixes ending in vowels	*nehnehier* 'to have already distributed'

After directional suffixes, the rules above are employed, except with the suffixes *-da*, *-la*, *-do*, *-wei* and *-pene*, where assimilation occurs, resulting in *-dahr*, *-lahr*, *-dohr*, *-wehr*, and *-penehr*.

Further discussion and examples of the use of this suffix are presented in section 5.7, which deals with aspect in Ponapean.

ALTERNATIONS IN VOWEL LENGTH IN THE VERB PARADIGM

5.4.6   At the beginning of this discussion of verbal suffixes, in section
5.4, we noted that most suffixes have more than one allomorph.
Most of these allomorphs were examined in the preceding sections. However, the allomorphs we have not yet discussed are
those which involve alternation in the length of the final vowel of
vowel final suffixes. This final vowel is sometimes long and
sometimes short. The following examples illustrate this alternation.

tangada	'to run up'
tangadahdo	'to run up here'

Note that, in the first example, the suffix *-da* ends in a short vowel.
In the second example, where this suffix is followed by *-do*, it ends
in a long vowel. It is pronounced *-dah-*.

We have already discussed two cases where final vowels are
lengthened. One was in section 3.5.1, where we noted that roots
that ended in short vowels in their free forms have long vowels in
their bound forms. The other case was discussed in section 3.5.2,
where it was noted that final vowels lengthen before enclitics.
Which of these two explanations should be employed to account
for alternations of vowel length in verbal suffixes is not entirely
clear, but there is some evidence that while verbal suffixes are
suffixes after roots, they function as enclitics after other suffixes.
Therefore, as with final root vowels before following enclitics, the
final vowel of a verbal suffix is lengthened only before forms of
the shape CV(C). Consider these examples.

tangkihdo	*tangkipene*
tangkihsang	

Note that the final vowel of the suffix *-ki* lengthens before *-do*
(CV) and *-sang* (CVC), but not before *-pene* (CVCV).

Additional examples of the lengthening of the final vowels of
verbal suffixes follow. Since our primary concern is with the form
of these examples, they will be left untranslated.

	Root + Suffix(es)	Pronounced
a)	*tang + ki*	*tangki*
	tang + ki + da	*tangkihda*
	tang + ki + da + do	*tangkihdahdo*
	tang + ki + da + do + sang	*tangkihdahdohsang*

b)   *wa + ki*   *wahki*
     wa + ki + da   *wahkihda*
     wa + ki + da + do   *wahkihdahdo*
     wa + ki + da + do + sang   *wahkihdahdohsang*

What is of special interest in this lengthening process is that if one of the two vowel initial suffixes *-ehng* or *-ehr* is employed in combination with any of the vowel final directional suffixes (resulting in forms like *-dahng* and *-dahr*, as noted in section 5.4.3), the final vowels of preceding suffixes do *not* lengthen. Examples are:

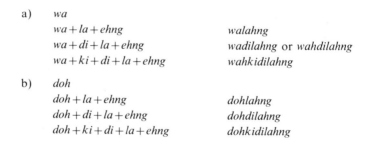

Root + Suffix(es)	Pronounced
tang + ki + da + ehng	*tangkidahng*
tang + ki + da + ehr	*tangkidahr*
tang + ki + da + do + ehng	*tangkidadohng*
tang + ki + da + do + ehr	*tangkidadohr*

The effect forms like *-dahng* and *-dahr* have on vowel final roots is also very complex, as illustrated by these examples.

a)   *wa*
     wa + la + ehng   *walahng*
     wa + di + la + ehng   *wadilahng* or *wahdilahng*
     wa + ki + di + la + ehng   *wahkidilahng*

b)   *doh*
     doh + la + ehng   *dohlahng*
     doh + di + la + ehng   *dohdilahng*
     doh + ki + di + la + ehng   *dohkidilahng*

Notice in the examples after (a), where the final vowel of the free form of the root is short, this vowel alternates in length depending upon the suffixes that follow. In the (b) examples, where the final root vowel is long, it does not. How these alternations in vowel length are to be accounted for is not clear. Further research is required.

THE VERB PHRASE

5.5   Now that we have examined the major classes of verbs and the many verbal affixes that exist in Ponapean, let us turn our attention to the **verb phrase**. A verb phrase may be defined as consisting of the following elements.

(Subject Pronoun) (Aspect Marker(s)) (Adverb(s)) VERB (Adverb(s))

VERB stands for 'verb plus any verbal affix(es)'. Elements enclosed within parentheses may or may not be present.

As this formulation illustrates, a verb phrase may consist of a single VERB. Examples of such verb phrases are italicized in the following sentences.

> Serio *sengiseng.*
> 'That child *is crying.*'

> Lampo *langada.*
> 'That lamp *was hung up.*'

> Soulik *peren.*
> 'Soulik *is happy.*'

Other words may also be present in a verb phrase. In the following sentence, all elements except a subject pronoun occur.

> Soulik *pahn pil peren kodouluhl.*
> Soulik *will also be extremely happy.*

The verb in this sentence is *peren* 'happy'. The words immediately preceding and following this verb, *pil* 'also' and *kodouluhl* 'extremely', are **adverbs**. The first word in this verb phrase, *pahn* (here translated as 'will'), is an **aspect marker**. Adverbs are the subject of section 5.6. Aspect markers are examined in the more general discussion of aspect presented in section 5.7.

Subject pronouns may also occur in a verb phrase, but only when the subject noun phrase of the sentence is not present. Therefore, consider the following sentence.

> a)   *Soulik peren.*
>   'Soulik is happy.'

If the audience to whom this sentence might be addressed understands that it is *Soulik* who is being talked about, then the following sentence is possible.

b)   *E peren.*
        'He is happy.'

This sentence simply consists of a verb phrase containing the subject pronoun *e* and the verb *peren*. It is assumed, however, that both preceding sentences, (a) and (b), are derived from a hypothetical sentence like the following.

c)   **Soulik e peren.*
        Soulik he happy

Therefore, from this sentence, (a) may be derived by deleting the subject pronoun *e*, and (b) may be derived by deleting the noun phrase *Soulik*. Except when the subject noun phrase of a sentence is **topicalized** (section **6.4.2**), a sentence like (c), however, is ungrammatical.

There are many reasons for believing that hypothetical sentence (c) must be the source of both sentences (a) and (b), and that in this hypothetical sentence, the subject pronoun should be considered part of the verb phrase. Some of the more important of these reasons follow.

First, in many Micronesian languages, structures like (c) *are* grammatical. Consider the following examples from Woleaian and Marshallese.

Woleaian: *Soulik ye ker.*
                   Soulik he happy
                   'Soulik is happy.'

(Woleaian *ye* corresponds to Ponapean *e*.)

Marshallese: *Soulik e ṃōṇōṇō.*
                   Soulik he happy
                   'Soulik is happy.'

Even in Pingelapese, a Ponapeic language, this next sentence is grammatical.

Pingelapese: *Soulik e peren.*
                     Soulik he happy
                     'Soulik is happy.'

Comparisons with still other Micronesian languages support the position that, historically, similar structures were also grammatical in Ponapean. Ponapean, however, underwent a change that resulted in a rule to the effect that if the subject noun phrase of a sentence is present, then the subject pronoun is not, and vice-versa. Also, in all the Micronesian languages that have subject pronouns that co-occur with subject noun phrases, these pronouns function as part of the verb phrase. This must similarly have been true of Ponapean. But apart from these historical considerations, there are other reasons for believing that subject pronouns should be treated in modern Ponapean as part of the verb phrase.

One fact about subject pronouns is that they may occur in a sentence *only* if a verb is present. Sentences without verbs are also possible in Ponapean. Such sentences, called **equational sentences**, are examined in section **6**.2.1. An example follows.

    Soulik sounpadahk emen.
    'Soulik is a teacher.'

If the noun phrase *Soulik* is pronominalized, the following sentence results.

    Ih sounpadahk emen.
    'He is a teacher.'

In this case, a subject pronoun is *not* employed, but rather an independent pronoun is. One logical way, then, to account for the fact that subject pronouns occur only in sentences that contain verbs is to say they are part of the verb phrase.

Another reason to consider subject pronouns as part of the verb phrase is that they parallel the behavior of object pronouns. Object pronouns, as we discussed in section **5**.4.2, occur as verbal suffixes and are clearly part of the verb phrase. Therefore, consider the next sentence.

    Limwei duhp seri kau.
    'Limwei bathed those children.'

If the audience for whom this sentence is intended knows that what Limwei bathed was several children, then the following sentence is also possible.

> *Limwei duhpirail.*
> 'Limwei bathed them.'

In this sentence, the object noun phrase *seri kau* 'those children' has been deleted, and the object pronoun *-irail* has been suffixed to the verb, thus functioning as part of the verb phrase and paralleling the behavior of subject pronouns.

The reaction of native speakers to questions about how sentences may be meaningfully divided up into parts also provides support for the argument that subject pronouns are part of the verb phrase. If asked how the following sentences may be divided into two parts, nearly every speaker of Ponapean will suggest the following divisions.

> (a) *Ohlo | daper mpweio.*
>   'That man | caught the ball.'
>
> (b) *E daper | mpweio.*
>   'He caught | the ball.'

Even though asking the speaker to divide these sentences into *two* parts may be loading the question, the results are interesting. In sentence (a), the two parts into which the sentence is divided are those of subject and predicate (discussed in section **6**.2.2). In sentence (b), however, where a subject noun phrase is not present, the division occurs between the verb phrase and the following object noun phrase. The subject pronoun *e* is treated as belonging to the same phrase as the verb *daper*.

Still other arguments that lend credence to the position that subject pronouns are part of the verb phrase come from the consideration of facts about the sound system of Ponapean. The most interesting of these observations involves the fact that intonation patterns in Ponapean must be analyzed in terms of the phrase, and, as we will note in section **6**.3.5, subject pronouns behave intonationally as part of the verb phrase.

There is little doubt that subject pronouns should be analyzed as part of the verb phrase in Ponapean. One consequence of this analysis, as we have already noted, is that it is possible for a sentence in Ponapean to consist only of a verb phrase. But since sentences like these come from sentences in which the subject noun phrase has been pronominalized, all sentences in Ponapean may be ultimately derived from sentences which do contain subject noun phrases.

ADVERBS

5.6 **Adverbs** are traditionally defined as words which modify verbs, adjectives, or other adverbs. For our purposes, this is not a satisfactory definition. Perhaps the best we can do in this grammar toward defining adverbs is to say that they are words which do not fit one of the other definitions of parts of speech.

The problem with the traditional definition of an adverb as a modifier of a verb, adjective, or another adverb may be illustrated by the following sentences, where three words that we wish to call adverbs—*nohn*, *dene*, and *lao*—are employed.

(a) *Ohlo nohn pohnkahke.*
man-that too lazy
'That man is too lazy.'

(b) *Dene ohlo ese lokaiahn Sapahn.*
It-is-said-that man-that know speech-of Japan
'It is said that that man knows Japanese.'

(c) *Kita awi ira lao kohdo.*
we wait they until come.
'Let's wait until they come.'

While in sentence (a) the adverb *nohn* 'too' modifies the adjective *pohnkahke* 'lazy', and thus fits the traditional definition of an adverb, the adverbs in sentences (b) and (c) have different functions. The adverb *dene* 'it is said that' in sentence (b) modifies not just a single word, but rather the entire sentence that follows. Adverbs which modify sentences we will call **sentence adverbs**. The adverb *lao* in sentence (c), which here is best translated 'until', is of still another type. It has the function of indicating a connection between two sentences. Adverbs like this we will call **conjunctive adverbs**. From these examples we can see that of the kinds of words we wish to call adverbs in this grammar, only those like *nohn* in sentence (a) meet the traditional definition. It is to adverbs like *nohn* that we wish to devote our attention here.

Adverbs of the types called sentence adverbs and conjunctive adverbs are better explained within the context of the sentence; consequently, they will be examined in the next chapter.

There are several important generalizaitions that we may make about adverbs like *nohn*. The first is that, as adverbs, none of these forms reduplicate. The second is that all of these adverbs normally occur in one of two positons—either between the aspect markers and the main verb, or immediately following the main verb. These are preferred rather than required positions, however, since a third characteristic of these adverbs is that they involve some freedom of position.

Twenty adverbs of this type are examined in this section. The forms of these adverbs follow. Their meanings will be considered in the discussions that follow.

nohn	*pwuwak*
inenen	*ahpwtehn*
mwur	*mwadangete*
ekis	*pil*
meid	*kehn*
ahpwide	*sekehn*
douluhl	*poaden*
kodouluhl	*mahs*
sekere	*uhd*
kalapw	*nek*

Nohn: This adverb, which has the alternate pronunciations *nohkin* and *nohk*, means 'too'. It occurs in sentences like the following.

E nohn doadoahk laud aio.
'He worked too hard yesterday.'

Soulik pahn nohn soupisek lakapw.
'Soulik will be too busy tomorrow.'

This adverb is also sometimes found before the aspect marker *kin* (though apparently not *pahn*). Therefore, both of these sentences are acceptable.

E kin nohn sakaula.
E nohn kin sakaula.
'He gets too drunk.'

The difference in meaning between these two sentences is largely one of emphasis. The first sentence employs normal word order and is a statement of fact. The second, where *nohn* is placed before *kin*, conveys the same information, but would normally only be employed in a warning. For example:

> *Ke dehr iang lahpo! E nohn kin sakaula!*
> 'Don't go with that guy! He gets too drunk!'

Inenen: This adverb, meaning 'very' or 'really', may be used only with stative verbs. Examples follow.

> *Mehn Pohnpei inenen kadek.*
> 'Ponapeans are very kind.'

> *Sehtet inenen enihep.*
> 'This shirt is very mildewed.'

> *Irail inenen ese.*
> 'They really know it.'

A sentence adverb, *uhdahn*, has a similar meaning. We will examine it in the next chapter.

Mwur: This adverb is probably best translated into English as 'a little'.

> *E kin mwur pweipwei.*
> 'He's a little crazy.'

> *Soulik mwur soumwahuda aio.*
> 'Soulik got a little sick yesterday.'

> *Koaros pahn mwur doadoahk.*
> 'Everyone will work a little.'

Ekis: The adverb *ekis* means 'a bit'.

> *E pahn ekis soumwahu lakapw.*
> 'He will be a bit sick tomorrow.'

> *Ohlo ekis alu oh ekis tang.*
> 'That man walked a bit and ran a bit.'

> *Sehto ekis mwerekirek.*
> 'That shirt is a bit wrinkled.'

Mwur and *ekis* are sometimes employed together, as in this sentence.

> *Ei pwoudo mwur ekis luwakahk.*
> 'My spouse is a little bit jealous.'

Reversing the order of these two adverbs to **ekis mwur* is not permissible.

Meid: The adverb *meid* 'truly' occurs only in sentences with a yes/no question intonation pattern. (See section **6.4.3** for further discussion of yes/no questions.) Examples of its usage follow.

> *Ke meid pai!*
> 'Aren't you truly lucky!'

> *E meid mwahu!*
> 'Isn't it truly good!'

Sentences like these we might call **exclamation questions**. These are sentences which are question-like in intonation, but are functionally emphatic. The adverb *pwa*, which is a sentence adverb discussed in the next chapter, functions in a similar manner.

Ahpwide: The adverb *ahpwide* is used in combination with adjectives suffixed by *-la* to indicate that the quality described by the adjective will be intensified. Examples follow.

> *Ke dehr mwenge laud, pwe ke pahn ahpwide mworouroula.*
> 'Don't eat a lot, because you will get even fatter.'

> *Ma serio sohte mwenge, e pahn ahpwide tihtihla.*
> 'If that child doesn't eat, he will get even skinnier.'

Some speakers employ *ahpwte* as an alternant of *ahpwide*.

Douluhl: The adverb *douluhl* means 'thoroughly', 'completely', or 'very'. Unlike the other adverbs we have thus far examined, *douluhl* occurs after the main verb, as in these examples.

> *E ese douluhl.*
> 'He knows it thoroughly.'

> *Soulik loalekeng douluhl.*
> 'Soulik is very intelligent.'

Kodouluhl: The adverb *kodouluhl* (apparently a fossilized causative form of *douluhl*) also follows the main verb in a sentence, and means 'extremely'.

E pwangadahr kodouluhl.
'He got extremely tired.'

Soulik loalekeng kodouluhl.
'Soulik is extremely intelligent.'

Sekere: This adverb means 'maybe' or 'perhaps'. It occurs in sentences like the following.

I pahn sekere laid lakapw.
'I will perhaps fish tomorrow.'

Soulik sekere sukusukuhl.
'Soulik is perhaps attending school.'

Irail kin sekere uhweng lahpo.
'They perhaps oppose that man.'

Kalapw: The adverb *kalapw* means 'frequently'. The following sentences illustrate its usage.

Liho kin kalapw seiloak.
'That woman frequently travels.'

Nei serio kalapw seng.
'My child frequently cries.'

Wahro pahn kalapw sepehlda.
'That canoe will frequently capsize.'

Pwuwak: Like *kalapw*, the adverb *pwuwak* may mean 'frequently', as in these examples.

E pwuwak keteu.
'It frequently rains.'

Kumwail pahn pwuwak menmeir.
'You will frequently be sleepy.'

With verbs which name activities requiring skill, the meaning of *pwuwak* is extended to include the idea of 'successfully'. Therefore, a sentence like *E pwuwak laid* means 'He frequently fishes (and he is successful at it)'. *Pwuwak* also occurs as an adjective meaning 'to have a special affinity for growing certain species of yams'. Whereas *pwuwak* as an adjective may reduplicate, *pwuwak* as an adverb may not.

Ahpwtehn: The adverb *ahpwtehn* means 'just' in a temporal sense.

> *Nei pwihko ahpwtehn mehla.*
> 'My pig just died.'

> *Soulik ahpwtehn kohdo.*
> 'Soulik just came.'

Mwadangete: This adverb, which also is sometimes shortened to *mwadang*, means 'quickly' as in these sentences.

> *E pahn mwadangete kohdo.*
> 'He will quickly come.'

> *E mwadangete lakid.*
> 'He quickly discarded it.'

Pil: This adverb means 'also'. It may be used in sentences like the following.

> *Liho pil neksang University of Hawaii.*
> 'That woman also graduated from the University of Hawaii.'

> *E pahn pil laid.*
> 'He will also fish.'

Pil may also occur before *pahn*, as in this sentence.

> *E pil pahn laid.*
> 'He also will fish.'

The sentence above is ambiguous. It may either mean '*He* also will fish', where it assumed others will fish as well, or 'He also will *fish*', in addition to other activities. The sentence in which *pahn* precedes *pil* has only this second meaning.

Kehn: The adverb *kehn* means 'easily'.

E kehn lingeringer.
'He is easily angered.'

Pilohlo kehn ohla.
'*Pilohlo* (a food) spoils easily.'

Sekehn: This adverb is made up of the two morphemes *sa-* (the negative prefix, here in a tightly bound form) and *kehn*. It means 'not easily'.

E sekehn lingeringer.
'He is not easily angered.'

Mahr sekehn ohla.
'Preserved breadfruit doesn't spoil easily.'

Poaden: This adverb means 'incessantly' or 'always'.

E poaden kapakap.
'He is incessantly praying.'

Mahs: The adverb *mahs* 'please' occurs immediately after verbs, as these examples illustrate.

Kihdo mahs soahlen.
'Please give me the salt.'

Pwekada mahs serien.
'Please pick up that child.'

Uhd: The adverb *uhd*, also pronounced *ihd* by some speakers, means 'to take one's turn at', as illustrated by the following examples.

Irail uhd doadoahk.
'They took their turn at working.'

Soulik pahn uhd laid.
'Soulik will take his turn at fishing.'

Nek: This form, hesitantly labeled as an adverb, may be translated 'alternatively' or 'instead', as in the following examples.

I nek wahdo.
'I alternatively could bring it (instead of someone else).'

I nek kohwei rehmw.
'I alternatively could visit your place (instead of not visiting it).'

The presence of 'could' in the translations of the preceding sentences is suggestive of the possibility that it might be more appropriate to label *nek* as a **modal**, rather than as an adverb. Indeed, the function of *nek* seems to be one of marking the **subjunctive mood**—that what is being talked about represents possiblity or desire, rather than fact. It is not clear, however, whether any formal criteria exist that would justify the establishment of a separate word class of modals. Other words that might traditionally be labeled as modals or as auxiliary verbs are discussed in section **6.5.3** under the heading *Infinitive Clauses*.

Adjectives are also found in combination with verbs, as in the following sentences.

   (a) *E lokaia suwed.*
        he talk bad
        'He is foul-mouthed.'

   (b) *E suwedin lokaia.*
        he bad-to talk
        'He's bad at talking.'

In neither of these examples, however, does the adjective function as an adverb. Instead, in sentence (a) the adjective *suwed* 'bad' is used after the verb *lokaia* 'to talk' to form a **compound verb**. Although Ponapean spelling conventions call for *lokaia suwed* to be written as two words, evidence that these two words together form a compound can be provided by employing a suffix like *-la* which, as the example below shows, occurs after *suwed* rather than *lokaia*. That is, it occurs at the end of this compound.

E lokaia suwedila.
'He became foul-mouthed.'

Further, this compound verb is of the subclass we labeled adjective, as shown by its use with the stative marker *me* in the next sentence.

E me lokaia suwed.
'He is foul-mouthed!'

Other examples of such compounds are listed below.

doadoahk laud	'hard-working'
alu inen	'straight-walking'
lokaia tohto	'argumentative'
pap pwand	'slow-swimming'
tang marahra	'fast-running'

In sentence (b) of the earlier examples, the adjective *suwed* precedes the verb *lokaia* and is used with the complementizer *-n*. How constructions like these work will be the subject of further study in sections **6**.5.1 and **6**.5.3.

ASPECT

5.7   Probably common to every language is the presence of one or more grammatical devices that may be employed to signal something about the 'time' of what is being expressed. Frequently, such indications of time are signaled by the use of temporal phrases (like 'in the morning') as well as by the use of words and affixes that occur in combination with verbs (like 'will walk' or 'walked'). Precisely how these signals work, though, or even what they signal, may vary considerably from one language to another. In this section, our concern is with how such signals of time work in Ponapean. More particularly, we will be interested in how time is expressed in the verb phrase. Although we will occasionally make reference to temporal phrases, we will postpone discussion of phrases like these until section **6**.3.2.

A familiar term used to talk about verbal expressions of time in a language like English is *tense*. Tense is used to specify the time of what is expressed by the verb relative to the time of the utterance. Therefore, each time a sentence is uttered in English, a decision must be made about tense. This consideration is crucial in determining what the form of the verb will be. Consider the following two sentences.

They walked to work.
They walk to work.

The difference between the forms of the verb 'to walk' in these sentences tells us something about when the action of 'walking' occurred. In the first sentence, we understand that the walking took place at some indefinite time in the past. 'Past' is signaled by the suffix '-ed'. In the second sentence, where this suffix is not present, the action described is essentially non-past. It is something that might occur, for example, every day.

While the concept of tense is useful for describing English, it is not for Ponapean. In fact, Ponapean may be described as a *tenseless* language. This is not to say that in Ponapean it is impossible to express notions of time. A sentence like 'I was born at 10:30 in the morning on January 17, 1944' can be expressed with as much precision in Ponapean as it is in English. What is meant by saying that Ponapean is tenseless is that it expresses considerations of time in a way different from English. Rather than using a tense system to signal time relations, Ponapean employs what we will call an **aspect system**. The basic difference between these two systems is this: in a tense system, *when* an event occurred is important; in an aspect system, the *time contour* of the event is crucial. What is meant by *time contour* will be explored in the following discussions.

Basically there are four distinctions of aspect in Ponapean. The action or state expressed by a particular verb may be marked as (1) unrealized, (2) habitual, (3) durative, or (4) perfective. How these aspects are signaled will be examined subsequently. First, it should be made clear that a verb unmarked for aspect is either the opposite of or neutral to these distinctions. Therefore, a verb occurring in a verb phrase without any indication of aspect may be viewed as naming an action or state which is realized, but neutral with respect to whether it is durative, habitual, or perfective. Consider the following Ponapean sentence and its English translations.

> *Soulik soumwahu.*
> 'Soulik was sick.'
>   or
> 'Soulik is sick.'

This sentence simply states that the state of being sick is or has been realized and is associated with 'Soulik'. As the translations above indicate, whether the state of being sick existed in the past or exists now is ambiguous. The time of Soulik's being sick is established either by context or by adding a temporal phrase like *nan sounpar samwalahro* 'last year' or *met* 'now', as in the following sentences.

>*Soulik soumwahu nan sounpar samwalahro.*
>'Soulik was sick last year.'

>*Soulik soumwahu met.*
>'Soulik is sick now.'

Since verbs occurring unmarked for aspect are considered to be realized, verbs naming actions, particularly those which do not normally involve long periods of time to perform, are often appropriately translated into English in the past tense, as in this next example.

>*Soulik pwupwidi.*
>'Soulik fell down.'

But even action verbs may be ambiguous as to whether they name a past or current action, as these next sentences illustrate.

>*Lahp teio laid aio.*
>'That other guy fished yesterday.'

>*Lahp teio laid met.*
>'That other guy fishes now.'

The basic point here is that a verb unmarked for aspect only signifies that the action, event, or condition it names is realized. How a verb may be marked for aspect to signal other facts about time is what we wish to consider now. As we shall see in the next sections, aspect is normally signalled in one of two ways. Either separate words called **aspect markers** precede the verb, or verbal affixes are employed.

UNREALIZED ASPECT

5.7.1   An action, event, or condition named by a verb may be marked for **unrealized aspect** by use of the aspect marker *pahn*. Often, *pahn* may be translated in English as 'will', as in these examples.

>*Pwopwoudo pahn wahdo rais.*
>'That couple will bring rice.'

Soulik pahn doahke lahpo.
'Soulik will fight that guy.'

Kitail pahn rik mwangas lakapw.
'We will gather ripe coconuts tomorrow.'

Pahn does not necessarily signal action in the future however. For example, consider the following sentence.

Pwopwoudo pahn wahdo rais aio, ahpw re manokehla.
'That couple would have brought rice yesterday, but they forgot it.'

Here *pahn* is used to signal that an action was to have taken place in the past. It is for this reason that *pahn*, rather than being described as a future marker, is better considered as marking that what is named by the verb is or was unrealized.

HABITUAL ASPECT

5.7.2   The aspect marker *kin* is used to signal that an action, state, or event named by a verb is a **habitual** one. Examples of the use of *kin* are presented below.

Soulik kin pirida kuloak isuh.
'Soulik gets up at seven o'clock.'

Aramas ngeder kin iang doadoahk.
'A great many people participate in the work.'

Sohte me kin poakpoake aramas akupwung.
'No one likes a petty person.'

Kin may also be used in sentences which specifically refer to actions that took place in the past. For example, compare this sentence with first one listed above.

Soulik kin pirida kuloak isuh nan sounpar samwalahro.
'Soulik got up at seven o'clock last year.'

Notice that although the phrase *nan sounpar samwalahro* 'last year' has been added to this sentence, neither *kin* nor the form of the verb are changed. Thus, *kin* may be used to signal habitual action either in the past, the present, or, as in the next sentence, in the future.

>*Sang ansowet kohla, i pahn kin kang rais.*
>'From now on, I will eat rice.'

In this sentence, both *pahn* and *kin* are employed, the order being *pahn* before *kin*. Other examples of these two aspect markers used in combination follow.

>*Lahpo pahn kin iang sukuhl University of Hawaii.*
>'That guy will attend school at the University of Hawaii.'

>*Soulik pahn kin loaleid ma e mweselsang Pohnpei.*
>'Soulik will be homesick if he leaves Ponape.'

DURATIVE ASPECT

5.7.3   **Durative aspect** in Ponapean is signaled by reduplication or, if the verb is inherently reduplicated, by the use of *wie*. The forms of reduplication were already examined in section 3.3.4. Its function to indicate durative aspect is what will be considered here. What is meant by durative aspect may be illustrated by comparing the following two sentences.

>(a) *I kang rais.*
>   'I ate rice.'

>(b) *I kangkang rais.*
>   'I am eating rice.'

In sentence (a), where the verb *kang* occurs unreduplicated, the verb indicates that the action of eating was realized. A sentence like this, as we pointed out earlier, might also mean 'I eat rice.' No further information about the time contour of this action is expressed. In sentence (b), on the other hand, reduplication is employed to signal that the action of eating involves some duration of time. This sentence is translated as 'I am eating rice', which apart from further context is its best translation. However, the use of reduplication is not restricted to present time. Since it is a marker of aspect rather than of tense, it may be used to talk about durative activities in the past, present, and future, as these sentences illustrate.

>*I kangkang rais aio ansou me Soulik kohdoh.*
>'I was eating rice yesterday when Soulik came.'

I kangkang rais ansowet.
'I am eating rice now.'

I pahn kangkang rais lakapw ansou me Soulik pahn kohdoh.
'I will be eating rice tomorrow when Soulik comes.'

As the last sentence illustrates, unrealized aspect may co-occur with durative aspect. Durative aspect may also co-occur with habitual aspect or unrealized and habitual action in combination. Examples are:

I kin kangkang rais.
'I (habitually) am eating rice.'

I pahn kin kangkang rais ansou me i pahn kohla Sapahn.
'I will (habitually) be eating rice when I go to Japan.'

If a verb which requires the use of *wie* occurs with the aspect markers *pahn* and *kin*, *wie* occurs immediately before the verb, as this sentence illustrates.

I pahn kin wie doadoahk ansou koaros.
'I will (habitually) be working all the time.'

Durative aspect may occur with verbs of all types in Ponapean, including adjectives, as in these sentences.

E kadakadek.
'He is being kind.'

E wie pweipwei.
'He is being crazy.'

E lemelemei.
'He is being cruel.'

E wie poupoulap.
'He is being too familar.'

The use of durative aspect with verbs naming relatively permanent states is uncommon, since verbs like these are inherently durative. The verb *masukun* 'to be blind' is such a verb. However, given the proper context, even a verb like this may take durative aspect. For example, in describing someone who suffers from spells of temporary blindness, the following sentence is possible.

> *Ohlo masamasukun.*
> 'That man is being blind.'

Certainly the great majority of, if not all, verbs in Ponapean may be reduplicated or combine with *wie* to indicate durative aspect.

PERFECTIVE ASPECT

5.7.4   The suffix *-ehr*, the various pronunciations of which were considered in section 5.4.5, is used to signal **perfective aspect**. Perfective aspect is used with verbs to indicate that an action, event, or condition has reached or is on its way toward reaching some kind of conclusion or state of completion. Examples of the use of *-ehr* to signal perfective aspect are presented below.

> *I kangehr rais.*
> 'I have eaten rice.'
>
> *Lahpo kolahr Saipan.*
> 'That guy has gone to Saipan.'
>
> *Soulik wadohr noumw pwuhko.*
> 'Soulik has brought your book.'
>
> *E esehier.*
> 'He has known it.' or 'He already knows it.'
>
> *E kadekehr.*
> 'He has been kind.'

It should be noted that sentences like the last one, where *-ehr* is suffixed directly to an adjective like *kadek* 'kind', are grammatical, but rare. A sentence like the following is more obviously acceptable.

> *E kadekalahr.*
> 'He has become kind.'

Adjectives like *kadek* name qualities which a person normally either does or does not have. By suffixing to these adjectives one of the directional suffixes used to indicate a change of state, the use of *-ehr* to indicate that the change of state is complete results in a more obviously meaningful form.

Perfective aspect may occur in combination with all other aspects. In combination with unrealized aspect, three meanings are possible, as illustrated by the following sentences.

(a) *I pahn mwemweitlahr Pohnpei.*
     'I am about to visit Ponape.'
          or
     'I am finally going to visit Ponape.'

(b) *I pahn samwalahr ansou me lahpo lelodoh.*
     'I will have left by the time that guy reaches here.'

In sentence (a), *pahn* in combination with *-ehr* may be used either to signal that an action is to take place in the immediate future, or that an action one has long anticipated is finally going to be carried out. Which of these two meanings is appropriate for a particular sentence must be determined by context. In sentence (b), where the time reference of the sentence is established as 'by the time that guy reaches here', *pahn* is used with *-ehr* to signal that the action will be completed at some time in the future, but not necessarily in the immediate future.

In combination with the habitual marker *kin*, *-ehr* is used to signal that one instance of an action, state, or condition that is habitual has been completed. For example, upon observing a known thief who suddenly has a lot of money, the following sentence employing the verb *pirap* 'to steal' might be appropriate.

Lahpo kin pirapehr.
'That guy has engaged in one of his customary acts of theft.'

Perfective aspect may also be used in combination with durative aspect, as these examples illustrate.

I lalaidehr.
'I have been fishing.'

Liho wie lopwolopwehr.
'That woman has been doing laundry.'

Seriet lingilingeringerehr.
'That child has been being angry.'

In general, we may say that all combinations of aspect are possible in Ponapean.

6.   Sentences

OVERVIEW

6.1   Now that we have made a number of basic observations about sounds, words, and phrases, let us broaden our investigation of Ponapean grammar to include the study of sentences. Ideally, our goal in this chapter would be to set forth a set of rules so precise that they would account for all of the sentences that are grammatical in Ponapean and exclude all of those that are ungrammatical. The word 'ideally' must be included in describing this goal, because in fact our discussion will fall short of this. Indeed, such a goal has never been achieved in describing any language, nor is it certain that it ever could be. This is due to the fact that language is extremely complicated, and the subject of sentence formation in particular is one about which we still have much to learn. The goals of this chapter, then, are much less ambitious than the previously described ideal.

We will begin this chapter by considering the structure of the **basic sentence**. After we have reached at least a working definition of such a basic sentence, we will see how other kinds of sentences may be produced through various kinds of modification. These include sentences of the type called **imperative sentences, thematic sentences, interrogative sentences**, and **negative sentences**. Finally, we will consider how basic sentences may occur in combination to form what are traditionally called **compound sentences** and **complex sentences**.

Much more could be written about any one of these topics than has been included here, and hopefully someday this task will be taken up. For the present, however, we shall have to be content with noting only some of the more obvious facts about Ponapean sentences. We begin by considering the basic structure of sentences.

THE BASIC STRUCTURE OF SENTENCES

6.2   To begin to understand the complexities involved in describing the structure of sentences, let us look at the following short text taken from a well-known Ponapean legend.

> *Keilahn aio, mie ehu seiloak pwarodohng Pohnpei. Ohl riemen kaunda. Eden emen Olisihpa ah eden emen Olosohpa. Ohl riemenet, ira me loalekeng oh pil koahiek en kohkohseli nan wasa apwal akan pwe ira kisehn aramas manaman de sarawi kan me kaparaparadahdohsang Kataupeidi. Ira wadahr aramas tohto kei oh dakehda lapalahn wahr oapwoat me kehu mehte pwoat ah serek silipwoat. Soangen wahr pwoatet kin kak wahda aramas epwiki ape. Irail ahpw kohdo pidolongehng nan kepidau kis, oh inenlongehng ni deke laud me mi limwahn werengen sahpw laud Pohnpei, me adaneki Soupaip, oh irail wiahda arail kousoan wasaho.*

A free translation of this passage follows.

> Long ago, there was a voyage that came here to Ponape. Two men directed it. One was named Olisihpa and the other was named Olosohpa. As for these two men, they were intelligent and also capable of traveling around to difficult places, because they were relatives of powerful or holy people that settled here from Kataupeidi. They took many people and boarded a great canoe that had just one mast, but three sails. This kind of canoe could carry a hundred or so people. They then came here, entered a small pass, and went straight to a large island named Soupaip that lies near the middle of the main island of Ponape, and they made their residence in that place.

Even a casual examination of such a brief text as this illustrates that there are many different ways of putting sentences together in Ponapean. A longer text would reveal an even greater variety of sentences. And when we stop to think that there is, in fact, no limit to how many sentences we might connect by 'and', or how many modifiers we might use with a noun, we are faced with the dilemma that in Ponapean, as in any language, there is no limit to the number of different possible sentences. The problem that we face, then, is how are we to talk about the structure of sentences?

BASIC SENTENCE TYPES

6.2.1   One way in which we can approach the problem of talking about the structure of sentences is to try to determine what the basic sentence types of a language are. We do this because we assume that once we know what these basic types are, then we will be able to determine the set of rules which will account for longer and more complicated sentences. Another way to view this task is that we are attempting to mirror what a native speaker of Ponapean knows. He knows, though probably not at a conscious level, what the basic sentence types of his language are and the rules that apply to them to enable him to produce an infinite number of sentences. He knows, for example, how to change a positive statement to a negative one, how to move parts of sentences around for the purposes of emphasis, how to connect two or more sentences together, and so on.

Based upon our present understanding of Ponapean, our position will be that there are only two basic sentence types, **equational sentences** and **verbal sentences**, which we will examine below. In subsequent sections of this chapter we will then attempt to present some of the ways in which these basic sentence types may be modified.

Equational Sentences

Equational sentences are sentences minimally composed of two noun phrases, one of which normally has the function of locating or identifying the other. Following are examples of sentences of this type.

Ohlo sounpadahk emen.
man-that teacher one
'That man is a teacher.'

Don mehn Amerika.
Don one-of America
'Don is an American.'

Tuhke pwoat mwo.
tree one there
'That is a tree.'

Iet noumw naipen.
here your knife-there
'Here is your knife.'

Verbal Sentences

Verbal sentences are sentences minimally composed of a noun phrase and a verb phrase. Following are examples of sentences of this type.

> *Lahpo noahrok.*
> 'That guy is greedy.'

> *Soulik pahn duhdu.*
> 'Soulik will bathe.'

> *Serepeino tangala.*
> 'That girl fled.'

> *Ohlo memeir.*
> 'That man is sleeping.'

How many noun phrases occur in a basic verbal sentence depends upon whether the verb is intransitive or transitive and what verbal affixes occur with the verb. The preceding example sentences all contained one noun phrase followed by one verb phrase, in which an intransitive verb was the head. If a transitive verb occurs as the head of the verb phrase, then two noun phrases must be present in the sentence, as illustrated by these examples.

> *Pwutako kinih nah pwutako.*
> 'That boy pinched his brother.'

> *Aramas akau kide nahso.*
> 'Those people littered the feasthouse.'

> *Lahpo dehm masiso.*
> 'That guy felt around for the matches.'

> *Soulik kilang kasdohn palapal.*
> 'Soulik saw a sword fighting movie.'

A second noun phrase may also occur in a verbal sentence when an intransitive verb occurs in combination with one of the suffixes *-ki, -ehng,* or *-sang,* as illustrated by the next examples.

> *Soulik pahn laidiki uhket.*
> 'Soulik will fish with this net.'

> *Pwutak riemeno papalahng wahro.*
> 'Those two boys swam toward the canoe.'

> *Limwei aluhlahsang ohlo.*
> 'Limwei walked away from that man.'

When transitive verbs occur in combination with one of these suffixes, then three noun phrases may occur in a basic verbal sentence.

Soulik pahn pariki tuhkè kan sileht.
'Soulik will cut those logs with this adze.'

Ewalt pahn lopukehng sehu ohlo.
'Ewalt will cut sugar cane for that man.'

Ohlo ekihsang Soulik koakono.
'That man hid the box from Soulik.'

No basic verbal sentences have been found which contain more than three noun phrases.

In all of the preceding verbal sentences, the order of the phrases was:

Noun Phrase Verb Phrase (Noun Phrase) (Noun Phrase)

There is one type of verbal sentence, however, in which a verb phrase may occur as the first phrase in the sentence. Examples are:

Mie rais.
exists rice
'Rice exists.' or 'There is rice.'

Mie nei pwuhk.
exists my book
'My book exists.' or 'I have a book.'

Sentences like these are called **existential** sentences; they establish the *existence* of something. The reversed order of the phrases in these sentences can probably be accounted for by a rule applying to existential sentences that reorders verb phrases before noun phrases. If this is true, then we may say that the order of phrases in all verbal sentences is the order described at the beginning of this paragraph.

THE BASIC SENTENCE DEFINED

6.2.2   Now that we have examined the two basic sentence types of

Ponapean, let us see what sort of general statement we may make concerning what a basic sentence is. In most traditional grammars we are taught that a sentence consists of a **subject** and a **predicate**. In fact, this is a workable definition. For example, all of the following Ponapean sentences, whether equational or verbal, can be divided into subjects and predicates.

Subject	Predicate
Ohlo	*sounpadahk emen.*
'That man	is a teacher.'
Don	*ohl emen.*
'Don	is a man.'
Soulik	*sehse.*
'Soulik	doesn't know.'
Olapahd	*wiahda Pakihn.*
Olapahd	made the island of Pakihn.'
Mehn mahs oko	*inenen kehlail.*
'Those people of long ago	were very strong.'
Ohl riemen	*kaunda wahro.*
'Two men	captained that canoe.'
Kidie	*ngalis Soulik.*
'This dog	bit Soulik.'
Lampo	*pahn pwupwidi.*
'That lamp	will fall down.'

Notice that the subjects of these sentences have the function of **referring** to something. In the first sentence the subject refers to *ohlo* 'that man', while in the last sentence it refers to *lampo* 'that lamp.' The predicates of these sentences, on the other hand, have the function of **relating** the subject to some condition or action. In the first sentence, the predicate relates the condition of being *sounpadahk emen* 'a teacher' to *ohlo* 'that man'. In the last sentence, it relates the action *pahn pwupwidi* 'will fall down' to the subject *lampo* 'that lamp'. We may further observe that all of these sentences are either equational or verbal. That is, they have one of the following two structures.

	Subject	Predicate
Equational:	Noun Phrase	Noun Phrase
Verbal:	Noun Phrase	Verb Phrase (Noun Phrase) (Noun Phrase)

Based upon these observations, we may note that a basic sentence in Ponapean consists of two parts—a noun phrase and a second part, which may consist either of a noun phrase, or a verb phrase followed by one or more noun phrases. Let us call this second part a **predicate phrase**. Thus, our first definition of a basic sentence follows.

A sentence consists of a noun phrase and a predicate phrase.

This statement, or rule if you like, represents a claim that speakers of Ponapean organize their sentences into two parts, or **constituents**. Whether or not this is the way we will ultimately want to characterize a Ponapean sentence is not certain, but for our purposes it will nearly suffice. 'Nearly' is used here, because in fact there are other elements in a basic sentence for which the rule above does not account.

OTHER ELEMENTS IN THE BASIC SENTENCE

6.3   There are two ways in which the definition of a basic sentence presented in the preceding section is incomplete.

The first is involved with the way we characterized a predicate phrase. While it is true that a predicate phrase may consist of either a noun phrase or a verb phrase in combination with noun phrases, there are also phrases of two other types that may optionally be present in the predicate. These are the kinds of phrases that we will call **locative phrases** (naming places) and **temporal phrases** (naming times). For example, consider the following sets of examples. The (a) set contains equational sentences and the (b) set, verbal sentences.

(a) *Ohlo sounpadahk emen Wene.*
     'That man is a teacher in Wene.'

     Ohlo sounpadahk emen nan pahr samwalahro.
     'That man was a teacher last year.'

     Ohlo sounpadahk emen Wene nan pahr samwalahro.
     'That man was a teacher in Wene last year.'

(b) *Ohlo mehla Wene.*
'That man died in Wene.'

Ohlo mehla nan pahr samwalahro.
'That man died last year.'

Ohlo mehla Wene nan pahr samwalahro.
'That man died in Wene last year.'

In these examples, we see that a predicate phrase may optionally contain both a locative and a temporal phrase.

The second way in which our definition of a basic sentence is incomplete is that it fails to account for the optional occurrence of **sentence adverbs**. Examples of sentences containing sentence adverbs follow.

Dene ohlo mehla.
'It is said that man died.'

Dene ohlo sounpadahk emen.
'It is said that man is a teacher.'

Since we have not previously discussed either sentence adverbs or locative and temporal phrases, that is the task we need to take up here. Thus, locative and temporal phrases will be examined in sections **6**.3.1 and **6**.3.2. However, since describing phrases of these types involves a number of complexities, a useful discussion of them will be somewhat lengthy. These section therefore represent a diversion from the primary focus of this chapter, which is the sentence. Consequently, the reader may feel free to read these sections later and go on to section **6**.3.3 which deals with sentence adverbs and **6**.3.4 which offers an expanded view of the basic sentence.

LOCATIVE PHRASES

6.3.1   A **locative phrase** may simply be defined as a phrase which tells where an action, event, or condition took place. Example locative phrases are italicized in the following sentences.

(a) Ohlo kohla *Kolonia.*
'That man went *to Kolonia.*'

(b) Ohlo kohla *ni ohpiso.*
'That man went *to that office.*'

(c) Ohlo kohla *mwo*.
      'That man went *there*.'

These examples illustrate locative phrases of three basic types. In sentence (a) a **locative noun phrase** is employed. In sentence (b) a **locative noun phrase introduced by a preposition** is used, while in sentence (c) a **demonstrative pronoun** occurs. In the following discussion, we will examine each of these kinds of locative phrases in more detail.

Locative Noun Phrases

A noun phrase may function as a locative phrase without a preceding preposition if the head noun of the phrase is a **locative noun**. A locative noun is a noun which names a place or a location. In the following discussion, we will divide our discussion of locative noun phrases into five parts, based upon the type of locative noun employed. The five types of locative nouns we will consider are: **proper nouns, prepositional nouns, relational nouns, locative nouns bound to prepositions**, and the **locative noun** *wasa* 'place'.

Proper Nouns: A proper noun which names a place may be used as a locative noun. Since proper nouns require no further modification, they may stand alone as locative noun phrases. Examples follow.

Pwutako kohsang *Pohnpei*.
'That boy comes from *Ponape*.'

I mwahuki mwemweitla *Wene*.
'I like to visit *Wene*.'

Lahpo mihmi *Pohrasapw*.
'That guy is staying in *Pohrasapw*.'

Prepositional Nouns: A second type of locative noun is that which we will call a **prepositional noun**. There are at least twelve nouns of this type, all of which are bound roots that occur in direct possessive constructions of the kind examined in section **4.8.2**. Following are ten of these nouns as they occur with the third person singular suffix -$\emptyset$ 'his, her, or its' variously translated below as 'his, him, or it' appropriate to the English context.

mpe	'next to him (with animate relationships)'
limwah	'next to him (with any relationship)'
mwoh	'ahead of him', 'before him'
mwuri	'after him', 'behind him'
nanwerenge	'midst of it'
pah	'below him'
powe	'above him'
loale	'inside it' or with reference to emotions 'inside him'
liki	'outside it' or with reference to an outward show of emotions 'outside him'
reh	'his location'

Two additional prepositional nouns are listed below as they occur with the third person dual suffix *-ra* 'their', appropriately translated for these forms as 'them.'

nanpwungara	'the location between them'
nanmadolara	'the area between them'

These two nouns, because of the nature of their meanings, normally only combine with plural suffixes. Other prepositional nouns, however, may take all possessive suffixes. Therefore, the full paradigm of *mpe* is as follows.

mpei	'next to me'
mpemw	'next to you'
mpe	'next to him'
mpat	'next to us (exclusive)'
mpata	'next to us (dual)'
mpatail	'next to us (plural)'
mpamwa	'next to you (dual)'
mpamwail	'next to you (plural)'
mpara	'next to them (dual)'
mparail	'next to them (plural)'

With the construct suffix, *mpe* may occur in a phrase like the following.

mpehn ohlo	'next to that man'

Six of the prepositional nouns listed above—*mpe, limwah, nanpwungara, mwoh, nanwerenge,* and *mwuri*—occur only with possessive pronoun suffixes. The remaining six—*reh, loale, pah, powe, nanmadol,* and *liki* —occur either with possessive pronoun suffixes or with singular demonstrative modifiers, but not with both at the same time. Therefore, a noun like *reh,* in addition to occurring with possessive suffixes, may occur in forms like the following.

reht	'this location'
rehn	'that location by you'
reho	'that location away from us'

Relational Nouns: A third type of locative noun is that which we will call a **relational noun**. There are at least five nouns of this type, as listed below.

il-	'distance'
kail-	'distance'
lepi-	'section, area'
pei-	'location'
pali-	'side'

A unique feature of relational nouns is that they all combine with some verbal suffixes. Consequently, the term **prepositional verb** has also been suggested as a label for these forms. The term relational noun seems preferable, however, since these forms function syntactically as *nouns*; they are called *relational* because, in at least one or another of their usages, they all establish locations relative to some implicit point of reference.

The relational nouns *il-* and *kail-* are bound forms. They seem to be synonymous, having a generalized meaning that might be translated as 'distance.' These two roots occur with verbal directional suffixes of the third and fourth positions, with the suffix *-sang* of the fifth position, and with object pronouns of the sixth position.

With directional suffixes of the third and fourth positions, the location established by the relational nouns *il-* and *kail-* is understood to be relative to some third point of reference understood by both the speaker and the listener. Examples of the root *il-* in combination with suffixes of third position follow. The root *kail-* behaves identically.

E mi iledi.	'It's at a location some distance downward (from it).'
E mi ilada.	'It's at a location some distance upward (from it).'
E mi ilehi.	'It's at a location some distance seaward (from it).'
E mi ilolong.	'It's at location some distance inland (from it).'

As the preceding examples illustrate, no demonstrative modifiers are employed when *il-* (or *kail-*) occur in combination with directional suffixes of the third position. In combination with suffixes of the fourth position, however, demonstrative modifiers must follow the resulting forms, as illustrated by the next set of examples.

E mi ilalaho.	'It's at a location some distance away from us (and it).'
E mi ilodoh(t).	'It's at a location some distance towards me (from it).'
E mi ilowehn.	'It's at a location some distance towards you (from it).'

The translations of these sentences are somewhat awkward, since English has no comparable forms.

With the suffix *-sang* plus a following object pronoun or noun phrase, the point of reference left unstated in the preceding examples may be expressed.

E mi ilehisanguhk.
'It's at a location some distance seaward from you.'

E mi ilehisang dekeho.
'It's at a location some distance seaward from that island.'

As these examples illustrate, it is possible, as with verbs, for more than one verbal suffix to follow a root.

The relational noun *lepi-* 'section' or 'area' combines with the same verbal suffixes as *il-* and *kail-* and the generalizations made above apply to this noun also. Only two additional points need be made. First, unlike *il-* or *kail-*, *lepi-* may be directly suffixed by singular demonstrative modifiers, as in these examples.

lepie(t)	'this section'
lepien	'that section, by you'
lepio	'that section, away from us'

Secondly, the two directional suffixes -*di* and -*da* take on additional meanings. The suffix -*di*, in addition to meaning 'downward', may also mean 'leeward'. The suffix -*da*, in addition to meaning 'upward', may also mean 'windward.'

The relational noun *pei-* combines only with verbal directional suffixes of the third position, with the following meanings.

peidi	'leeward'
peidak	'windward'
peiei	'seaward'
peilong	'inland'

(The suffix -*dak* in *peidak* is an archaic form of the suffix -*da* 'upwards'.) When used in a locative phrase, these forms must be followed by a demonstrative modifier. For example:

I kohsang peilongo.
'I came from inland.'

The final relational noun to be considered here is *pali* 'side'. *Pali*, like *lepi-*, may combine directly with singular demonstrative modifiers, as in these examples.

paliet	'this side'
palien	'that side, by you'
palio	'that side, away from us'

Pali also occurs with verbal directional suffixes of the fourth position plus the suffix -*sang* and a following noun phrase or object pronoun. In the following examples, the third person singular object pronoun ∅ 'him, her, or it' is employed.

palilahsang	'side away from us (and it)'
palidohsang	'side towards me (from it)'
paliweh	'side towards you (from it)'

Notice that the last form here is irregular. *Paliweh* occurs instead of the expected *paliweisang*.

The root *pali* is also found in the following compound words which name locations.

(a)	*palihdam*	'outrigger side of a canoe'
	palikasa	'side of a canoe opposite the outrigger'

	paliepeng	'north'
	palieir	'south'
	palimese	'east'
	palikapi	'west'
(b)	*palimaun*	'right side'
	palimeing	'left side'

The locative nouns listed under (a) may stand alone without further affixation. Examples are:

Wehio pwarada palihdam.
'That turtle surfaced on the outrigger side.'

Sohpwo kohla palimese.
'That ship went east.'

The locative nouns listed under (b) may stand alone, or they may occur with possessive suffixes, as in these examples.

Ohlo pahn mwohndi palimaun.
'That man will sit on the right side.'

Ohlo pahn mwohndi palimauni.
'That man will sit to the right of me.'

Both *palimaun* and *palimeing* are Class I nouns.

Locative Nouns Bound to Prepositions: Some locative nouns in Ponapean occur bound to the prepositions *ni* and *nan*. Three of the prepositional nouns we earlier examined were of this type. These were the nouns beginning with *nan* (listed *nanwerenge*, *nanpwungara*, and *nanmadolara*). We treated these three nouns as prepositional nouns, however, because they may occur in direct patterns of possession. The nouns bound to prepositions that we will examine in this section may not. Examples of the kind of nouns we will consider here are listed below.

With *ni*		With *nan*	
niaul	'slope'	*nanmadau*	'ocean'
		nanwel	'mangrove swamp'
		nankep	'inlet'
		nansed	'ocean, sea'
		nanras	'ground level of a feasthouse'

When used in locative phrases, these nouns combine with demonstrative modifiers, as these examples illustrate.

> *Re kohla niaulo.*
> 'They went to the slope.'

> *Re kesik nanwelo.*
> 'They hunted in that forest.'

We treat nouns like these as locative nouns rather than as noun
phrases introduced by prepositions because the preposition here
is bound to the following noun. Evidence for this is of two kinds.
First, these nouns do not occur without the preceding preposition
with the same meaning. Second, in the case of forms involving a
preposition plus a following monosyllabic noun, the lengthening
of the vowel characteristic of such nouns in isolation does not
occur. Therefore, *nanras* is from *nan* plus *rahs*. *Rahs* in isolation
does not mean 'the ground level of a feasthouse', but rather 'the
place of the earth oven'. Also *rahs* in isolation contains a long
vowel. In combination with *nan*, it does not.

   The Noun *Wasa*: Still one other noun that may occur as the
headword of a locative phrase without a preceding preposition is
the noun *wasa*, meaning 'place'. It combines with demonstrative
modifiers, as in these examples.

> *E tangala wasaho.*
> 'He fled to that place.'

> *Serepeino pwupwsang wasaht.*
> 'That girl fell from this place.'

Wasa also occurs as the head noun of more complex locative
phrases like the following.

> *E pelehda wahro wasa me e pelehdi ie tuhkeho.*
> 'He carved out the canoe at the place where he cut down the tree.'

Constructions like these will be examined in section **6**.5.2.

Locative Noun Phrases Introduced by Prepositions

   Except when the headword of a locative noun phrase is a
locative noun of one of the types previously discussed, a locative

noun phrase must be introduced by a preposition, as in these examples.

E tangala ni imwen winio.
'He ran to the hospital.'

Ohlo memeir nan ihmwo.
'That man is sleeping in that house.'

As these sentences illustrate, there are two prepositions in Ponapean: *ni* and *nan*. We will examine these in further detail below.

When the preposition *ni* is used with locative phrases, it may be translated as 'to' or 'at', or may simply remain untranslated. Examples are:

E wahla ni nahso.
'He carried it to the feasthouse.'

E mihmi ni imweio.
'He is staying at my house.'

E kohsang ni ihmw sarawio.
'He came from the church.'

The preposition *ni* has an alternate pronunciation *nin* which occurs before words beginning with coronal consonants (*d*, *t*, *s*, *l*, *n*, and *r*), as illustrated in the following examples.

Locative Phrase with *ni*	Also Pronounced	English
ni dahuo	*nin dahuo*	'to that channel'
ni takaio	*nin takaio*	'to that rock'
ni sidohwaho	*nin sidohwaho*	'to that store'
ni lapakeho	*nin lapakeho*	'to that flood'
ni nahso	*nin nahso*	'to that feasthouse'
ni rahpo	*nin rahpo*	'to that raft'

With words beginning with other consonants, *nin* may not be used. **Nin mallo,* for example, is incorrect. It should also be noted that some speakers use *nin* only when this preposition is bound to the following noun. Therefore, as we will note in section 6.3.2, *nisoutik* 'evening' has an alternate *ninsoutik*, which is accepted by all speakers.

The preposition *nan* may be translated 'in' or 'on' or left untranslated. Examples follow.

Kilelo mi nan kapango.
'That picture is in that suitcase.'

E ntingihdi nan tehn doaropweho.
'He wrote it on that piece of paper.'

E kohla nan skohso.
'He went to the airport.'

The preposition *nan* is used to establish a location within a space
defined either in terms of two or three dimensions. Consequently,
'in' is typically the most appropriate translation of *nan*. Note in
the second example sentence previously cited, however, that *nan*
is translated 'on'. *Nan* corresponds to the English preposition 'on'
only when a location within a two dimensional space is being
referred to. (A piece of paper is normally thought of in terms of
width and length, but not height.) When a three dimensional
space is involved, *nan* never corresponds to 'on'. Instead, the
prepositional noun *powe* 'above him, her, or it' does, as illustrated
by the following sentence.

Pinselo mi pohn tehpelo.
pencil-that exist above-of table-that
'The pencil is on the table.'

Demonstrative Pronouns in Locative Phrases

Both locative noun phrases and locative noun phrases introduced by prepositions may be replaced by the demonstrative
pronouns *met* 'here', *men* 'there, by you', and *mwo* 'there, away
from you and me'. Examples follow.

E wahdo met.
'He carried it here.'

I kak wahwei men.
'I can carry it there (by you).'

I wahsang mwo.
'I carried it from there (away from us).'

(For a more complete discussion of these demonstrative pronouns, see section 4.5.3.)

TEMPORAL PHRASES

6.3.2   Similar in structure and function to locative phrases are the kinds of phrases we will call **temporal phrases**. But, whereas locative phrases tell where something occurred, temporal phrases tell *when* it occurred. Like locative phrases, temporal phrases are of three basic types. These three types are illustrated in the following sentences.

> (a)   Lahpo pwurodo *aio*.
>   'That guy returned *yesterday*.'
>
> (b)   Serepeino pahn mwemweitla Kolonia *nan wihket*.
>   'That girl will visit Kolonia *this week*.'
>
> (c)   E lalaid *met*.
>   'He's fishing *now*.'

In sentence (a), a **temporal noun phrase** is employed. In sentence (b), a **temporal noun phrase introduced by a preposition** is used, while in sentence (c), a **demonstrative pronoun** occurs. Following the procedure we employed in the previous section on locative phrases, we will organize our discussion of temporal phrases according to these three types.

Temporal Noun Phrases

A noun phrase may function as a temporal noun phrase without a preceding preposition if the head noun of the phrase is a **temporal noun**. A temporal noun is a noun that names a time or a unit of time. In this section, four types of temporal nouns will be examined. These four types are: **temporal nouns, temporal nouns bound to prepositions, prepositional nouns**, and the **temporal noun** *ansou* 'time'.

     Temporal Nouns: Some temporal nouns occur alone in temporal phrases without further modification. Examples of such nouns follow.

aio	'yesterday'	*mahs*	'in the past'
rahnwet	'today'	*ngkapwan*	'a while ago'
lakapw	'tomorrow'	*mwuhr*	'later'
pali	'day after tomorrow'		
peilah	'two days after tomorrow'		

The nouns listed in the first column name days in relation to today while those in the second name an indefinite time either in the past or future. Examples of these temporal nouns used in sentences follow.

> *Soulik rik mwangas aio.*
> 'Soulik gathered copra yesterday.'

> *Mehn Pohnpei kin pelipel mahs.*
> 'Ponapeans did tattooing in the past.'

> *Pwopwoudo wahdo ngkapwan.*
> 'That couple brought it a while ago.'

Ningkapwan occurs as an alternant of *ngkapwan* for some speakers.

Temporal noun phrases which name specific times involve the use of the temporal nouns *kuloak* 'clock' and *minit* 'minute', both of which are borrowed from English. These nouns are used in expressions like the following.

kuloak eisek	'ten o'clock'
kuloak eisek elep	'half past ten'
minit limau mwohn kuloak eisek	'five minutes before ten o'clock'
minit limau daulih kuloak eisek	'five minutes after ten o'clock'

Sentences in which temporal noun phrases like these may occur are the following.

> *Mihting pahn tepida minit eisek limau mwohn kuloak riau.*
> 'The meeting will begin fifteen minutes before two o'clock.'

> *I kin mwengehn souwas kuloak eisek ehu elep.*
> 'I eat lunch at eleven thirty.'

Temporal noun phrases naming specific dates also occur without preceding prepositions, as in these examples.

> *Ohlo ipwidi Senweri eisek, kid duwepwiki rieisek duwau.*
> 'That man was born January 10, 1929.'

> *Pwutako pahn neksang sukuhl Suhn riau.*
> 'That boy will graduate from school June 2nd.'

Expressions like these involve the use of a temporal noun naming a month plus a following numeral expression naming the day and possibly the year. A complete list of the names of the months in Ponapean follows.

Senweri	'January'	*Sulai*	'July'
Pepuweri	'February'	*Oakos*	'August'
Mahs	'March'	*Septempe*	'September'
Epreil	'April'	*Oakoatope*	'October'
Mei	'May'	*Nopempe*	'November'
Suhn	'June'	*Tisempe*	'December'

All of these words, of course, are borrowed from English. Ponapean, though, did have its own calender prior to Western contact that included names for months, days, and phases of the moon. Today, these terms are no longer in use and are known by relatively few speakers. Later in this section we will note that nouns which name months, except when employed in naming specific dates, normally occur with the preposition *nan*.

Temporal Nouns Bound to Prepositions: In the preceding discussion of locative phrases, we noted that some locative nouns occur bound to prepositions. *Nanwel* 'forest' was one example. Similarly, there are a number of temporal nouns which also occur bound to prepositions. Some of these are listed below.

(a)	*nisohrahn*	'pre-dawn morning hours'
	nimenseng	'morning'
	nisouwas	'noon'
	nisoutik	'evening'
	nipwong	'night'
(b)	*Niehd*	'Monday'
	Niare	'Tuesday'
	Niesil	'Wednesday'
	Niepeng	'Thursday'
	Nialem	'Friday'
(c)	*nanrek*	'season of plenty'
	nanisol	'season of scarcity'

As these examples illustrate, temporal nouns bound to prepositions are basically of three types. Listed under (a) are the names for parts of the day. Listed under (b) are the names of the first five days of the week. Notice that these names are made up of the preposition *ni* plus a numeral from the *ehd* counting system which we examined in section **4**.4.5. The names of the remaining two days of the week are *Rahn Kaunop* 'Saturday' and *Rahn Sarawi* 'Sunday'. Listed under (c) are some seasons of the year. These temporal nouns may occur alone in a temporal phrase, or they may occur with other modifiers. The following sentences employing *nimenseng* 'morning' illustrate these possibilities.

(a) *Ohlo kin doadoahk nimenseng.*
    'That man works in the morning.'

(b) *Ohlo pahn doadoahk nimenseng en lakapw.*
    'That man will work tomorrow morning.'

(c) *Ohlo doadoahk nimensengo.*
    'That man worked this morning.'

In sentence (a), *nimenseng* is employed alone with a generic meaning 'in the morning' without reference to any specific morning. In sentence (b), *nimenseng* occurs in the construct construction *nimenseng en lakapw*, literally 'morning of tomorrow' or 'tomorrow morning'. In sentence (c), *nimenseng* occurs with the demonstrative modifier *-o*, which signals that the morning referred to is the one that occurred earlier in the day. More generally, the demonstrative *-o* may be used with parts of the day to refer to any time past to the previous midnight, or, for some speakers, even to the previous evening. The demonstrative *-et* may also be used with words like these to refer either to the present time or to any time coming until daybreak of the following day. Assuming, then, that one were speaking at noon, 'this morning' would be *nimensengo*, while 'this noon' would be *nisouwaset* and 'this evening' would be *nisoutiket*.

What we have said about temporal nouns bound to prepositions naming parts of the day applies as well to those naming days of the week or seasons. Therefore, the demonstratives *-o* and *-et* may also be used with these nouns with the meanings 'previous' or 'last' for *-o*, and with the meanings 'present', 'following', or 'coming' for *-et*. With these nouns, though, the modifiers *samwalahro* 'last' and *kohkohdo* 'coming' are also commonly used, as illustrated in the following sentences.

Soulik iang kamadipwo Niesil samwalahro.
'Soulik participated in the feast last Monday.'

Kitail pahn kang mwahng nanisol kohkohdo.
'We will eat taro in this coming season of scarcity.'

Prepositional Nouns: Some of the prepositional nouns that we examined in the preceding discussion of locative nouns are also used with temporal meanings. Among these are the two prepositional nouns *mwoh* 'before (it)' and *mwuri* 'after (it)'. Examples of these nouns used temporally are presented in the following sentences.

E pahn kohdo mwohn lahpo.
'He will come before that guy.'

E pahn kohdo mwohi.
'He will come before me.'

Soulik kak doadoahk mwurin kamadipwo.
'Soulik can work after the feast.'

Soulik kak doadoahk mwuri.
'Soulik can work after it.'

The Noun *Ansou*: Still one other noun that may occur as the head noun in a temporal phrase without a preceding preposition is the noun *ansou* 'time'. It combines with the demonstrative modifiers *-o* and *-et*, as in these examples.

E sohte mihmi wasaht ansowo.
'He wasn't here at that time.'

E memeir ansowet.
'He is sleeping now.'

Like *wasa, ansou* also occurs as the head noun of more complex temporal phrases, like the following.

E memeir ansou me nah serio pwupwidio.
'He was sleeping when his child fell down.'

Constructions like these are examined in section **6**.5.2.

Temporal Noun Phrases Introduced by Prepositions

Except when the head word of a temporal phrase is one of the types we previously examined, a temporal phrase must be introduced by one of the two prepositions, *ni* or *nan*.

The preposition *ni*, which also occurs as *nin* under the conditions described in the preceding discussion, is used to mean 'at (the time of)' when referring to some specific time. It occurs in phrases like these.

> *Soulik lemmwida ni eh kilangada enio.*
> 'Soulik got frightened at the time he saw the ghost.'
>
> *John lel met ni ei mwesemweselsang wasaht.*
> 'John arrived here at the time I was leaving this place.'
>
> *I mworouroula ni ei mihmi Pohnpeio.*
> 'I got fat at the time I was in Ponape.'

The preposition *nan* is used when specifying some time within a larger period of time, as in these examples.

> *Irail pahn pwurodo nan wihk kohkohdo.*
> 'They will return next week.'
>
> *I pahn kohla Hawaii nan Septempe.*
> 'I am going to Hawaii in September.'
>
> *E kin angin nan Tisempe.*
> 'It is windy in December.'

Demonstrative Pronouns in Temporal Phrases

Locative phrases, as we previously noted, may be replaced by the demonstrative pronouns *met*, *men*, and *mwo*. In the case of temporal phrases, however, only the demonstrative pronoun *met* may be used. Examples are:

> *Sarawi wiewiahwi met.*
> 'Services are taking place now.'
>
> *Ke lesila met!*
> 'You've had it now!'

SENTENCE ADVERBS

6.3.3   **Sentence adverbs**, as defined here, are basically of two types—those which modify entire sentences and normally occur in sentence initial position, and those which modify parts of sentences and have considerable freedom of position. Examples of sentence adverbs of the first type follow.

> *Dene* Kepina pahn kohdo lakapw.
> '*It is said* the Governor will come tomorrow.'

> *Likamwete* Soulik kohdo aio.
> '*Apparently* Soulik came yesterday.'

> *Ele* kitail pahn mwesel lakapw.
> '*Perhaps* we will leave tomorrow.'

> *Paiente* ke kanengamah.
> '*Luckily* you are patient.'

> *Pala* kowe me ese!
> '*As if* you are the one who knows!'

Other sentence adverbs of this type include *ipwadeke* 'is it correct to assume that', *mwein* 'maybe', *uhdahn* 'it is certain that' and *mehlel* 'it is true that'.

The effect of these adverbs is to indicate the speaker's attitude about the certainty, or possibly the desirability, of the information contained in the following sentence. While these adverbs normally occur at the beginning of the sentence they modify, some may also be moved between the subject noun phrase and the predicate phrase, as in these examples.

> *Mwein ohlo aluhla Kolonia.*
> *Ohlo mwein aluhla Kolonia.*
> 'Maybe that man walked to Kolonia.'

> *Uhdahn Soulik pahn pwangada.*
> *Soulik uhdahn pahn pwangada.*
> 'It is certain that Soulik will get tired.'

One of these adverbs, *mehlel*, may also occur in sentence final position when the predicate phrase of the sentence has an adjective as its head. An example is:

> *Ohlo doadoahk laud mehlel.*
> 'That man is hard-working!'

Here *mehlel* has the function of signaling emphasis.

Another sentence adverb used to signal emphasis that may be employed with sentences of all types is *pwa*. *Pwa*, however, is unique among sentence adverbs of this first type because it occurs *only* in sentence final position. Examples of its usage are:

Ke paiamwahu pwa!
'You are lucky!'

Kitail kamam sakau pwa!
'We enjoy kava!'

Kowe me ese pwa!
'You are the one who knows!'

Sentence adverbs of the second type are characterized by their freedom of position within the sentence. Two such adverbs are *pein* and *-te*.

The adverb *pein* may occur before either noun phrases or verb phrases, as illustrated by the following sentences.

(a) *Pein ohlo diarada ah sapwung.*
     'That man himself found his mistake.'

(b) *Ohlo diarada pein ah sapwung.*
     'That man found his own mistake.'

(c) *Ohlo pein diarada ah sapwung.*
     'That man found his mistake on his own.'

As these examples show, *pein* has a **reflexive** function. In sentence (a), it modifies the subject noun phrase and means '-self'. *Pein* may also be used before independent pronouns with this same meaning, as in these examples.

Pein ih diarada ah sapwung.
'He himself found his mistake.'

Pein ngehi diarada ei sapwung.
'I myself found my mistake.'

In sentence (b), *pein* modifies a possessive noun phrase, in this case in the object position. Here *pein* is best translated 'own'. In sentence (c), *pein* modifies the verb phrase, with the meaning 'on one's own' or 'of one's own accord'. Thus, sentences like the following are also possible.

Ohlo pein kohdo.
'That man came on his own.'

Pwutako pein pwurodo.
'That boy returned on his own.'

If the verb phrase contains an object pronoun with the same referent as the subject, then *pein* in this position may mean '-self', as in these examples.

Irail pein duhpirail.
'They bathed themselves.'

I pein duhpie.
'I bathed myself.'

The enclitic adverb *-te* means 'just' or 'only' when following a noun phrase. Examples are:

Ohlohte kangala rais koaros.
'Just that man ate up all the rice.'

Ohlo kin kang raiste.
'That man eats only rice.'

This adverb also occurs after reduplicated verbs, but with the meaning of 'still' or 'continuing', as in these examples.

Lahpo tangatangete.
'That guy is still running.'

Soulik mwengemwengehte.
'Soulik is still eating.'

Kita nek koasoakoasoaite eten.
'We can continue talking this evening.'

A final point to be made here is that it is possible for a sentence to contain more than one sentence adverb. Two sentence adverbs of the first type may occur together, as in the following sentence.

Mwein ele Olapahd kodon emen.
'Maybe perhaps Olapahd was a giant.'

Two sentence adverbs of the second type may also occur together, as in this next sentence.

I pein duduhpiehte.
'I am still bathing myself.'

Or, sentence adverbs of both types may occur in a single sentence, as in this next sentence.

Likamwete irail pein duhpirail.
'Apparently they bathed themselves.'

AN EXPANDED VIEW OF THE BASIC SENTENCE

6.3.4   Based upon the observations made in sections **6**.3.1 through **6**.3.3, we may expand our definition of a basic sentence as follows.

A basic sentence consists of a noun phrase and a predicate phrase plus, optionally, one or more sentence adverbs.

Our understanding of what a predicate phrase is must also be expanded.

A predicate phrase consists of a noun phrase or a verb phrase in combination with zero to two noun phrases PLUS an optional locative and/or temporal phrase.

A more formal way to state these rules follows. The abbreviations NP and VP are used to stand for *noun phrase* and *verb phrase* respectively. Items enclosed in parentheses are optional. The curly brackets surrounding NP and VP (NP) (NP) in the second rule mean that one must choose one or the other of these two ways of forming a predicate phrase, but not both.

Sentence → (Sentence Adverb) NP Predicate Phrase

Predicate Phrase → $\left\{ \begin{array}{l} \text{NP} \\ \text{VP (NP) (NP)} \end{array} \right\}$ (Locative Phrase) (Temporal Phrase)

BASIC SENTENCE INTONATION

6.3.5   One additional property of sentences that we have not yet considered is their patterns of **intonation**. The term intonation refers to the melodic properties of speech that are produced by variations in the pitch of the voice. Not very much is known about intonation in Ponapean, but we can at least make some general observations about intonation in basic sentences.

The following examples illustrate the intonation patterns of basic affirmative sentences. In these examples, pitch is graphically illustrated by the relative height of the underlining, with higher pitch being indicated by higher lines.

Limwei *sounpadahk emen.*

'Limwei is a teacher.'

Limwei *pahn duhdu.*

'Limwei will bathe.'

Limwei *pahn duhp* *seri kat.*

'Limwei will bathe these children.'

Limwei *pahn duhp* *seri kat* *ni pillapo.*

'Limwei will bathe these children at the river.'

Limwei *pahn duhp* *seri kat* *ni pillapo* *pwohnget.*

'Limwei will bathe these children at the river tonight.'

Notice that the overall intonation pattern of these sentences is falling. Each phrase is pronounced with slightly lower pitch than the preceding one. Also note that the end of each phrase is signalled by a slight rise or a slight fall in pitch. A slight rise marks that the end of the phrase has been reached, but not the end of the sentence. A slight fall indicates that the end of both the phrase and the sentence have been reached.

As we noted in section 5.5, subject pronouns behave intonationally as part of the verb phrase, as illustrated by these examples.

E pahn duhdu.
'She will bathe.'

E pahn duhp   *seri kat.*

'She will bathe these children.'

A complete study of intonation (and stress, about which almost nothing is known) remains to be undertaken.

MODIFICATIONS OF THE BASIC SENTENCE

6.4 Now that we have examined the structure of basic sentences, let us turn our attention to how sentences like these may be modified to produce still other sentence types. Basically, the ways in which sentences may be modified are by deleting sentence elements, by moving elements of the sentence around, by adding elements, or by substituting elements. In a more formal grammar of Ponapean our task would be to state precisely how these patterns of modification work, but for our purposes here we will instead focus our attention on some of their major results.

One way in which sentences may be modified is through pronominalization. Some basic observations about pronouns and pronominalization were presented in sections **4**.5.3 through **4**.7.4 of chapter 4 and in section 5.5 of chapter 5. In this section our concern will be with other kinds of modifications that result in the types of sentences we will call **imperative sentences**, **thematic sentences**, **interrogative sentences**, and **negative sentences**. All of these sentence types may be derived from basic sentences.

IMPERATIVE SENTENCES

6.4.1 **Imperative sentences** are sentences which express commands. Examples follow.

Mwohndi!
'Sit down!'

Kangala raiso!
'Eat up that rice!'

Wahla pwuhke paho!
'Take this book down there!'

These sentences are all derived from verbal sentences by the deletion of the subject pronoun, which we assume to be *ke* 'you'.

One might wish to argue, of course, that *ke* never was in these sentences and that imperative sentences ought to be treated as basic sentence types. Evidence against this position, however, occurs when we note that in some kinds of imperative sentences, the pronoun 'you' is retained.

When commands are negated, then *ke* 'you' is normally retained, as in these examples.

> *Ke dehr mwohndi!*
> 'Don't sit down!'

> *Ke dehr kangala raiso!*
> 'Don't eat that rice!'

> *Ke dehr wahla pwuhke paho!*
> 'Don't take this book down there!'

In commands like these, *ke* is not deleted except when the command is intended as a general directive. Therefore, the command 'Don't smoke!' might be more likely to appear on a sign as *Dehr sumwoak*!, rather than *Ke dehr sumwoak*!

When a non-singular form of the second person pronoun 'you' is employed, it must always be retained, as in these examples.

> *Kumwa mwohndi!*
> 'Sit down (you two)!'

> *Kumwail mwohndi!'*
> 'Sit down (you all)!'

> *Kumwa kangala raiso!*
> 'Eat up that rice (you two)!'

> *Kumwail kangala raiso!*
> 'Eat up that rice (you all)!'

Also, when commands occur in honorific speech, the honorific form of the pronoun *ke*, which is *komw*, must be retained. Examples are;

> *Komw ketdi!*
> 'Sit down!'

Komw sakanla raiso!
'Eat up that rice!'

Komw ketkihla pwuhke paho.
'Take this book down there!'

It thus seems reasonable to assume that all types of imperative sentences result from modifications of basic verbal sentences.

THEMATIC SENTENCES

6.4.2   The kinds of sentences that we will call **thematic sentences** are
those in which one noun phrase has been singled out for emphasis
as the sentence **theme**. A noun phrase functioning as a theme has
a different grammatical relationship to the rest of the sentence
than a normal subject noun phrase does. Consider, for example,
sentence (a) in contrast to sentences (b) and (c).

(a)   *Ohl riemeno kin doadoahk Kolonia.*
      'Those two men work in Kolonia.'

(b)   *Ohl riemeno me kin doadoahk Kolonia.*
      'Those two men are the ones who work in Kolonia.'

(c)   *Ohl riemeno, ira kin doadoahk Kolonia*
      'As for those two men, they work in Kolonia.'

Notice that the noun phrase *ohl riemeno* 'those two men' that
functions as the subject of sentence (a) is emphasized as the theme
of sentences (b) and (c). This emphasis is accomplished in
sentence (b) by the use of a grammatical device called **focusing**,
while in sentence (c) another grammatical device called **topi-calization** is employed. Further discussions of focusing and topicalization follow.

Focusing

A noun phrase can be **focused** by placing it at the beginning of the
sentence and preceding the remainder of the sentence by the
pronoun *me*. Any noun phrase in a sentence may be focused. For
example, the object noun phrase *liho* 'that woman' of sentence (a)
occurs as a focused noun phrase in sentence (b).

(a) *Soulik poakoapoake liho.*
'Soulik loves that woman.'

(b) *Liho me Soulik poakoapoake.*
'That woman is who Soulik loves.'

An important distinction between these sentences is that whereas (a) is a verbal sentence, (b) is equational. *Liho* 'that woman' is a noun phrase and so is *me Soulik poakoapoake*, literally, 'one Soulik loves'. All focused sentences are equational.

The preceding example illustrates the focusing of an object noun phrase, but other noun phrases, as we noted, may also be focused. For example, contrast sentence (a) below with sentences (b), (c), and (d).

(a) *Lahpo pahn inauriki kisin pwehlet wahro.*
'That guy will lash that canoe with this sennit.'

(b) *Lahpo me pahn inauriki kisin pwehlet wahro.*
'That guy is who will lash that canoe with this sennit.'

(c) *Wahro me lahpo pahn inauriki kisin pwehlet.*
'That canoe is what that guy will lash with this sennit.'

(d) *Kisin pwehlet me lahpo pahn inauriki wahro.*
'This sennit is what that guy will lash that canoe with.'

Sentence (a) illustrates normal word order. Sentences (b) through (d), however, involve focusing. In sentence (b), it is the subject noun phrase *lahpo* 'that guy' that is focused. Since this noun phrase is already in initial position, focusing is signalled here only by the use of *me*. In sentence (c), the object noun phrase *wahro* 'that canoe' is focused, while in sentence (d) it is the instrumental noun phrase *kisin pwehlet* that is focused. Still other examples of focused noun phrases follow.

With Subject Noun Phrases Focused:

Ohla me wia.
'That man is who did it.'

Ira me dake wahr oapwoat.
'They are who boarded the canoe.'

With Object Noun Phrases Focused:

> *Arail doadoahk me irail tapiada.*
> 'Their work is what they started.'

> *Mwahr koanoat me ohlo alehdi.*
> 'A high title is what that man got.'

With Noun Phrases Introduced by *-ki* Focused:

> *Uhket me Soulik laidiki.*
> 'This net is what Soulik fished with.'

> *Sileht me i pahn pariki tuhke kan.*
> 'This adze is what I will cut those logs with.'

With Noun Phrases Introduced by *-ehng* Focused:

> *Wahro me i pahn papalahng.*
> 'That canoe is what I will swim towards.'

> *Ohlo me i pahn lopukehng sehu.*
> 'That man is who I will cut sugar cane for.'

With Noun Phrases Introduced by *-sang* Focused:

> *Ohlo me i pahn aluhlahsang.*
> 'That man is who I will walk away from.'

> *Nehn pwihko me e sepehsang.*
> 'That pig's leg is what he cut off.'

Locative and temporal phrases, which we noted in sections 6.3.1 and 6.3.2 are noun phrases of a special type, may also be focused. For example, consider the following pair of sentences, where in sentence (b) the locative noun phrase *Ruk* 'Truk' is focused.

(a) *Ohlo mwemweitla Ruk.*
    'That man visited Truk.'

(b) *Ruk me ohlo mwemweitla ie.*
    'Truk is where that man visited.'

Notice that the focusing of a locative noun phrase involves not only moving that phrase to initial position and employing *me*, but additionally the **locative pronoun** *ie* 'there' must be placed in the position originally occupied by the locative phrase. Other examples of focused locative phrases follow.

> *Pohrasapw me lahpo mihmi ie.*
> 'Pohrasapw is where that guy is staying.'
>
> *Ni ohpiso me Soulik kohla ie.*
> 'To the office is where Soulik went.'
>
> *Mwo me ohlo pwupwidi ie.*
> 'There is where that guy fell down.'

Temporal phrases may also be focused, as illustrated in the second of the two following sentences.

(a) *Pwopwoudo wahdo aio.*
   'That couple brought it yesterday.'

(b) *Aio me pwopwoudo wahdo.*
   'Yesterday is when that couple brought it.'

Notice that when temporal phrases are focused, no pronoun comparable to the locative pronoun *ie* occurs.

All of the examples we have examined thus far have involved the focusing of a noun phrase of a verbal sentence. Focusing may also occur in equational sentences, but, apparently with sentences of this type, it is only possible to focus the subject noun phrase, as in these examples.

> *Ohlo me sounpadahk emen.*
> 'That man is the one who is a teacher.'
>
> *Don me mehn Amerika.*
> 'Don is the one who is an American.'

Equational sentences involving the use of demonstrative pronouns may under no circumstances be focused.

With further study, no doubt a great deal more could be said about focusing. The preceding discussion, though, should be adequate to provide a basis for understanding the extensive use of focusing that will be encountered in the discussion of question word questions.

Topicalization

Like focusing, topicalization involves emphasizing a noun phrase by moving it into the initial position of a sentence. But whereas focusing results in an equational sentence—a sentence which is of a subject-predicate type—topicalization results in a sentence of a **topic-comment** type. An example follows.

Ohl riemenet, ira loalekeng.
'As for these two men, they were intelligent.'

The noun phrase *ohl riemenet* 'these two men' is the **topic** of this sentence, and the complete sentence that follows, *ira loalekeng* 'they were intelligent', is the **comment**.

Out of context, topicalized sentences sometimes sound odd, but in connected speech they are relatively common. The example above was taken from the short paragraph presented at the beginning of section **6**.2. Speaking of an early voyage to Ponape, this passage in part stated:

Ohl riemen kaunda. Eden emen Olisihpa ah eden emen Olosohpa. Ohl riemenet, ira loalekeng. . . .

'Two men directed it. One was named Olisihpa and one was named Olosohpa. As for these two men, they were intelligent. . . . '

The last sentence is the one involving topicalization.

Additional examples of topicalized noun phrases follow.

Lahpo, e sehse laid.
'As for that guy, he doesn't know how to fish.'

Ohl akau, i sohte mwahukinirail.
'As for those men, I don't like them.'

Notice in these sentences that a pronoun occurs in place of the subject or complement noun phrase that has been topicalized. When locative or temporal phrases are topicalized, however, no such pronoun occurs. Examples are:

Ni sidohwaho, i anahne kohla.
'As for the store, I need to go there.'

Lakapw, i pahn kommoal
'As for tomorrow, I will rest.'

It is also possible for temporal phrases, but *not* locative phrases, to be moved into sentence initial position by a device different from either focusing or topicalization. An example is:

> *Lakapw i pahn kommoal.*
> 'Tomorrow I will rest.'

This sentence might be considered a stylistic alternant of the sentence *I pahn kommoal lakapw.* 'I will rest tomorrow.' The distinction between a temporal phrase that is stylistically pre-posed and one that is topicalized is signaled primarily by differences in intonation and pause. A topicalized temporal phrase ends with higher rising pitch and is followed by a longer pause between it and the rest of the sentence.

Elaine Good (personal communication) has pointed out that it is *not* possible to topicalize either a proper noun or an indefinite noun phrase. The following Ponapean sentences, therefore, are ungrammatical. (The corresponding English sentences are acceptable.)

> **Joe, i mwahuki.*
> 'As for Joe, I like him.'

> **Hawaii, i men mwemweitla.*
> 'As for Hawaii, I want to visit there.'

> **Mwahmw, i iouki.*
> 'As for fish, I consider it delicious.'

Given the proper context, apparently all other noun phrases in a sentence may be topicalized.

INTERROGATIVE SENTENCES

6.4.3 **Interrogative sentences** are sentences which ask questions. There are two major types of questions: **yes/no questions** and **question-word questions.** Each of these types is examined below.

Yes/No Questions

Questions that can be answered by either 'yes' or 'no' are distinguished from affirmative sentences by their patterns of intonation. The differences between the intonation patterns of statements and yes/no questions are illustrated by the following examples. As in the discussion of intonation presented in section **6**.3.5, pitch is graphically illustrated by the relative height of the underlining, with higher pitch being indicated by higher lines.

Statement	Yes/No Question
Ih mehn Ruk.	*Ih mehn Ruk?*
'He is Trukese.'	'Is he Trukese?'
Ohlo ahpwtehn kohdo.	*Ohlo ahpwtehn koh do?*
'That man just came.'	'Did that man just come?'
Ohlo duhdu nan pillapo.	*Ohlo duhdu nan pillap o?*

'That man bathed in the river.'   'Did that man bathe in the river?'

The slight variations in pitch that occur at the end of phrases behave the same way in both statements and questions. The overall pitch patterns of statements and yes/no questions, though, are quite different. Statements are characterized by an overall falling pitch pattern, with each phrase marked by successively lower pitch. Yes/no questions, on the other hand, are characterized by an overall level pitch pattern, with higher pitch only on the last syllable.

Question Word Questions

Question word questions differ from yes/no questions in two major ways. First, unlike yes/no questions, the normal intonation pattern of question word questions is the same as that of statements. Second, question word questions employ a class of words called **interrogatives** which signal which part of the sentence requires further specification. A list of the thirteen interrogatives that occur in Ponapean follow.

ihs	'who'
ia	'where, what'
mehnia	'which'

depe	'how many'
iahd	'when'
da	'what'
mehnda	'why, to what purpose'
pwekida	'why'
apweda	'why not, what else, what other alternative'
ed-	'proceed by what means'
depehne	'what relation to (him, her, or it)'
paid	'and who else'
keus	'who are you'

How these interrogatives work in question word questions along with further information about other morphemes they combine with is presented in the following discussions.

Ihs: The interrogative *ihs* means 'who'. Examples of its use in verbal sentences follow.

(a) *Ihs me soumwahu?*
'Who is sick?'

Ihs me pwupwidi?
'Who fell down?'

Ihs me kadarodo kisakis wet?
'Who sent this gift?'

(b) *Ihs me e pahn iang?*
'Who is he going with?'

Ihs me ohlo rapahki?
'Who did that man look for?'

Ihs me Soulik doakoa?
'Who did Soulik stab?'

Notice that whether *ihs* corresponds to the subject of the verb, as it does in the examples under (a), or to the object of the verb, as it does in the examples under (b), it is normally focused, with the use of *me* being obligatory. A sentence like *Ihs soumwahu?* is ungrammatical, and a sentence like *E pahn iang ihs?* is uncommon.

Ihs may also be used in equational sentences, as in these examples.

Ihs sounpadahko?
'Who is that teacher?'

Ihs ohlo?
'Who is that man?'

In these sentences, too, *ihs* must appear in the position of the first noun phrase, but *me* is not employed.

Ihs also occurs in possessive constructions, as the following sentences illustrate.

Kenen ihs dahlo?
'Whose plate of food is that?'

Nimen ihs uhpwo?
'Whose drinking coconut is that?'

En ihs rausiso?
'Whose trousers are those?'

Semen ihs me mehla?
'Whose father died?'

In these examples, *ihs* may be translated 'whose'. It occurs in the position that, in a statement, would be occupied by a noun phrase representing the possessor.

Finally, *ihs* may combine with the **enumerative suffix** *-nge* as *ihsnge* to mean 'who (plural)', as in these examples.

Ihsnge kumwail?
'Who (pl.) are you?'

Ihsnge me ke iang?
'Who (pl.) did you go with?'

Nimen ihsnge uhpw akau?
'Whose (pl.) drinking coconuts are those?'

Ia: The question word *ia* may mean either 'where' or 'what', depending upon the kind of sentence in which it occurs. The more common meaning of *ia* is 'where', as illustrated by the following sentences.

Ke pahn kohla ia?
'Where are you going?'

Ira pampap ia?
'Where are they swimming?'

Ohlo kohsang ia?
'Where does that man come from?'

In these examples, *ia* occurs in the position that would be occupied by a locative phrase in a corresponding affirmative sentence. *Ia* may also occur at the beginning of sentences like these, but in this case it occurs with the locative noun *wasa* 'place' (in conventional spelling written *iawasa*), and as in the focusing of locative phrases, the locative pronoun *ie* occurs in the position originally occupied by *ia*. Examples are:

Iawasa ke pahn kohla ie?
'Where is it that you are going?'

Iawasa re pampap ie?
'Where is it that they are swimming?'

Iawasa ohlo kohsang ie?
'Where is it that man comes from?'

Sentences like these apparently have meanings that are like those of focused sentences, but they differ from other focused sentences by employing *wasa* rather than *me* before the remainder of the sentence. Consequently, both of the following sentences are of doubtful grammaticality.

(?) *Iawasa me ke pahn kohla ie?*
(?) *Ia ke pahn kohla ie?*

The interrogative *ia* is also employed to mean 'where' in equational sentences like the following.

Ia kowe?
'Where are you?'

Ia imwen winien?
'Where is the hospital?'

Ia ohpisen?
'Where is the office?'

It is only in equational sentences that *ia* may be used to mean 'what'. This meaning is appropriate, though, only if the second noun phrase has as its head a directly possessed noun that names a quality or attribute, rather than a physical object. Examples follow.

> *Ia edemw?*
> 'What is your name?'

> *Ia wehwe?*
> 'What is its meaning?'
>   or
> 'What does it mean?'

> *Ia mwomwe?*
> 'What is its appearance?'
>   or
> 'What does it look like?'

With some nouns, a freer English translation of *ia* is 'how', as in these examples.

> *Ia iremw?*
> 'What is your condition?'
>   or
> 'How are you?'

> *Ia duwen omw kohdo?*
> 'What is the manner of your coming?'
>   or
> 'How did you come?'

Like *ihs*, *ia* also occurs with the enumerative suffix *-nge* in the form *iahnge*. *Iahnge* may only be used in equational sentences, where it means 'where (plural)' in the sense 'enumerate the locations of' or 'what (plural)', also in an enumerative sense. Examples follow.

> *Iahnge ohl akan?*
> 'Where are (enumerate the locations of) those men?'

> *Iahnge edemw?*
> 'What are (enumerate) the names you have gone by?'

Mehnia: The interrogative *mehnia* means 'which'. It is composed of three morphemes: the replacive pronoun *me*, the construct suffix *-n*, and the interrogative *ia*. Literally it means 'one-of-where'. *Mehnia* occurs in noun phrases and precedes the head noun, as in these examples.

> *E wahdo mehnia lohs?*
> 'Which mat did he bring?'

> *Ke men kilang mehnia kasdo?*
> 'Which movie do you want to see?'

Complement noun phrases (direct objects or noun phrases introduced by verbal suffixes) containing *mehnia* are also commonly focused, as in these examples.

> *Mehnia lohs me e wahdo?*
> 'Which mat is it that he brought?'

> *Mehnia kasdo me ke men kilang?*
> 'Which movie is it that you want to see?'

Whereas focusing is optional when *mehnia* occurs in complement noun phrases, it is obligatory when *mehnia* occurs in subject noun phrases. Examples are:

> *Mehnia serepein me keieu masamwahu?*
> 'Which girl is it that is the prettiest?'

> *Mehnia sohp me pahn kohla Pingelap?*
> 'Which ship is it that is going to Pingelap?'

In focused sentences involving *mehnia*, *me* is sometimes deleted in informal speech. Other interrogatives that behave like *mehnia* are *depe* 'how many', *iahd* 'when', and *da* 'what'. Therefore, all of these interrogatives permit the deletion of *me*, are obligatorily focused in subject noun phrases, and are optionally focused in complement phrases.

If the identity of the head noun in a noun phrase containing *mehnia* is known to the listener(s), then it may be deleted and *mehnia* may stand in place of the entire noun phrase, as in these examples.

> *Mehnia me e wahdo?*
> 'Which did he bring?'

Mehnia me pahn kohla Pingelap?
'Which one will go to Pingelap?'

Like the preceding two interrogatives we have examined, *mehnia* may also combine with the enumerative suffix *-nge* to mean 'which (plural)'.

Mehniahnge lohs me e wahdo?
'Which mats did he bring?'

Mehniahnge sohp me pahn kohla Pingelap?
'Which ships will go to Pingelap?'

Depe: The interrogative *depe* means 'how many'. It occurs in noun phrases in the position of numerals. Examples of its usage follow.

Ke pwainda iaht depe?
'How many yards did you buy?'

Lahpo kolehdi mwahmw depe?
'How many fish did that guy get?'

Pwihno kemehla pwihk depe?
'How many pigs did that group kill?'

As noted in the last discussion, complement noun prases containing *depe* are optionally focused, while subject noun phrases containing *depe* are obligatorily focused. *Me* may be deleted in informal speech.

Iaht depe me ke pwainda?
'How many yards did you buy?'

Pwihk depe me pwihno kemehla?
'How many pigs did that group kill?'

Amamas depe me iang kamadipwo?
'How many people participated in that feast?'

Sukuhl depe me mi nan wehin Kiti?
'How many schools are there in the municipality of Kiti?'

Like numerals, the interrogative *depe* may combine with the causative prefix *ka-*. With numerals, as we noted in section **4.4.8**, *ka-* is used to form ordinals; therefore, *ka-* prefixed to *riau* 'two' results in *kariau* 'second'. With *depe*, the prefixing of *ka-* results in *kedepe*, the meaning of which is 'what rank'. What is especially interesting about *kedepe* is that it is an **interrogative verb**, a verb which signals a question. The following sentence illustrates how it might be used.

> *Ke kedepe?*
> 'What rank are you?'

Out of context, this question is ambiguous. It might be an inquiry about one's position in a contest or one's standing with respect to another in terms of age. More generally, it may be used in any situation where the question of rank is relevant. The response to a question like this would involve the use of an ordinal numeral.

Iahd: The interrogative *iahd* means 'when'. It occurs in the position of a temporal phrase, as the following examples illustrate.

> *Ke kohdo iahd?*
> 'When did you come?'
>
> *Re pahn mwenge iahd?*
> 'When will they eat?'
>
> *Ohlo mehla iahd?*
> 'When did that man die?'

As the next examples illustrate, *iahd* may also be focused.

> *Iahd me ke kohdo?*
> 'When was it that you came?'
>
> *Iahd me re pahn mwenge?*
> 'When is it that they will eat?'
>
> *Iahd me ohlo mehla?*
> 'When was it that that man died?'

Me may be deleted in informal speech.

Da: The interrogative *da* may be broadly translated 'what'. Its specific meaning, however, depends upon the kind of construction in which it appears. Following the head noun in noun phrases, *da* means 'what kind of', as in these questions.

Soulik padokehdi kehp da?
'What kind of yam did Soulik plant?'

Serio sasaik mwahmw da?
'What kind of fish is that child catching?'

Complement noun phrases containing *da* may be optionally focused; subject noun phrases containing *da* are obligatorily focused. *Me* is sometimes deleted in informal speech.

Kehp da me Soulik padokehdi?
'What kind of yam is it that Soulik planted?'

Mwahmw da me serio sasaik?
'What kind of fish is it that that child is catching?'

Mahn da me kak kangala aramas?
'What kind of animal is it that can eat people?'

Pwoht da me kin sepehlda?
'What kind of boat is it that turns over?'

Questions like these are frequently shortened by deletion to sentence fragments like the following.

Kehp da?
'What kind of yam?'

Mwahmw da?
'What kind of fish?'

These questions are particularly interesting in contrast to the following, where *da* appears initially with the meaning 'what do you mean by'.

Da kehp?
'What do you mean by yam?'

Da mwakereker?
'What do you mean by constellation?'

Da also occurs in construct constructions, where it may be translated 'what for'.

> *Sopin da?*
> 'What is the ship for?

The response to a question like this might be *sopin laid* 'fishing ship', where *laid* is the verb 'to fish'.

This interrogative is also used to stand in the place of entire noun phrases. Used this way in verbal sentences, it is pronounced *dah* rather than *da*, the vowel lengthening here being a result of the application of the monosyllabic noun vowel lengthening rule. Examples follow.

> *Re kukih dah?*
> 'What did they cook?'
>
> *Kitail pahn kowih dah?*
> 'What are we going to chase?'

Dah may also be focused according to the principles we discussed for *da*. When *dah* occurs with *me*, however, they are by convention written together as *dahme*. Examples follow.

> *Dahme re kukih?*
> 'What is it that they cooked?'
>
> *Dahme kitail pahn kowih?*
> 'What is it that we are going to chase?'
>
> *Dahme pwupwidi?*
> 'What is it that fell down?'
>
> *Dahme ngalisuhk?*
> 'What is it that bit you?'

Dahme is also used in 'why' questions. Questions like these are formed by suffixing *-ki* to the verb of the sentence, as in these examples.

> *Dahme ke tangki?*
> 'Why did you run?'
>
> *Dahme ke men kohkihdo Pohnpei?*
> 'Why do you want to come to Ponape?'
>
> *Dahme ke mwahukihki kang sakau?*
> 'Why do you like to drink kava?'

In equational sentences, *da* occurs in combination with the bound morphemes *-kot* and *-kei* in the forms *dahkot* 'what (singular)' and *dahkei* 'what (plural)'. Examples follow.

Dahkot met?
'What is this?'

Dahkei met?
'What are these?'

In verbal sentences, 'what (plural)' is expressed by use of the enumerative suffix *-nge* in the form *dahnge*. *Dahnge* is always focused, as the following examples illustrate.

Dahnge me ohla?
'What (plural) was broken?'

Dahnge me ke pahn idang?
'What (plural) are you going to mash?'

Finally, *da* occurs with other morphemes in three additional interrogatives, all of which have the general meaning of 'why'. Each of these is discussed below.

Mehnda: The interrogative *mehnda*, from the pronoun *me* plus the construct suffix *-n* plus *da*, means 'why' or 'to what purpose'. It always occurs at the beginning of sentences, as in the following examples.

Mehnda ke wia?
'Why did you do it?'

Mehnda ke sopohla.
'Why did you elope?'

Mehnda is also used alone as an interjection or with the subordinator *ma* 'if' to mean 'never mind'. The use of *mehnda* with *ma* is examined in section **6**.5.1.

Pwekida: The interrogative *pwekida*, from *pwe* 'because' plus the instrumental suffix *-ki* plus *-da*, also means 'why'. Unlike *mehnda*, however, *pwekida* only occurs alone; it never occurs as part of a larger sentence. Therefore, in response to a statement like *Soulik sohte pahn kohdo* 'Soulik won't come', one might ask *Pwekida?* 'Why?'. But, a sentence like **Pwekida Soulik sohte* *pahn kohdo*? is ungrammatical. An alternate pronunciation of *pwekida* is *pwehda*.

Apweda: The interrogative *apweda*, like *pwekida*, occurs only as a one word question and never as part of a sentence. *Apweda*, possibly from *ahpw* 'but' plus *da*, means 'Why not?' 'What else?' or 'What other alternative is there?'

Ed-: The bound morpheme *ed-*, like *kedepe*, is an interrogative verb. It broadly means 'to proceed by what means'. It combines with directional suffixes, as in the following questions.

Re pahn edala?
'How will they go there?'

Soulik edodo?
'How did Soulik come here?'

Depehne: In addition to interrogative verbs, there are also **interrogative nouns** in Ponapean. The interrogative *depehne* is one such example. *Depehne* always occurs in direct patterns of possession, the form given here being the third person singular, meaning 'what relation to him, her, or it'. 'Relation' here is used both with reference to physical locations and connections of persons by kin or clan. Thus, both of the following sentences are possible.

Depehnen imwen Souliko?
'Where is it in relation to Soulik's house?'

Depehnen lahpo?
'How is he related to that guy?'

The answer to the first question would involve the use of a prepositional or relational noun, while the answer to the second would involve a noun expressing a family or clan relationship.

In the preceding examples, *depehne* occurs in a construct form with a following noun phrase. Suffixed by possessive pronouns, *depehne* follows the pattern of Class III nouns. Questions like the following are therefore also possible.

Depehnei?
'Where is it in relation to me?'
        or
'How is he related to me?'

Depehnarail?
'Where is it in relation to them?'
or
'How is he related to them?'

An alternate pronunciation of *depehne* is *dehne*.

Paid: Another interrogative noun is *paid*. *Paid* occurs in equational sentences with the meaning 'and who else'. Following are examples.

Ih paid?
'He and who else?'

Soulik paid?
'Soulik and who else?'

Keus: The final interrogative that we will consider is *keus*, meaning 'Who are you?' or 'Who goes there?'. *Keus* is no longer in common use. It is employed at the present time primarily in the context of legends with reference to one of the guards during the reign of the *Saudeleurs* who challenged those approaching his post with '*Keus*?'. It is believed by some speakers of Ponapean that this interrogative comes from *kowe ihs*, literally 'you who'. In contemporary Ponapean, however, *kowe ihs* is ungrammatical, the proper word order of a question like this being *ihs kowe*.

NEGATIVE SENTENCES

6.4.4   In section 5.3, where we examined verbal prefixes, we noted that some verbs in Ponapean may be negated by the use of the prefixes *sa-* and *sou-*. For example, a verb like *pwung* 'correct' may combine with the prefix *sa-* to produce *sapwung* 'incorrect', while a verb like *pisek* may combine with the prefix *sou-* to produce *soupisek* 'busy'. With these negative prefixes, it is therefore possible to negate a single word in a sentence. This is one kind of negation. Our examination of negation in this section, however, has a different focus. Here our concern is not with just how a single word may be negated, but rather it is with how sentences may be negated.

The negation of sentences in Ponapean involves the use of a class of words that we will call **negators**. A list of these negators, along with alternate forms where they occur, are presented below.

kaidehn	(*kaidehkin, kaidehk, kaidehnte*)
sohte	
solahr	(*sohla*)
soher	
saikinte	(*saik, kaikinte, kaik*)
sou	
dehr	(*deh*)
dehpa	

To examine the differences in meaning and function of these various negators, it will be useful to organize the following discussion according to how negation works with two basic sentence types—equational and verbal—and with two modified sentence types—imperative and interrogative.

Negative Equational Sentences

Equational sentences are negated by the use of the negator *kaidehn*. The use of *kaidehn* is illustrated below, where an affirmative equational sentence is followed by its negative counterpart.

Affirmative: *Ih sounpadahk emen.*
                    'He is a teacher.'

Negative: *Kaidehn ih sounpadahk emen.*
                    'He is not a teacher.'

As this example illustrates, the negator *kaidehn* precedes the sentence it negates. Other examples of the use of *kaidehn* follow.

Kaidehn ngehi mehn Iap.
'I am not Yapese.'

Kaidehn ohlo Nahnmwarki.
'That man is not a Nahnmwarki.'

Kaidehn weren Soulik mwo.
'That is not Soulik's canoe there.'

The negator *kaidehn* has an alternate form *kaidehkin*, which is sometimes shortened to *kaidehk*.

Kaidehn also occurs in combination with the sentence adverb

-*te* in the form *kaidehnte*. *Kaidehnte* is used in emphatic negation, as in these examples.

> *Kaidehnte ohlo sounpadahk emen!*
> 'That man is not a teacher!'
>
> *Kaidehnte ngehi mehn Iap!*
> 'I am not Yapese!'

Negative Verbal Sentences

Verbal sentences may be negated by the use of the negators *sohte*, *solahr*, *soher*, and *saikinte*. The most common of these is *sohte*. Its use is illustrated in the negative sentence below.

Affirmative:	*Nohno pahn men pehle mwengeho.*
	'Mother will want to reheat that food.'
Negative:	*Nohno sohte pahn men pehle mwengeho.*
	'Mother will not want to reheat that food.'

Notice that the negator *sohte* occurs before the predicate phrase. In general, all negators of verbal sentences appear in this position. Additional examples of the use of *sohte* follow.

> *I sohte pahn mwadong.*
> 'I will not play.'
>
> *Soulik sohte kilang Marce.*
> 'Soulik didn't see Marce.'
>
> *Re sohte nsensuwed.*
> 'They aren't unhappy.'

Sohte may also be used to negate existential sentences.

Affirmative:	*Mie saip wasaht.*
	'There are sardines here.'
Negative:	*Sohte saip wasaht.*
	'There are no sardines here.'

In existential sentences, the negator *sohte* replaces the verb *mie*. Other examples of this use of *sohte* follow.

Sohte aramas nan ihmwo.
'There are no people in that house.'

Sohte sinek Pohnpei.
'There are no snakes in Ponape.'

Another negator that may be employed in verbal sentences is *solahr*, which may be translated 'no longer'. Examples of the use of this negator follow.

I solahr pahn kang mwengehn wai.
'I will no longer eat imported food.'

I solahr soumwahu.
'I am no longer sick.'

I solahr men pweidi rehmw.
'I no longer want to stay overnight at your place.'

Like *sohte*, *solahr* may also be used in existential sentences.

Solahr saip wasaht.
'There are no longer any sardines here.'

Solahr masis nan sidohwaho.
'There are no longer any matches in that store.'

A common alternate of *solahr* is *sohla*.

Another negator that means 'no longer' is *soher*. *Soher*, however, differs in two respects from *solahr*. First, *soher* may not be used in existential sentences; *solahr* may. Second, *soher* has been found only in combination with the aspect marker *pahn*; this is not true of *solahr*. Examples of the use of *soher* follow.

Soulik soher pahn duhkihla ah peneinei.
'Soulik will no longer be burdened with the support of his family.'

I soher pahn kang rais.
'I will no longer eat rice.'

Pwihko soher pahn pitsang nan kehlo.
'That pig will no longer escape from that pen.'

Still one other negator that occurs in verbal sentences is *saikinte* 'not yet'. Like *soher*, *saikinte* may not be used in existential sentences. Following are examples of the use of *sai-kinte*.

> *Pahpa saikinte pwurodo.*
> 'Father has not yet returned.'

> *I saikinte onopada.*
> 'I haven't yet prepared it.'

> *E saikinte pakairiki.*
> 'He hasn't yet announced it.'

Saikinte is sometimes also pronounced *kaikinte*, and these forms may be shortened to *saik* and *kaik* respectively.

Negative Interrogative Sentences

One negator we have not yet examined, *sou*, occurs only in yes/no verbal questions like the following.

> *Ke sou iang kohla?*
> 'Didn't you go along?'

> *Serio sou menmwenge?*
> 'Isn't that child hungry?'

> *Irail sou pahn pwangadahr?*
> 'Won't they get tired?'

In all of these cases, *sou* may be replaced by *sohte* with no resulting difference in meaning. But, whereas *sohte* may also be used in statements or in negative existential questions, *sou* is restricted in its usage to questions like those above.

Other negative yes/no questions are formed, as expected, simply by employing the appropriate intonation pattern. In these cases, the negator is the same as that employed in statements. For example:

> *Kaidehn ih mehn Iap?*
> 'Isn't he Yapese?'

> *E saikinte kohdo?*
> 'Hasn't he come yet?'

Sohte rais wasaht?
'Isn't there any rice here?'

Pahpa solahr pahn sumwoak?
'Isn't father going to smoke any longer?'

The response to negative yes/no questions may be either *ei* 'yes' or *soh* 'no'. However, the presence of the negator in the question must be taken into consideration in responding, as illustrated by these examples.

Ke menmwenge?	*Ei, i menmwenge.*
Are you hungry?	Yes, I am hungry.
Ke sou menmwenge?	*Soh, i menmwenge.*
Aren't you hungry?	No, I am hungry.

Both responses indicate that the speaker is hungry. But in the second response *soh* 'no' is employed rather than *ei* 'yes'. *Soh* here negates the negative sentence. The sentence that follows affirms that the speaker is hungry.

Negative Imperative Sentences

Imperative sentences, which express commands, are negated by the use of *dehr* or *dehpa*. Examples where *dehr* is employed follow.

Ke dehr mwohndi!
'Don't sit down!'

Ke dehr wiahda tiahk suwed!
'Don't behave badly!'

Ke dehr wahla naipo likin ihmwet!
'Don't take that knife outside this house!'

A common alternate of *dehr* is *deh*.

The negator *dehpa* is used in commands with the meaning 'not ever', as in these examples.

Ke dehpa sumwoak!
'Don't ever smoke!'

Ke dehpa nim kahs!
'Don't ever drink gasoline!'

Ke dehpa pap mwo!
'Don't ever swim there!'

Whereas *dehr* is neutral with respect to time—a command employing *dehr* might either mean 'Don't do it now!' or 'Don't ever do it!'—*dehpa* forbids that the action named by the verb *ever* be performed.

BASIC SENTENCES IN COMBINATION

6.5   Thus far in this chapter we have been primarily concerned with describing basic sentences and ways in which they may be modified. If we were to go back and examine the paragraph from the Ponapean legend presented in section **6**.2, or if we were to study any good sample of Ponapean speech, it would soon become apparent that what we have not yet considered is the fact that every speaker of Ponapean commonly employs sentences that themselves are made up of two or more basic sentences in combination. Though sentences like these may be very long and very complicated, relatively simple examples may also be found. Consider the following sentence.

(a)   *Dahlo pwupwidihsang pohn tehpelo, ahpw e sohte ohla.*
'The dish fell off the table, but it didn't break.'

It is obvious that within this sentence, the two following sentences occur.

(b)   *Dahlo pwupwidihsang pohn tehpelo.*
'The dish fell off the table.'

(c)   *E sohte ohla.*
'It didn't break.'

A term that we will find useful to refer to a sentence which is itself part of a larger sentence is **clause**. We may thus describe sentence (a) as consisting of two clauses—clause (b) and clause (c)—linked together by the word *ahpw* 'but'.

The use of a word like *ahpw* represents only one of three basic ways in which clauses may be combined in Ponapean. Our task in the remainder of this chapter will be to examine these three ways. They will be discussed under the headings **conjoined clauses**, **relative clauses**, and **nominal clauses**.

Conjoined Clauses

6.5.1   When two or more clauses are joined together in sequence through the use of linking words of the types that we will call **conjunctions** and **conjunctive adverbs**, we will speak of them as **conjoined clauses**. How linking words are employed in conjoining clauses is explored further below.

Conjunctions

Conjunctions are of two types—**coordinators** and **subordinators**. *Coordinators* are employed to link together clauses in a *coordinate* relationship. That is, each clause is of equal rank; one does not depend on another for its meaning. *Subordinators* are employed to link together clauses in a *subordinate* relationship. In this case, one clause depends upon another for its full meaning. A list of the coordinators and subordinators that we will examine in this section follows.

Coordinators		Subordinators	
oh	'and'	*ma*	'if'
ah	'and, however'	*pwe*	'because'
ahpw	'but'	*pwehki*	'because of'
de	'or'	*pwehde*	'since'
		mahkete	'otherwise'

Coordinators: The following sentences illustrate ways in which the coordinators listed above may be used.

oh: *Soulik pahn mwenge oh e pahn meir.*
'Soulik will eat and he will sleep.'

Ih iouki rais oh Pedro iouki rais.
'He likes rice and Pedro likes rice.'

ah: *I laid, ah e meir.*
'I fished, and he slept.'

I sohte iouki mwengeho, ah i pwainda.
'I don't like that food; however, I bought it.'

ahpw: *Dahlo pwupwidi, ahpw e sohte ohla.*
'The dish fell, but it didn't break.'

Takaio tikitik, ahpw e toutou.
'That rock is small, but it is heavy.'

de: *Kita pahn laid de kita pahn suksakau?*
         'Shall we fish or shall we make kava?'

         Ke pahn doadoahk de ke pahn meir?
         'Are you going to work or are you going to sleep?'

The difference in meaning between the first two of these coordinators is somewhat subtle. Both may be translated 'and', but *oh* is employed where the relationship between the conjoined clauses is essentially a parallel one, whereas *ah* signals a contrastive relationship. Hence, *ah* may also sometimes appropriately be translated 'however'.

When clauses conjoined by coordinators contain identical constituents, then all but one of the occurrences of the constituent are usually deleted. Consider the following sentence.

Soulik iouki mahi oh Limwei iouki mahi.
'Soulik likes breadfruit and Limwei likes breadfruit.'

In this sentence the verb phrase *iouki mahi* 'likes breadfruit' occurs twice. The first occurrence may be deleted to form the following more normal sentence.

Soulik oh Limwei iouki mahi.
'Soulik and Limwei like breadfruit.'

Additional examples illustrating deletion of this nature occur in the second of each of the following pairs of sentences.

(a) *Soulik diarada tala riau oh Soulik diarada naip pwoat.*
     'Soulik found two dollars and Soulik found a knife.'

     Soulik diarada tala riau oh naip pwoat.
     'Soulik found two dollars and a knife.'

(b) *I kohla Kolonia, ah lahpo pil kohla Kolonia.*
     'I went to Kolonia; however, that guy also went to Kolonia.'

     I kohla Kolonia, ah lahpo pil kohla.
     'I went to Kolonia; however, that guy also went.'

(c) *E masamwahu, ahpw e pweipwei.*
'He is handsome, but he is stupid.'

E masamwahu, ahpw pweipwei.
'He is handsome, but stupid.'

(d) *Ke pahn iang pwihnet de ke pahn iang pwihno?*
'Are you going with this group or are you going with that group?'

Ke pahn iang pwihnet de pwihno?
'Are you going with this group or that group?'

All of the examples we have looked at thus far have involved the conjoining of just two clauses. In theory, there is no limit to how many clauses might be linked together this way. Consider a sentence like the following:

Soulik oh Ewalt oh Casiano oh Damian oh Pendu oh Marce oh Masaki pahn doadoahk lakapw.
'Soulik and Ewalt and Casiano and Damian and Pendu and Marce and Masaki will work tomorrow.'

The number of names that might be linked together in a sentence like this is constrained only by limitations of memory.

An additional interesting point illustrated by the preceding example sentence is that the coordinator *oh* differs in an important way from its English counterpart 'and'. In English, when a number of phrases are linked together by the use of 'and', all occurrences of 'and' except the last may be deleted. Therefore, the English translation above might be more commonly expressed:

'Soulik, Ewalt, Casiano, Damian, Pendu, Marce, and Masaki will work tomorrow.'

In Ponapean, however, similar deletions of *oh* are impermissible. Though deletion of this sort does sometimes occur in the speech of younger Ponapeans, it is felt to be a consequence of the influence of English and is not considered correct by older speakers.

One case in which *oh* may be deleted in Ponapean, but not in English, is illustrated by the following sentences.

(a) *Soulik tangala oh Soulik doadoahk.*
'Soulik ran there and Soulik worked.'

(b) *Soulik tangala oh doadoahk.*
'Soulik ran there and worked.'

(c) *Soulik tangala doadoahk.*
'Soulik ran there (and) worked.'

All of these sentences may be given the same interpretation; that
is, a person named Soulik ran somewhere and worked. However,
most speakers of Ponapean would find sentence (a) awkward, if
not ungrammatical. The expected processes of deletion have not
been employed. Sentences (b) and (c) represent ways in which this
sentence might be improved. In sentence (b), the second occurrence of *Soulik* is deleted. In sentence (c), the coordinator *oh* is
additionally dropped. Apparently, however, the deletion of *oh* in
such sentences may take place only after intransitive verbs of
motion. Additional examples follow.

Ohlo seila laid.
'That man paddled there (and) fished.'

E mwohndi kommoal.
'He sat down (and) rested.'

E kohla wendi meir.
'He went there (and) lay down (and) slept.'

The role of intransitive verbs of motion in the deletion of
conjunctions will be brought up again in a subsequent discussion
of the conjunctive adverb *en*. Also, we will note in section **6**.5.3
that it is possible for two verbs to appear in sequence where the
first verb is transitive, as in *anahne mwenge* 'need to eat'. The
explanation of constructions like these, however, does not involve
the deletion of conjunctions. Rather, the second verb here represents an **infinitive clause**.

Still one other important point that we need to note is that
not all sentences that have noun phrases connected by *oh* result
from the conjoining of two clauses. Consider a sentence like the
following.

E mwohd nanpwungen Soulik oh lahpo.
'He sat between Soulik and that guy.'

A sentence like this could not be derived from the following
sentence. It makes no sense.

*E mwohd nanpwungen Soulik oh e mwohd nanpwungen lahpo.
*'He sat between Soulik and he sat between that guy.'

We therefore need to have a provision in our grammar for allowing two or more noun phrases to be connected by *oh*, as well as two or more clauses. Further justification for this position is offered by the ambiguity of a sentence like the following.

Soulik oh Limwei pwopwoud.
'Soulik and Limwei are married.'

This sentence has two possible meanings.

(a) 'Soulik and Limwei are married (to each other).'

(b) 'Soulik and Limwei are married (but not necessarily to each other).'

Meaning (a) would result from conjoining two noun phrases, while sentence (b) would result from conjoining two clauses and then deleting an identical constituent. However, if meaning (a) is intended, ambiguity may be avoided by using a construction like the following.

Soulik ih Limwei pwopwoud.
'Soulik and Limwei are married.'

In this sentence, the independent pronoun *ih* 'he, she or it' is employed in place of the coordinator *oh*. The only possible meaning of this sentence is that Soulik and Limwei are married to each other.

Subordinators: The five subordinators listed at the beginning of this section were *ma*, *pwe*, *pwehki*, *pwehde*, and *mahkete*. The meanings and functions of these words are examined below.

The subordinator *ma* means 'if'. It may be employed in sentences like the following.

Wahdo mahs ehu kamara ma ke kohla Sapahn.
'Please bring me a camera if you go to Japan.'

Sendin pehmwen pahn kensda ma ke idih iahia.
'Your finger will ulcerate if you point at a rainbow.'

In these examples, the **subordinate clause** (the clause introduced
by the subordinator *ma*) follows the main clause. A clause
introduced by *ma* may also occur first, though, as in these
sentences.

Ma ke kohla Sapahn, wahdo mahs ehu kamara.
'If you go to Japan, please bring me a camera.'

Ma ke idih iahia, sendin pehmwen pahn kensda.
'If you point at a rainbow, your finger will ulcerate.'

The subordinator *pwe* means 'because'. Examples of its
usage are:

Kitail mwesel pwe e pahn keteudi.
'Let's leave because it is going to rain.'

Limwei sohte mwahukinira pwe ira lehk.
'Limwei doesn't like them because they are selfish.'

A subordinate clause introduced by *pwe* must follow the main
clause.

The subordinator *pwehki* means 'because of'. Examples of
its usage are:

Limwei sohte mwahukinira pwehki ara lehko.
'Limwei doesn't like them because of their selfishness.'

I pwang pwehki ei doadoahko.
'I'm tired because of my work.'

This subordinator (from *pwe* plus *ki*) differs from *pwe* in two
ways. First, whereas a subordinate clause introduced by *pwe* must
follow the main clause, one introduced by *pwehki* may either
precede or follow. Thus, the two example sentences above may
alternatively be expressed:

Pwehki ara lehko, Limwei sohte mwahukinira.
'Because of their selfishness, Limwei doesn't like them.'

Pwehki ei doadoahko, i pwang.
'Because of my work, I'm tired.'

Second, whereas any clause that follows *pwe* may stand alone as a sentence, only a gerundive clause may follow *pwehki*. (Gerundive clauses will be examined in section **6**.5.3.) Note the differences that exist between the subordinate clauses in the following sentences.

> *Limwei sohte mwahukinira pwe ira lehk.*
> 'Limwei doesn't like them because they are selfish.'

> *Limwei sohte mwahukinira pwehki are lehko.*
> 'Limwei doesn't like them because of their selfishness.'

One other word meaning 'because of' that we might note here is *ahki*. Unlike either *pwe* or *pwehki*, however, *ahki* is never used as a subordinator to conjoin clauses. Instead, it is used only in response to 'why' questions, as in the following interchange.

(a) *Dahme Limwei sohte mwahukinirahki?*
'Why doesn't Limwei like them?'

(b) *Ahki ara lehko.*
'Because of their selfishness.'

A response employing *pwehki* would also be correct here. With both *pwehki* and *ahki*, a gerundive clause follows.

The subordinator *pwehde* 'since' is apparently somewhat uncommon. Some speakers register doubt as to whether or not they ever use this form. Examples like the following illustrate its usage.

> *Ohl oko uhdahn pahn kohdo pwehde ira me kaun.*
> 'Those men will surely come since they are the leaders.'

> *Koh me pahn wiliankitail pwehde kowe me keieu marahra.*
> 'You are the one who will represent us since you are the fastest.'

The subordinator *mahkete*, sometimes shortened to *mahk* or even *mah*, means 'otherwise'. Examples illustrating its usage are:

> *Ata kohla mwenge, mahkete kita kanekehla doadoahko.*
> our go-there eat, otherwise we finish-up work-that
> 'If it hadn't been for our going to eat, we would have finished that work.'

Omw lehken, mahkete aramas poakoapoakeiuk.
your selfishness-there, otherwise people like-you
'If it weren't for your selfishness, people would like you.'

Notice that *mahkete*, unlike the other subordinators we have examined, introduces the main rather than the subordinate clause. Also note that the subordinate clause is gerundive.

Conjunctive Adverbs

Another group of words that play an important role in conjoining clauses are **conjunctive adverbs**. The forms of these adverbs follow. Their meanings will be considered later.

peien	*en*
de	*lao*
eri	*apw*
pa	

What distinguishes these words from conjunctions is their position in the sentence. Unlike conjunctions, they do not occur between clauses, but rather within clauses. They occur as part of the verb phrase of the subordinate clause after subject pronouns (if present) and before aspect markers. Further details concerning each of these adverbs follow.

The conjunctive adverb *peien* means 'happen to'. One way in which it may be used is in subordinate clauses introduced by the subordinator *ma* 'if'.

Ma e peien kohdo, ke kak pakairiki.
'If he happens to come, you can announce it.'

Ma ke peien kohla laid, wahdo mahs emen mwahmw.
'If you happen to go fishing, please bring me one fish.'

Peien also occurs in combination with the subordinator *pwe* and the conjunctive adverb *de*.

De is used in combination with the subordinator *pwe* to mean 'lest', as illustrated by these examples.

Kanaieng pwe ke de pwupwidi!
'Be careful lest you fall!'

Wahda mehn pap pwe ke de duhla!
'Take a life jacket lest you drown!'

If *peien* 'happen to' is used in combination with *pwe* and *de*, then *pwe . . . de* is better translated 'in case'.

> *Wahda mehn pap pwe pwohto de peien sepehlda.*
> 'Take a life jacket in case the boat happens to capsize.'

> *Kumwa mihmi pwe lahpo de peien kohdo.*
> 'You (two) wait in case that guy happens to come.'

It is probable that the negative *dehr* that we examined in section **6.4.4** is from *de* plus the completive suffix *-ehr*. In fact, *dehr* may also occur in combination with *pwe*, as in this command.

> *Kanaieng pwe ke dehr pwupwidi!*
> 'Be careful you don't fall down (again)!'

A comparison of this example with the first one presented in this paragraph indicates that there is a subtle distinction in meaning between the use of *de* and *dehr* in sentences like these.

The conjunctive adverb *eri* combines with *oh* 'and' to mean, depending on context, 'then' or 'so', as in the following examples.

> *I doadoahk lao nek oh ngehi eri kohla.*
> 'I worked until finished and then I went there.'

> *E laid aio oh ih eri kolehdi wehi ehu.*
> 'He fished yesterday and so he caught a turtle.'

One distinctive fact about the use of *eri* is that if the subject noun phrase of the clause in which it occurs is pronominalized, the pronoun must be in an independent rather than a subject form. The following sentence, a variant of the second example cited above, is therefore ungrammatical.

> **E laid aio oh e eri kolehdi wehi ehu.*

Another point is that the conjunction *oh* is sometimes deleted before clauses containing *eri*. Thus, the following sentence is acceptable.

> *E laid aio ih eri kolehdi wehi ehu.*

Finally, we might note that it is possible for *eri* to occur in independent sentences. Examples are:

(a) *Ira eri pwurodo wasaht.*
'They then returned to this place.'

(b) *Eri, iet duwen mwomwarail.*
'Well, here is what they looked like.'

In example (a), *eri* occurs in the position characteristic of conjunctive adverbs. Sentences of this type occur when the main clause is known to the listener (s). In sentence (b), *eri* precedes the sentence. Here, *eri* is used to call the listener's attention to the fact that new information is coming that will expand upon information previously provided. Both of these usages of *eri* are extremely common in narratives.

The conjunctive adverb *pa* has three different meanings, depending upon the kind of sentence in which it occurs. In combination with *pwe*, it means 'since (contrary to expectations)', as in the following examples.

Likamwete re sohte iang, pwe i pa sohte kilang.
'Apparently they didn't participate, since (contrary to expectations) I didn't see them.'

Mwein e sohte nda, pwe i pa sehse.
'Maybe he didn't say, since (contrary to your expectations) I don't know.'

The 'contrary to expectations' meaning of *pa* is also implicit in sentences where it is used with *ah* 'and'. In this case, however, *pa* carries a meaning closer to 'suddenly (contrary to expectations)'. Examples follow, where the parentheses around *ah* indicate that it is sometimes deleted with no change in meaning.

Se mwomwohd (ah) mwangaso pa pwupwidi.
'We were sitting and suddenly (contrary to our expectations) the ripe coconut fell.'

Re mwengemwenge (ah) ohlo pa pwerisang.
'They were eating and suddenly (contrary to their expectations) that man appeared.'

A third usage of *pa* is illustrated by the next sentences.

I pa pahn awiawioh pwang!
'I'll be waiting and waiting until I'm exhausted!'

> *I pa mwengemwengeoh lok!*
> 'I ate and ate until I suffered!'

Here *pa* functions in an idiom that is used to express that some activity is ongoing until a new state is reached. The suffix *-oh*, pronounced with extra length and high pitch, is used to signal the unusual duration of the activity. *Pa* is used to further emphasize this duration.

The conjunctive adverb *en* in combination with the conjunction *pwe* means 'so as to be able to' or 'in order to'. This adverb, in addition to occurring as *en*, also has the form *-n* after words ending in non-high vowels (vowels other than *i* or *u*). Thus, a pronoun like *ke* 'you' followed by this adverb will occur as *ken*, *e* 'he, she, or it' will occur as *en*, etc. Examples follow.

> *Kitail kohla laid pwe kitail en kang mwahmw.*
> 'Let's go fish so that we can eat fish.'

> *Menpihro pihrdo pwe en kang sehu.*
> 'The bird flew here so that it could eat sugar cane.'

Now note the following sentences.

> (a) *Irail kohla pwe irail en laid.*
>   'They went there so that they could fish.'

> (b) *Irail kolahn laid.*
>   'They went there in order to fish.'

Though English calls for somewhat different translations of these two sentences, in Ponapean they mean the same thing. Their identical meanings are a consequence of the fact that sentence (b) is derived from sentence (a) by the process of deletion we examined in the discussion of the conjunction *oh*. Thus, in sentence (b) the second occurrence of *irail* is deleted, along with *pwe*. Like *oh*, *pwe* may apparently only be deleted in such sentences when it follows an intransitive verb of motion. After deletion, the conjunctive adverb *en* follows the verb to signal the difference in meaning between sentences like the following.

> *Irail kohla laid.*
> 'They went there (and) fished.'

Irail kolahn laid.
'They went there in order to fish.'

Further discussion of *en* and its role in infinitive clauses is presented in section **6**.5.3.

Unlike the conjunctive adverbs we have examined thus far, *lao* 'until' never occurs in combination with conjunctions. Instead, it is used alone to link clauses, as the following sentences illustrate.

Kita awi ira lao kohdo.
we (dual) wait they (dual) until come-here
'Let's wait until they come.'

I sohte pahn kohla e lao kohdo.
I not will go-there he until come-here
'I won't go until he comes.'

If the subjects of the clauses linked by *lao* are identical, then the subject preceding *lao* must be deleted. Thus, sentence (a) below is ungrammatical. Instead, sentence (b), which is derived from sentence (a), is employed.

(a)   **E doadoahk e lao nek.*
      he work he until finish

(b)   *E doadoahk lao nek.*
      'He worked until finished.'

The conjunctive adverb *apw* 'and then', like *lao*, is used alone to link clauses. However, as the parentheses in the examples below indicate, the deletion of the subject preceding *apw* is optional, not obligatory, if it is identical to the subject of the first clause.

(a)   *I pahn mwenge (i) apw mweselsang wasaht.*
      'I will eat and then (I'll) leave this place.'

(b)   *E doadoahk lao nek (e) apw kohla Kolonia.*
      'He worked until finished and then (he) went to Kolonia.'

Pronouns ending in non-high vowels (vowels other than *i* or *u*) often fuse with a following *apw* so that *ke* plus *apw* is pronounced *kahpw*, *e* plus *apw* is pronounced *ahpw*, and so on. Sentence (b) above might therefore be pronounced as follows when the subject pronoun *e* is not deleted.

> *E doadoahk lao nek ahpw kohla Kolonia.*

A second way in which *apw* is used is illustrated by the following sentences.

> *I apw pahn men iang.*
> 'I really would like to come.'
>
> *I apw pwangadahr.*
> 'I'm really tired.'
>
> *Ke apw wahdo mehkot.*
> 'Be sure to bring something.'

In these examples, *apw* does not have a conjunctive function, but rather is used as an intensifier. Notice, however, that it still appears in the position characteristic of conjunctive adverbs. Therefore, as the first sentence illustrates, it precedes an aspect marker like *pahn*. Regular adverbs of intensity would follow.

RELATIVE CLAUSES

6.5.2   Another way in which a sentence may occur within a larger sentence is as a **relative clause**. A relative clause is a clause which has the function of modifying a noun phrase. Example relative clauses are italicized in the following sentences.

(a) Ohl *me kohsang Ruko* uhdahn kadek.
    'That man *that came from Truk* is very kind.'

(b) Mwahmw *me e wahdo aioh* mat.
    'The fish *that he brought yesterday* is spoiled.'

(c) I ese ohl *me pahn kohdo lakapwo.*
    'I know the man *who is going to come tomorrow.*'

(d) I kangala rais *me ke pehleho.*
    'I ate up the rice *that you reheated.*'

Each of the sentences above is formed from two basic sentences Sentence (a), for example, contains these two.

(e) *Ohlo uhdahn kadek.*
     'That man is very kind.'

(f) *Ohlo kohsang Ruk.*
     'That man comes from Truk.'

In order for a sentence to function as a relative clause, it must contain a noun phrase identical to the noun phrase it is to modify. Since sentence (f) contains the noun phrase *ohlo* 'that man', and so does sentence (e), sentence (f) may be embedded in sentence (e), as follows.

(g) *Ohlo (Ohlo kohsang Ruk)—uhdahn kadek.*

The structure above is a hypothetical one from which we may derive sentence (a) by making three changes. Omitting details, these changes are: (1) in the embedded sentence, focus the noun phrase that is identical to the one being modified, (2) delete the identical noun phrase in the embedded sentence, and (3) move the demonstrative modifier in the noun phrase being modified to the end of the embedded sentence. From structure (g), we may therefore derive sentence (a) above as follows.

(g)   *Ohlo (Ohlo kohsang Ruk)—uhdahn kadek.*
(1) Focus: *Ohlo (Ohlo me kohsang Ruk)—uhdahn kadek.*
(2) Delete: *Ohlo (Ø me kohsang Ruk)—uhdahn kadek.*
(3) Move Dem.:   *Ohl (Ø me kohsang Ruk) o—uhdahn kadek.*
(a)   *Ohl me kohsang Ruko uhdahn kadek.*

Sentences (b), (c), and (d) may be similarly derived.

From: *Mwahmwo (E wahdo mwahmwo aio)—mat.*
Result: *Mwahmw me e wahdo aioh mat.*

From: *I ese—ohlo (Ohlo pahn kohdo lakapw).*
Result: *I ese ohl me pahn kohdo lakapwo.*

From: *I kangala—raiso (Ke pehle raiso).*
Result: *I kangala rais me ke pehleho.*

By assuming that the identical noun phrase in the embedded sentence must be focused, we are able to explain two facts about relative clauses in Ponapean. First, this assumption explains the presence of *me* in relative clauses. As we noted in section **6**.4.2, *me* occurs in sentences in which a noun phrase has been focused. Second, it provides an explanation for the structure of sentences like the following.

> *I pasakapwala wasa me Soulik kin mi ieho.*
> 'I visited for the first time the place where Soulik lives.'

This sentence may be derived from the following structure.

> *I pasakapwala—wasaho (Soulik kin mi wasaho).*
> I visit-first-time—place-that (Soulik *kin* exist place-that).

In the embedded sentence, the locative noun phrase *wasaho* 'place-that' is the one that must be focused. Note that when it is focused, the locative pronoun *ie* occurs in its place. As we have already noted in section **6**.4.2, *ie* appears in sentences only as the result of *focusing* a locative noun phrase. The form *ieho* results from *ie* plus the enclitic demonstrative modifier *-o*. *Wasaho* similarly results from *wasa* plus *-o*.

The change which moves the demonstrative modifier of the noun phrase being modified to a position following the relative clause is motivated by the fact that a noun phrase plus a following relative clause together function as a larger noun phrase. And, as we noted in section **4**.5.1, demonstrative modifiers always occur as the last element in such phrases. This fact, however, leads to the interesting result that certain kinds of sentences are problematic in Ponapean. For example, consider the following English sentence:

> That dog that bit this child will be killed.

Though perhaps awkward, this is a perfectly grammatical sentence. Basically, it derives from a structure like the following.

> That dog (that dog bit this child)—will be killed.

One might assume, therefore, that a similar Ponapean sentence could be derived from this structure.

> *Kidio (Kidio ngalis seriet)—pahn kamala.*
> dog-that (dog-that bit child-this)—will be-killed

By making the three changes we previously discussed, the following sentence would result.

> *Kidi me ngalis serieto pahn kamala.*

But this sentence is of questionable grammaticality. After moving the demonstrative modifier *-o* of the first noun phrase *kidio* 'that dog' to the end of the relative clause, two demonstrative modifiers occur in succession; both *-et* 'this' and *-o* 'that' follow *seri* 'child'. Many (but not all) speakers reject such sequences and maintain that only one demonstrative modifier may occur at the end of a noun phrase. This does not mean that for these speakers it is impossible to express such an idea in Ponapean. One solution might be an utterance like the following:

> *Kidio—E ngalis seriet.—pahn kamala.*
> 'That dog—He bit this child.—will be killed.'

But, *E ngalis seriet* is not a relative clause. It is simply a sentence inserted after the noun phrase *kidio* as a kind of afterthought. One additional point we might note here is that while it is possible in English to say 'that dog will be killed which bit this child', where the relative clause 'which bit this child' is moved to the end of the sentence, a parallel change is not possible in Ponapean.

So far, all the examples of relative clauses we have examined have occurred in subject, object, or locative noun phrases. Relative clauses may, however, occur in any noun phrase in a sentence. We might also note that *me* may be deleted in any relative clause. Following are additional examples.

> *Ohl (me) kohdo aioh sarekedo sakau pwoat.*
> 'The man that came yesterday dug up a kava plant.'

> *Soulik laidiki uhk (me) ahpwtehn pweipweidaho.*
> 'Soulik fished with the net that was just purchased.'

> *I papalahng wahr (me) mwowihdio.*
> 'I swam to that canoe that was swamped.'

> *I aluhlahsang ohl (me) lingeringero.*
> 'I walked away from that man who was angry.'

> *Ohlo mwemweitla wasa (me) kasarawio.*
> 'That man visited the place that is sacred.'

> *Pwopwoudo wahdo rahn (me) liho mehla.*
> 'That couple brought it the day that woman died.'

It is also possible for one sentence to contain multiple relative clauses, as in this next example.

> *I tuweng ohl (me) netkihla pwoht (me) wiawihda deke (me) Soulik ipwidi ieho.*
> 'I met the man who sold the boat that was made on the island where Soulik was born.'

Adjectives which occur in noun phrases begin their life, too, as relative clauses. Consider the following sentence.

> *Kidi toantoalo ngongngong.*
> 'That black dog is barking.'

Adjectives, as we have noted, are simply a class of intransitive verbs. Thus, we may derive a sentence like this from the following two sentences.

> *Kidio ngongngong.*
> 'That dog is barking.'
>
> *Kidio toantoal.*
> 'That dog is black.'

By embedding the second sentence in the first, the following structure results.

> *Kidio (Kidio toantoal)—ngongngong.*

Then by making the three changes previously described, we may derive this sentence.

> *Kidi me toantoalo ngongngong.*

Finally, by deleting *me*, the sentence first considered results.

> *Kidi toantoalo ngongngong.*

An important way in which adjectives introduced by relative clauses differ from other verbs, however, is in the position they may take in the noun phrase. First, consider the following two sentences.

(a) *Pwutak silimen (me) reireio kohdo aio.*
     'Those three boys who are tall came yesterday.'

(b) *Pwutak reirei silimeno kohdo aio.*
     'Those three tall boys came yesterday.'

These two sentences have essentially the same meaning, but structurally they are different. Notice in sentence (a) that the adjective *reirei* 'tall' occurs in a relative clause after the numeral *silimen* 'three'. *Me* in this sentence is optional. If *me* is deleted, however, then sentence (a) may also be expressed as in (b). Therefore, the adjective may be moved into a position immediately after the head noun with other elements in the phrase following. This kind of movement of a modifier is possible only with adjectives. Therefore, while sentence (c) below which employs the general intransitive verb *lalaid* 'fishing' is grammatical, sentence (d) is not.

c)   *Pwutak silimen (me) lalaido kohdo aio.*
     'Those three boys who are fishing came yesterday.'

d)   **Pwutak lalaid silimeno kohdo aio.*
     *'Those three fishing boys came yesterday.'

A final point about adjectives is that when two or more are present in a noun phrase, the order in which they occur is not optional, but is determined according to meaning. Among the more common kinds of adjectives, this ordering is as follows.

Noun (material) (size) (shape) (color)

That is, adjectives denoting materials precede those denoting size, those denoting size precede those denoting shape, and so on. Some examples follow.

dahl pwonopwon weitahtaho
'that round red dish'

dahl kalaimwun pwonopwon weitahtaho
'that big round red dish'

dahl mete kalaimwun pwonopwon weitahtaho
'that big round red metal dish'

Obviously, not all kinds of adjectives are covered by the formula given above, nor is it likely that this ordering is absolute.

NOMINAL CLAUSES

6.5.3   Thus far we have explored two major ways in which basic sentences can be combined to form a larger sentence. First we considered sentences that were conjoined through the use of conjunctions and/or conjunctive adverbs, and we called sentences in this relationship conjoined clauses. Then we examined the use of a sentence as a modifier of a noun phrase, and we labeled sentences with this function relative clauses. Now we will turn our attention to a third major way in which a sentence may occur within a larger sentence. This third way is when a sentence as a whole acts as a noun phrase. Sentences with this function we will call **nominal clauses**.

Nominal clauses are of three basic types: **gerundive clauses**, **finite clauses**, and **infinitive clauses**. Examples of each are presented below.

Gerundive Clause:

En pwutako sengo kelingeringer.
'*That boy's crying* is irritating.'

Finite Clause:

Ohlo nda *me Soulik kohla laid aio.*
'That man said *that Soulik went fishing yesterday.*'

Infinitive Clause:

I idingki Soulik *en kohla.*
'I forced Soulik *to go.*'

Further discussion and additional examples of each of these types of nominal clauses follow.

Gerundive Clauses

When a sentence occurs in a possessive construction and functions as a noun phrase, we will call it a **gerundive clause**. Example gerundive clauses are italicized in the following sentences.

En pwutako pirapo kapwuriamweie.
'*That boy's stealing it* astonished me.'

En pwutako kengwinio nek.
'*That boy's medicine-taking* is finished.'

En pwutako daper mpweio kaselel.
'*That boy's catching the ball* was fine.'

Each of these clauses may be derived from a sentence. For example, the gerundive clauses listed below in the left column may be related to the corresponding sentences listed to the right.

Gerundive Clause	Sentence
en pwutako pirapo	*Pwutako pirap.*
'that boy's stealing it'	'That boy stole it.'
en pwutako kengwinio	*Pwutako kengwini.*
'that boy's medicine-taking'	'That boy medicine-took.'
en pwutako daper mpweio	*Pwutako daper mpweio.*
'that boy's catching the ball'	'That boy caught the ball.'

The relationship between these clauses and sentences may be characterized as follows.

en + Sentence + (Demonstrative Modifier)

That is, these examples of gerundive clauses consist of *en*, a sentence, and if the action, event, or condition referred to is specific, a demonstrative modifier.

   In the formulation above, *en* results from the combining of two morphemes—the general possessive classifier *a-* and the construct suffix *-n*. While the general classifier is always used in gerundive clauses, it may combine with other suffixes than *-n*. The construct suffix is employed only when the subject noun phrase of the next sentence contains a noun, as in the following examples. (The abbreviation *Cl* stands for 'classifier'.)

Sentence	Gerundive Clause
Pwutako seng.	*en pwutako sengo*

| boy-that cry | Cl-n boy-that cry-that |
| 'That boy cried.' | 'that boy's crying' |

Liho seng.	*en liho sengo*
woman-that cry	Cl-n woman-that cry-that
'That woman cried.'	'that woman's crying'

Soulik seng.	*en Soulik sengo*
Soulik cry	Cl-n Soulik cry-that
'Soulik cried.'	'Soulik's crying'

If the subject noun phrase is replaced by a pronoun, then *a-* combines with a possessive pronoun suffix that agrees in person and number with that pronoun, and replaces it. Examples are:

I seng.	*ei sengo*
I cry	Cl-my cry-that
'I cried.'	'my crying'

Kumwail seng.	*amwail sengo*
you (pl.) cry	Cl-your (pl.) cry-that
'You cried.'	'your crying'

Irail seng.	*arail sengo*
they (pl.) cry	Cl-their (pl.) cry-that
'They cried.'	'their crying'

Gerundive clauses may occur in any position in a sentence where a noun phrase may occur. Additional examples follow.

I tamataman *omw wahdo pwuhko.*
'I remember *your bringing the book.*'

I suwediki *arail katairongo.*
'I dislike *their making noise.*'

E suwedehng *arail doadoahko.*
'It is bad in relation to *their working.*'

Sileho adahdehng *aht palawaro.*
'That adze was sharpened for *our canoe-making.*'

I tangasang *arail peio.*
'I fled from *their fighting.*'

Omw sapwasapw kesempwalsang *omw pahn mwemweitla Hawaiio.*
'*Your owning land* is more important than *your visiting Hawaii.*'

Finite Clauses

Another way in which a sentence may function as a noun phrase
is when it occurs as a **finite clause**. A finite clause is the easiest
kind of clause to recognize. It is the most sentence-like, since the
sentence it contains does not undergo the modifications of
possession as gerundive clauses do, nor the reductions by deletion
characteristic of infinitive clauses. There are essentially four kinds
of finite clauses. They are: **direct quotation clauses**, *me* **clauses**,
yes/no question clauses, and **question word question clauses.**

Direct quotation clauses occur as objects of transitive verbs
and are presented as verbatim repetitions of some utterance from
another speech occasion. Examples are:

> *Soulik nda, "Lahpo nohn pwerisek."*
> 'Soulik said, "That guy is too industrious." '

> *Serepeino ndahieng pwutako, "Ke dehr likamw!"*
> 'That girl said to the boy, "Don't lie!" '

> *Ohlo sapeng, "I sohte wehwehki."*
> 'That man answered, "I don't understand it." '

> *Liho idek reh, "Ke pahn mwesel lakapw?"*
> 'That woman asked of him, "Are you going to leave tomorrow?" '

In spoken Ponapean, a slight pause precedes a direct quotation
clause. Clauses like these, of course, occur most commonly in
narration.

Me **clauses** are so labeled because they consist of a sentence,
always affirmative, preceded by the word *me*. Clauses of this kind
are typically found as objects of transitive verbs of reporting,
perceiving, or mental activity. Examples follow.

> *I manokehla me ke kohsang Ruk.*
> I forget that you come-from Truk
> 'I forgot that you came from Truk.'

> *Soulik rong me serepeino sohte mwahukinuhk.*
> Soulik hear that girl-that not like-you
> 'Soulik heard that girl doesn't like you.'

> *Se mwelehkih me e sohte pahn pwurodo.*
> We suspect that he not will return-here
> 'We suspect that he won't return.'

> *I ese me irail pil mweselsang wasaht.*
> I know that they also leave-from place-this
> 'I know that they also left this place.'

A few additional examples of verbs that may be followed by *me* clauses are *wehwehki* 'to understand', *akamaiki* 'to dispute', *tamataman* 'to remember', and *kamehlele* 'to believe'. With all of these verbs, including those in the example sentences above, the use of *me* is obligatory. However, there are a few verbs with which *me* may or may not occur. For example, consider the following two sentences.

(a) *I leme me ohlo pahn kohdo.*
    'I thought that that man would come here.'

(b) *I leme ohlo pahn kohdo.*
    'I thought that man would come here.'

Notice that whereas *me* precedes the sentence *ohlo pahn kohdo* 'that man will come' in sentence (a), it is not present in sentence (b). Some speakers feel there is a distinction in meaning between these two sentences. This distinction may be characterized as follows. In sentence (a), the speaker is reporting a fact that he had presumed to be true. Whether or not it was in fact true is irrelevant. In sentence (b), the omission of *me* is interpreted as signaling that the speaker made no such presumption about the truth of the information contained in the following sentence. That is, he thought that the man was coming, but there still remained some doubt in his mind. Thus, a subtle difference in meaning between sentences (a) and (b) is perceived by some speakers. Others, however, reject these differing interpretations and insist that, with certain verbs, the use of *me* is simply optional. Two other verbs that behave like *leme* with respect to *me* are *kilang* 'to see' and *koapwoaroapwoarki* 'to hope'.

Yes/no question clauses differ from *me* clauses in two respects. First, whereas the sentence occurring in a *me* clause is always affirmative, that in a yes/no question clause is, as the name of this clause type implies, a yes/no question. Secondly, whereas *me* clauses are introduced by the word *me*, yes/no question clauses are introduced by the word *ma*, meaning 'if' or 'whether'. An example follows.

I men ese ma mie kamadipw rahnwet.
'I want to know if there is a feast today.'

The sentence *Mie kamadipw rahnwet?* 'Is there a feast today?' is the yes/no question that occurs in this clause. Additional examples are:

E idek ma e pahn iang mwenge?
'He asked if he was going to join in eating.'

Ke kilang ma e doakoahdi mwahmwo?
'Did you see if he speared that fish?'

Ke rong ma mie sohp peidi aio?
'Did you hear if a ship arrived yesterday?'

Ke ese ma olen waio ahn kang sasimi?
'Do you know if that American is used to eating raw fish?'

Question word question clauses, like yes/no question clauses, involve the use of an interrogative sentence. As the name of this clause type also indicates, the kind of interrogative sentence involved is that which employs a question word. Unlike yes/no question clauses, however, no word like *ma* precedes clauses of this type. The only constraint in these clauses is that the phrase containing the question word must be focused within the clause. Consider the following example.

E idek iahd me ke men laid.
'He asked when you want to fish.'

The question word question clause in this sentence is *iahd me ke men laid* 'when do you want to fish'. The question word *iahd* is focused in this clause. A sentence like the following, where *iahd* is not focused, is ungrammatical.

*E idek ke men laid iahd.

Additional examples of question word question clauses are:

Ke ese ihs me widekihla karisihno?
'Do you know who spilled the kerosene?'

Ke tamataman aramas depe me iang mi ni mehlaho?
'Do you remember how many people were at the funeral?'

I manokehla dahme e nda me ke pahn wahdo.
'I forgot what he said you were to bring.'

Ke rong iawasa lahpo kamakamala ie?
'Did you hear where that guy was killed?'

Infinitive Clauses

The term **infinitive clause** will be used to label the types of clauses italicized in the following sentences.

I idingki *Soulik en kohla.*
'I forced *Soulik to go.*'

Lahpo kaweidiki *Soulik en pwurala.*
'That guy advised *Soulik to return.*'

I kahng *Soulik en soumwahu.*
'I hate *for Soulik to be sick.*'

I ahn *kang sasimi.*
'I am accustomed *to eating raw fish.*'

I men *doadoahk.*
'I want *to work.*'

Precisely how infinitive clauses are formed in Ponapean is not very well understood, but several generalizations about such clauses are possible. First, infinitive clauses always occur after transitive verbs. Second, not all transitive verbs can be followed by infinitive clauses; only some can. Further, among those verbs that permit following infinitive clauses, there is some variation in how individual verbs interact with such clauses.

The nature of the variation noted above is illustrated by the following sentences.

(a) *I mweidehng Soulik en sumwoak.*
'I permitted Soulik to smoke.'

I pein mweidehngie i en sumwoak.
'I permitted myself to smoke.'

(b)   *I anahne Soulik en doadoahk.*
      'I need (for) Soulik to work.'

      I anahne doadoahk.
      'I need to work.'

(c)   **I ahn Soulik en nim pihru.*
      *'I am accustomed for Soulik to drink beer.'

      I ahn nim pihru.
      'I am accustomed to drinking beer.'

These pairs of sentences illustrate at least three variables in terms of how transitive verbs interact with infinitive clauses.

The verb *mweidehng* 'to permit' is illustrative of one class of verbs in Ponapean. The two sentences listed after (a) employing this verb are possibly derived from structures roughly like the following.

I mweidehng Soulik (Soulik sumwoak)
I permit-to Soulik (Soulik smoke)

I mweidehngie (I sumwoak)
I permit-to-me (I smoke)

The first sentence after (a) may be derived from the first structure above by deleting the second occurrence of *Soulik* and inserting *en* before *sumwoak*. The second sentence after (a) is derived from the second structure above also by the insertion of *en*, but no deletion takes place. Instead, the reflexive marker *pein* is inserted into the first verb phrase. Other verbs that behave like *mweidehng* are *idingki* 'to force', and *kaweidiki* 'to advise'.

The verb *anahne* 'to need' employed in the (b) pair of sentences is illustrative of the way in which most transitive verbs interact with infinitive clauses. The sentences listed after (b) are possibly derived from the following structures.

I anahne (Soulik doadoahk)
I need (Soulik work)

I anahne (I doadoahk)
I need (I work)

The first sentence listed after (b) is derived from the first structure above by inserting *en* before the verb *doadoahk*. The second sentence after (b) is derived from the second structure by deleting the second occurrence of *I* 'I'. *En* is not inserted. Other verbs that behave like *anahne* are *song* 'to try', *kahng* 'to hate, to refuse', *pwungki* 'to approve of', *mwahuki* 'to like', and *lemehda* 'to decide'.

The verb *ahn* 'to be accustomed to' employed in the (c) pair of sentences is characteristic of a small set of verbs that permit infinitive clauses only when the subject of the underlying infinitive clause is identical to the subject of the main clause. Therefore, the first structure is not permitted; the second is.

> **I ahn (Soulik nim pihru)*
> I accustomed (Soulik drink beer)
>
> *I ahn (I nim pihru)*
> I accustomed (I drink beer)

Another verb like *ahn* is *iang* 'to participate'.

It is not the case that all transitive verbs that may be followed by infinitive clauses behave like one of the three verbs examined above. Other classificatory criteria, and consequently other classes of verbs, exist. For example, some verbs permit *only* a following infinitive clause. *Mweidehng*, examined above, is such a verb, and so is the verb *men* 'to want'. But, *men* behaves like *anahne* in terms of its interaction with infinitive clauses, as illustrated by the following examples.

> *I men Soulik en pwurala.*
> 'I want Soulik to return.'
>
> *I men pwurala.*
> 'I want to return.'

The verb *kak* 'to be able' is similar to *men* in that, at least in underlying structures, it must be followed by an infinitive clause. But, *kak* permits this clause to be deleted; *men* does not. Examples are:

> *I men kilang serepeino.*
> 'I want to see that girl.'
>
> **I men.*
> *I want.

I kak kilang serepeino.
'I am able to see that girl.'

I kak.
'I am able.'

If the infinitive clause following *kak* is known to the listener (s), it may be deleted. More often, such sentence fragments are simply reduced to *Kak.*

The option of deleting a following infinitive clause provides the basis for a minor distinction between *men* and *kak.* A more important difference between these two verbs is that, in terms of interacting with following infinitive clauses, *kak* behaves like *ahn.* Therefore, it permits only infinitive clauses in which the underlying subject is identical to the subject of the main clause. This fact is clearly a consequence of the meaning of *kak.* One cannot be 'able' for another.

In a more traditional grammar of Ponapean, verbs like *men* and *kak* might be analyzed as **auxiliary verbs**. However, it is impossible to effectively define such a class of verbs. What seems to be the case is that transitive verbs vary considerably in terms of what types of clauses they may be followed by. A full study of this topic, as well as of how the use of *en* in infinitive clauses relates to the use of *en* as a conjunctive adverb, remains to be undertaken.

7. Honorific Speech

OVERVIEW

7.1   The purpose of the preceding chapters of this grammar was to provide a description of the major structural features of Ponapean. But, in one important respect, this grammar remains far from complete. From the point of view of the native speaker of Ponapean, this grammar has thus far failed to take note of what he considers to be the most interesting and, from a social point of view, the most important aspect of his language. The omission, to be taken up in this chapter, is the use of **honorific speech** or, as it is sometimes called, **high language**.

The study of honorific speech is important for a number of reasons. One is that, although other Austronesian languages employ honorific patterns of speech, Ponapean is the only Micronesian language that has developed this speech style to any degree of complexity. The use of honorific speech is thus one of the defining characteristics of Ponapean. A second reason is that, since not all speakers of Ponapean are able to use honorific speech with equal facility, command of this speech style is typically equated with sophistication, cultivation, and the ability to speak Ponapean well.

In looking at honorific speech from a grammatical point of view, as we shall in this chapter, we will discover that the degree to which honorific speech differs from the common language is not very great. Basically, the major difference lies in the choice of vocabulary that one uses. The sound system and the grammatical structures of this speech style are essentially the same as those of the common language.

What makes the use of honorific speech so challenging to the native speaker is the task of learning this special vocabulary and knowing *when* to use it. The usage of honorific speech is ul-

timately tied up with so many non-linguistic facts about Ponapean culture that a thorough study of this subject is as much the
task of anthropology or sociology as it is of linguistics. Consequently, the observations made in this chapter represent only a
small part of what there is to be said about this subject. It is
hoped, however, that the reader will be able to discover from this
discussion at least what the major features of honorific speech
are, and how they relate to the structural features of the language
presented in the previous chapters.

THE SOCIAL CONTEXT OF HONORIFIC SPEECH

7.2   It is probably safe to say that no matter what language we speak,
the *style* of speech we employ is governed to some degree by the
social situation in which we are involved. Sometimes the
differences between one speech style and another are so subtle
that they go largely unnoticed. In other cases, a particular speech
style may be so well defined that it plays a major role in how one
individual interacts with another. The latter is the case of Ponapean honorific speech.
           The principal function of honorific speech is to show *respect*.
Therefore, its use is inextricably bound up with considerations of
social status. Who one is speaking to or about—whether superiors, peers, or inferiors—determines when and how this speech
style is to be employed. The issue of how status relationships are
established on Ponape is, of course, one of great complexity that
goes well beyond the scope of this grammar. But, for the reader
who knows nothing about the social structure of this island, the
following general observations about Ponapean polity will prove
useful in understanding the content of this chapter.
           Although the question of status in modern Ponape is tied to
a number of factors, including wealth, position within the church
or government, and education, the clearest indicator of social
position is the *title* one holds. Ponapean titles indicate rank
within the traditional political system. In this system, Ponape is
divided into five municipalities: Madolenihmw, Uh, Net, Kiti,
and Sokehs. In each of these municipalities, there are two lines
of chiefs. The highest chief in one line is called the *Nahnmwarki*
and the highest chief in the other, the *Nahnken*. Below each of
these chiefs there are numerous other title holders, the first eleven
of which are considered to be the most important. Precisely
which titles are included in these positions varies somewhat from

one municipality to another, but in the municipality of Madolenihmw, for example, the first twelve titles in each line, including the *Nahnmwarki* and *Nahnken*, are as follows.

(1)	Nahnmwarki	Nahnken
(2)	Wasahi	Nahlaimw
(3)	Dauk	Nahnsahu Ririn
(4)	Noahs	Nahnapas
(5)	Nahnawa	Nahnmadaun Idehd
(6)	Nahnpei	Souwel Lapalap
(7)	Nahn Kiroun Pohn Dake	Lepen Ririn
(8)	Nahlik Lapalap	Ou Ririn
(9)	Nahnihd Lapalap	Oun Pohnpei
(10)	Lempwei Lapalap	Nahn Pohnpei
(11)	Saudel	Kaniki Ririn
(12)	Oundolen Ririn	Nahnsaumw en Wehi

Holders of other titles outside of these twelve range in importance from the holders of relatively important titles, which are called *koanoat*, to holders of lesser titles, which may be either municipal titles (*wehi* titles) or titles which are only for sections of land within the municipality (*kousapw* titles). In spite of the very large number of titles that exist (most adults hold a title), all titles are ranked, with probably no two titles being precisely equivalent. Where identical titles within different municipalities are involved, the rank of the municipality in traditional importance will determine which of the titles is higher.

The use of honorific speech is tied to the rank of these titles. Which form of speech one uses depends upon to whom one is speaking, or in some cases, about whom one is speaking. With these basic facts about the Ponapean title system in mind, let us go on to look at honorific vocabulary.

HONORIFIC VOCABULARY

7.3   Honorific speech is principally exemplified by the use of special morphemes and words that substitute for certain common language nouns, verbs, pronouns, and possessive classifiers. As a first step toward understanding this honorific vocabulary, it will be useful to establish two levels of usage. The labels that we will use for these two levels are those set forth by Paul Garvin and Saul Riesenberg in their informative paper "Respect Behavior on

Ponape: An Ethnolinguistic Study." (See Bibliography for publication details.)

The highest of these levels of usage is labeled **royal honorific**. Speech of this level is used only with the *Nahnmwarki* and the *Nahnken*. The second of these two levels is called **respect honorific**. This speech style is used with all other superiors or with respected equals. Garvin and Riesenberg state (p. 203) that in Ponapean terminology "respect honorific speech is *lòkaya͡ n͡ mέyŋ* [*lokaiahn meing*], speech of gentlemen; royal honorific speech is either *lòkaya͡ n͡ pàto·ŋ͡ sówpeyti* [*lokaiahn patohng soupeidi*], speech of talking-to Sowpeyti (highest chiefs), or *lokàya͡ n͡ impὲ͡ n͡ sówpeyti* [*lokaiahn mpehn soupeidi*], speech of in-the-presence of Sowpeyti." Many speakers of Ponapean, however, disagree with this terminology and instead report that the term *meing* alone is used to refer to the level of *royal honorific*, and that the term *lokaiahn wahu* 'speech-of respect' is used as a general term for *all* honorific speech. The terms *lokaiahn patohng soupeidi* and *lokaiahn mpehn soupeidi*, they believe, are simply literal descriptions of the situations in which honorific speech is used. Further, a number of speakers have noted that the term *meing* is coming to be used as an equivalent of *lokaiahn wahu*.

It is not surprising that some differences exist between the analyses of honorific speech presented in this grammar and in Garvin and Riesenberg's paper. Reliable data on honorific speech are difficult to obtain and are somewhat variable from one speaker to another. Probably only a relatively small percentage of Ponapean speakers have extensive control of honorific patterns of speech, and many of these individuals are reluctant to share their special knowledge. While we were fortunate to obtain an extensive list of honorific vocabulary from Linter Hebel on Ponape, much of the analysis concerning the usage of the vocabulary was carried out in Hawaii, where access to a large number of speakers, particularly older speakers, was highly restricted.

Since the purpose of this chapter is to present only some of the major features of honorific speech and is not to provide a comment on Garvin and Riesenberg's work, further references to points of difference between this analysis and theirs will not be provided. The serious student of honorific speech is urged to consult both of these works.

NOUNS AND VERBS

7.3.1   Within the vocabulary of Ponapean, there are at least several hundred honorific morphemes. The majority of these belong to the major word classes of nouns and verbs. The distribution of these morphemes generally follows one of three patterns. Corresponding to a particular common language form (1) both a respect and a royal honorific form occur, (2) only a single honorific form occurs which is used at both these levels, or (3) only a single honorific form occurs which is restricted to the royal honorific level. Following are examples of each of these patterns. Where more than one form is listed in a single column, these represent alternate forms.

Pattern I:

Common	Respect Honorific	Royal Honorific	English
paliwar	kahlap	erekiso	body
mese	wasaile	sihleng	face
moange	tapwi	koadokenmei/ peipei	head
likinpaiki	likinsekiri	likinioar/ likinleng	back of the head
peh	lime	limeiso	hand, arm
sowe	pelikie	pelikiso	back
pahnadi	pahnkupwur	mwareiso	chest
kapahrek	mahsen	rerenpwaiso	speech
mwenginingin	mwokuhku	loiloitik/ mwoluhlu	whisper
seisei	kotokot	tahta	haircut
uhda	apehda	ninlengida/ ketda	stand
wendi	seidi	kipedi	lie down
kouruhr	kiparamat	rarenei	laugh
pek	pidekila	loakewel	defecate
idek	keinemwe	keidek	ask
med	tip	likier/ idier	full
uhpw	pehn	pwihleng	drinking coconut
meir	seimwoak	derir	sleep
peren	kupwur peren	keremwoaliso	happy, joyful
kopwou	palang	ohdou	basket
pwoud	werek	likend	spouse
nim	dake	urak	drink

ngile	*kepitie*	*elinge*	voice
likuwer	*malipe*	*ediniei*	call
mehla	*matala*	*pweula*	die
mwohndi	*ketdi*	*mwoalehdi*	sit down
lokaia	*mahsen*	*pahngok*	speak
kapakap	*kasakas*	*loulou*	pray
sakaula	*luhmwuhmw*	*keinihn*	intoxicated
sokon	*irar*	*irareileng* (NM)	cane
		irareiso (NK)	

Pattern II:

Common	Respect and Royal Honorific	English
timwe	*keinuhnu/sisipwai*	nose
loh	*dinapw*	tongue
tepinwere	*tepinkasang*	neck
neh	*aluweluwe*	leg, foot
pipihs	*koamwosod*	urinate
pwourda	*kipada*	get up
pirida	*ohpalawasa*	wake up
mmwus	*kaliali*	vomit
lisoarop	*ohpweiso*	hat
soumwahu	*luhmwuhmw*	sick
pahnpeh	*pahnpwoal*	armpit
lingeringer	*engieng*	angry
mwukumwuk	*dawado*	gargle
ahu	*dawas*	mouth
sara	*dawaspeseng*	open one's mouth
ouraman	*eliman*	dream
pai	*iasenei*	fortunate
mour	*ieias*	alive
pitenmoang reirei	*pwilipeipei*	long hair
kei	*marekeiso*	annoint
manokehla	*meliehla*	forget
koul	*melikahka*	sing
ese	*mwahngih*	know
dehu	*mwoahl*	area, location
pwang	*ngir*	tired
tihnsewe	*pelikie*	back, backbone
lipahned	*pilen pahnmweli*	gossip
ned	*ingir*	smell

sali	*irap*	meat or fish course
suwediki	*kalahdiki*	dislike
mwengehn mvenseng	*kapwarsou*	breakfast
rong	*kapaidoke* (tr.) *kapaidok* (intr.)	hear
mwohndi	*keipwekidi*	sit down
ngkoal	*kepeukuhk*	sennit
likinsepe	*likinmwoale*	cheek

Pattern III:

Common and Respect Honorific	Royal Honorific	English
padi	*dekehnering*	eyebrow
ririnmese	*ririnderihleng/ nihnihrek*	eyelash
sendin peh	*rekeleng*	finger
sendin neh	*rekepwel*	toe
pwuriamwei	*eimwolu*	astonishment
kihl	*ihrekiso*	skin
epwinek	*mahlengida*	to wash one's face
peuk	*malimalih*	to blow
kommoal	*nanmwoalehdi*	to rest
mwaramwar	*nihn*	garland
kaikai	*pahrehre*	chin, jaw
kenei sakau	*pailol*	meal after kava
pilen ewe	*pilen dawas*	saliva
pitenwel	*pitenpeipei*	strand of hair
pitenmoang	*pitentepwitepw*	hair, of the head
ilek	*poarone*	dispatch
lemeleme	*mwuserehre*	think
pihl	*ngke*	water (drinking)
tenihr	*irilapiso*	fan
tahmw	*isilap*	forehead
ngile	*kapitie*	voice
dahng	*kapahiso/kepehiso*	thigh
wasahn wideh	*kereiso*	bathing place for the feet
likengkengenihmat	*kilahsoupwa*	incest
nsenamwahu	*keremwell* (n)	contentment
	kerekeremwell (adj)	content

Note that most of the preceding forms name body parts, items in common use, or bodily activities. Also note that two morphemes commonly reoccur. These are -*iso* and -*leng*. The morpheme -*iso*, which occurs in words like *erekisio* 'body', *limeiso* 'hand', *pelikiso* 'back', and *rerenpwaiso* 'speech', may be translated 'lord'. The morpheme -*leng*, which occurs in words like *likinleng* 'back of the head', *ninlengida* 'stand', *pwihleng* 'drinking coconut', *ririnderihleng* 'eyelash', and *rekeleng* 'finger', is a bound form of the noun *lahng*, which means 'heaven' or 'sky'. The meanings of both these morphemes refer to the exalted status of the individuals with whom they are used.

In at least one instance, the choice of the morphemes -*iso* and -*leng* is differentiated according to who is being addressed. When speaking to the *Nahnmwarki*, the word for 'cane' is *irareileng*; when speaking to the *Nahnken*, it is *irareiso*. Thus, for some forms, distinctions of usage are elaborated beyond the three levels we previously noted. This is especially true of some of the honorific classifiers that are examined in section 7.4.

THE VERBS *ket* AND *pato*

7.3.2   Two honorific verbs have meanings so generalized that it is difficult to discuss them apart from context. These are the verbs *ket* and *pato*. The basic distinction between these forms is one that we have not previously encountered. While *ket* is an honorific form, used at either the respect or royal honorific levels, *pato* is a **humiliative** form. It is employed in the presence of superiors or respected equals, either when speaking of one's self or one's own group, or when speaking to or of another who is of lesser rank than some other participant in the conversation.

Ket and *pato* may occur alone without further affixation in place of the verb *mi* 'to exist', as in these examples.

> *I pato paho.*
> I exist down-there
> 'I was down there.'

> *Komw ket paho.*
> you exist down-there
> 'You were down there.'

In combination with directional suffixes, these two verbs may substitute for most common verbs of motion for which there is not already an honorific form, as illustrated by these examples.

Common	Humiliative	Honorific	English
kohla	patohla	ketla	'go there'
kohsang	patohsang	ketsang	'come from'
kohwei	patohwei	ketwei	'go toward you'
aluhla	patohla	ketla	'walk there'
mwohndi	patohdi	ketdi	'sit down'

Another use of the verbs *ket* and *pato* is that they may occur with the conjunctive adverb *-n* before other verbs which have no special honorific form, or where the honorific form is unknown to the speaker. Some examples are:

Common	Humiliative	Honorific	English
laid	patohwen laid	ketin laid	'to fish'
sapal	patohwen sapal	ketin sapal	'to walk'
seiloak	patohwen seiloak	ketin seiloak	'to travel'
kamadipw	patohwen kamadipw	ketin kamadipw	'to feast'

Both of these verbs also have transitive forms. These are *patohwan* and *ketki*. The transitive form *patohwan* is used as a humiliative counterpart to some common honorific transitive verbs, as in these examples.

Common	Humiliative	Honorific	English
ese	patohwan	mwahngih	'to know'
nda	patohwan	masanih	'to say'
kilang	patohwan	masanih	'to see'

With other common transitive verbs for which there are no special honorific forms, the root *ketki* is employed with, in some cases, following verbal suffixes.

ale	patohwan	ketki	'to take'
wahla	patohwanla	ketkihla	'to carry there'
kihieng	patohwanehng	ketkieng	'to give'

HONORIFIC PRONOUNS

7.3.3   Honorific forms exist not only for nouns and verbs, but for personal pronouns as well. Only the second and third person singular forms of these pronouns are different, however. The dual and plural forms are the same. The honorific pronoun forms are listed below.

	Independent	Subject	Object	Possessive
2nd	*komwi/ihr*	*komw/re*	*-komwi/-ihr*	*-mwi/-r*
3rd	*ihr*	*re*	*-ihr*	*-r*

For the second person singular forms, meaning 'you', two forms are given under each column. The first is the respect honorific form; the second is the royal honorific form. The third person singular forms are all royal honorific. Also note that the second person royal honorific forms are identical to the third person forms, and that these third person honorific forms are identical to the common language third person plural alternants.

The use of common language third person plural pronouns for honorific second person singular forms apparently has two motivations. First, the use of third person rather than second person forms serves to symbolically remove the person being addressed from the normal plane of the speaker-hearer relationship. Second, plural forms are appropriate because, when talking to a high chief, one must address his *eni* 'spirit' as well.

Like common object pronouns, honorific object pronouns occur suffixed to verbs. Examples are:

Ngehi me pahn patowahnihrla.
'I am the one who will take you (royal) there.'

Ngehi me pahn patowahnkomwihla.
'I am the one who will take you (respect) there.'

Honorific possessive pronouns are examined in the next section as part of the more general topic of honorific possession.

HONORIFIC POSSESSION

7.4   To discuss honorific patterns of possession, it will be useful to distinguish between two types of constructions—humiliative possessive constructions and honorific possessive constructions. The differences between these types of constructions are outlined below.

HUMILIATIVE POSSESSIVE CONSTRUCTIONS

7.4.1   **Humiliative possessive constructions** are employed under circumstances paralleling the use of the verb *pato*. Thus, when speaking of something one owns or possesses in the presence of respected equals or superiors, a humiliative possessive construction must be employed. An example of such a construction follows.

> *ei tungoal pwihk*
> 'my pig'

Ei 'my' is the first person singular possessed form of the general classifier *a-*; *tungoal* signals that the construction is humiliative; and *pwihk* in this case is the noun representing the thing possessed.

Regardless of the meaning of the noun representing the thing possessed, humiliative constructions always employ a suffixed form of the general possessive classifier in combination with *tungoal*. Compare, for example, the following phrases, where common language possessive constructions are contrasted with humiliative constructions.

Common Constructions	Humiliative Constructions
(a) *moangei* 'my head'	*ei tungoal moahng* 'my head'
ngilei 'my voice'	*ei tungoal ngihl* 'my voice'
kili 'my skin'	*ei tungoal kihl* 'my skin'
(b) *ei seht* 'my shirt'	*ei tungoal seht* 'my shirt'
nei seri 'my child'	*ei tungoal seri* 'my child'
werei sidohsa 'my automobile'	*ei tungoal sidohsa* 'my automobile'

Note that in the common language, depending upon the noun representing the thing possessed, either a direct possessive construction is employed, as in the examples under (a), or an indirect possessive construction is used, as in the examples under (b). In humiliative possessive constructions, all nouns enter into indirect constructions. But, whereas in the common language different possessive classifiers are employed in indirect constructions, in humiliative constructions the general classifier *a-* always occurs.

Humiliative possessive constructions may also be employed when speaking to another. When speaking to someone clearly of lower status in the presence of a superior, then constructions like the following are possible.

omw tungoal moahng
'your head'

omw tungoal seht
'your shirt'

When speaking to a respected equal or a superior in the presence of someone of high rank, then the respect honorific possessive suffix *-mwi* is employed with the classifier *a-* to form constructions like these:

omwi tungoal moahng
'your head'

omwi tungoal seht
'your shirt'

The use of *-mwi* signals respect for the person being spoken to, but *tungoal* signals that one of a higher rank is present.

When speaking of a third party of lower status than the person being spoken to, then constructions like the following would be employed.

ah tungoal seht
'his shirt'

en ohlo ah tungoal seht
'that man's shirt'

Tungoal may also be used as a noun and as an intransitive verb. As a noun, it has the general meaning of 'food' or 'drink'. As an intransitive verb, it means 'to eat' or 'to drink'. The corresponding transitive form of the verb is *tungoale*.

HONORIFIC POSSESSIVE CONSTRUCTIONS

7.4.2   Honorific possessive constructions grammatically parallel common language possessive constructions, except that honorific classifiers, honorific pronouns, and honorific nouns are employed.

Direct honorific possessive constructions are formed by suffixing the possessive pronouns *-mwi* 'your (respect honorific)' or *-r* 'your/his (royal honorific)' to the noun representing the thing possessed. Examples are:

> *kahlepemwi*
> 'your body'
>
> *sihlengihr*
> 'your (his) face'

Some speakers of Ponapean feel that nouns at the royal honorific level do not normally combine with possessive suffixes, since these forms are used with only the highest chiefs, and context would make it clear who is being talked about. Thus, if one used the word *sihleng* 'face (royal honorific)', it would be obvious whose face was being referred to. Other speakers reject this position and believe that *sihlengihr* is the correct form. Still other speakers prefer *sihlengimwi* as the royal honorific form, their position being that since *sihleng* is in itself a royal form, the respect honorific suffix may be used without diminishing the level of usage of the word.

The suffix *-r* combines in an unexpected way with preceding roots. In the preceding example, *sihleng* is a Class I noun; it has the final base vowel *i*. When suffixed by *-r*, this base vowel occurs *long*, as in *sihlengihr*. Except before *-r*, these final base vowels do *not* occur long, as illustrated by the following examples.

Root	Common	Respect	Royal	English
sawi-	*sawimw*	*sawimwi*	*sawihr*	'your clan'
mware-	*mwaremw*	*mwaremwi*	*mwarahr*	'your title'
ria-	*riemw*	*riemwi*	*riahr*	'your sibling'

Note that the base vowels *i* and *a* lengthen before *-r*, but not before other suffixes. Further, the distinction between the final base vowels *e* and *a* has been lost for these honorific forms. Roots with *e* as the base vowel are treated like *a* roots. Therefore, *mware-* in combination with *-r* results in *mwarahr*, not **mwarehr*.

Honorific classifiers are used in indirect possessive constructions. Corresponding to the common language classifiers for food and drink (*kene* and *nime* respectively) are the following three honorific classifiers.

koanoat
pwenieu
sahk

These classifiers do not normally occur with possessive suffixes. Some speakers, however, do report using *sekemwi*.

Which classifier should be employed with a particular individual depends in part upon the rank of the other individuals who are present at the time of the utterance. At a feast, for example, where the *Nahnmwarki* is present, the classifier *koanoat* could be used only with him and with individuals bearing traditionally important *koanoat* titles outside of the *Nahnmwarki* line. Four such titles are:

Lepen Palikir
Lepen Net
Soulikin Awak
Lepen Moar

The classifier *pwenieu* is used with the wives of these title holders. If no holders of any of these titles are present, then *koanoat* may be used with the *Dauk*, and humiliative constructions with all others. If the *Dauk* is not present, then *koanoat* may be used only with high *koanoat* title holders outside of the line of the *Nahnmwarki*. If no high *koanoat* title holder is present, then the classifier *sahk* is used with highest title holder and his wife, and humiliative constructions with all others. *Sahk* is always used with the *Nahnken* and his wife.

The words *koanoat*, *pwenieu*, and *sahk* also function as nouns at the royal honorific level. These nouns mean either 'food' or 'drink'. The respect honorific forms of these nouns are *kepin koanoat*, *kepin pwenieu*, and *kepin sahk*. If the highest title holder present is *koanoat*, then the food and drink of all others in *kepin koanoat*. If *pwenieu* is appropriate with the highest title holder present, then *kepin pwenieu* is used with others, and similarly *kepin sahk* is used with others in the presence of a title holder for whom *sahk* is appropriate. Also related to the nouns *koanoat* and *sahk* are the following verbs, meaning 'to eat' or 'to drink'.

Intransitive	Transitive
koanoat	*koanoate*
sak	*sakan*

The use of these verbs parallels the use of the corresponding classifiers and nouns.

The use of other honorific classifiers in Ponapean is less complicated. Following is a list of the third person singular forms of five honorific classifiers, along with the common language classifiers to which they correspond.

Honorific Classifier	Common Classifier	Classifier Type
sapwellime	*ah* and *nah*	general and dominant
nillime	*sapwe*	land
tehnpese	*imwe*	dwellings
tehnwere	*were*	vehicles
moatoare	*kie*	things to sleep on

All of these classifiers may combine with *-mwi* and *-r*, as illustrated below.

Respect Honorific	Royal Honorific
sapwellimemwi	*sapwellimahr*
nillimemwi	*nillimahr*
tehnpesemwi	*tehnpasahr*
tehnweremwi	*tehnwarahr*
moatoaremwi	*moatoarahr*

Each of the royal honorific forms above also has an alternant where no possessive suffix is employed. Therefore, *sapwellim* may be used as alternant of *sapwellimahr* at the royal level. Other honorific classifiers are formed by suffixing *-mwi* or *-r* to the roots of common language classifiers.

OTHER FEATURES OF HONORIFIC SPEECH

7.5   Two additional features of honorific speech that we have not yet considered are its sound system correlates and the special set of greetings that are employed in this speech style. Each of these features is examined below.

SOUND SYSTEM CORRELATES

7.5.1   The only instance where honorific speech has obvious sound system correlates is in the exaggerated prolongation of vowels in a few common words and expressions. In the common greeting *kaselehlie*, the already long vowel *eh* may be prolonged two to three times its normal length when addressing a superior or respected equal. Similarly, the vowel *e* in the word *ei* 'yes' and the initial vowel *ih* in *ihieng* 'excuse me (used when passing in front of others)' are lengthened more than normal when one wishes to signal respect.

It is possible that the phenomenon of using extra vowel length to signal respect provides the explanation for why final short base vowels are lengthened before *-r*. Therefore, one would expect that the root *sapwellima-* in combination with the possessive suffix *-r* would result in *sapwellimar*; the correct form instead is *sapwellimahr*. The lengthening of the vowel in the final syllable may thus be a result of this phenomenon.

GREETINGS

7.5.2   The basic greeting in Ponapean is *kaselehlie*. In honorific speech, as we noted in the preceding section, the long vowel *eh* is further prolonged in this greeting to signal respect. Still further elaborations of this basic greeting occur, however, when approaching the dwelling or vehicle of a superior, or when greeting him personally.

When approaching the dwelling of someone with whom the use of honorific speech is appropriate, then the occupant(s) of that dwelling are greeted:

> *Kaselehlie tehnpasen!*
> Greetings empty-nest-there!

Similarly, when greeting the occupant(s) of a vehicle bearing a superior, the following greeting is employed.

> *Kaselehlie tehnwaren!*
> Greetings empty-vehicle-there!

The pattern of avoiding a direct greeting to the people in these situations, and of addressing the dwelling or vehicle as being 'empty', provides still another example of how honorific speech is removed from the normal plane of the speaker/listener relationship.

Special greetings are also employed with holders of certain high titles. When greeting a *Nahnmwarki, Kaselehlie Wasa Lapalap* 'Greetings Honored Place' may be employed, or the *Nahnmwarki* may be addressed through the use of his alternate title. The alternate titles for the *Nahnmwarki*-s of three municipalities are listed below.

Municipality	Alternate Title
Madolenihmw	*Isipahu*
Uh	*Sahngoro*
Kiti	*Soukise*

For example, the *Nahnmwarki* of Madolenihmw may be greeted *Kaselehlie Isipahu* 'Greetings Isipahu' or, more politely, *Kaselehlie maing Isipahu* 'Greetings sir Isipahu'. The choice of *wasa lapalap* or the alternate title as a preferred greeting varies somewhat from one municipality to another. In no case, however, would a *Nahnmwarki* be addressed directly as *Nahnmwarki*. The alternate title *Isoeni* was formerly used for the *Nahnmwarki* of Sokehs. The alternate title for the *Nahnmwarki* of Net, if one exists, is not known.

The proper greeting to a *Nahnken* is *Kaselehlie Isohka*. Holders of the four titles listed in the preceding section, which are considered *koanoat* even in the presence of the *Nahnmwarki*, are addressed as *pwoud*. The alternate title of the *Wasai* is *Nahnpwutak*, for the *Dauk* it is *Nahniau*, and for the *Noahs* it is *Nahnno*. Lower titles in the *Nahnmwarki* line and titles below the *Nahnken* in that line are addressed as *Iso*, but some variation exists here, depending upon the municipality. Any title holder entitled to the offering of 'first fruits', the offering of a portion of a crop or catch when it first comes into season, may be addressed as *Mwohnsapwaka*.

Appendix: Ponapean Orthography

Ponapean has now been written for well over one hundred years. Out of this experience has evolved a relatively systematic spelling system. At present, it is probably safe to say that Ponapean comes closer to having a widely accepted, standard orthography than any other language in the Trust Territory. However, as anyone who has had occasion to write Ponapean knows, there still remain many areas of indecision concerning the spelling of this language. In an effort to deal with these problems, a Ponapean Orthography Workshop was organized under the auspices of the Trust Territory government and the Pacific and Asian Linguistics Institute of the University of Hawaii.

The initial meeting of this workshop was conducted in Kolonia, Ponape from the 10th to the 21st of January, 1972. Its purpose was to provide an opportunity for representatives of the Ponapean community to meet with several consultants in order to consider how the Ponapean spelling system might be standardized. Participating in this workshop were:

Committee Members	Local Consultant
Fr. Paulino Cantero, S. J.	Rev. Harold Hanlin
Mr. Godaro Gallen	
Mr. Linter Hebel	P.A.L.I. Consultants
Mr. Santiago Joab	Mr. Kenneth Rehg
Mr. Ewalt Joseph	Mr. Damian Sohl
Mr. Pensile Laurence	
Mr. Martiniano Rodriguez	
Mr. Leonard Santos	

The outcome of this first workshop was a set of tentative recommendations regarding spelling procedures for Ponapean.

The practical implications of these recommendations were then studied for one year. On January 29, 1973 a majority of the above-named committee members in consultation with Rev. Harold Hanlin, Fr. William McGarry, and Mr. Damian Sohl met to formulate a final set of recommendations. These recommendations were recorded in a report that was circulated to various governmental agencies on Ponape.

The spelling practices employed in this grammar are largely consistent with the spelling recommendations made in that report. In the *Summary of Recommendations* that follows, some minor modifications of the original statement of these recommendations have been made. In all cases, however, these are modifications of style and organization, never of substance. Cross-references are provided to those sections of the grammar in which certain recommendations have already been discussed. Those recommendations not previously considered are given fuller treatment. In some instances, comments are also included that suggest certain recommendations will require further refinement or revision, either because they lack popularity or because they were based upon an incomplete understanding of the grammatical phenomenon involved.

SUMMARY OF RECOMMENDATIONS

1.0   SOUNDS AND SYMBOLS

1.1   DIALECT CONSIDERATIONS

Spellings that reflect Northern (or Main) dialect pronunciations are to be employed by all speakers of Ponapean.

One question which has long interfered with the standardization of Ponapean orthography has been the question of which dialect should be reflected in the way words are spelled. A number of alternative solutions to this problem were considered at the Workshop, three of which follow. (1) Employ one symbol that can variously stand for /ɛ/ in the Northern dialect and /ɔ/ in the Kiti dialect. (2) Allow all speakers of Ponapean to spell in accord with their own pronunciation. (3) Select one of the two major dialects as a standard.

The first alternative was rejected on the basis that it had been unsuccessfully tried before. The second alternative, which would allow all speakers to write words as they pronounce them, was rejected because the committee felt that to accept this solution was to abandon the goal of standardization. Alternative three remained, and the Northern dialect was chosen as the standard.

The reasons for selecting the Northern dialect were: (1) except for some variation in vowel qualities, the two dialects are very similar; (2) many Kiti teachers already teach their children Northern dialect spellings; and (3) the majority of speakers of Ponapean speak the Northern dialect. While no opposition to this decision was voiced at the Workshop, it has met with some resistance in Kiti. (See also sections 1.4, 2.2, and 2.6.7.)

1.2　THE ALPHABET

The Ponapean alphabet is to employ twenty symbols—sixteen single letters and four digraphs. The alphabetic order to be employed is:

a e i o oa u h k l m mw n ng p pw r s d t w

When alphabetizing words, those containing short vowels will be listed before those containing the same long vowel. Thus, *pa* will be listed before *pah*.

(See sections 2.5 through 2.7 for a discussion of the phonemes these symbols represent. Section 2.7.3 deals with one of the problems of this alphabet.)

1.3　DOUBLED CONSONANTS

Within a single word, write doubled consonants as they are pronounced, but spell /mwmw/ as *mmw*, /mwpw/ as *mpw*, and /ww/ as *uw*.

A recommendation was also set forth by the committee that *ii* should never be written to indicate a vowel/glide or double glide sequence. It now seems preferable, however, to permit *ii* based on data presented in sections 2.7.3 and 3.3.4. (Also see section 2.5.7.)

1.4　PROTHETIC VOWELS

The vowels *i* and *u* that optionally occur before words beginning with the consonant clusters *mp*, *mpw*, *nd*, *nt*, *ns*, and *ngk* are *not* to be written.

(See section 2.9.2.)

2.0   WORD DIVISION

2.1   Prefixes

All prefixes are to be written attached to the word they precede. All resulting sound changes are to be reflected by the spelling.

(See sections 3.3.2, 3.7.4, and 5.3.)

2.2   Possessive Suffixes

All possessive suffixes are to be written attached to the noun they follow. All resulting sound changes are to be reflected by the spelling.

(See section 4.8.)

2.3   Verbal Suffixes

All verbal suffixes are to be written attached to the verb stem. All resulting sound changes are to be reflected by the spelling. However, when *ong* and *sang* function as prepositions and do not follow a verb stem, they are to be written as separate words.

(See section 5.4.)

2.4   Comparative and Superlative Constructions

The suffixes *-sang* and *-ie* are to be written attached to adjectives in comparative constructions. All resulting sound changes are to be reflected by the spelling.

(See section 5.4.4.)

2.5   The Construct Suffix

The construct suffix *-n* is to be written attached to the preceding word if that word is one syllable in length or if it ends in a vowel. Elsewhere, it is to be written *en*.

This recommendation was prompted by the observation that the construct morpheme behaves sometimes as a suffix and sometimes as an enclitic. The conditions under which it behaves one way or the other, however, are not well understood. It is likely that this recommendation will need to be further refined before any procedure for writing this morpheme gains wide acceptance. Some deviation from this recommendation occurs in this grammar. (See sections 4.8 and 4.9.)

2.6   OTHER SUFFIXES

All other morphemes labeled as suffixes in this grammar are to be written attached to the root they follow. All resulting sound changes are to be reflected by the spelling.

(See sections 3.7.4 and 5.2.3.)

2.7   ENCLITICS

(1)   **Demonstrative Modifiers—All singular demonstrative modifiers are to be written attached to the word they follow. All resulting sound changes are to be reflected by the spelling. Plural demonstrative modifiers are to be written as separate words, with or without a preceding vowel, as they are pronounced.**

(2)   **Numeral Classifiers—Numeral classifiers used as indefinite articles are to be written as separate words, with or without a preceding vowel, as they are pronounced.**

(3)   **Sentence Adverbs—The sentence adverb *-te* is to be written attached to the word it follows, except after a proper name. In the latter case it is to be written as a separate word.**

(See sections 3.4 *Enclitics*, 4.5.1 *Demonstrative Modifiers*, 4.4.4 *The Use of Numeral Classifiers*, and 6.3.3 *Sentence Adverbs*.)

2.8   COMPOUND WORDS

Only compound words involving sound changes are to be written together.

(See section 3.6.2.)

2.9   QUESTION WORDS

Ia, *da* (*h*), and *ihs* are to be written as separate words, except in the forms *iahnge*, *dahnge*, *ihsnge*, *mehnia*, *dahme*, *dahkot*, *dahkei*, and *mehnda*.

(See section 6.4.3.)

3.0   OTHER ORTHOGRAPHIC ISSUES

3.1   LOAN WORDS

All loan words borrowed into Ponapean prior to World War II are to be spelled as Ponapean words. Subsequent loans, of English origin, are to retain their English spelling.

Participants at the Workshop set forth this recommendation for two reasons. First, many recent borrowings from English are not fully assimilated into the language. Thus, there is a great deal of variation in how these words are pronounced and consequently considerable uncertainty as to how they should be spelled in Ponapean. Second, since Ponapean schoolchildren study English, the retention of the English spelling for these words would mean that only one spelling would have to be learned. This recommendation, however, is the subject of some debate among Ponapean educators. Many feel that all loan words that have been fully assimilated into Ponapean should be spelled as Ponapean words.

(See section 1.5.)

3.2   PUNCTUATION AND CAPITALIZATION

English punctuation and capitalization procedures are to be adopted for Ponapean.

In addition to capitalizing the first word of sentences, personal names, place names, days of the week, months of the year, etc., it was also recommended that all traditional titles and all honorific pronouns be capitalized. It was also recommended, following the practice for English, that the first person singular subject and independent pronouns (*i* and *ngehi*) be capitalized, but this recommendation has met with some resistance. It runs counter to traditional practice, and it is argued that the capitalization of first person pronouns conflicts with the Ponapean cultural ideal of modesty and deference in dealing with others.

Copies of the original report on the Ponapean Orthography Workshop may be obtained from the Ponape Department of Education.

Bibliography

Ambrosio de Valencina, Frey. 1892. Diccionario hispano-kanaka ó sea modesta collectión de las voces más usuales y conocidas de esta lengua de la Ascencion ó Ponape. Imprenta del Asito de Huerfanos de Nuestra Senora, Tambobong. Also attributed to A. M. de Arinez.

Bender, Byron W. 1971. Micronesian languages. In: Current trends in linguistics, Thomas A. Sebeok, ed. Volume 8, Part 1, Linguistics in Oceania, pp. 426–465. The Hague, Mouton.

———. 1973. Parallelisms in the morphophonemics of several Micronesian languages. Oceanic Linguistics 12 (1 & 2): 455–477.

Burdick, Alan. 1970. Dictionary of the Ponapean language. Ponape District Department of Education. Mimeographed.

C., A. 1880–1. Quelques mots de la langue de Puynipet (île de l'Ascension) dans l'archipel des Carolines. Actes de la Soc. Philologique 2: 75–116.

Cantero, Paulino. 1950. Ponapean-English dictionary. Ponape District. Mimeographed.

Christian, F. W. 1897. Notes from the Caroline Islands, Ponape. Onomatopoeas, or imitative sounds. Journal of the Polynesian Society 6: 187–200.

———. 1898. Table of letter-changes in the dialects of Pinape and Kusaie (Eastern Carolines). Journal of the Polynesian Society 7: 64–72.

Doane, E. T. 1860. The Ebon and Ponapi dialects compared. The Friend 9: 9–11, 14–15. Morning Star Papers, 1861.

———. 1896. A comparison of the languages of Ponape and Hawaii with notes . . . by S. H. Ray. Roy. Soc. N. S. W. Proc. 29: 420–453.

Dyen, Isidore. 1962. The lexicostatistical classification of the Malayo-polynesian languages. Language 38: 38–46.

Fischer, John L. 1955. Language and folklore in Truk and Ponape: A study in cultural integration. Ph.D. dissertation, Harvard University, Cambridge, Mass.

————, with the assistance of Ann M. Fischer. 1957. The Eastern Carolines. HRAF Behavior Science Monograph. New Haven: HRAF Press. Reprinted with minor additions 1966 and 1970. New Haven: HRAF Press.

————. 1959. Meter in Eastern Carolinian oral literature. Journal of American Folklore 72 (283): 47–52.

————. 1965. The stylistic significance of consonantal *sandhi* in Trukese and Ponapean. American Anthropologist 67 (6), Part I: 1495–1502. Reprinted 1972 with additions. In: Directions in Sociolinguistics: The Ethnology of Communication, J. J. Gumperz and Dell Hymes, eds., pp. 498–511. New York: Holt, Rinehart and Winston.

————. 1966 Interrogatives in Ponapean: Some semantic and grammatical aspects. In: Report of the 17th Annual Round Table Meeting on Linguistics and Language Studies. Georgetown University Monograph Series on Languages and Linguistics, No. 19, Francis P. Dineen, ed., pp. 1–17. Washington, D. C.: Georgetown University Press.

————. 1966. Syntax and social structure: Truk and Ponape. In: Sociolinguistics, William Bright, ed., Proceedings of the U. C. L. A. Sociolinguistics Conference, 1964, pp. 168–187. The Hague: Mouton and Co.

————. 1969. Honorific speech and social structure: A comparison of Japanese and Ponapean. Journal of the Polynesian Society 78 (3): 417–422.

Garvin, Paul L. 1949. Linguistic study of Ponape. CIMA Report, No. 2. Washington, D. C.: Pacific Science Board.

————. 1954. Delimitation of syntactic units. Language 30 (3): 345–348.

————. 1954. Literacy as a problem in language and culture. In: Report of the 5th Annual Round Table Meeting on Linguistics and Language Teaching. Georgetown University Monograph Series on Languages and Linguistics, Monograph No. 7, Hugo J. Mueller, ed., pp. 117–129. Washington, D. C.: Georgetown University Press.

————. 1958. Syntactic units and operations. Proceedings of the 8th International Congress of Linguists, pp. 626–632. Oslo: Oslo University Press.

————. 1959. The standard language problem: Concepts and methods. Anthropological Linguistics 1(3): 28–31.

————. 1962. A study of inductive method in syntax. Word 18 (1 & 2): 107–120.

————. 1962. Ponapean morphophonemics. Phonetica 8(2): 115–127.

————. 1971. The sound pattern of Ponapean. Travaux du Cercle Linguistiques de Prague 4 (1): 47–61.

———— and Saul H. Riesenberg. 1952. Respect behavior on Ponape: An ethnolinguistic study. American Anthropologist 54(2), Part 1: 201–220.

Girschner, Max. 1906. Grammatik der Ponapesprache. Mitt. des Seminars für Orient. Sprachen, Berlin (Ostasiatische Studien Abteil) I(9): 73–126.

———. 1910. Zur Sprache von Ponpae und der Zentralkarolinen. Anthropos 5: 560–563.

———. 1912. Papuanischer Mischkarakter der Sprachen von Ponape und der Zentralkarolinen. Anthropos 7: 503–504.

Glassman, Sidney F. 1952. The flora of Ponape. B. P. Bishop Museum Bulletin No. 209. Honolulu: Bishop Museum Press.

Grace, George W. 1959. The position of the Polynesian language within the Austronesian (Malayo-Polynesian) language family. International Journal of American Linguistics Supplement, Vol. 25, No. 3. Indiana University Publications in Anthropology and Linguistics, Memoir 16. Baltimore: Waverly Press.

———. 1970. Languages in Oceania. Working Papers in Linguistics 2 (3): 1–24. Honolulu: Department of Linguistics, University of Hawaii.

Gulick, Luther Halsey. 1858. Notes on the grammar of the Ponape dialect. Honolulu: Commercial Advertiser Press.

———. 1880. A vocabulary of the Ponape dialect. Ponape-English and English-Ponape: with a grammatical sketch. Journal of the American Oriental Society 10: 1–109.

Hahl, A. 1904. Ein Beitrag zur Kenntnis der Umgangssprache von Ponape. Mitt. des Seminars für Orient. Sprachen, Berlin 7: 1–30.

Harrison, Sheldon P. 1976. Mokilese-English dictionary. PALI Language Texts: Micronesia. Honolulu: University Press of Hawaii.

———. 1976. Mokilese reference grammar. PALI Language Texts: Micronesia. Honolulu: University Press of Hawaii.

Howells, William W. 1973. The Pacific islanders. New York: Scribner's.

Lee, Kee-dong. 1973. Verbal aspect in Kusaiean and Ponapean. Working Papers in Linguistics 5(9): 23–66. Honolulu: Department of Linguistics, University of Hawaii.

Marshall, Mac and James D. Nason. 1975. Micronesia 1944–1974. A bibliography of anthropological and related source materials. New Haven: HRAF Press.

Matsuoka, Shizuo. 1928. Study of the language of the central Carolines. Tokyo: Kyodo Kenkyusha. [In Japanese.]

———. 1930. Study of the language of Ponape. Tokyo: Kyodo Kenkyusha. [In Japanese.]

Newell, J. E. 1893. Chief's language in Samoa. With note on chief's language in Lifu and Ponape by S. H. Ray. 9th Internat. Congr. of Orientalists Trans. 2: 784–801. Edinburgh: Ballantyne Press.

Pawley, Andrew. 1972. On the internal relationships of Eastern Oceanic languages. In: Studies in Oceanic Culture History, Volume 3, Roger

C. Green and Marion Kelly, eds. Pacific Anthropological Records, No. 13, pp. 1–142. Honolulu: Department of Anthropology, B. P. Bishop Museum.

———— and Roger C. Green. 1973. Dating the dispersal of the Oceanic languages. Oceanic Linguistics 12(1 & 2): 1–67.

Rehg, Kenneth L. 1973. On the history of Ponapean phonology. Working Papers in Linguistics 5(8): 17–55. Honolulu: Department of Linguistics, University of Hawaii.

Rehg, Kenneth, and Damian Sohl. 1969. Kitail Lokaiahn Pohnpei: Introductory lessons in Ponapean. Washington, D. C.: United States Peace Corps. Offset.

Rehg, Kenneth, and Damian Sohl. 1979. Ponapean-English dictionary. PALI Language Texts: Micronesia. Honolulu: The University Press of Hawaii.

Riesenberg, Saul H. 1948, Magic and medicine in Ponape. Southwestern Journal of Anthropology [now called Journal of Anthropological Research] 4 (4): 406–429.

————. 1968. The native polity of Ponape. Smithsonian Contributions to Anthropology, Vol. 10. Washington, D. C.: Smithsonian Institution Press.

———— and John L. Fischer. 1955. Some Ponapean proverbs. Journal of American Folklore 68 (267): 9–18.

Sohn, Ho-min. 1973. Relative clause formation in Micronesian languages. Oceanic Linguistics 12 (1 & 2): 353–392.

Sugita, Hiroshi. 1973. Comparison of verb-object relationships in Micronesian languages. Oceanic Linguistics 12 (1 & 2): 393–406.

Sugiura, Kenichi. 1940. Words of respect in Ponape Islands. Anthrop. Society of Tokyo Journal 55: 479–488. [In Japanese.]

Taylor, C. R. H. 1965. A Pacific bibliography: printed matter relating to the native peoples of Polynesia, Melanesia, and Micronesia. 2nd ed. Oxford: Clarendon Press.

Index